FINANCIAL MATHEMATICS:
Theory and Practice

Robert L. Brown
University of Waterloo

Steve Kopp
University of Western Ontario

MCGRAW-HILL RYERSON LIMITED

Toronto   Montréal   Boston   Burr Ridge, IL   Dubuque, IA   Madison, WI   New York
San Francisco   St. Louis   Bangkok   Bogotá   Caracas   Kuala Lumpur   Lisbon   London
Madrid   Mexico City   Milan   New Delhi   Santiago   Seoul   Singapore   Sydney   Taipei

Financial Mathematics: Theory and Practice

Product Development Manager, Learning Solutions: Jason Giles
Learning Solutions Custom Print Specialist: Katherine Gaskin
Learning Solutions Manager: Jeff Snook
Senior Sponsoring Editor: Kimberley Veevers
Supervising Editor: Stephanie Gay

Cover Design: Katherine Gaskin

2 3 4 5 6 7 8 9   QG   1 9 8 7 6 5 4 3 2

Printed and bound in U.S.A.

Contents

Preface

Welcome to an alternative approach to the teaching and learning of financial mathematics!

We have a combined 68 years of teaching experience in actuarial science in general, and financial mathematics in particular. (Robert is now retired from the University of Waterloo, where he taught actuarial science for 40 years, and Steve is currently in his 28th year of teaching actuarial science and statistics at the University of Western Ontario.) In those 68 years, we have always lamented the fact that while there were multiple references available to our students, we had to spend extra time in preparation of our classes and assignments to fill in certain pedagogical deficiencies in any one of these references. Thus, our desire to enter the textbook listings for this discipline.

Our textbook is designed for mathematics / actuarial students with a strong grounding in, and understanding of, a basic first-year calculus curriculum. Our target audience contains students who plan to write the established actuarial examinations as made available around the world and, some day, to have a career in the actuarial or finance professions.

This textbook is designed to provide the reader with a generic approach to understanding financial mathematics with respect to a wide range of financial transactions, including annuities, mortgages, personal loans, and bonds, as well as a limited knowledge of advanced topics such as duration and immunization. All examples are solved from absolute first principles and we propose that any student should solve all financial mathematics problems in the same way; that is, from absolute first principles.

As previously stated, this textbook assumes a knowledge of introductory calculus, so problems are posed whose solutions may require the use of derivatives, or integrals, or both. A comfort with exponents and logarithms is also assumed.

We would be remiss if we did not thank Jeff Snook, Kimberly Veevers, and Stephanie Gay at McGraw-Hill Ryerson, and Javid Ali at the University of Waterloo, for their essential assistance in creating this textbook.

This textbook acknowledges the existence of modern financial calculators and spreadsheets and uses these technologies where appropriate. However, in each and every instance, our goal is to have the student be equipped to understand each solution from fundamental principles.

Our passion for, and interest in, financial mathematics remains undiminished. It is our sincere hope that this textbook provides the student with an improved understanding of the fascinating calculations that underlie most financial transactions.

Robert Brown, Victoria, British Columbia
Steve Kopp, London, Ontario

CHAPTER 1

The Time Value of Money

Learning Objectives

Money is invested or borrowed in thousands of transactions every day. When an investment is cashed in or when money is repaid, a fee is collected or charged. That fee is called interest.

Interest can be viewed as the "rent" one pays for the use of someone else's money. If it is your money being used, it is you who will receive this rent in the form of interest. If you are using someone else's money, you will be the one who pays this rent.

Because of interest, money has different values at different times. For example, if you put $1000 in a bank account that pays interest at a rate of 4% per year, what is your bank account worth at the end of one year?

The answer is $1040. This can be illustrated in the following time diagram. (Note: We will use time diagrams in the solutions to all questions in this book and we suggest you do the same.)

$$\begin{array}{ccc} \$1000 & & \$1040 \\ \downarrow & +4\% \text{ of } 1000 = \$40 & \downarrow \\ \rule{1cm}{0.4pt}\!\!\cdots\!\!\rule{1cm}{0.4pt} & & \\ 0 & & 1 \end{array}$$

How much is your bank account worth at the end of two years? Is it $1080 or is it $1081.60? (The difference of $1.60 is the payment of 4% interest on the $40 of interest earned in year one.)

The answer of $1080 is correct if you are earning "simple interest". The answer of $1081.60 is correct if you are earning "compound interest". We will cover both of these concepts in Chapter 1.

Upon completing this chapter, you will be able to do the following:

- Understand and use the accumulation and amount functions.
- Understand and work with an effective rate of interest.
- Understand the difference between simple interest and compound interest and use them in problem solving.
- Calculate the accumulated value, or future value, of a single sum of money invested today.
- Calculate the value today of a payment due sometime in the future.
- Understand and use a rate of discount.
- Understand nominal rates of interest and discount, and use them in problem solving.
- Calculate interest that is compounded continuously.
- Calculate the accumulated or present value of an investment where the interest rate changes over time.

Accumulation and Amount Functions

Let's begin with an investor who starts out with an original amount of capital invested. This amount is called the *principal* and will be denoted by P. The total amount of capital the investor has at the end of a defined period of time is called the *accumulated value* and will be denoted by S. The difference between the accumulated value and the principal is the *amount of interest*, denoted I, earned on the investment. We will refer to this as just *interest*. Note that we assume that no further capital is either added or withdrawn.

Thus

$$S - P = I$$

We will begin with the case in which $P = \$1$. From this, we define an *accumulation function*, $a(t)$, which gives the accumulated value, at time $t \geq 0$, of the original investment of \$1. The accumulation function $a(t)$ has the following properties:

- $a(0) = 1$
- $a(t)$ increases with time if our rate of return is positive (**Note:** Negative returns are possible and will be discussed in later chapters.)
- We will consider $a(t)$ to be continuous even though interest payments are often made discretely at defined points in time.

If, instead, we assume an original investment of P, then we can define an *amount function*, $A(t)$. $A(t)$ has the following properties:

- $A(0) = P$
- $A(t) = Pa(t)$
- $A(t)$ increases with time if our rate of return is positive.
- We will consider $A(t)$ to be continuous.

Finally, we define I_n to be the amount of interest earned in the unit of time from $(n - 1)$ to (n). Thus,

$$I_n = \text{accumulated amount at end of period } n$$
$$- \text{ accumulated amount at end of period } n - 1$$

or

$$I_n = A(n) - A(n - 1)$$

The following four graphs illustrate the most common forms of growth for $A(t)$.

Note that these could be graphs for $a(t)$ if we start with $P = 1$.

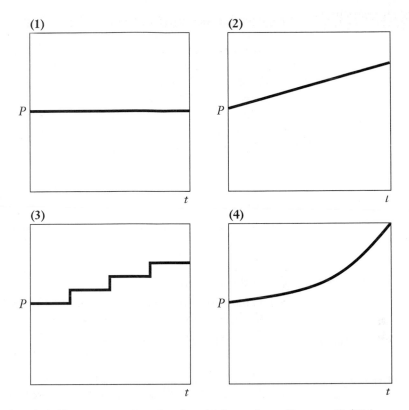

Graph 1 illustrates a situation in which we have "invested" $P but we are receiving no interest on our capital. That is, $S = P$ and $I = 0$.

In Graph 2, $A(t)$ rises linearly. This would be the case if our capital, P, is earning simple interest (see Section 1.4). The slope of the curve represents the rate of return on our investment.

In Graph 3, $A(t)$ is a step function. At the end of each defined period, $A(t)$ rises by a set amount, which remains constant over time. Thus, once again, we are earning simple interest, but that interest, I, is being credited to us at discrete points in time.

Lastly, Graph 4 represents a context upon which most of this textbook is founded. The value of the amount function, $A(t)$, increases exponentially. This illustrates the growth pattern associated with compound interest. In this environment, I increases over time, but the rate of return remains constant, as will be explained in section 1.5.

EXAMPLE 1   You are given an accumulation function $a(t) = b(t - 2)^3 + ct + d$. You are also given $a(1) = 1.47$ and $a(2) = 1.64$. If \$250 is invested at $t = 0$, what is the accumulated value at $t = 4.5$?

Solution   Step 1. $a(0) = 1 = b(0 - 2)^3 + c(0) + d = -8b + d$
Step 2. $a(1) = 1.47 = b(1 - 2)^3 + c + d = -b + c + d$
Step 3. $a(2) = 1.64 = b(2 - 2)^3 + 2c + d = 2c + d$

From 1, we obtain $d = 1 + 8b$.

From 3, we obtain $1.64 = 2c + 1 + 8b$, which gives $c = 0.32 - 4b$.

From 2, $a(1) = 1.47 = -b + c + d = -b + 0.32 - 4b + 1 + 8b = 3b + 1.32$, which solves for $b = 0.05$.

$$c = 0.32 - 4(0.05) = 0.12$$
$$d = 1 + 8(0.05) = 1.40$$

Thus,

$$
\begin{aligned}
A(4.5) &= 250[a(4.5)] \\
&= 250[0.05(4.5 - 2)^3 + 0.12(4.5) + 1.40] \\
&= 250(2.72125) \\
&= \$680.31
\end{aligned}
$$

EXAMPLE 2   Given the accumulation function $a(t) = 0.10(t - 2)^3 + 0.05t + 1.8$:

a) What is the accumulated value at $t = 15$ of $500 invested at $t = 6$?
b) If $1000 is invested at $t = 0$, what is I_5?

Solution a   First calculate the initial investment, P.

$$500 = P\,a(6) = P[0.10(6-2)^3 + 0.05(6) + 1.8] = P(8.5)$$

$$P = \frac{500}{8.5} = 58.82352941$$

Thus,

$$
\begin{aligned}
A(15) &= 58.82352941[a(15)] \\
&= 58.8235294[0.10(15-2)^3 + 0.05(15) + 1.8] \\
&= \$13\ 073.53
\end{aligned}
$$

Solution b $I_5 = A(5) - A(4) = 1000[a(5) - a(4)] = 1000[4.75 - 2.8] = \$1950$

Exercise 1.1

1. Given $A(t) = \dfrac{1000}{50 - t}$ for $0 \leq t < 50$, calculate P and $a(10)$.

2. Given the amount function $A(t) = 2t^2 + 3t + 10$:
   a) Determine $a(t)$.
   b) Determine I_n.

3. Prove that $I_1 + I_2 + \cdots + I_n = A(n) - A(0)$.

4. Calculate the amount of interest earned between time $t = 3$ and $t = 8$ if:
   a) $I_n = n$
   b) $I_n = 2^n$

5. You are told that $a(t) = at^2 + b$ and that $1000 invested at time 0 accumulates to $1200 at time 2. Calculate the value of the $1000 at time 10.

The Effective Rate of Interest

The definition of the **effective rate of interest** is as follows:

> The effective rate of interest is the amount of money that one unit of capital, invested at the beginning of a period, will earn during the period, where interest is paid at the end of the period. We will denote the effective rate of interest by i.

We further need to assume that during this period of time there are no additions or withdrawals of capital.

By the definition, we can see that $i = a(1) - a(0)$.

Since $a(1)$ and $a(0)$ describe the *accumulation function* for the first investment period, we can define i_1 as the effective rate of interest earned in the first investment period:

$$i_1 = a(1) - a(0)$$

It is also true that:

$$i_1 = \frac{A(1) - A(0)}{A(0)}$$

since $a(0) = 1$ and $A(t) = Pa(t)$.

We could also write i_1 as:

$$i_1 = \frac{I_1}{A(0)}$$

since $I_1 = a(1) - a(0)$, where I_1 is the dollar amount of interest earned in the first investment period.

We can generalize this relationship and state that the effective rate of interest earned in the nth investment period, $(n - 1, n)$ is:

$$i_n = \frac{A(n) - A(n - 1)}{A(n - 1)} = \frac{I_n}{A(n - 1)}$$

As we can see, the effective rate of interest in any period, i_n, is the ratio of the amount of interest earned during the period to the amount of principal invested at the beginning of the period.

Note that i is expressed as a percentage. This means that if $i = 6\%$, then any calculations that use i will use $i = 0.06$.

EXAMPLE 1   In section 1.1, Example 2, we defined the accumulation function $a(t) = 0.10(t - 2)^3 + 0.05t + 1.8$. Calculate the effective rates of interest i_1, i_2, i_5, and i_{20}.

Solution $i_1 = \dfrac{a(1) - a(0)}{a(0)} = \dfrac{1.75}{1} - 1 = 0.75 = 75.00\%$

$i_2 = \dfrac{a(2) - a(1)}{a(1)} = \dfrac{1.90 - 1.75}{1.75} = 0.085714285 = 8.57\%$

$$i_5 = \frac{a(5) - a(4)}{a(4)} = \frac{4.75 - 2.8}{2.8} = 0.696428571 = 69.64\%$$

$$i_{20} = \frac{a(20) - a(19)}{a(19)} = \frac{586 - 494.05}{494.05} = 0.186114765 = 18.61\%$$

As you can see, this particular accumulation function leads to rather interesting effective rates of interest.

Exercise 1.2

1. Suppose you invest \$5000 at time 0 and $a(t) = 1 + 0.03t$.
   a) Calculate i_4.
   b) Calculate i_{10}.

2. You are given $A(t) = 1000 + 40t$.
   a) Calculate I_5 and i_5.
   b) Calculate I_{20} and i_{20}.

3. You are given $A(t) = 100(1.05)^t$.
   a) Calculate I_5 and i_5.
   b) Calculate I_{20} and i_{20}.

4. At the end of year 5, an investment has grown to \$750. This investment has earned annual effective rates of interest equal to $i_n = 0.0075n - 0.0015$ since issue. What was the size of the initial investment made at time 0?

| Section 1.3 | **Simple Interest** |

In early times, the principal lent and the interest paid might be tangible goods (e.g., grain). Now, they are most commonly in the form of money. The practice of charging interest is as old as the earliest written records of humanity. Four thousand years ago, the laws of Babylon referred to interest payments on debts.

Short-term transactions often use simple interest. Under simple interest, the interest earned (or paid) is computed on the original principal during the whole time, or term, of the loan at the stated annual rate of interest.

We shall use the following notation:

P = the principal, or the present value of S, or the discounted value of S, or the proceeds.
I = simple interest.
S = the amount, or the accumulated value of P, or the future value of P, or the maturity value of P; that is, $S = P + I$.
r = annual rate of simple interest.
t = time in years.

Simple interest is calculated by means of the formula

$$\boxed{I = Prt} \tag{1}$$

From the definition of the amount S we have

$$S = P + I$$

By substituting for $I = Prt$, we obtain S in terms of P, r, and t:

$$S = P + Prt$$

$$\boxed{S = P(1 + rt)} \qquad (2)$$

> The factor $(1 + rt)$ in formula **(2)** is called an **accumulation factor at a simple interest rate r** and the process of calculating S from P by formula **(2)** is called **accumulation at a simple interest rate r**.

We can display the relationship between S and P on a time diagram.

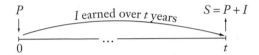

Alternatively,

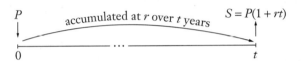

Value of t

The time t must be in years. When the time is given in months, then

$$t = \frac{\text{number of months}}{12}$$

When the time is given in days, there are two different varieties of simple interest in use:

1. **Exact interest**, where $t = \dfrac{\text{number of days}}{365}$

   i.e., the year is taken as 365 days (leap year or not).

2. **Ordinary interest**, where $t = \dfrac{\text{number of days}}{360}$

   i.e., the year is taken as 360 days.

CALCULATION TIP:

The general practice in Canada is to use exact interest, whereas the general practice in the United States and in international business transactions is to use ordinary interest (also referred to as the Banker's Rule). In this textbook, exact interest is used all the time unless specified otherwise.

When the time is given by two dates we calculate the exact number of days between the two dates from a table listing the serial number of each day of the year. The exact time is obtained as the difference between serial numbers of the given dates. In leap years (years divisible by 4) an extra day is added to February.

> **OBSERVATION:**
>
> When calculating the number of days between two dates, the most common practice is to count the starting date, but not the ending date. The reason is that financial institutions calculate interest each day on the closing balance of a loan or savings account. On the day a loan is taken out or a deposit is made, there is a non-zero balance at the end of that day, whereas on the day a loan is paid off or the deposit is fully withdrawn, there is a zero balance at the end of that day.
>
> However, it is easier to assume the opposite when using the table on the inside back cover. That is, unless otherwise stated, you should assume that interest is not calculated on the starting date, but is calculated on the ending date. That way, in order to determine the number of days between two dates, all you have to do is subtract the two values you find from the table on the inside back cover. Example 1 will illustrate this.

EXAMPLE 1 A loan of \$15 000 is taken out. If the interest rate on the loan is 7%, how much interest is due and what is the amount repaid if

a) The loan is due in 7 months;

b) The loan was taken out on April 7 and is due in 7 months?

Solution a We have $P = 15\,000$, $r = 0.07$ and since the actual date the loan was taken out is not given, we use $t = \frac{7}{12}$.

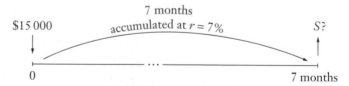

Interest due, $I = Prt = \$15\,000 \times 0.07 \times \frac{7}{12} = \$612.50$

Amount repaid = Future or accumulated value,

$$S = P + I = \$15\,000 + \$612.50 = \$15\,612.50$$

Alternatively, we can obtain the above answer in one calculation:

$$S = P(1 + rt) = \$15\,000[1 + 0.07(\tfrac{7}{12})] = \$15\,612.50$$

Solution b Since a date is given when the loan was actually taken out, we must use days. Seven months after April 7 is November 7. Using the table on the inside back cover, we find that April 7 is day 97 and November 7 is day 311. The exact number of days between the two dates is $311 - 97 = 214$. Thus, $t = \frac{214}{365}$.

Interest due, $I = Prt = \$15\,000 \times 0.07 \times \frac{214}{365} = \$615.62$

Future value, $S = P + I = \$15\,000 + \$615.62 = \$15\,615.62$

Alternatively,

$$S = P(1 + rt) = \$15\,000[1 + 0.07(\tfrac{214}{365})] = \$15\,615.62$$

EXAMPLE 2   Determine the exact and ordinary simple interest on a 90-day loan of $8000 at $8\frac{1}{2}\%$.

Solution   We have $P = 8000$, $r = 0.085$, numerator of $t = 90$ days.

Exact interest, $I = Prt = \$8000 \times 0.085 \times \frac{90}{365} = \$167.67$

Ordinary interest, $I = Prt = \$8000 \times 0.085 \times \frac{90}{360} = \$170.00$

OBSERVATION:

Notice that ordinary interest is always greater than the exact interest and thus it brings increased revenue to the lender.

EXAMPLE 3   A loan of $100 is to be repaid with $120 at the end of 2 months. What was the annual simple interest rate?

Solution   We have $P = 100$, $I = 20$, $t = \frac{2}{12}$, and

$$r = \frac{I}{Pt} = \frac{20}{100 \times \frac{2}{12}} = 120\%$$

EXAMPLE 4   How long will it take $3000 to earn $60 interest at 6% simple interest?

Solution   We have $P = 3000$, $I = 60$, $r = 0.06$, and

$$t = \frac{I}{Pr} = \frac{20}{3000 \times 0.06} = \frac{1}{3} = 4 \text{ months}$$

EXAMPLE 5 A deposit of $1500 is made into a fund on March 18. The fund earns simple interest at 5%. On August 5, the interest rate changes to 4.5%. How much is in the fund on October 23?

Solution Using the table on the inside back cover, we determine the number of days between March 18 and August 5 = $217 - 77 = 140$ and the number of days between August 5 and October 23 = $296 - 217 = 79$.

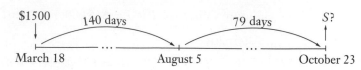

S = original deposit + interest for 140 days + interest for 79 days
$= \$1500 + (\$1500 \times 0.05 \times \frac{140}{365}) + (\$1500 \times 0.045 \times \frac{79}{365})$
$= \$(1500 + 28.77 + 14.61)$
$= \$1543.38$

Effective Rate of Interest

Under simple interest, the *accumulation function* is:

$$a(t) = 1 + rt$$

and the *amount function* is:

$$A(t) = P(1 + rt)$$

Suppose your investment earns a constant rate of simple interest, r, every year. Then, the effective rate of interest in year n is:

$$i_n = \frac{I_n}{A(n-1)}$$
$$= \frac{A(n) - A(n-1)}{A(n-1)}$$
$$= \frac{P[1 + rn] - P[1 + r(n-1)]}{P[1 + r(n-1)]}$$
$$= \frac{r}{1 + r(n-1)}$$

As you can see, as n increases, the value of i_n decreases, which means that if your investment earns the same rate of simple interest every year, you will end up with a decreasing effective rate of interest. That is, your effective rate of interest will get smaller each succeeding year of the investment.

EXAMPLE 6 An investment of $600 is earning 6% interest each year. What is the effective rate of interest earned in year 1, year 2, year 5, and year 10?

Solution $i_1 = \frac{a(1) - a(0)}{a(0)} = \frac{1.06 - 1}{1} = 0.06 = 6.00\%$

$i_2 = \frac{a(2) - a(1)}{a(1)} = \frac{1.12 - 1.06}{1.06} = \frac{0.06}{1.06} = 0.0566038 = 5.66\%$

$$i_5 = \frac{a(5) - a(4)}{a(4)} = \frac{1.30 - 1.24}{1.24} = \frac{0.06}{1.24} = 0.048387 = 4.84\%$$

$$i_{10} = \frac{a(10) - a(9)}{a(9)} = \frac{1.60 - 1.54}{1.54} = \frac{0.06}{1.54} = 0.038961 = 3.90\%$$

Exercise 1.3

1. Determine the maturity value of
   a) a $2500 loan for 18 months at 12% simple interest,
   b) a $1200 loan for 120 days at 8.5% ordinary simple interest,
   c) a $10 000 loan for 64 days at 7% exact simple interest, and
   d) a $5000 loan taken out on June 23 and due on December 15 at 6% exact simple interest.

2. At what rate of simple interest will
   a) $1000 accumulate to $1420 in $2\frac{1}{2}$ years,
   b) money double itself in 7 years,
   c) $500 accumulate $10 interest in 2 months, and
   d) $800 accumulate to $850 from March 18 to October 18?

3. How many days will it take
   a) $1000 to accumulate to at least $1200 at 5.5% simple interest,
   b) $1600 to earn at least $30 of interest at 3.5% simple interest, and
   c) $5000 to accumulate to at least $5100 at 9% simple interest?

4. Determine the ordinary and exact simple interest on $5000 for 90 days at $10\frac{1}{2}\%$.

5. A student lends his friend $50 for 1 month. At the end of the month he asks for repayment of the $50 plus purchase of a chocolate bar worth $2.50. What simple interest rate is implied?

6. What principal will accumulate to $5100 in 6 months if the simple interest rate is 9%?

7. What principal will accumulate to $580 in 120 days at 18% simple interest?

8. Determine the accumulated value of $1000 over 65 days at $6\frac{1}{2}\%$ using both ordinary and exact simple interest.

9. A man borrows $1000 on February 16 at 7.25% simple interest. What amount must he repay in 7 months?

10. A sum of $2000 is invested from May 18, 2010, to April 8, 2011, at 4.5% simple interest. Determine the amount of interest earned.

11. On May 13, 2010, Jacob invested $4000. On February 1, 2011, he intends to pay Fred $4300 for a used car. The bank assured Jacob that his investment would be adequate to cover the purchase. Determine the minimum simple interest rate that Jacob's money must be earning.

12. Determine the effective rate of interest i_3 that is equivalent to the following rates of simple interest.
    a) $i = 2\%$
    b) $i = 7\%$

13. You are given that $1500 accumulates to $1600 over two years at a rate of simple interest of i. Determine the effective rate of interest in year 2, i_2.

Section 1.4 **Compound Interest**

Recall the example from the introduction to this chapter:

If you invest $1000 for one year where the rate of return is 4% per annum, then at the end of one year you will have $1040. This is true under both a simple interest assumption and a compound interest assumption.

How much is this investment worth after two years if the rate of return remains at 4% per annum?

As we have seen, if we have a rate of simple interest, the answer is $A(2) = 1000[1 + (0.04)(2)] = \$1080$.

But if we have a rate of compound interest, then the $40 of interest earned in year one, immediately earns interest itself at 4%, which is an additional $40(0.04) = \$1.60$, and we end up with $1081.60 at the end of two years.

As stated, this is called "compound interest" and is the most common model that is applied for time periods in excess of one year.

Note: Simple interest models are often used for time periods of less than one year and if $t = 1$, our answers are identical under either model.

Under compound interest, the *accumulation function* is:

$$a(t) = (1 + i)^t$$

and the *amount function* is:

$$\boxed{A(t) = P(1 + i)^t, \, t \geq 0} \tag{3}$$

If our interest rate is a constant of i, then the effective rate of interest in period n is:

$$i_n = \frac{A(n) - A(n-1)}{A(n-1)}$$

$$= \frac{P(1+i)^n - P(1+i)^{n-1}}{P(1+i)^{n-1}}$$

$$= \frac{(1+i) - 1}{1}$$

$$= i, \text{ which is independent of } n$$

Thus, a constant rate of compound interest implies a constant effective rate of interest. This is not true for simple interest as we have shown.

If we assume a continuous function for each of compound interest, $a(t) = (1 + i)^t$ and simple interest, $a(t) = (1 + i \times t)$, then we can graph these functions as follows:

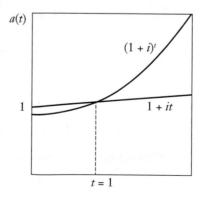

From the graph we can see that:

$$1 + it > (1 + i)^t, 0 < t < 1$$
$$1 + it = (1 + i)^t = 1 + i, t = 1$$
$$1 + it < (1 + i)^t, t > 1$$

This can be proven algebraically by doing a binomial expansion on $(1 + i)^t$ and comparing that expansion (you need only go to three terms) to $1 + it$. This is left as an exercise.

EXAMPLE 1 For a \$1000 investment earning $i = 5\%$ per annum, calculate the accumulated value of the investment at times, $t = \frac{1}{2}$, $t = 1$, $t = 2$, and $t = 3$ under both compound and simple interest.

Solution

Time	$A(t)$ — Compound Interest	$A(t)$ — Simple Interest
$\frac{1}{2}$	$1000(1.05)^{\left(\frac{1}{2}\right)} = 1024.70$	$1000\left[1 + \left(\frac{1}{2}\right)0.05\right] = 1025.00$
1	$1000(1.05) = 1050.00$	$1000[1 + (1)(0.05)] = 1050.00$
2	$1000(1.05)^2 = 1102.50$	$1000[1 + (2)(0.05)] = 1100.00$
3	$1000(1.05)^3 = 1157.63$	$1000[1 + (3)(0.05)] = 1150.00$

We can also calculate the effective rate of interest:

Time	Compound Interest	Simple Interest
1	$i_1 = \dfrac{A(1) - A(0)}{A(0)} = \dfrac{1050 - 1000}{1000} = 0.05$	$i_1 = \dfrac{A(1) - A(0)}{A(0)} = \dfrac{1050 - 1000}{1000} = 0.05$
2	$i_2 = \dfrac{A(2) - A(1)}{A(1)} = \dfrac{1102.50 - 1050}{1050} = 0.05$	$i_2 = \dfrac{A(2) - A(1)}{A(1)} = \dfrac{1100 - 1050}{1050} = 0.0476$
3	$i_3 = \dfrac{A(3) - A(2)}{A(2)} = \dfrac{1157.63 - 1102.50}{1102.50} = 0.05$	$i_3 = \dfrac{A(3) - A(2)}{A(2)} = \dfrac{1150 - 1100}{1100} = 0.0455$

Under compound interest theory, we assume that once interest (I) is earned, it is immediately reinvested at the same rate. This is not always possible, and this complication is explored later in the book.

We can verify the fact that under compound interest, $a(t) = (1 + i)^t$ as follows: In year 1, \$1 is invested at rate i, so at the end of that year we have \$$(1 + i)$. In year 2, \$$(1 + i)$ is invested at rate i, so at the end of that year we have

$$(1 + i) + i(1 + i) = (1 + i)^2.$$

This pattern continues. For the time period $(t - 1, t)$ we have:

$$(1 + i)^{t-1} + i(1 + i)^{t-1} = (1 + i)^{t-1}(1 + i) = (1 + i)^t$$

Note that this model can be applied for all values of t, both integer and fractional.

Exercise 1.4

Part A

Problems 1 to 8 make use of the following table. In each case calculate the accumulated value and the compound interest earned.

No.	Principal	Interest Rate	Time
1.	$100	$5\frac{1}{2}\%$	5 years
2.	$500	3%	2 years
3.	$220	8.8%	3 years
4.	$1000	9%	6 years
5.	$50	6%	4 years
6.	$800	$7\frac{3}{4}\%$	10 years
7.	$300	8%	3 years
8.	$1000	10%	2 years

9. Accumulate $500 for one year at
   a) $i = 4\%$, b) $i = 8\%$, c) $i = 12\%$.

10. How much money will be required on December 31, 2012, to repay a loan of $2000 made December 31, 2009, if $i = 7\%$?

11. In 1492, Queen Isabella sponsored Christopher Columbus' journey by giving him $10 000. If $i = 3\%$, how much money would be in the account in 2010? If the bank account earned a simple interest rate of 3%, how much money would be in the account in 2010?

Part B

1. Using a computer spreadsheet, set up a table and plot the graph showing the growth of $1000 at compound interest rates $i = 4\%$, 7%, 10% and time = 5, 10, 15, 20, and 25 years.

2. Prove, using the binomial expansion of $(1 + i)^t$:
   a) $1 + it > (1 + i)^t$, if $0 < t < 1$
   b) $1 + it = (1 + i)^t = 1 + i$, if $t = 1$
   c) $1 + it < (1 + i)^t$, if $t > 1$

Section 1.5 | **Present Value**

To this point, we have used both compound and simple interest to determine accumulated, or future values, of money transactions. It is also possible to determine *present values* of payments due in the future. An example will illustrate this concept.

EXAMPLE 1 A payment of $S = \$1$ is due to be paid exactly t years from now. What is the value today of this $1 if the rate of compound interest is i per annum?

Solution We arrange our data on a time diagram.

Under compound interest, $a(t) = a(0)(1 + i)^t$.

In this situation, we know $a(t) = 1$.

Thus,

$$a(0) = \frac{1}{(1 + i)^t} = (1 + i)^{-t}$$

The factor, $(1 + i)^{-t}$, is used to determine present values at a rate of interest and is called the *discount factor*. This process is called "discounting at a rate of interest".

In most actuarial literature, the symbol v is used for $(1 + i)^{-1}$ so that $v^t = (1 + i)^{-t}$. However, we will tend to use $(1 + i)^{-t}$ directly in this text book.

We can also determine present values at a simple rate of interest as follows:

EXAMPLE 2   Determine the value today of \$1 due to be paid exactly t years from now if the rate of simple interest is i per annum.

Solution   We have the same time diagram:

Under simple interest, $a(t) = a(0)(1 + it)$.

In this situation, we know $a(t) = 1$.

Thus,

$$a(0) = \frac{1}{(1 + it)} = (1 + it)^{-1}$$

Note 1: We normally restrict the use of the symbol v to applications using compound interest.

Note 2: The above formulae can also be used for fractional periods of time.

Note 3: From this point on, all present-value questions will assume compound interest unless otherwise explicitly stated.

In General

If the future amount is $A(t)$, then the present value of this amount under compound interest is:

$$\boxed{A(0) = P = A(t)(1 + i)^{-t}} \tag{4}$$

Under simple interest, it is:

$$\boxed{A(0) = P = A(t)(1 + it)^{-1}} \tag{5}$$

EXAMPLE 3   Determine the present value of $S = \$1000$ to be paid 27 months from now if interest is 5% per annum effective.

Solution

The $1000 will be paid in 27 months or 2.25 years from now.

Thus,

$$
\begin{aligned}
P\,a(2.25) &= \$1000 \\
P(1.05)^{2.25} &= \$1000 \\
P &= \$1000(1.05)^{-2.25} \\
&= \$896.03
\end{aligned}
$$

EXAMPLE 4   A borrower offers to pay a lender $500 in one year, $300 in two years, and $200 in three years. If $i = 4\%$, how much was lent out today?

Solution

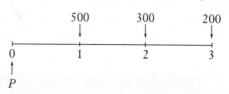

Thus,

$$
\begin{aligned}
P &= 500(1.04)^{-1} + 300(1.04)^{-2} + 200(1.04)^{-3} \\
&= \$935.94
\end{aligned}
$$

It should be clear that:

$$
v^t = [a(t)]^{-1} = a^{-1}(t) = \frac{1}{a(t)}
$$

And, that for $t \geq 0$:

under simple interest: $a^{-1}(t) = \dfrac{1}{1 + it}$

under compound interest: $a^{-1}(t) = \dfrac{1}{(1 + i)^t} = (1 + i)^{-t} = v^t$

EXAMPLE 5   Determine what amount must be invested at a rate of interest of 5% to accumulate $S = \$5000$ at the end of four years under a) simple interest; b) compound interest.

Solution

Solution a $P = 5000a^{-1}(4) = 5000[1 + (0.05)(4)]^{-1} = \$4166.67$

Solution b $P = 5000a^{-1}(4) = 5000(1.05)^{-1} = \$4113.51$
Did you anticipate the fact that b) < a)?

Exercise 1.5

Part A

Calculate the discounted value in problems 1 to 5.

No.	Amount	Interest Rate	Time
1.	$100	6%	3 years
2.	$50	$8\frac{1}{2}$%	2 years
3.	$2000	11.8%	10 years
4.	$500	10%	5 years
5.	$800	5%	3 years

6. What amount of money invested today will grow to $1000 at the end of 5 years if $i = 8\%$?

7. How much would have to be deposited today in an investment fund paying $i = 10.4\%$ to have $2000 in 3 years time?

8. What is the discounted value of $2500 due in 10 years if $i = 9.6\%$?

9. On her 20th birthday, a woman receives $1000 as a result of a deposit her parents made on the day she was born. How large was that deposit if it earned interest at $i = 6\%$?

10. A note dated October 1, 2010, calls for the payment of $800 in 7 years. On October 1, 2011, it is sold at a price that will yield the investor $i = 12\%$. How much is paid for the note?

11. A note for $250 dated August 1, 2010, is due with compound interest at $i = 9\%$ 4 years after date. On November 1, 2011, the holder of the note has it discounted by a lender who charges $i = 7.5\%$. What are the proceeds?

12. A note for $1000 dated January 1, 2011, is due with interest at 6% compounded annually five years after date. On July 1, 2012, the holder of the note has it discounted by a lender who charges 7% compounded annually. Determine the proceeds.

Part B

1. The management of a company must decide between two proposals. The following information is available:

	Investment	Net Cash Inflow at End of		
Proposal	Now	Year 1	Year 2	Year 3
A	80 000	95 400	39 000	12 000
B	100 000	35 000	58 000	80 000

Advise management regarding the proposal that should be selected, assuming that on projects of this type the company can earn $i = 14\%$.

| Section 1.6 | **Discount** |

There are rare situations in which, instead of paying interest on a loan at the end of the loan period, the "interest" is deducted at the time of the loan (i.e., the "interest" is paid up front). This process is called "discounting the loan" and the rate of discount is represented by the symbol d.

For example, a bank might loan you $1000 at a rate of discount $d = 8\%$. They will calculate the interest in advance, $1000(0.08) = \$80$, and give you $1000 - \$80 = \$920$ now and ask you to pay back $1000 in one year.

The Effective Rate of Discount

The effective rate of discount for year n, d_n, is the ratio of the cost of a loan (called the amount of interest or discount) to the amount invested at the *end* of the year.

$$d_n = \frac{A(n) - An - 1}{A(n)} = \frac{I_n}{A(n)}$$

Recall the definition for the effective rate of interest:

$$i_n = \frac{A(n) - A(n-1)}{A(n-1)} = \frac{I_n}{A(n-1)}$$

Note the difference between interest and discount:

Discount: Paid/due at the beginning of the year calculated on the balance at the end of the year.

Interest: Paid/due at the end of the year calculated on the balance at the beginning of the year.

Under compound interest, the effective rate of discount is constant from year to year.

$$\begin{aligned}
d_n &= \frac{A(n) - A(n-1)}{A(n)} = \frac{I_n}{A(n)} \\
&= \frac{a(n) - a(n-1)}{a(n)} \\
&= \frac{(1+i)^n - (1+i)^{n-1}}{(1+i)^n} \\
&= \frac{i}{1+i}
\end{aligned}$$

Relationship between Interest Rate and Discount Rate

Under compound interest, we have the relationship:

$$d = \frac{i}{1+i}$$

and thus,

$$i = \frac{d}{1-d}$$

This can be arrived at logically. If a \$1 loan is discounted at rate, d, you effectively get a net loan of $1 - d$ and pay back \$1. The cost of the loan is d. The rate of interest for this transaction is the cost of the loan (d) related to the amount invested at the beginning of the year $(1-d)$.

Thus,

$$i = \frac{d}{1-d}$$

EXAMPLE 1   If a discounted loan is offered at a rate of discount $d = 8\%$, what is the equivalent rate of interest?

Solution
$$i = \frac{d}{1 - d} = \frac{0.08}{1 - 0.08} = \frac{0.08}{0.92} = 0.0869565 = 8.70\%$$

This says that getting a discounted loan at $d = 8\%$ is equivalent to getting the same loan at an interest rate of 8.70%.

Another Relationship

$$d = \frac{i}{1 + i} = i(1 + i)^{-1} = iv$$

This relationship is logical, since d is interest paid at the beginning of the year.

EXAMPLE 2   Show that $1 - d = (1 + i)^{-1} = v$.

Solution
$$1 - d = 1 - \frac{i}{1 + i} = \frac{(1 + i) - i}{1 + i} = (1 + i)^{-1} = v$$

Note: Both $(1 + i)^{-1} = v$ and $1 - d$ are the present value of \$1 to be paid at the end of the year.

Accumulating and Discounting with a Discount Rate

In theory, you can also accumulate a sum of money with a discount rate and you can calculate the discounted, or present value of a future sum of money using a discount rate.

Accumulation Functions under d
Compound discount: $a(t) = (1 - d)^{-t}$
Simple discount: $a(t) = (1 - dt)^{-1}$

Discount Functions under d
Compound discount: $a^{-1}(t) = (1 - d)^t$
Simple discount: $a^{-1}(t) = (1 - dt)$

EXAMPLE 3   Determine what amount must be invested at a rate of discount $d = 5\%$, to have \$1000 at the end of four years, under a) compound discount; b) simple discount.

Solution

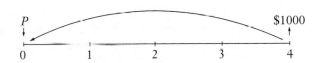

Solution a $P = 1000(1 - 0.05)^4 = 1000(0.95)^4 = \$814.51$

Solution b $P = 1000[1 - (0.05)(4)] = 1000(1 - 0.20) = \$800$

EXAMPLE 4 If a discounted two-year loan is taken out and we receive a total of $2000 today, what is the actual size of the loan taken out if the discount rate is $d = 7\%$ and we are being charged a) compound discount; b) simple discount?

Solution

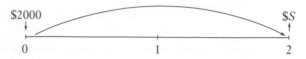

Solution a $S = 2000(1 - 0.07)^{-2} = 2000(0.93)^{-2} = \$2312.41$

In other words, a discounted loan of $2312.41 is taken out. Interest of $2312.41 - 2000 = \$312.41$ is paid in advance (at time of loan) and the remainder, $2000, is received. At the end of two years, the original loan amount of $2312.41 is paid back.

Note that the equivalent rate of interest is:

$$i = \frac{d}{1-d} = \frac{0.07}{1-0.07} = 0.0752688$$

and we could calculate the future value as:

$$S = 2000(1.0752688)^2 = \$2312.41$$

Solution b $S = 2000[1 - (0.07)(2)]^{-1} = 1000(1 - 0.14)^{-1} = \$2325.58$

Exercise 1.6

Part A

1. Julia borrows $1000 at a discount rate $d = 4\%$ for 2 years. How much money does she have the use of if:
   a) d is a compound discount rate?
   b) d is a simple discount rate?

2. Levy needs to borrow money to repay a debt. He has the choice of an annual effective interest rate of 5.1% or an annual effective discount rate of 4.9%. Which should he choose?

3. Li Li knows that when she graduates in 4 years time she will receive $10 000 from her grandmother. However, she needs money today to pay her tuition. If $d = 5\%$, how much money will the present value of $10 000 provide to pay her bills today?

4. Wendy wants to buy some furniture costing $7000. She will repay the loan in 3 years. If $d = 7\%$, how much will she repay?

5. An investor deposits $2000 today. If the discount rate is $d = 5\%$, what is the accumulated value at the end of 5 years given:
   a) compound discount?
   b) simple discount?
   Predict which answer will be larger.

6. What discount rate is equivalent to $i = 8\%$?

7. Using a simple discount rate of 4% per annum, calculate the present value of a payment of $5000 due in 3 months.

8. A $30 000 car loan is repaid by one payment of $38 526.34 after 36 months. What is the annual effective discount rate?

9. Calculate what amount must be invested at a rate of discount of 7% per annum to accumulate $1000 at the end of 3 years given:
   a) compound discount;
   b) simple discount.

10. A store normally offers a 10% discount on accounts paid at the time of delivery. If the customer delays payment for 1 month and then pays the bill in full, what is the effective rate of simple discount? (Assume a month is $\frac{1}{12}$ of a year.)

11. A bank offers a 272-day discounted loan at a simple discount rate of 12%.
    a) How much money would a borrower receive if he asked for a $5000 loan?
    b) What size loan should the borrower ask for in order to actually receive $5000?
    c) What is the equivalent simple interest rate that is being charged on the loan?

12. A promissory note with face value $2000 is due in 175 days and bears 7% simple interest. After 60 days it is sold for $2030. What simple discount rate can the purchaser expect to earn?

13. A discounted loan of $3000 at a simple discount rate of 6.5% is offered to Mr. Jones. If the actual amount of money that Mr. Jones receives is $2869.11, when is the $3000 due to be paid back?

14. A borrower receives $1500 today and must pay back $1580 in 200 days. If this is a discounted loan, what rate of simple discount is assumed?

15. What rate of simple interest is equivalent to a simple discount rate of
    a) 10% over the period March 13 to September 2?
    b) 6.5% over 9 months?
    c) 4.8% over 15 weeks?

16. What rate of simple discount is equivalent to a simple interest rate of
    a) 5% over the period April 25 to August 16?
    b) 12% over 11 months?
    c) 7.5% over 182 days?

Part B

1. Recall that $d_n = \dfrac{I_n}{A(n)}$.
    a) Determine d_5 equivalent to a simple interest rate $i = 4\%$.
    b) Determine d_5 equivalent to a compound interest rate $i = 4\%$.

2. Assuming compound discount, prove that d_n is constant for all n.

3. Given $A(t) = (1.04)^{1/2}(1 + 0.035t)$:
    a) Calculate d_4.
    b) Calculate i_4.

4. Brett and Jean open new bank accounts on their common day of graduation. Brett deposits $500 into his bank account while Jean deposits $250 into her account. Each account grows at rate d compounded per annum. If the growth in Brett's account in year 11 is equal to the growth in Jean's account in year 17, what is the value of that common growth?

Section 1.7 **Nominal Rates of Interest and Discount**

Nominal Rate of Interest

Recall the definition of an effective rate of interest from section 1.2:

> The effective rate of interest, i, is the amount of money that one unit of capital, invested at the beginning of a period will earn during the period, where the interest is paid at the end of the period.

To this point, all of our "periods" have been one year in length. But this does not have to be the case. We can have periods of 6 months, 3 months, or 1 month in duration (or any length of time, other than 1 year). When interest is paid (or earned) more frequently than once a year, the annual rate of interest is called a "nominal rate".

The following is an example of the terminology that can be used for a nominal rate of interest:

- 5% per annum compounded quarterly
- 5% per annum convertible quarterly
- 5% per annum payable quarterly

The above is saying that the annual rate of interest is 5%, but where interest is paid, or compounded, or converted, at the end of each 3-month period (or quarter year).

In this book, the following notation will be used:

$$i^{(m)} = \text{nominal rate of interest, compounded } m \text{ times a year}$$

Note 1: $i^{(m)}$ is stated as an annual rate of interest.

Note 2: The length of time between interest calculations is called the "interest conversion period" or just "interest period".

Note 3: $\frac{i^{(m)}}{m}$ = effective rate of interest per interest period = effective rate of interest per mth of a year.

In our example above, $i^{(4)} = 5\%$, which means interest is calculated and paid at the end of every 3-month period at the rate of $i = \frac{0.05}{4} = 0.0125$ per quarter year.

Relationship between i and $i^{(m)}$

In general:

> Two rates of interest are said to be **equivalent** if a given amount of principal invested for the same length of time at either rate produces the same accumulated values.

Normally it is advisable to compare rates over a one-year period of time. Let's invest $1 for one year.

- $1 invested at i will grow to $\$(1 + i)$ at the end of one year.
- $1 invested at $i^{(m)}$ will earn interest at $\frac{i^{(m)}}{m}$ at the end of each mth of a year, after which it will earn interest.

Year	End of Period	Interest	Accumulated Value
$\frac{1}{m}$	1	$\frac{i^{(m)}}{m}$	$\left(1+\frac{i^{(m)}}{m}\right)$
$\frac{2}{m}$	2	$\left(1+\frac{i^{(m)}}{m}\right)\frac{i^{(m)}}{m}$	$\left(1+\frac{i^{(m)}}{m}\right)+\left(1+\frac{i^{(m)}}{m}\right)\frac{i^{(m)}}{m}=\left(1+\frac{i^{(m)}}{m}\right)^2$
$\frac{3}{m}$	3	$\left(1+\frac{i^{(m)}}{m}\right)^2\frac{i^{(m)}}{m}$	$\left(1+\frac{i^{(m)}}{m}\right)^2+\left(1+\frac{i^{(m)}}{m}\right)^2\frac{i^{(m)}}{m}=\left(1+\frac{i^{(m)}}{m}\right)^3$
$\vdots$	$\vdots$	$\vdots$	$\vdots$
1	m	$\left(1+\frac{i^{(m)}}{m}\right)^{m-1}\frac{i^{(m)}}{m}$	$\left(1+\frac{i^{(m)}}{m}\right)^m$

- Thus, \$1 invested at $i^{(m)}$ will grow to $\left(1+\frac{i^{(m)}}{m}\right)^m$ at the end of one year.

For i and $i^{(m)}$ to be equivalent, they must accumulate to the same amount at the end of any number of years, such as one year. Thus,

$$1+i=\left(1+\frac{i^{(m)}}{m}\right)^m$$

which solves for:

$$i=\left(1+\frac{i^{(m)}}{m}\right)^m-1$$

or

$$i^{(m)}=m(1+i)^{\frac{1}{m}}-1$$

EXAMPLE 1 Determine what annual rate of interest is equivalent to $i^{(4)}=5\%$.

Solution
$$1+i^{(1)}=\left(1+\frac{0.05}{4}\right)^4=(1.0125)^4$$
$$i^{(1)}=(1.0125)^4-1=0.050945337=5.0945337\%$$

EXAMPLE 2 What nominal rate of interest, compounded monthly, is equivalent to $i^{(1)}=9.5\%$?

Solution We wish to calculate the equivalent $i^{(12)}$. Accumulating \$1 for 1 year at each interest rate and equating, we get:
$$1.095=\left(1+\frac{i^{(12)}}{12}\right)^{12}$$
$$i^{(12)}=12\left[(1.095)^{\left(\frac{1}{12}\right)}-1\right]=12(0.007591534)=0.091098411=9.1098411\%$$

EXAMPLE 3   What nominal rate of interest, compounded semi-annually, is equivalent to 8% compounded daily?

Solution   We are given $i^{(365)} = 8\%$ and we wish to calculate the equivalent $i^{(2)}$. Accumulating \$1 for one year at each interest rate and equating, we get:

$$\left(1 + \frac{i^{(2)}}{2}\right)^2 = \left(1 + \frac{0.08}{365}\right)^{365}$$

$$i^{(2)} = 2\left[(1.000219178)^{\left(\frac{365}{2}\right)} - 1\right] = 0.081612425 = 8.1612425\%$$

EXAMPLE 4   You are looking to invest some money and have narrowed your choices to the following three banks:

Bank A offers $i^{(2)} = 9\%$
Bank B offers $i^{(4)} = 8.95\%$
Bank C offers $i^{(12)} = 8.80\%$

Rank the banks from highest to lowest rates of return.

Solution   Calculate the equivalent annual effective rates of return.

Bank A: $i = \left(1 + \frac{0.09}{2}\right)^2 - 1 = 0.092025$

Bank B: $i = \left(1 + \frac{0.0895}{4}\right)^4 - 1 = 0.0925489$

Bank C: $i = \left(1 + \frac{0.0880}{12}\right)^{12} - 1 = 0.09163754$

Bank B has the highest interest rate, followed by Bank A. Bank C has the lowest rate.

For equivalent nominal rates of interest,

$$i^{(1)} > i^{(2)} > i^{(4)} > i^{(6)} > i^{(12)} > i^{(24)} > i^{(52)} > i^{(365)}$$

In other words, the more times interest is paid (or compounded) each year, the lower the nominal rate needs to be to give the same amount of interest.

Accumulating and Discounting with Nominal Rates of Interest

Suppose we wish to accumulate \$1 for t years at a nominal rate of interest of $\frac{i^{(m)}}{m}$.

We let n = term of the investment in interest periods = mt.

1. Accumulation function: $a(t) = \left(1 + \frac{i^{(m)}}{m}\right)^{mt} = \left(1 + \frac{i^{(m)}}{m}\right)^n$

2. Discount factor: $v^n = \left(1 + \frac{i^{(m)}}{m}\right)^{-mt} = \left(1 + \frac{i^{(m)}}{m}\right)^{-n}$

EXAMPLE 5   Determine the accumulated value of $5000 over 10 years at $i^{(12)} = 6\%$.

Solution   The effective rate of interest per month is $\frac{0.06}{12} = 0.005$.

Investment period $= 10$ years $\times 12 = 120$ months

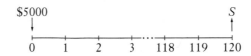

$$S = 5000(1.005)^{120} = 5000(1.819396734) = \$9096.98$$

EXAMPLE 6   You owe someone $8000 in 3 years time. If the interest rate on the loan is $i^{(4)} = 9\%$, how much did you borrow today?

Solution   The effective rate of interest per quarter is $\frac{0.09}{4} = 0.0225$.

Investment period $= 3$ years $\times 4 = 12$ quarters

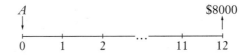

$$A = 8000(1.0225)^{-12} = 8000(0.765667477) = \$6125.34$$

Nominal Rate of Discount

We can also define a nominal rate of discount, $d^{(m)}$, in which interest is calculated (compounded, paid) at the beginning of every mth of a year:

$d^{(m)} =$ nominal rate of discount payable (compounded, convertible) m times a year

$\frac{d^{(m)}}{m} =$ effective rate of discount per mth of a year

Accumulating and Discounting with Nominal Rates of Discount

In theory, we can accumulate and discount sums of money with a nominal rate of discount. Suppose we wish to accumulate $1 for t years at a nominal rate of discount of $\frac{d^{(m)}}{m}$. We let $n =$ term of the investment in interest periods $= mt$.

1. Accumulation function, $a(t) = \left(1 - \frac{d^{(m)}}{m}\right)^{-mt} = \left(1 - \frac{d^{(m)}}{m}\right)^{-n}$

2. Discount factor, $v^n = \left(1 - \frac{d^{(m)}}{m}\right)^{mt} = \left(1 - \frac{d^{(m)}}{m}\right)^{n}$

EXAMPLE 7   What is the present value of \$3000 due at the end of 2 years at a nominal rate of discount $d^{(4)} = 8\%$?

Solution   The effective rate of discount per quarter is $\dfrac{0.08}{4} = 0.02$.

Investment period = 2 years × 4 = 8 quarters

$$A = 3000(1 - 0.02)^8 = 3000(0.98)^8 = 3000(0.850763023) = \$2552.29$$

EXAMPLE 8   You invest \$10 000 today at $d^{(2)} = 6\%$. How much will you have 42 months later?

Solution   The effective rate of discount per half year is $\dfrac{0.06}{2} = 0.03$.

Investment period = 42 months = 3.5 years = 3.5 × 2 = 7 half years

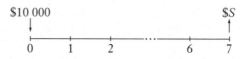

$$S = 10\,000(1 - 0.03)^{-7} = 10\,000(0.97)^{-7} = 10\,000(1.23765004) = \$12\,376.50$$

EXAMPLE 9   What effective rate of discount, d, per year is equivalent to $d^{(12)} = 9\%$?

Solution   To calculate equivalent rates of interest or discount, you accumulate \$1 for 1 year at each rate and set the two values equal to one another and solve.
- \$1 invested for 1 year at d grows to $(1 - d)^{-1}$ at the end of 1 year.
- \$1 invested for 1 year at $d^{(12)}$ grows to $\left(1 - \frac{0.09}{12}\right)^{-12}$ at the end of 1 year.

Thus,

$$(1 - d)^{-1} = \left(1 - \tfrac{0.09}{12}\right)^{-12}$$

$$(1 - d) = \left(1 - \tfrac{0.09}{12}\right)^{12}$$

which solves for:

$$d = 1 - (0.9925)^{12} = 0.086378765 = 8.64\%$$

EXAMPLE 10   What nominal rate of interest, compound monthly, is equivalent to $d^{(4)} = 8\%$?

Solution   Invest $1 for 1 year at both rates and equate:

$$\left(1 + \frac{i^{(12)}}{12}\right)^{12} = \left(1 - \frac{d^{(4)}}{4}\right)^{-4}$$

or

$$\left(1 + \frac{i^{(12)}}{12}\right)^{12} = \left(1 - \frac{0.08}{4}\right)^{-4}$$

which solves for:

$$i^{(12)} = 12\left[(0.98)^{-\left(\frac{4}{12}\right)} - 1\right] = 12(0.006756962) = 0.081083541 = 8.11\%$$

Note: Calculating equivalent interest or discount rates by investing $1 for 1 year works only for compound interest and compound discount. To calculate equivalent simple interest or simple discount rates, you must have an investment period over which you need to calculate the equivalent rates. Then you can invest $1 over that investment period.

CALCULATION TIP:

It is assumed that students will be using pocket calculators equipped with the functions y^x and $\log x$ to solve the problems in *Mathematics of Finance*. In the examples in this textbook, we have used all digits of the factors provided by a pocket calculator and rounded off to the nearest cent *only* in the final answer.

The table and graph below show the effect of time and rate on the growth of money at compound interest.

Growth of $10 000 at Compound Interest Rate $i^{(12)}$				
Years	6%	8%	10%	12%
5	13 488.50	14 898.46	16 453.09	18 166.97
10	18 193.97	22 196.40	27 070.41	33 003.87
15	24 540.94	33 069.21	44 539.20	59 958.02
20	33 102.04	49 268.03	73 280.74	108 925.54
25	44 649.70	73 401.76	120 569.45	197 884.66
30	60 225.75	109 357.30	198 373.99	359 496.41
35	81 235.51	162 925.50	326 386.50	653 095.95
40	109 564.54	242 733.86	537 006.63	1 186 477.25

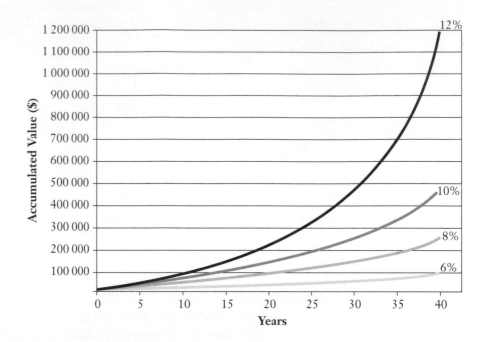

Using a Computer Spreadsheet

A computer spreadsheet is tailor made for many of the financial calculations that will be studied in this textbook. There are several spreadsheets available (such as Excel, Lotus Symphony, KSpread, OpenOffice.org Calc, Gnumeric, and Numbers) and all can generate the required calculations very well. In this text, we will present Excel spreadsheets.

We will illustrate the formulas needed to perform the calculations of Example 2 on a spreadsheet. The entries in an Excel spreadsheet are summarized below. It is assumed that the initial investment, $10 000, is entered in cell B11 (typed in as 10 000, no commas or dollar sign).

CELL	ENTER	INTERPRETATION
A1	'Years'	'End of Year'
B1	0.06	Should format so that it appears as 6%
C1	0.08	Should format so that it appears as 8%
D1	0.10	Should format so that it appears as 10%
E1	0.12	Should format so that it appears as 12%

In A2 to A9, type 5, 10, 15, 20, 25, 30, 35, and 40. In B2, we need to type the formula that will accumulate the initial investment (given in B11) to the end of 5 years at the given interest rate. Remember that the given interest rate needs to be divided by 12 (to obtain the monthly rate) and the exponent must be multiplied by 12 (to give the term in months). In B2 we type,

$$= \$B\$11*(1 + B\$1/12)^\wedge(\$A2*12)$$

To generate the rest of the values, copy B2 into C2 to E2 and then copy into B3 to E9.

Note that dollar signs before and after a letter (B11) mean the value in that cell will not change when you copy the formula. A dollar sign after the letter (B$1) means the value in that cell will change when you copy across a row, but not when you copy down a column. A dollar sign before the letter ($A2) means the value in that cell will change when you copy down a column, but not when you copy across a row.

A copy of the resulting spreadsheet is given below.

	A	B	C	D	E
1	Years	6%	8%	10%	12%
2	5	13,488.50	14,898.46	16,453.09	18,166.97
3	10	18,193.97	22,196.40	27,070.41	33,003.87
4	15	24,540.94	33,069.21	44,539.20	59,958.02
5	20	33,102.04	49,268.03	73,280.74	108,925.54
6	25	44,649.70	73,401.76	120,569.45	197,884.66
7	30	60,225.75	109,357.30	198,373.99	359,496.41
8	35	81,235.51	162,925.50	326,386.50	653,095.95
9	40	109,574.54	242,733.86	537,006.63	1,186,477.25
10					
11	Principal= $	10,000			

Exercise 1.7

Part A

1. Determine the annual effective rate (two decimals) equivalent to the following rates:
   a) $i^{(2)} = 7\%$; b) $i^{(4)} = 3\%$; c) $i^{(4)} = 8\%$;
   d) $i^{(365)} = 12\%$; e) $i^{(12)} = 9\%$.

2. Determine the nominal rate (two decimals) equivalent to the given annual effective rate:
   a) $i^{(1)} = 6\%$ determine $i^{(2)}$;
   b) $i^{(1)} = 9\%$ determine $i^{(4)}$;
   c) $i^{(1)} = 10\%$ determine $i^{(12)}$;
   d) $i^{(1)} = 17\%$ determine $i^{(365)}$;
   e) $i^{(1)} = 4.5\%$ determine $i^{(52)}$.

3. Determine the nominal rate (two decimals) equivalent to the given nominal rate:
   a) $i^{(2)} = 8\%$, determine $i^{(4)}$;
   b) $i^{(4)} = 6\%$, determine $i^{(2)}$;
   c) $i^{(12)} = 18\%$, determine $i^{(4)}$;
   d) $i^{(6)} = 10\%$, determine $i^{(12)}$;
   e) $i^{(4)} = 8\%$, determine $i^{(2)}$;
   f) $i^{(52)} = 4\%$, determine $i^{(2)}$;
   g) $i^{(2)} = 5\frac{1}{4}\%$, determine $i^{(12)}$;
   h) $i^{(4)} = 12.79\%$, determine $i^{(365)}$.

4. What simple interest rate is equivalent to $i^{(12)} = 5.7\%$ if money is invested for 2 years?

5. What simple interest rate is equivalent to $i^{(365)} = 8\%$ if money is invested for 3 years?

6. If the interest on the outstanding balance of a credit card account is charged at $1\frac{3}{4}\%$ per month, what is the annual effective rate of interest?

7. A trust company offers guaranteed investment certificates paying $i^{(2)} = 4.9\%$ and $i^{(1)} = 5\%$. Which option yields the higher annual effective rate of interest?

8. Which rate gives the best and the worst rate of return on your investment?
   a) $i^{(12)} = 15\%$, $i^{(2)} = 15\frac{1}{2}\%$, $i^{(365)} = 14.9\%$
   b) $i^{(12)} = 6\%$, $i^{(2)} = 6\frac{1}{2}\%$, $i^{(365)} = 5.9\%$.

9. Bank A has an annual effective interest rate of 10%. Bank B has a nominal interest rate of $9\frac{3}{4}\%$. What is the minimum frequency of compounding for bank B in order that the rate at bank B be at least as attractive as that at bank

A? What would be the answer if bank A offered 5% and bank B offered 4.75%?

10. Determine the accumulated value of $100 over 5 years at an 8% nominal rate compounded:
a) annually; b) semi-annually; c) quarterly; d) monthly; e) daily.

11. Parents put $1000 into a savings account at the birth of their daughter. If the account earns interest at 6% compounded monthly, how much money will be in the account when their daughter is 18 years old?

12. Determine the accumulated value of $1000 at the end of 1 year at
a) $i^{(1)} = 6.136\%$; b) $i^{(2)} = 6.045\%$; c) $i^{(4)} = 6\%$; d) $i^{(12)} = 5.970\%$.

13. An obligation of $2000 is due December 31, 2014. What is the value of this obligation on June 30, 2010, at $i^{(4)} = 5.5\%$?

14. A man can buy a piece of land for $400 000 cash or payments of $230 000 down and $200 000 in 5 years. If he can earn $i^{(2)} = 4\%$, which plan is better?

15. Calculate the total value on July 1, 2010, of payments of $1000 on July 1, 2000, and $600 on July 1, 2017, if $i^{(2)} = 9\%$.

16. If money is worth $i^{(1)} = 10\%$, determine the present value of a debt of $3000 with interest at $11\frac{1}{2}\%$ compounded semi-annually due in 5 years.

17. Determine the annual effective interest rate, $i^{(1)}$, (to two decimals) equivalent to a nominal discount rate of $d^{(4)} = 7\%$.

18. Calculate the present value of $1000 due in 5 years at each of the following rates:
a) $i^{(4)} = 8\%$; b) $i^{(365)} = 5\%$; c) $d^{(2)} = 10\%$; d) $d^{(12)} = 9\%$.

19. Calculate the accumulated value at $t = 10$ years of $5000 invested today at each of the following rates:
a) $i^{(12)} = 8\%$; b) $i^{(2)} = 5\%$; c) $d^{(4)} = 6\%$; d) $d^{(365)} = 7\%$.

20. a) Determine $d^{(4)}$ equivalent to a simple rate of interest $i = 8\%$.
b) Determine $d^{(4)}$ equivalent to a simple rate of discount $d = 8\%$.

Part B

1. Twenty thousand dollars is invested for 5 years at a nominal rate of 6%. Determine the accumulated value of the investment if the rate is compounded with frequencies $m = 1, 2, 4, 12$, and 365 using
a) the fundamental compound interest formula;
b) equivalent annual effective rates;
c) equivalent nominal rates compounded monthly. Compare your answers in a), b), and c).

2. A bank pays 6% per annum on its savings accounts. At the end of every 3 years a 2% bonus is paid on the balance. Determine the annual effective rate of interest, $i^{(1)}$, earned by an investor if the deposit is withdrawn:
a) in 2 years, b) in 3 years, c) in 4 years.

3. A fund earns interest at the nominal rate of 8.04% compounded quarterly. At the end of each quarter, just after interest is credited, an expense charge equal to 0.50% of the fund is withdrawn. Determine the annual effective yield realized by the fund.

4. An insurance company says you can pay for your life insurance by paying $100 at the beginning of each year or $51.50 at the beginning of each half-year. They say the rate of interest underlying this calculation is $i^{(2)} = 3\%$. What is the true value of $i^{(2)}$?

5. In general, the *annual effective rate of interest* is the ratio of the amount of interest earned during the year to the amount of principal invested at the beginning of the year.
a) Show that, at a simple interest rate r, the annual effective rate of interest for the nth year is $\dfrac{r}{1 + r(n - 1)}$, which is a decreasing function of n. Thus a constant rate of simple interest implies a decreasing annual effective rate of interest.
b) Show that, at a compound interest rate i per year, the annual effective rate of interest for the nth year is i, which is independent of n. Thus a constant rate of compound interest implies a constant annual effective rate of interest.

6. Melinda has a savings account that earns interest at 6% per annum. She opened her account with $1000 on December 31. How much interest will she earn during the first year if
a) the interest is compounded daily;
b) the interest is calculated daily and paid into the account on June 30 and December 31;
c) the interest is calculated daily and paid into the account at the end of each month?

7. Determine the compound interest earned on an investment of $10 000 for 10 years at a nominal rate of 5.4% compounded with frequencies $m = 1, 2, 4, 12, 52$, and 365.

8. A note for $2500 dated January 1, 2011, is due with interest at $i^{(12)} = 12\%$ 40 months later. On May 1, 2011, the holder of the note has it discounted by Financial Consultants Inc. at $i^{(4)} = 13\frac{1}{4}\%$. On the same day, Financial Consultants Inc. sells the note to a bank that discounts notes at $i^{(1)} = 13\%$. What is the profit made by Financial Consultants Inc.?

9. Determine the compound discount if $1000, due in 5 years with interest at $i^{(1)} = 7\frac{1}{2}\%$, is discounted at a nominal rate of 6% compounded with frequencies $m = 1, 2, 4, 12, 52$, and 365.

10. Given that $0 < d < 1$, show that:
a) $(1 - d)^t < 1 - dt$, if $0 < t < 1$;
b) $(1 - d)^t = 1 - dt$, if $t = 1$;
c) $(1 - d)^t > 1 - dt$, if $t > 1$.

11. If i and d are equivalent rates of simple interest and simple discount over t periods, show that $i - d = idt$.

| Section 1.8 | **Forces of Interest and Discount** |

In any text on calculus one will find the equation

$$\lim_{m \to \infty} \left(1 + \frac{x}{m}\right)^m = e^x$$

where the number $e \doteq 2.718$ has an infinite expansion and is the base of the natural logarithms.

This equation will be useful in compound interest problems where a nominal rate of interest is compounded continuously. Continuous compounding is an important topic for actuaries to develop theoretical models in actuarial science.

We have already dealt with problems where the nominal rate i has been compounded as often as daily. For example, consider the nominal rate of interest $i^{(m)} = 12\%$ compounded at different frequencies and compare the accumulated value of $1 over a 1-year period (so-called annual accumulation factors). The results can be summarized in the following table.

$$i^{(m)} = 12\%$$

m	**Annual Accumulation Factor**
1	$(1.12)^1 = 1.12$
2	$\left(1 + \frac{0.12}{4}\right)^2 = 1.1236$
4	$\left(1 + \frac{0.12}{4}\right)^4 = 1.12550881$
12	$\left(1 + \frac{0.12}{4}\right)^{12} = 1.12682503$
52	$\left(1 + \frac{0.12}{4}\right)^{52} = 1.127340987$
365	$\left(1 + \frac{0.12}{4}\right)^{365} = 1.127474614$

From the above table we can see that as the frequency m of compounding increases, the annual accumulation factor also increases and approaches an upper bound as m is increased without limit, i.e., $m \to \infty$. To determine this upper bound that represents the annual accumulation factor at nominal rate 12% compounded continuously (i.e., $\delta = 12\%$), we wish to calculate:

$$\lim_{m \to \infty}\left(1 + \tfrac{0.12}{m}\right)^m$$

Using the equation

$$\lim_{m \to \infty}\left(1 + \tfrac{x}{m}\right)^m = e^x$$

we obtain

$$\lim_{m \to \infty}\left(1 + \tfrac{0.12}{m}\right)^m = e^{0.12} = 1.127496852$$

Thus, if $i^{(\infty)} = \delta = 12\%$, then the equivalent effective annual rate of interest is $i = 12.7496852\%$.

Alternative Derivation of the Force of Interest

It is possible to derive relationships between $i^{(1)}$, $i^{(m)}$, and $\delta =$ the force of interest, in a more mathematically disciplined approach.

Suppose you have an investment, $A(0)$, earning $i^{(4)}$.

At the end of the first quarter,

$$A\left(\tfrac{1}{4}\right) = A(0)\left(1 + \tfrac{i^{(4)}}{4}\right)$$

Amount of interest earned in the first three months $= A\left(\tfrac{1}{4}\right) - A(0)$

We can generalize this result to any three-month period.

Amount of interest earned in any three-month period $= A\left(t + \tfrac{1}{4}\right) - A(t)$

The effective rate of interest earned for this three-month period is:

$$\frac{i^{(4)}}{4} = \frac{A(t + 1/4) - A(t)}{A(t)} = \frac{a(t + 1/4) - A(t)}{a(t)}$$

and

$$i^{(4)} = 4\left[\frac{a(t + 1/4) - a(t)}{a(t)}\right]$$

If you were earning a nominal rate of interest compounded monthly, then we would be interested in the amount of interest earned in any monthly period and interested in the nominal rate of interest compounded monthly,

$$i^{(12)} = 12\left[\frac{a(t + 1/12) - a(t)}{a(t)}\right]$$

Generalizing this to any nominal rate, we obtain:

$$i^{(m)} = m\left[\frac{a(t + 1/m) - a(t)}{a(t)}\right]$$

If we take the limit of $i^{(m)}$ as $m \to \infty$, we get

$$\delta_t = i^{(\infty)} = \lim_{m \to \infty} m\left[\frac{a(t + 1/m) - a(t)}{a(t)}\right]$$

Let $h = \frac{1}{m}$, so that as $h \to 0$, $m \to \infty$,

$$\delta_t = i^{(\infty)} = \lim_{h \to 0}\left[\frac{a(t + h) - a(t)}{ha(t)}\right] = \frac{1}{a(t)}\lim_{h \to 0}\left[\frac{a(t + h) - a(t)}{h}\right] = \frac{1}{a(t)}\frac{d}{dt}a(t) = \frac{a'(t)}{a(t)}$$

Note 1: $\delta_t = i^{(\infty)}$ is called the *force of interest.*

Note 2: If $a(t + 1) - a(t)$ is the amount of growth in an investment of \$1 from time t to $t + 1$, then $a'(t)dt$ represents the instantaneous amount of growth of the investment at exact time t.

Note 3: Thus, $\delta_t = i^{(\infty)} = \frac{a'(t)}{a(t)}$ is a measure of the relative instantaneous rate of growth at exact time t (that is, δ_t is a measure of the intensity with which interest is operating at exact time t).

Note 4: δ_t may change as t changes.

Alternatively,

$$\delta_t = i^{(\infty)} = \frac{d}{dt}\ln a(t) = \frac{a'(t)}{a(t)}$$

Integrating both sides, we get:

$$a(t) = e^{\int_0^t \delta_r dr}$$

and

$$A(t) = A(0)e^{\int_0^t \delta_r dr}$$

The above formula can be used to accumulate (or take the present value of) a sum of money for t years when the force of interest varies over the t years. An example of this will be presented in section 1.9.

Constant Force of Interest

In a compound interest situation, the accumulation function is $a(t) = (1 + i)^t$.
Thus,

$$\delta_t = i^{(\infty)} = \frac{d}{dt}\ln a(t) = \frac{d}{dt}\ln(1 + i)^t = \frac{d}{dt}t\cdot\ln(1 + i) = \ln(1 + i)$$

We see that if the effective rate of compound interest is constant, then the force of interest is constant.

$$\delta = \ln(1 + i)$$

Accumulating and Discounting Under a Constant Force of Interest

Accumulation Function

$$a(t) = e^{t\delta} \text{ and } A(t) = A(0)e^{t\delta}$$

Discount Factor

$$v^t = e^{-t\delta}$$

EXAMPLE 1   Determine

a) The rates $i^{(2)}$ and $i^{(4)}$ that are equivalent to $\delta = 6\%$.

b) The rate δ that is equivalent to $i^{(1)} = 9\%$ and $i^{(12)} = 9\%$.

Solution a   Using the principles of section 2.2, we equate the annual accumulation factors at each interest rate and obtain:

$$(1 + i)^2 = e^{0.06}$$
$$i = e^{0.06/2} - 1$$
$$i = 0.030454534$$
$$i^{(2)} = 2i = 0.060909067$$
$$i^{(2)} \doteq 6.09\%$$

$$(1 + i)^4 = e^{0.06}$$
$$i = e^{0.06/4} - 1$$
$$i = 0.015113064$$
$$i^{(4)} = 4i = 0.060452258$$
$$i^{(4)} \doteq 6.05\%$$

Solution b   Again using the principles of accumulating \$1 for 1 year under each interest rate, we obtain:

$$(1.09) = e^{\delta}$$
$$\delta = \ln(1.09) = 0.086177696 \doteq 8.62\%$$

$$(1.0075)^{12} = e^{\delta}$$
$$\delta = 12 \ln(1.0075) = 0.089664178 \doteq 8.97\%$$

OBSERVATION:

We can generalize the results of Example 1a) and state that for rates of interest that are equivalent,

$$i^{(1)} > i^{(2)} > i^{(4)} > i^{(12)} > i^{(365)} > \delta.$$

The accumulated value S of principal P at rate $i^{(m)}$ for t years is

$$S = P\left(1 + \frac{i^{(m)}}{m}\right)^{mt} = P\left[\left(1 + \frac{i^{(m)}}{m}\right)^{m}\right]^{t}$$

If interest is compounded continuously

$$\boxed{S = \lim_{m \to \infty} P\left[\left(1 + \frac{i^{(m)}}{m}\right)^{m}\right]^{t} = Pe^{\delta t}} \tag{6}$$

Similarly we can develop the formula for the discounted value P, given S, δ, and t.

$$\boxed{P = Se^{-\delta t}} \tag{7}$$

The following examples illustrate how the formula $S = Pe^{\delta t}$, can be used to determine the accumulated value S, the discounted value P, the rate δ, the effective rate i, and time in years t.

EXAMPLE 2 Determine the accumulated value of \$5000 over 15 months at a nominal rate of 8% compounded continuously.

Solution We have $\delta = 0.08$, $t = \frac{15}{12} = 1.25$ and so can calculate the accumulated value S of \$5000:

$$S = 5000\, e^{(0.08)(1.25)} = \$5525.85$$

EXAMPLE 3 You owe \$2500 in 9 months and another \$2800 in 27 months. How much did you borrow today if you are charged interest at 5% compounded continuously?

Solution
$$\begin{aligned}
P &= \text{present value of \$2500} + \text{present value of \$2800} \\
&= 2500e^{-(0.05)(9/12)} + 2500e^{-(0.05)(27/12)} \\
&= 2500e^{-(0.05)(0.75)} + 2500e^{-(0.05)(2.25)} \\
&= 2407.99 + 2502.07 \\
&= \$4910.06
\end{aligned}$$

EXAMPLE 4 A mutual fund deposit of \$1000 increased in value by \$560 over 30 months. Determine

    a) the continuous rate of increase;
    b) the annual effective rate of increase.

Solution a We have $P = 1000$, $S = 1560$, $t = \frac{30}{12} = 2.5$, and can solve the equation for δ.

$$\begin{aligned}
1000e^{\delta(2.5)} &= 1560 \\
e^{2.5\delta} &= 1.560 \\
2.5\delta &= \ln 1.560 \\
\delta &= \frac{\ln 1.560}{2.5} \\
\delta &= 0.177874329 \\
\delta &\doteq 17.79\%
\end{aligned}$$

Solution b We want to determine the equivalent annual effective rate $i^{(1)}$ for a given rate $\delta = 0.177874329$ by comparing the accumulated value of $1 at the end of 1 year:

$1 at $i^{(1)}$ will accumulate to $1 + i$

$1 at $\delta = 0.177874329$ will accumulate to $e^{0.177874329}$

Thus

$$1 + i = e^{0.177874329}$$
$$i = e^{0.177874329} - 1$$
$$i = 0.194675175$$
$$i \doteq 19.47\%$$

We can also determine $i^{(1)}$ by solving the equation

$$1000(1 + i)^{2.5} = 1560$$
$$(1 + i)^{2.5} = 1.560$$
$$1 + i = (1.560)^{1/2.5}$$
$$i = (1.560)^{1/2.5} - 1$$
$$i = 0.194675175$$
$$i^{(1)} \doteq 19.47\%$$

EXAMPLE 5 How long will it take to triple your investment at 6.25% compounded continuously?

Solution We have $P = x$, $S = 3x$, $\delta = 0.0625$ and can solve the equation below for time t in years.

$$xe^{0.0625t} = 3x$$
$$e^{0.0625t} = 3$$
$$0.0625t = \ln 3$$
$$t = \frac{\ln 3}{0.0625}$$
$$t = 17.5777966 \text{ years}$$
$$t \doteq 17 \text{ years, 6 months, 28 days}$$

Lastly, we leave it to the student to show that $\lim_{n \to \infty} d^{(n)} = \delta$.

Exercise 1.8

Part A

1. Fifteen hundred dollars is invested for 18 months at a nominal rate of 9%. Determine the accumulated value if interest is compounded a) annually; b) monthly; c) continuously.

2. A debt of $8000 is due in 5 years. Determine the original loan amount if the interest rate is 8% compounded a) quarterly; b) daily; c) continuously.

3. At what nominal rate compounded continuously will your investment increase 50% in value in 3 years? Determine also the equivalent annual effective rate.

4. By what date will $800 deposited on February 4, 2009, be worth at least $1200
   a) at 6% compounded daily;
   b) at 6% compounded continuously?

5. If money doubles at a certain rate of interest compounded continuously in 5 years, how long will it take for the same amount of money to triple in value?

6. Shirley must borrow $1000 for 2 years. She is offered the money at
   a) 8% compounded continuously;
   b) $8\frac{1}{4}$% compounded semi-annually;
   c) $8\frac{1}{2}$% simple interest.

   Which offer should she accept?

Part B

1. What simple interest rate is equivalent to the force of interest $\delta = 7$% if money is invested for 5 years?

2. If the population of the world doubles every 25 years, how long does it take to increase by 50%? Assume population growth takes place continuously at a uniform rate.

3. The force of interest is $\delta = 10$%. At what time should a single payment of $2500 be made so as to be equivalent to payments of $1000 in 1.25 years and $1500 in 6.5 years?

4. How long will it take $250 to accumulate to $400, if the force of interest is $\delta = 7$% for the first 2 years and $\delta = 8$% thereafter?

5. Jill borrowed $1000 and wants to pay off the debt by payments of $400 at the end of 3 months and 2 equal payments at the end of 6 months and 12 months. What will these payments be if the force of interest is $\delta = 10$%?

6. What simple discount rate is equivalent to 8% compounded continuously if money is invested for 4 years?

Section 1.9 **Varying Rates**

The previous sections have assumed that the rate of compound interest relevant to any particular problem remains unchanged throughout the term of the problem. However, this need not be the case and, in practice, interest rates vary with considerable frequency. For instance, banks, trust companies, and credit unions vary their deposit rates with changes in market conditions.

In situations like this, an investor is most often interested in two things: how much will their investment accumulate to and what was the return on investment (ROI).

This complication of changing interest rates is not really a difficulty as the problems may be solved by completing the appropriate compound interest calculations in stages. As shown in the following examples, intermediate values are determined at each date that has an interest rate change. No new compound interest techniques are required and these problems may be considered to be two or more compound interest problems, simply expressed in one question.

EXAMPLE 1 Marc invested $1000 in a savings account. The account paid interest at $i^{(1)} = 6\%$ for 6 years followed by $i^{(1)} = 4\%$ thereafter. How much did Marc have in the account after 8 years? What annual effective rate of return, i, did he earn each year over the 8 years?

Solution The time diagram below sets out the two stages in the calculation and the two interest rates.

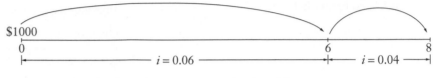

$$\$1000$$
$$\begin{array}{ccc} 0 & 6 & 8 \end{array}$$
$$i = 0.06 \qquad i = 0.04$$

Accumulated value after 6 years $= 1000(1.06)^6$
$$\doteq 1418.52$$
Accumulated value after 8 years $= 1418.52(1.04)^2$
$$\doteq 1534.27$$

or

Accumulated value after 8 years $= 1000(1.06)^6(1.04)^2$
$$\doteq 1534.27$$

To calculate Marc's annual effective rate of return over 8 years, we use the principles of section 1.7. The accumulated value of $1 over 8 years at i is $(1 + i)^8$. The accumulated value of $1 over 8 years at the given interest rates is $(1.06)^6(1.04)^2$. Thus,

$$(1 + i)^8 = (1.06)^6(1.04)^2 = 1.534270272$$
$$i = (1.534270272)^{1/8} - 1$$
$$i = 0.054964228$$
$$i \doteq 5.50\%$$

OBSERVATION:

When compound interest rates vary, an average interest rate must *never* be calculated. Each compound interest rate must be allowed to have its full effect.

EXAMPLE 2 Cheryl took out a loan and must repay $10 000 in 10 years. The interest rates on the loan were $i^{(4)} = 8\%$ for the first 3 years, $i^{(2)} = 10\%$ for the next 5 years, and $i^{(1)} = 9\%$ for the last 2 years. What was the original amount of the loan? What annual effective rate of interest was Cheryl charged over the 10-year period?

Solution This problem should be tackled in three stages, moving from the value in 10 years time toward the present value, stopping at each date that has an interest rate change. The following time diagram illustrates the problem:

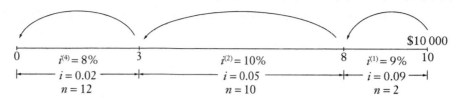

The three stages in this solution are:

Step 1   Value in 8 years time $= 10\ 000(1.09)^{-2}$
$$\doteq 8416.80$$

Step 2   Value in 3 years time $= 8416.80(1.05)^{-10}$
$$\doteq 5167.19$$

Step 3   Value now $= 5167.19(1.02)^{-12}$
$$\doteq 4074.29$$

This solution may also be expressed as:

$$\text{Present value} = \$10\ 000(1.02)^{-12}(1.05)^{-10}(1.09)^{-2}$$
$$= \$4074.29$$

There are two ways to determine the annual effective rate of interest, i.

$\$4074.29 = \$10\ 000(1 + i)^{-10}$, which solves for $i = 9.39\%$

OR: Accumulate \$1 for 10 years at i and set equal to the accumulated value of \$1 at the given interest rates.

$$(1 + i)^{10} = (1.02)^{12}(1.05)^{10}(1.09)^2$$
$$i = (2.45441529)^{1/10} - 1 = 0.09394328 \doteq 9.39\%$$

EXAMPLE 3   A student owes \$200 in 6 months and \$300 in 15 months. What single payment now will repay these debts if the interest rate is $i^{(4)} = 12\%$ for 9 months and $i^{(4)} = 8\%$ thereafter?

Solution   We arrange the data as set out in the following time diagram, where X is the single payment and time is expressed in quarters.

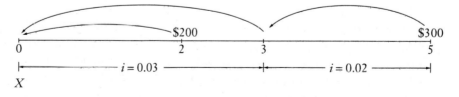

$$\text{The present value of the } \$200 \text{ debt} = 200(1.03)^{-2}$$
$$\doteq 188.52$$

$$\text{The value at time 3 of the } \$300 \text{ debt} = 300(1.02)^{-2}$$
$$\doteq 288.35$$

$$\text{The present value of the } \$300 \text{ debt} = 288.35(1.03)^{-3}$$
$$\doteq 263.88$$

$$\text{Hence the present value of both debts} = \$188.52 + \$263.88$$
$$= \$452.40$$

This solution may also be expressed as
$$X = 200(1.03)^{-2} + 300(1.02)^{-2}(1.03)^{-3}$$
$$\doteq 188.52 + 263.88$$
$$= 452.40$$

The following example illustrates varying continuously compounded interest (that is, situations in which δ_t varies with t).

EXAMPLE 4   Calculate the accumulated value of $1250 at the end of 5 years if $\delta_t = \dfrac{1}{1 + \frac{1}{2}t}$.

Solution   We know that $a(t) = e^{\int_0^t \delta_r\,dr}$.
We have:

$$\int_0^5 \frac{1}{1 + \frac{1}{2}t}\,dt = 2\ln\left(1 + \tfrac{1}{2}t\right)\big|_{t=0}^{t=5} = 2[\ln(3.5) - \ln(1)] = 2\ln(3.5) = \ln(3.5)^2$$

Thus,

$$A(5) = 1250e^{\ln(3.5)^2} = 1250(3.5)^2 = 1250(12.25) = \$15\ 312.50$$

Exercise 1.9

Part A

1. How much will $2000 accumulate to in 12 years if the interest rate is $i^{(1)} = 11\%$ for the first 6 years and $i^{(1)} = 9\%$ for the next 6 years?

2. What is the present value of $1000 in 6 years if $i^{(1)} = 8\%$ for 2 years and $i^{(1)} = 7\%$ thereafter?

3. Carol deposited $500 into her credit union account on January 1, 2007. What will be in the account on January 1, 2012, if $i^{(2)} = 5\%$ for 2007, $i^{(2)} = 6\%$ for 2008 and 2009, and $i^{(2)} = 4.5\%$ for 2010 and 2011? What effective rate of return did Carol earn over the 5-year period?

4. Two thousand dollars are invested for 10 years at the following interest rates:
   $i^{(2)} = 5\%$ for years 1, 2, and 3;
   $i^{(4)} = 8\%$ for years 4, 5, 6, and 7; and
   $i^{(12)} = 6\%$ for years 8, 9, and 10.
   Determine the accumulated value and the com-

pound interest earned. What equivalent nominal rate, $i^{(2)}$, was earned over the 10-year period?

5. What sum of money due on July 1, 2011, is equivalent to $2000 due on January 1, 2005, if $d^{(2)} = 10\%$ for 2005 and 2006, and $d^{(2)} = 9\%$ thereafter?

6. A debt of $5000 is due at the end of 5 years. It is proposed that $X be paid now with another $X paid in 10 years time to liquidate the debt. Calculate the value of X if the effective interest rate is 6.1% for the first 6 years and 4.8% for the next 4 years.

7. A company wishes to replace the following three debts:
$20 000 due on July 1, 2008
$30 000 due on January 1, 2011 and
$35 000 due on July 1, 2014
with a single debt of $Y payable on January 1, 2011. Calculate the value of Y if $i^{(2)} = 12\%$ prior to January 1, 2011 and $i^{(2)} = 10\%$ after January 1, 2011.

8. A young couple owns a block of land worth $290 000. They are offered a 20% deposit and 2 equal payments of $150 000 each at the end of years 2 and 4. If money is worth $i^{(2)} = 8\%$ for the first 2 years and $i^{(4)} = 12\%$ for the next 2 years, should they accept the offer?

9. A person can buy a lot for $155 000 cash outright or $60 000 down, $60 000 in 2 years, and $60 000 in 5 years. Which option is better if money can be invested at
a) $i^{(12)} = 7.2\%$?
b) $i^{(4)} = 7.5\%$ for the first 3 years and $i^{(4)} = 4\%$ for the next 2 years?

10. Determine the annual effective rate of interest that is equivalent to $i^{(4)} = 6\%$ for 2 years followed by $i^{(12)} = 8\%$ for 4 years.

11. Determine the annual effective rate of discount, d, over 6 years, that is equivalent to $d^{(4)} = 4\%$ for 2 years followed by $d^{(2)} = 9\%$ for the next 4 years.

12. Calculate the accumulated value of $1000 at the end of 5 years if $\delta_t = (1 + t)^{-1}$.

13. Calculate the annual effective interest rate, $i^{(1)}$, equivalent to $\delta_t = 0.01t$ for the period $0 \le t \le 2$.

14. Determine the accumulated value of $100 at the end of 10 years if $\delta_t = 0.04(1 + t)^{-2}$.

15. An investment is made for one year in a fund where the accumulation function is a second degree polynomial. The fund earns $i^{(2)} = 5\%$ in the first six months. Over the entire year, the fund yields $i^{(1)} = 7\%$ effective. What is $\delta_{0.75}$?

16. Given $\delta_t = 0.01 + 0.004t$, determine the accumulated value over 5 years of $1000 invested today.

17. What is the level effective rate of interest, $i^{(1)}$, over a 5-year period if the fund earns $d^{(4)} = 6\%$ for the next 2 years, $d^{(2)} = 7\%$ for the next 2 years and $d^{(12)} = 8\%$ in the last year?

18. Given $\delta_t = 2(1 - 2t)^{-1}$, determine $a(t)$.

19. Given $\delta_t = t^2(1 + t^3)^{-1}$ calculate the present value of $300 due at $t = 5$.

20. The force of interest, δt is:
$$\delta_t = \begin{cases} 0.03 & 0 < t \le 4 \\ 0.01(t^2 - t) & t > 5 \end{cases}$$
Calculate the present value of $5000 payable at time $t = 10$.

Part B

1. Show algebraically that
$$(1 + i)^n \times (1 + j)^n \ne \left(1 + \frac{i + j}{2}\right)^{2n}$$
and hence conclude that compound interest rates should not be averaged.

2. Guo invests $500 for 4 years. The nominal interest rate remains 8% each year although in the first year it is compounded semi-annually, in the second year compounded quarterly, in the third year compounded monthly, and in the fourth year compounded daily. What is the accumulated value? How much greater is this value than the corresponding value assuming that the first rate had remained unchanged for the 4 years?

3. Calculate the payment due on July 1, 2011, that is equivalent to $1000 due on January 1, 2008, plus $2000 due on March 1, 2013, if $i^{(4)} = 8\%$ prior to July 1, 2011, and $i^{(12)} = 12\%$ thereafter.

4. Determine the lump sum that is needed to be invested today in order to receive $20 000 in 8 years and another $30 000 in 15 years if

$i^{(1)} = 12\%$ for years 1, 2, and 3;
$i^{(2)} = 10\%$ for years 4, 5, 6, 7, 8, and 9;
$i^{(4)} = 8\%$ for years 10, 11, and 12; and
$i^{(12)} = 9\%$ for years 13, 14, and 15.

5. $1000 was deposited on January 1, 2006, and $2000 was deposited in an account on July 1, 2008. Interest was paid on the account at $d^{(4)} = 7\%$ from January 1, 2006, to October 1, 2008, and at $d^{(2)} = 5\%$ from October 1, 2008, until April 1, 2010. Determine the amount in the account on April 1, 2010, and determine the equivalent nominal interest rate compounded monthly actually earned on the investment over the period.

6. A sum of money is left invested for 3 years. In the first year, it earns interest at $i^{(12)} = 4\%$. In the second year, the rate of interest earned is $i^{(4)} = 8\%$, and in the third year the rate of interest changes to $i^{(365)} = 5.5\%$. Calculate the level rate of interest, $i^{(1)}$, that would give the same accumulated value at the end of 3 years.

7. What compound interest rate, $i^{(4)}$, is equivalent over a 3-year period to a simple interest rate of 6% the first year, followed by a simple discount rate of 8% for the next 2 years?

8. Determine the following derivatives:
   a) $\frac{d}{di}v$, b) $\frac{d}{di}\delta$, c) $\frac{d}{di}d$, d) $\frac{d}{d\delta}i$, e) $\frac{d}{d\delta}d$

9. Determine an expression for δ_t at:
   a) simple interest rate, i, per annum;
   b) simple discount rate, d, per annum.

10. At time $t = 0$, $1000 is deposited into each of Fund A and Fund B. Fund A accumulates at $d^{(4)} = 8\%$. Fund B accumulates $\delta = at^2$. At time $t = 4$, the accumulated value of the two funds is equal. Determine a.

Section 1.10   **Summary and Review Exercises**

- $a(t)$, is the accumulation function, where $a(0) = 1$.
  - Under simple interest, $a(t) = 1 + rt$.
  - Under compound interest, $a(t) = (1 + i)^t$.
- $A(t)$ is the amount function, where $A(0) = P$.
  - Under simple interest, $A(t) = P(1 + rt)$.
  - Under compound interest, $A(t) = P(1 + i)^t$.
- The accumulated value of P at the end of t years is:
  - $P(1 + rt)$ at simple interest, where $(1 + rt)$ is the accumulation factor at simple interest rate r and
  - $P(1 + i)^t$ at compound interest where $(1 + i)^t$ is the accumulation factor at compound interest rate i.
- The present value of S due in t years is:
  - $S(1 + rt)^{-1}$ at simple interest, where $(1 + rt)^{-1}$ is the discount value factor at simple interest rate i, and
  - $S(1 + i)^{-t} = Sv^t$ at compound interest, where $(1 + i)^{-t} = v^t$ is the discount value factor at compound interest rate i.
- Interest paid in advance is called discount and denoted, d so that $d = i(1 + i)^{-1} = \frac{i}{1 + i}$.
- The present value of S due in t years is:
  - $S(1 - d)^t$ where $(1 - d)^t$ is the present value factor at compound discount rate d, and
  - $S(1 - dt)$ where $(1 - dt)$ is the present value factor at simple discount rate d.

- The accumulated value of P at the end of t years is:
  - $P(1 - d)^{-t}$, where $(1 - d)^{-t}$ is an accumulation factor at compound discount rate d, and
  - $P(1 - dt)^{-1}$, where $(1 - dt)^{-1}$ is an accumulation factor at simple discount rate d.

- Equivalent rates: Two rates are equivalent if they have the same effect on money over the same period of time. (**Note:** At simple rates of interest and discount, the equivalent rates are dependent on the period of time.)

- The accumulated value of P at the end of n periods at the interest rate $i = \frac{i^{(m)}}{m}$ per interest period is given by $P(1 + i)^n$ where $(1 + i)^n$ is the accumulation factor at compound interest.

- The discounted value of S due at the end of n periods at the interest rate $i = \frac{i^{(m)}}{m}$ per interest period is given by $S(1 + i)^{-n}$ where $(1 + i)^{-n}$ is the discount factor at compound interest.

- The accumulated value of P at the end of t years at force of interest δ is given by $Pe^{\delta t}$, where $e^{\delta t}$ is the accumulation factor at continuous compounding.

- The discounted value of S due in t years at force of interest δ is given by $Se^{-\delta t}$, where $e^{-\delta t}$ is called a discount factor at continuous compounding.

Review Exercise 1.10

1. Determine the total value on June 1, 2011, of $1000 due on December 1, 2006, and $800 due on December 1, 2016, at $i^{(2)} = 6.38\%$.

2. A person deposits $1500 into a mutual fund. If the fund earns 9.8% per annum compounded daily for 10 years, what will be the accumulated value of the initial deposit?

3. You are given $a(t) = xt^2 + yt + z$, $a(1) = 1.08$ and $a(2) = 1.17$. If $5000 is invested at $t = 0$, determine the accumulated value at $t = 6.5$.

4. You are given $A(t) = t^2 + 4t + 5$. Determine:
   a) $a(n)$
   b) I_n
   c) δ_n

5. The XYZ company has had an increase in sales of 4% per annum. If sales in 2010 are $680\,000$, what would be the estimated sales for 2015?

6. Calculate the amount of interest earned between 5 and 10 years after the date of an investment of $100 if interest is paid semi-annually at $i^{(2)} = 7\%$.

7. Given $a(t) = xt^2 + y$ and that $2000 invested at time $t = 0$ accumulates to $2500 at time $t = 3$, calculate the accumulated value at time $t = 5$.

8. A trust company offers guaranteed investment certificates paying $i^{(2)} = 6\frac{3}{4}\%$, $i^{(4)} = 6\frac{1}{4}\%$, or $i^{(12)} = 6\frac{1}{8}\%$. Rate the options from best to worst.

9. Given $A(t) = 500 + 20t$, determine:
   a) I_{10} and i_{10}
   b) I_{20} and i_{20}

10. Given a deposit of $1000 at time $t = 0$, determine the accumulated value at time $t = 10$, given:
    a) $i = 5.5\%$,
    b) $i^{(4)} = 6\%$,
    c) $d = 4\%$,
    d) $d^{(12)} = 9\%$, and
    e) $\delta = 7\%$.

11. If Susan borrows $1000 today at $i^{(12)} = 7.2\%$,
    a) How much does she repay in 4 years?
    b) What is the equivalent annual effective rate of interest?

12. If you borrow $2000 today, how much will you have to repay in 5 years if:
    a) $i^{(1)} = 4\%$,
    b) $i^{(365)} = 7\%$,
    c) $d = 6\%$
    d) $d^{(4)} = 8\%$,
    e) $\delta = 5\%$.

13. Given $i = 5\%$ per annum effective, determine the equivalent rates:
    a) $i^{(12)}$
    b) d
    c) $d^{(4)}$
    d) δ

14. Rajiv needs to borrow some money today. He has the choice of two rates:
    $i^{(2)} = 10.2\%$ or $d^{(4)} = 9.6\%$. Which should he choose?

15. At what nominal rate compounded a) monthly, b) daily, c) continuously, will money triple in value in 10 years?

16. Paul has deposited $1000 in a savings account paying interest at $i^{(1)} = 4.5\%$ and now finds that his deposits have accumulated to $1246.18. If he had been able to invest the $1000 over the same period in a guaranteed investment certificate paying interest at $i^{(1)} = 6\%$, to what sum would his $1000 now have accumulated?

17. A piece of land can be purchased by paying $500 000 cash or $200 000 down and equal payments of $200 000 at the end of two and four years respectively. To pay cash, the buyer would have to withdraw money from an investment earning interest at rate $i^{(2)} = 8\%$. Which option is better and by how much?

18. A note for $2000 dated October 6, 2009 is due with compound interest at $i^{(12)} = 8\%$, two years after the date. On January 16, 2011, the holder of the note has it discounted by a lender who charges $i^{(4)} = 9\%$. Determine the proceeds and the compound discount.

19. Jackie invested $500 in an investment fund. Determine the accumulated value of her investment at the end of 6 years, if the interest rate was $i^{(2)} = 5.3\%$ for the first two years, $i^{(12)} = 7\%$ for the next three years, and $i^{(365)} = 4.5\%$ for the last year. What effective rate, i, did she earn over the 6 years?

20. Calculate the present value of $2000 due in $5\frac{1}{2}$ years if $i^{(4)} = 8\%$ for the first two years and $i^{(12)} = 10\%$ thereafter.

21. Calculate the accumulated value of $1000 at the end of 5 years using:
    a) annual effective interest rate of 6%;
    b) nominal interest rate of 6% compounded monthly;
    c) force of interest of 6% per annum.

22. Julie bought $2000 in Savings Bonds that paid interest at $i^{(1)} = 5\%$ with interest accruing at a simple interest rate for each month before November 1 (i.e., for any partial year). How much will she receive for the bonds if they are cashed in 5 years and 3 months after the date of issue?

23. If $\delta_t = (1 + 0.5t)^{-1}$ calculate the
    a) accumulated value of $1000 at the end of 10 years,
    b) equivalent effective rate, i, over 10 years,
    c) equivalent rate, $d^{(12)}$, over 10 years.

24. You borrow $4000 now and agree to pay $X in 3 months, $2X in 7 months, and $2X in 12 months. Determine X, if interest is at 9% compounded a) monthly; b) continuously.

25. You hold a promissory note that will pay you $2000 ten years from now. Calculate the present value of the note if:
    a) $i^{(4)} = 6\%$ for $0 \leq t \leq 4$ and
    b) $i^{(12)} = 7\%$ for $4 < t \leq 10$.

26. Repeat question 25 using:
    a) $d^{(2)} = 4\%$ for $0 \leq t \leq 4$ and
    b) $d^{(365)} = 5\%$ for $4 < t \leq 10$.

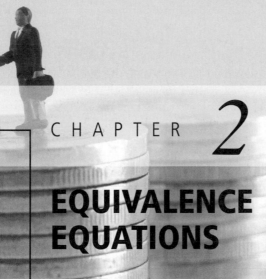

CHAPTER 2

EQUIVALENCE EQUATIONS

Learning Objectives

In Chapter 1, we learned how to perform financial calculations using simple and compound interest and using simple and compound discount. We also worked with nominal rates of interest and discount. Most financial transactions involve compound interest rates. Beginning with this chapter, the rest of this textbook is devoted to financial calculations using compound interest, unless stated otherwise.

Upon completing this chapter, you will be able to do the following:

- Calculate equivalent debts and payments using an equation of value.
- Determine how long it will take to earn a certain amount of interest.
- Calculate the rate of return on an investment.
- Solve non-financial problems that involve geometric growth.
- Calculate the price of Treasury bills in both Canada and the United States.

Section 2.1 ## Equations of Value

All financial decisions must take into account the basic idea that **money has time value**. In other words, receiving $100 today is not the same as receiving $100 one year ago, nor receiving $100 one year from now if there is a positive interest rate. In a financial transaction involving money due on different dates, every sum of money should have an attached date, the date on which it falls due. That is, the mathematics of finance deals with **dated values**. This is one of the most important facts in the mathematics of finance.

Illustration: At a simple interest rate of 8%, $100 due in one year is considered to be equivalent to $108 in two years since $100 would accumulate to $108 in one year. In the same way

$$\$100(1 + 0.08)^{-1} = \$92.59$$

would be considered an equivalent sum today.

Another way to look at this is to suppose you were offered $92.59 today, or $100 one year from now, or $108 two years from now. Which one would you choose? Most people would probably take the $92.59 today because it is money in their hands. However, from a financial point of view, all three values are the same, or are equivalent, since you could take the $92.59 and invest it for one year at 8%, after which you would have $100. This $100 could then be invested for one more year at 8% after which it would have accumulated to $108. Note that the three dated values are not equivalent at some other rate of interest.

In general, we compare dated values by the following **definition of equivalence**:

> $X due on a given date is equivalent at a given compound interest rate i to Y due n periods later, if $Y = X(1 + i)^n$ or $X = Y(1 + i)^{-n}$

The following diagram illustrates dated values equivalent to a given dated value X.

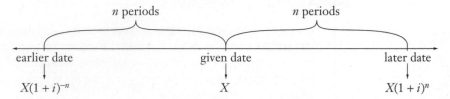

Based on the time diagram above we can state the following simple rules:

> 1. When we move money forward in time, we accumulate, i.e., we multiply the sum by an accumulation factor $(1 + i)^n$.
>
> 2. When we move backward in time, we discount, i.e., we multiply the sum by a discount factor $(1 + i)^{-n}$.

The following property of equivalent dated values, called the *property of transitivity*, holds under compound interest:

At a given compound interest rate, if X is equivalent to Y, and Y is equivalent to Z, then X is equivalent to Z.

To prove this property we arrange our data on a time diagram.

$$\begin{array}{ccccc} & X & & Y & & Z \\ \hline 0 & & n_1 & & n_2 & & n_3 \end{array}$$

If X is equivalent to Y, then $Y = X(1 + i)^{n_2 - n_1}$
If Y is equivalent to Z, then $Z = Y(1 + i)^{n_3 - n_2}$

Eliminating Y from the second equation we obtain

$$Z = X(1 + i)^{n_2 - n_1}(1 + i)^{n_3 - n_2} = X(1 + i)^{n_3 - n_1}$$

Thus Z is equivalent to X.

EXAMPLE 1 A debt of $5000 is due at the end of 3 years. Determine an equivalent debt due at the end of a) 3 months; b) 3 years 9 months, if $i^{(4)} = 4\%$.

Solution We arrange the data on a time diagram below.

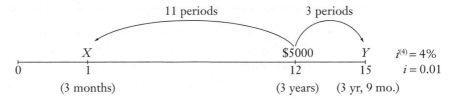

By definition of equivalence

$$X = \$5000(1.01)^{-11} = \$4481.62$$
$$Y = \$5000(1.01)^{3} = \$5151.51$$

Note that X and Y are equivalent by verifying

$$Y = X(1.01)^{14} \quad \text{or} \quad \$5151.51 = \$4481.62(1.01)^{14}$$

The sum of a set of dated values, due on different dates, has no meaning. We have to replace all the dated values by equivalent dated values, due on the same date. The sum of the equivalent values is called the **dated value of the set**.

At compound interest the following property is true: *The various dated values of the same set are equivalent.* The proof is left as an exercise. See problem 1 of Part B of Exercise 2.1.

EXAMPLE 2 A person owes $200 due in 6 months and $300 due in 15 months. What single payment a) now, b) in 12 months, will liquidate these obligations if money is worth $i^{(12)} = 6\%$?

Solution We arrange the data on the diagram below. Let X be the single payment due now and Y be the single payment due in 12 months.

To calculate the equivalent dated value X, we must discount the $200 debt for 6 months and discount the $300 debt for 15 months.

$$X = \$200(1.005)^{-6} + \$300(1.005)^{-15} = \$194.10 + \$278.38 = \$472.48$$

To calculate the equivalent dated value Y, we must accumulate the $200 debt from time 6 to time 12, or 6 periods, and discount the $300 debt from time 15 to time 12, or 3 periods.

$$Y = \$200(1.005)^{6} + \$300(1.005)^{-3} = \$206.08 + \$295.54 = \$501.62$$

We can verify the property of transitivity of X and Y by showing that

$$Y = X(1.005)^{12} = \$472.48(1.005)^{12} = \$501.62$$
$$\text{or} \quad X = Y(1.005)^{-12} = \$501.62(1.005)^{-12} = \$472.48$$

One of the most important problems in the mathematics of finance is the replacing of a given set of payments by an equivalent set. Two sets of payments are equivalent at a given compound interest rate if the dated values of the sets, on any common date, are equal. An equation stating that the dated values, on a common date, of two sets of payments are equal is called an **equation of value** or an **equation of equivalence**. The date used is called the **focal date** or the **comparison date** or the **valuation date**.

The procedure for setting up and solving an equation of value is stated below.

Step 1   Draw a good time diagram showing the dated values of debts on one side of the time line and the dated values of payments on the other side. The times on the line should be stated in terms of interest compounding periods.

Step 2   Select one, and only one, focal date and accumulate/discount all dated values to the focal date using the specified compound interest rate.

Step 3   Set up an equation of value at the focal date:

dated value of payments = dated value of debts.

Step 4   Solve the equation of value using methods of algebra.

The following examples illustrate the use of equations of value in the mathematics of finance.

EXAMPLE 3   A debt of \$1000 with interest at $i^{(4)} = 10\%$ will be repaid by a payment of \$200 at the end of 3 months and three equal payments at the ends of 6, 9, and 12 months. What will these payments be?

Solution   We arrange all the dated values on a time diagram.

debt:	\$1000					$i^{(4)} = 10\%$
	0	1	2	3	4	$i = 0.025$
payments:		\$200	X	X	X	

Any date can be selected as a focal date. We show the calculation using the end of 12 months and the present time.

Equation of value at the end of 12 months:

dated value of the payments = dated value of the debts
$$200(1.025)^3 + X(1.025)^2 + X(1.025)^1 + X = 1000(1.025)^4$$
$$215.38 + 1.050625X + 1.025X + X = 1103.81$$
$$3.075625X = 888.43$$
$$X \doteq 288.86$$

Equation of value at the present time:

$$200(1.025)^{-1} + X(1.025)^{-2} + X(1.025)^{-3} + X(1.025)^{-4} = 1000.00$$
$$195.12 + 0.951814396X + 0.928599411X + 0.905950645X = 1000.00$$
$$2.786364452X = 804.88$$
$$X \doteq 288.86$$

<u>**CALCULATION TIP:**</u>

Choose a convenient focal date, one that simplifies your calculations, when using equations of value at compound interest.

EXAMPLE 4   A man leaves an estate of $500 000 that is invested at $i^{(12)} = 2.4\%$. At the time of his death, he has two children aged 13 and 18. Each child is to receive an equal amount from the estate when they reach age 21. How much does each child get?

Solution   The older child will get X in 3 years (36 months); the younger child will get X in 8 years (96 months). We arrange the dated values on a time diagram.

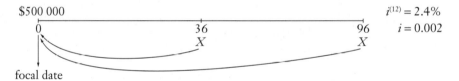

Equation of value at present:

$$X(1.002)^{-36} + X(1.002)^{-96} = 500\ 000$$
$$0.930597807X + 0.825465131X = 500\ 000$$
$$1.756062939X = 500\ 000$$
$$X \doteq \$284\ 727.84$$

Each child will receive $284 727.84

The following calculation checks the correctness of the answer:

Amount in fund at the end of 3 years = $500 000$(1.002)^{36}$ = $537 289.04
Payment to the older child = $284 727.84
Balance in the fund = $252 561.20
Amount in fund after 5 more years = $252 561.20$(1.002)^{60}$ = $284 727.83

The 1-cent difference is due to rounding.

EXAMPLE 5   Stephanie owes $8000 due at the end of 3 years with interest at $i^{(2)} = 8\%$. The lender agrees to allow her to pay back the loan early with a payment of $3000 at the end of 9 months and X at the end of 27 months. If the lender can reinvest any payments at $i^{(4)} = 5\%$, what is X?

Solution   In this example, there are two interest rates: 8% is the interest rate on the original loan, while 5% is the rate that will be used in the equation of value.

First we need to calculate the maturity value of the loan, which is due in 3 years (6 half-years):

$$S = 8000(1.04)^6 = 10\ 122.55$$

We now set up our time diagram, with $10 122.55 as the original debt and using quarter-years as the times.

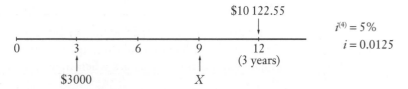

Equation of value at time 9:

$$3000(1.0125)^6 + X = 10122.55(1.0125)^{-3}$$
$$3232.149542 + X = 9752.250203$$
$$X \doteq 6520.10$$

A payment of $3000 at the end of 9 months and $6520.10 at the end of 27 months is equivalent to a debt of $10 122.55 at the end of 3 years.

To check this is the correct answer:

Payment at end of 9 month, invested at $i^{(4)} = 5\%$, $3000(1.0125)^6 =$ $3232.15
Payment at end of 27 months = $\underline{\$6520.10}$
Balance $9752.25

Balance invested at $i^{(4)} = 5\%$ to end of 3 years = $9752.25(1.0125)^3 = \$10122.55$ which is equal to the original debt owed at the end of 3 years.

An equation of value can be set up for problems involving simple interest or simple discount. The procedure is exactly the same, except the choice of focal date will change your final answer. That is because the property of transitivity does not hold when using simple interest or simple discount accumulation functions or discount functions. Thus, both parties to a financial transaction must agree on which focal date to use.

> **OBSERVATION:**
>
> In mathematics, an equivalence relation must satisfy the property of transitivity. Thus, strictly speaking, the equivalence of dated values at a simple interest rate is not an equivalence relation, and that is why when using simple interest you will get a different answer depending on what focal date is used. However, the choice of focal date under compound interest will not affect the final answer because the equivalence of dated values at a compound interest rate is an equivalence relation.

EXAMPLE 6 A person owes $300 due in 3 months and $500 due in 8 months. The lender agrees to allow the person to pay off these two debts with a single payment. What single payment a) now; b) in 6 months; c) in 1 year will liquidate these obligations if money is worth 8% simple interest?

Solution

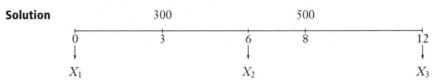

We calculate equivalent dated values of both obligations at the three different times and arrange them in the table below.

Obligations	Now	In 6 Months	In 1 Year
First	$300\left[1 + (0.08)\left(\frac{3}{12}\right)\right]^{-1} = 294.12$	$300\left[1 + (0.08)\left(\frac{3}{12}\right)\right] = 306.00$	$300\left[1 + (0.08)\left(\frac{9}{12}\right)\right] = 318.00$
Second	$500\left[1 + (0.08)\left(\frac{8}{12}\right)\right]^{-1} = 474.68$	$500\left[1 + (0.08)\left(\frac{2}{12}\right)\right]^{-1} = 493.42$	$500\left[1 + (0.08)\left(\frac{4}{12}\right)\right] = 513.33$
Sum	$X_1 = 768.80$	$X_2 = 799.42$	$X_3 = 831.33$

EXAMPLE 7 Debts of $500 due 20 days ago and $400 due in 50 days are to be settled by a payment of $600 now and a final payment 90 days from now. Determine the value of the final payment at a simple interest rate of 11% with a focal date at the present.

Solution We arrange the dated values on a time diagram.

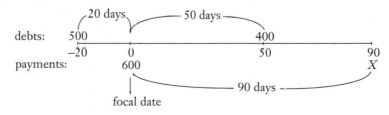

Equation of value at the present time:

dated value of payments = dated value of debts

$$X[1 + (0.11)(\tfrac{90}{365})]^{-1} + 600 = 500[1 + (0.11)(\tfrac{20}{365})] + 400[1 + (0.11)(\tfrac{50}{365})]^{-1}$$
$$0.973592958X + 600 = 503.01 + 394.06$$
$$0.973592958X = 297.07$$
$$X \doteq 305.13$$

The final payment to be made in 90 days is $305.13.

Exercise 2.1

Part A

1. If money is worth $i^{(4)} = 6\%$ determine the sum of money due at the end of 15 years equivalent to $1000 due at the end of 6 years.

2. What sum of money, due at the end of 5 years, is equivalent to $1800 due at the end of 12 years if money is worth $i^{(2)} = 11\tfrac{3}{4}\%$?

3. An obligation of $2500 falls due at the end of 7 years. Determine an equivalent debt at the end of a) 3 years and b) 10 years, if $i^{(12)} = 9\%$.

4. One thousand dollars is due at the end of 2 years and $1500 at the end of 4 years. If money is worth $i^{(4)} = 8\%$, calculate an equivalent single amount at the end of 3 years.

5. Eight hundred dollars is due at the end of 4 years and $700 at the end of 8 years. If money is worth $i^{(12)} = 3\%$, determine an equivalent single amount at a) the end of 2 years; b) the end of 6 years; c) the end of 10 years. Show your answers are equivalent.

6. A debt of $2000 is due at the end of 8 years. If $1000 is paid at the end of 3 years, what single payment at the end of 7 years would liquidate the debt if money is worth $i^{(2)} = 7\%$?

7. A person borrows $4000 at $i^{(4)} = 6\%$. He promises to pay $1000 at the end of one year, $2000 at the end of 2 years, and the balance at the end of 3 years. What will the final payment be?

8. A consumer buys goods worth $1500. She pays $300 down and will pay $500 at the end of 6 months. If the store charges $i^{(12)} = 18\%$ on the unpaid balance, what final payment will be necessary at the end of one year?

9. A debt of $1000 is due at the end of 4 years. If money is worth $i^{(12)} = 8\%$, and $375 is paid at the end of 1 year, what equal payments at the end of 2 and 3 years respectively would liquidate the debt?

10. On September 1, 2009, Paul borrowed $3000, agreeing to pay interest at 12% compounded quarterly. He paid $900 on March 1, 2010, and $1200 on December 1, 2010.
    a) What equal payments on June 1, 2011, and December 1, 2011, will be needed to settle the debt?
    b) If Paul paid $900 on March 1, 2010, $1200 on December 1, 2010, and $900 on March 1, 2011, what would be his outstanding balance on September 1, 2011?

11. A woman's bank account showed the following deposits and withdrawals:

	Deposits	Withdrawals
January 1, 2010	$200	
July 1, 2010	$150	
January 1, 2011		$250
July 1, 2011	$100	

If the account earns $i^{(2)} = 6\%$, determine the balance in the account on January 1, 2012.

12. Instead of paying $400 at the end of 5 years and $300 at the end of 10 years, a man agrees to pay X at the end of 3 years and $2X$ at the end of 6 years. Determine X if $i^{(1)} = 10\%$.

13. A man stipulates in his will that $50 000 from his estate is to be placed in a fund from which his three children are to each receive an equal amount when they reach age 21. When the man dies, the children are ages 19, 15, and 13. If this fund earns interest at $i^{(2)} = 6\%$, how much does each receive?

14. To pay off a loan of $4000 at $i^{(12)} = 7.2\%$, Ms. Fil agrees to make three payments in 3, 7, and 12 months respectively. The second and third payment are to be double the first. What is the size of the first payment?

15. Mrs. Singh borrows $3000, due with interest at $i^{(12)} = 9\%$ in 2 years. The lender agrees to let Mrs. Singh repay the loan with a payment of $1000 in 6 months, $1500 in 12 months, and X in 30 months. If money is worth $i^{(2)} = 6\%$, what is the value of X?

16. Thérèse owes $500 due in 4 months and $700 due in 9 months. If money is worth 7% simple interest, what single payment a) now; b) in 6 months; c) in 1 year, will liquidate these obligations?

17. Andrew owes Nicola $500 in 3 months and $200 in 6 months both due with simple interest at 6%. If Nicola accepts $300 now, how much will Andrew be required to repay at the end of 1 year, provided they agree to use a simple interest rate of 8% and a focal date at the end of 1 year?

18. A person borrows $1000 to be repaid with two equal instalments, one in 6 months, the other at the end of 1 year. What will be the size of these payments if the simple interest rate is 8% and the focal date is 1 year hence? What if the focal date is today?

19. Mrs. Adams has two options available in repaying a loan. She can pay $200 at the end of 5 months and $300 at the end of 10 months, or she can pay X at the end of 3 months and $2X$ at the end of 6 months. Determine X if simple interest is at 12% and the focal date is 6 months hence and the options are equivalent. What is the answer if the focal date is 3 months hence and the options are equivalent?

Part B

1. a) Prove the following property in the case of a set of two dated values: the various dated values of the same set are equivalent at compound interest.
   b) Show, algebraically, why this is not true for simple interest.

2. If money is worth $i^{(1)} = 8\%$, what single sum of money payable at the end of 2 years will equitably replace $1000 due today plus a $2000 debt due at the end of 4 years with interest at $12\frac{1}{2}\%$ per annum compounded semi-annually?

3. On January 1, 2010, Mr. Planz borrowed $5000 to be repaid in a lump-sum payment with interest at $i^{(4)} = 9\%$ on January 1, 2016. It is now January 1, 2012. Mr. Planz would like to pay $500 today and complete the liquidation with equal payments on January 1, 2014, and January 1, 2016. If money is now worth $i^{(4)} = 8\%$, what will these payments be?

4. You are given two loans, with each loan to be repaid by a single payment in the future. Each payment will include both principal and interest. The first loan is repaid by a $3000 payment at the end of 4 years. The interest is accrued at $i^{(2)} = 10\%$. The second loan is repaid by a $4000 payment at the end of 5 years. The interest is accrued at $i^{(2)} = 8\%$. These two loans are to be consolidated. The consolidated loan is to be repaid by two equal instalments of X, with interest at $i^{(2)} = 12\%$. The first payment is due immediately and the second payment is due one year from now. Calculate X.

5. You are given the following data on three series of payments:

	Payment at End of Year			Accumulated Value at End of Year 18
	6	12	18	
Series A	240	200	300	X
Series B	0	360	700	$X + 100$
Series C	Y	600	0	X

Assume interest is compounded annually. Calculate Y.

Section 2.2 — Determining the Rate and Time

Determining the Rate: When S, P, and n are given, we can substitute the given values into the fundamental compound interest formula $S = P(1 + i)^n$ and solve it for the unknown interest rate i.

$$S = P(1 + i)^n$$
$$(1 + i)^n = \frac{S}{P}$$
$$1 + i = \left(\frac{S}{P}\right)^{1/n}$$

$$\boxed{i = \left(\frac{S}{P}\right)^{1/n} - 1} \tag{8a}$$

CALCULATION TIP:

Using the power key of our calculator, we calculate the exact value of i. The nominal annual rate of interest is determined by multiplying the effective rate i by the number of compounding periods per year, $i^{(m)} = mi$, and then rounding off to the nearest hundredth of a percent.

EXAMPLE 1 At what nominal rate $i^{(12)}$ will money triple itself in 12 years?

Solution We can use any sum of money as the principal. Let $P = x$, then $S = 3x$, and $n = 12 \times 12 = 144$.

Substituting in $S = P(1 + i)^n$ we obtain an equation for the unknown interest rate i per month

$$3x = x(1 + i)^{144}$$
$$(1 + i)^{144} = 3$$

Solving the exponential equation $(1 + i)^{144} = 3$ directly for i and then using a pocket calculator we have

$$(1 + i)^{144} = 3$$
$$1 + i = 3^{1/144}$$
$$i = 3^{1/144} - 1$$
$$i = 0.007658429$$
$$i^{(12)} = 12i = 0.091901147$$
$$i^{(12)} \doteq 9.19\%$$

Using a Financial Calculator

Many of the calculations that have been presented so far in this textbook can be performed using a financial calculator. However, for most of the exercises, it is easiest to set up an equation of value and solve for the answer using the symbols and formulas presented in this text, using a calculator to do only the basic math. There has been no real need for a financial calculator.

However, there are situations where a financial calculator can lead to quicker answers, and calculating the value of i is one such situation.

There are many different financial calculators on the market. Four good ones are: Sharp EL-733A, Hewlett Packard 10B, Texas Instruments BA-35, and Texas Instruments BA-II Plus. We will illustrate the calculations using the notation from the Texas Instruments BA-II Plus calculator.

In Example 1, we have $PV = -1$ (note that you need a negative sign in front of the present value), $FV = S = 3$, and $n = 144$ (the term is always entered as the number of interest periods). The steps are as follows:

$$-1 \quad \boxed{PV} \quad 3 \quad \boxed{FV} \quad 144 \quad \boxed{N} \quad \boxed{CPT} \quad \boxed{I/Y}$$
$$0.765842888 \text{ (per month)}$$

Note that the answer is given as a percentage. That is, the monthly rate is 0.765842888%. To obtain the nominal rate, we need to multiply by 12:

$$i^{(12)} = 12(0.76584288)\% = 9.190114656\% \doteq 9.19\%$$

EXAMPLE 2   Suppose you would like to earn $600 of interest over 21 months on an initial investment of $2500. What nominal rate of interest, $i^{(4)}$, is needed?

Solution   We have $P = 2500$, $S = 2500 + 600 = 3100$, $n = 1.75 \times 4 = 7$ quarters, and $i = i^{(4)}/4$. Setting up the equation and solving, we get

$$3100 = 2500 \, (1 + i)^7$$
$$1 + i = (1.24)^{1/7}$$
$$i = (1.24)^{1/7} - 1$$
$$i = 0.031207244$$
$$i^{(4)} = 4i = 0.124828974$$
$$i^{(4)} \doteq 12.48$$

Using the BA-II Plus calculator:

$$-2500 \quad \boxed{PV} \quad 3100 \quad \boxed{FV} \quad 7 \quad \boxed{N} \quad \boxed{CPT} \quad \boxed{I/Y}$$
$$3.120724362 \text{ (per quarter)}$$

To obtain the nominal rate,

$$i^{(4)} = 4(3.120724362)\% = 12.482897\% \doteq 12.48\%$$

Determining the Time: When S, P, and i are given, we can substitute the given values into the fundamental compound amount formula $S = P(1 + i)^n$ and solve it for the unknown n using logarithms.

In this textbook we assume that students have pocket calculators with a built-in common logarithmic function $\log x$ and its inverse function 10^x.

Solving the formula $S = P(1 + i)^n$ for n we obtain:

$$(1 + i)^n = \frac{S}{P}$$

$$n \log(1 + i) = \log\left(\frac{S}{P}\right)$$

$$\boxed{n = \frac{\log\left(\frac{S}{P}\right)}{\log(1 + i)}} \tag{8b}$$

EXAMPLE 3 How long will it take \$500 to accumulate to \$850 at $i^{(12)} = 12\%$?

Solution Let n represent the number of months, then we have

$$500(1.01)^n = 850$$
$$(1.01)^n = \tfrac{850}{500}$$
$$(1.01)^n = 1.7$$

We have

$$n \log 1.01 = \log 1.7$$
$$n = \frac{\log 1.7}{\log 1.01}$$
$$n = 53.3277 \text{ months}$$
$$n = 4.4440 \text{ years}$$
$$= 4 \text{ years, } \underbrace{5 \text{ months,}}_{\substack{0.4440 \times 12 \\ = 5.328}} \underbrace{10 \text{ days}}_{\substack{0.328 \times 30 \\ = 9.84 \doteq 10}}$$

Alternative Solution The accumulated value of \$500 for 53 periods at $i^{(12)} = 12\%$ is $500(1.01)^{53} =$ \$847.23. Now we calculate how long it will take \$847.23 to accumulate \$2.77 simple interest at rate 12%.

$$t = \frac{i}{Pr} = \frac{2.77}{847.23 \times 0.12} = 0.027245652 \text{ years} \doteq 10 \text{ days}$$

Thus the time is 4 years, 5 months, and 10 days.

Using a Financial Calculator

To calculate n using the BA-II Plus calculator, we have $PV = -500$, $FV = 850$, and $I/Y = 1$ (the interest rate is the effective rate per compounding period, entered as a number, not a decimal). The steps are as follows:

$$-500 \quad \boxed{PV} \quad 850 \quad \boxed{FV} \quad 1 \quad \boxed{I/Y} \quad \boxed{CPT} \quad \boxed{N}$$

53.32769924 (months)

CALCULATION TIP:

When calculating unknown n from the fundamental compound interest formula **(7)**, use logarithms (that is, the exact method) in all exercises. The difference between the answers by the exact and the practical method is negligible.

EXAMPLE 4   Payments of \$100, \$200, and \$500 are paid at the end of years 2, 3, and 8 respectively. If $i^{(1)} = 5\%$ per annum effective, determine the time, t, at which a single payment of \$800 would be equivalent.

Solution

Using time 0 as the focal date.

$$800(1.05)^{-t} = 100(1.05)^{-2} + 200(1.05)^{-3} + 500(1.05)^{-8}$$
$$800(1.05)^{-t} = 601.89$$
$$(1.05)^{t} = \frac{800}{601.89} = 1.32915$$
$$t = \frac{\log 1.32915}{\log 1.05} = 5.832 \text{ years}$$

EXAMPLE 5   Jerry invests \$1000 today in a fund earning $i^{(2)} = 5\%$. How long will it take for his money to double?

Solution   We have $P = 1000$, $S = 2000$, $i = 0.025$ and will let n represent the number of half-years. Setting up the equation, we obtain

$$1000(1.025)^{n} = 2000$$
$$(1.025)^{n} = 2$$
$$n \log 1.025 = \log 2$$
$$n = \frac{\log 2}{\log 1.025}$$
$$n = 28.0710 \text{ half years}$$
$$= 14.0355 \text{ years}$$
$$= 14 \text{ years}, \quad \underbrace{0 \text{ months}}_{\substack{0.0355 \times 12 \\ = 0.426}}, \quad \underbrace{13 \text{ days}}_{\substack{0.4260 \times 30 \\ = 12.78 \doteq 13}}$$

Note: If the interest rate had been $i^{(2)} = 10\%$, $n = 7$ years, 1 month, 8 days.
Using the BA-II Plus calculator and $i = 0.05/2 = 0.025$ per half-year,

$$-1000 \quad \boxed{PV} \quad 2000 \quad \boxed{FV} \quad 2.5 \quad \boxed{I/Y} \quad \boxed{CPT} \quad \boxed{N}$$

28.07103453 (half-years)

Using $i = 0.10/2 = 0.05$ per half-year,

$$-1000 \quad \boxed{PV} \quad 2000 \quad \boxed{FV} \quad 5 \quad \boxed{I/Y} \quad \boxed{CPT} \quad \boxed{N}$$

14.20669908 (half-year)

Rule of 70

A quick estimate for the amount of time needed for money to double in value can be obtained using the "Rule of 70." According to this rule, the number of interest periods needed for money to double in value is approximately equal to 70 divided by the effective rate of interest per period.

Using this rule in Example 5, we obtain,

i) If $i^{(2)} = 5\%$, then $i = 0.025$ and $n \doteq 70/2.5 = 28.0$ half-years. Compare this to the correct answer of 28.0710.

ii) If $i^{(2)} = 10\%$, then $i = 0.05$ and $n \doteq 70/5 = 14.0$ half-years. Compare this to the correct answer of 14.2067.

EXAMPLE 6 At what rate of interest, $i^{(2)}$, would an investment of $1000 immediately and $2000 in 3 years accumulate to $5000 in 10 years?

Solution

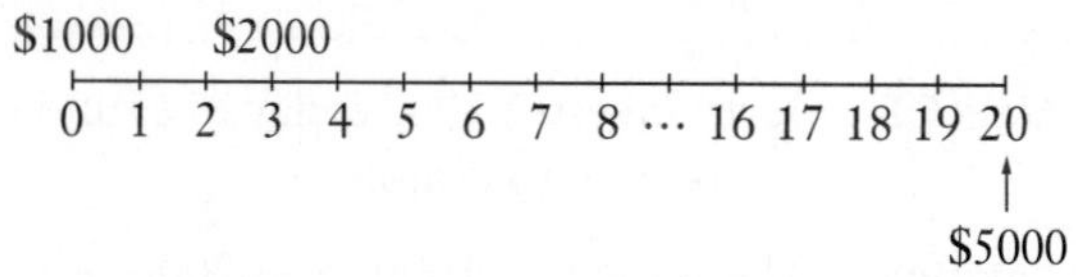

$1000 \quad $2000

```
├──┼──┼──┼──┼──┼──┼──┼──┼ ··· ┼──┼──┼──┼──┤
0  1  2  3  4  5  6  7  8    16 17 18 19 20
```
$5000

Using the end of 10 years (time 20) as the focal date,

$$1000(1 + i)^{20} + 2000(1 + i)^{14} = 5000$$

This cannot be solved algebraically. Instead you need to use "trial and error".

$i = \dfrac{i^{(2)}}{2}$	**LHS**
0.05	$6613.16
0.04	$5654.48
0.035	$5227.18
0.033	$5065.18
0.0322	$5001.76
0.03218	$5000.18

Rounding to five decimal points should be enough accuracy. Thus, the desired nominal rate of interest, $i^{(2)} = 2(0.03218) = 6.436\%$.

EXAMPLE 7 A deposit of $882.92 today will allow you to withdraw $1000 in 4 years and another $1200 in 8 years. What effective rate of interest is assumed?

Solution

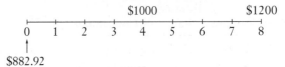

Using time 8 as our focal date:

$$882.92(1 + i)^8 = 1000(1 + i)^4 + 1200$$
$$882.92(1 + i)^8 - 1000(1 + i)^4 - 1200 = 0$$

This is a quadratic equation in the form $ax^2 + bx + c = 0$, where $x = (1 + i)^4$, $a = 882.92$, $b = -1000$, and $c = -1200$.

Thus

$$x = \frac{-b \pm \sqrt{b^2 - 4ac}}{2a}$$
$$= \frac{1000 \pm \sqrt{(-1000)^2 - 4(882.92)(-1200)}}{2(882.92)}$$
$$= -0.729778 \text{ or } +1.862383472$$

$$(1 + i)^4 = 1.862383472$$
$$i = (1.862383472)^{\frac{1}{4}} - 1$$
$$= 0.168200203$$
$$= 16.82\%$$

Exercise 2.2

Part A

In problems 1 to 4 calculate the nominal rate of interest.

No.	Principal	Amount	Time	Conversion
1.	$2000	$3000.00	3 years 9 months	quarterly
2.	$ 100	$ 150.00	4 years 7 months	monthly
3.	$ 200	$ 600.00	15 years	annually
4.	$1000	$1581.72	3 years 6 months	semi-annually

In problems 5 to 8 determine the time.

No.	Principal	Amount	Interest Rate	Conversion
5.	$2000	$2800	4%	quarterly
6.	$ 100	$ 130	9%	semi-annually
7.	$ 500	$ 800	6%	monthly
8.	$1800	$2200	8%	quarterly

9. An investment fund advertises that it will guarantee to double your money in 10 years. What rate of interest $i^{(1)}$ is implied?

10. If an investment grows 50% in 4 years, what rate of interest $i^{(4)}$ is being earned?

11. From 2006 to 2011, the earnings per share of common stock of a company increased from $4.71 to $9.38. What was the compounded annual rate of increase?

12. At what rate $i^{(365)}$ will an investment of $4000 grow to $6000 in 3 years?

13. How long will it take to double your deposit in a savings account that accumulates at
    a) $i^{(1)} = 4.56\%$?   b) $i^{(365)} = 7\%$?
    c) Redo a) and b) using the Rule of 70.

14. How long will it take for $800 to grow to $1500 in a fund earning interest at rate 9.8% compounded semi-annually?

15. How long will it take to increase your investment by 50% at rate 5% compounded daily?

16. The present value of $1000 due in $2n$ years plus the present value of $2000 due in $4n$ years is $1388.68. If the interest rate is $i^{(12)} = 9.60\%$, what is the value of n?

17. You need to buy some furniture that costs $12 900 in cash today. Alternatively, you can make a payment of $4429 today, followed by $4429 in 3 months, and $4429 in 6 months. For the second option, the furniture company claims they are only charging you interest at a rate of $i^{(1)} = 3\%$ (12 900 × 1.03 = 13 287, $\frac{13\,287}{3} =$ $4429). What is the true rate of interest, $i^{(1)}$, you are being charged? [*Hint:* Calculate $i^{(4)}$ first.]

Part B

1. At a given rate of interest, $i^{(2)}$, money will double in value in 8 years. If you invest $1000 at this rate of interest, how much money will you have
   a) in 5 years?
   b) in 10 years?

2. If money doubles at a certain rate of interest compounded daily in 6 years, how long will it take for the same amount of money to triple in value?

3. Draw a graph showing the time needed to double your money at rate $i^{(1)}$ for the rates 2%, 4%, 6%, ..., 20%. Calculate the exact answers and the answers using the Rule of 70.

4. Determine how long $1 must be left to accumulate at $i^{(12)} = 4.5\%$ for it to amount to twice the accumulated value of another $1 deposited at the same time at $i^{(2)} = 2.5\%$.

5. Money doubles in t years at rate of interest $i^{(1)}$. At what rate of interest, i^*, will money double in $\frac{t}{2}$ years?

6. You deposit $800 in an account paying $i^{(2)} = 9\%$, and $600 in a second account paying $i^{(2)} = 7\%$. When will the first account have twice the accumulated value of the second account?

7. Account A starts now with $100 and pays $i^{(1)} = 4\%$. After 2 years an additional $25 is deposited in account A. Account B is opened 1 year from now with a deposit of $95 and pays $i^{(1)} = 8\%$. When (in years and days) will Account B have $1\frac{1}{2}$ times the accumulated value in Account A if simple interest is allowed for part of a year?

8. In how many years and days should a single payment of $2000 be made in order to be equivalent to payments of $500 now and $800 in 3 years if interest is $i^{(1)} = 8\%$ and simple interest is allowed for part of a year?

9. Bradley puts $100 into Fund X and $100 into Fund Y. Fund Y earns compound interest at the annual rate of $i > 0$, and X earns simple interest at the annual rate of $1.05i$. At the end of 2 years, the amount in Fund Y equals the amount in Fund X. Calculate the amount in Fund Y at the end of 5 years.

10. Jeffrey borrows $1000 from Shirley at an annual effective interest rate i. He agrees to pay back $1000 after 6 years and $1366.87 after 12 years. At time $t = 9$, Jeffrey repays the outstanding balance instead. What is the amount of this payment?

11. Jeffrey deposits $10 into a fund at time $t = 0$ and $20 at time $t = 15$ years. Interest is credited at a nominal discount rate of d compounded quarterly for the first 10 years, and a nominal interest rate of 6% compounded semi-annually thereafter. The accumulated balance in the fund at the end of 30 years is $100. Calculate $d^{(4)}$.

12. The force of interest is $\delta_t = 0.02t$, where t is the number of years from January 1, 2011. If $1 is invested on January 1, 2013, how much is in the fund on January 1, 2018?

13. The accumulated value of $1 at time t, $0 \le t \le 1$ is given by a second-degree polynomial in t. You are given that the nominal rate of interest convertible semi-annually for the first half of the year is 5% per annum, and the effective rate of interest for the year is 4% per annum. Calculate δ_t at $t = \frac{3}{4}$.

14. The present value of $1000 due in $2n$ years plus the present value of $2000 due in $4n$ years is $1388.68.
    a) What is the value of n if interest is being earned at a simple interest rate of 9.60% and the focal date used is time 0?
    b) What is the value of n if interest is being earned at a simple interest rate of 9.60% and the focal date used is time $4n$?
    c) What is the value of n if interest is being earned at a simple discount rate of 9.60% and the focal date used is time 0.

Section 2.3 | **Other Applications of Compound Interest Theory, Inflation, and the "Real" Rate of Interest**

We know that the more money you invest at some given interest rate, i, the more dollars of interest you will earn. Further, once you earn a dollar's worth of interest, it becomes a part of the invested money and earns interest itself. The latter characteristic is referred to as multiplicative or geometric growth and is what differentiates compound interest from simple interest.

In any problem where there is geometric growth, even in nonfinancial situations, we can use the theory of compound interest.

EXAMPLE 1   A tree, measured in 2007, contains an estimated 150 cubic metres of wood. If the tree grows at a rate of 3% per annum, how much wood would it contain in 2017?

Solution   This is just geometric growth, so we can use compound interest theory. We have $P = 150$, $i = 0.03$, and $n = 10$. Thus, in 2017,

$$\text{Amount of wood, } S = 150(1.03)^{10}$$
$$\doteq 202 \text{ cubic metres}$$

EXAMPLE 2   The population of Canada in July 1997 was 30.3 million people. In July 2007 it was 33.4 million people.

a) What was the annual growth rate from July 1997 to July 2007?
b) At this rate of growth, when will the population reach 40 million people?

Solution a   We have $P = 30.3$, $S = 33.4$, $n = 10$, and we wish to determine $i = i^{(1)}$. Hence,

$$30.3(1 + i)^{10} = 33.4$$
$$(1 + i)^{10} = \tfrac{33.4}{30.3}$$
$$1 + i = (\tfrac{33.4}{30.3})^{1/10}$$
$$1 + i = 1.00978841$$
$$i \doteq 0.98\%$$

Solution b   We have $i = 0.0098$ from a), $P = 33.4$, $S = 40$, and we wish to determine n. Therefore,

$$33.4(1.0098)^n = 40$$
$$(1.0098)^n = \tfrac{40}{33.4}$$
$$n \log(1.0098) = \log \tfrac{40}{33.4}$$
$$n \doteq 18.49 \text{ years}$$
$$\doteq 18 \text{ years 6 months}$$

Therefore the population will reach 40 million sometime in January 2026 assuming the same rate of growth.

EXAMPLE 3   In 1980, Nolan Ryan, a pitcher for the Houston Astros, became the first million-dollar-a-year major league baseball player. In 2001, Alex Rodriguez signed a contract with the Texas Rangers that paid him an average of $25.2 million per season.

a) What is the annual rate of salary inflation from 1980 to 2001?
b) In 2008, Rodriguez had his contract renegotiated so that he earned an average of $28.0 million a year with the New York Yankees. What was the annual rate of growth in his salary from 2001 to 2008?
c) If this growth continues, what would be his expected salary in 2013?

Solution a We have $P = 1\,000\,000$, $S = 25\,200\,000$, $n = 2001 - 1980 = 21$ years. Thus,

$$1\,000\,000(1 + i)^{21} = 25\,200\,000$$
$$(1 + i)^{21} = 25.2$$
$$1 + i = (25.2)^{1/21}$$
$$1 + i = 1.166093459$$
$$i = 16.61\%$$

Solution b We have $P = 25.2$, $S = 28.0$, $n = 7$
Thus,

$$25.2(1 + i)^7 = 28.0$$
$$(1 + i)^7 = 28.0/25.2 = 1.1111111$$
$$(1 + i) = (1.1111111)^{1/7}$$
$$1 + i = 1.015165347$$
$$i = 1.52\%$$

Solution c In the 2013 season, Rodriguez should expect to re-sign for:

$$S = 28.0(1.015165347)^5 = \$30.2 \text{ million}$$

Inflation and the "Real" Rate of Interest

One very valuable use of compound interest theory is the analysis of rates of inflation. A widely used measure of inflation is the annual change in the Consumer Price Index. It measures the annual effective rate of change in the cost of a specified "basket" of consumer items.*

EXAMPLE 4 In June 2002 the Consumer Price Index was set at 100. In November 2008 the index was 113.00. That means that if goods cost an average of $100 in June 2002, they cost $113.00 in November 2008.

  a) Over that 6-year, 5-month period, what was the average annual compound percentage rate of change?
  b) If that rate of inflation were to continue, how long would it take before the purchasing power of a June 2002 dollar was only 80¢?

*The following Web site describes the CPI and also includes an inflation calculator. **www.bankofcanada.ca/en/rates/inflation_calc.html**

Solution a We have $P = 100, S = 113.00, n = 6\frac{5}{12}$ and we wish to determine $i = i^{(1)} =$ rate of inflation. Hence,

$$100(1 + i)^{6\frac{5}{12}} = 113.00$$
$$(1 + i)^{6\frac{5}{12}} = 1.1300$$
$$i = (1.1300)^{\frac{1}{6.41666}} - 1$$
$$= 1.92\%$$

Solution b In order to use the fundamental compound interest formula, we set $P = 0.80$, $S = 1, i = 0.0192$ and solve for n.

$$0.80(1.0192)^n = 1$$
$$(1.0192)^n = \frac{1}{0.80}$$
$$n \log 1.0192 = -\log 0.8$$
$$n \doteq 11.73 \text{ years}$$

The last example illustrated the effect of the rate of inflation as measured by the Consumer Price Index (CPI). Inflation rates vary from country to country and from time to time and can be relatively difficult to predict very far into the future. It is also possible to experience a period of time where prices drop and the CPI decreases. This is called deflation.

There is often a relationship between interest rates and rates of inflation. To illustrate this point, let's suppose that today you have $100 and you could buy a basket of goods with that $100. Suppose there is an inflation rate of 5%. This same basket of goods will now cost $105 at the end of the year. If you have not invested your $100, then at the end of the year it would be worth only $100/(1.05) = $95.24. In other words, if you wanted to buy that same basket of goods, you would be able to afford only 95.24% of the goods in the basket and would have to throw out 4.76% of them.

Had you invested your $100 at $i = 5\%$, you would have had $105 at the end of the year and would have been able to buy the exact same basket of goods. And if you had earned more than 5%, you would have been ahead of the game at the end of the year. (For example, if you earned 8%, you would have had $108 at the end of the year and it would have bought $108/1.05 = $102.86 worth of goods, an increase of 2.86%.)

Investors need to take into account the rate of inflation when calculating the rate of return they have earned on an investment. When doing so, investors are calculating what is referred to as the "real" rate of return.

If i is the annual rate of interest being paid in the marketplace and r is the annual rate of inflation, then $1 invested at the beginning of the year will grow to $(1 + i)$ at the end of the year. However, its purchasing power is equal to only $\left(\dfrac{1 + i}{1 + r}\right)$. Hence, the real rate of return is

$$\boxed{i_{real} = \frac{1 + i}{1 + r} - 1 = \frac{i - r}{1 + r}} \tag{10}$$

To make a meaningful comparison of interest and inflation, both rates should refer to the same one-year period.

EXAMPLE 5   Jack invested $1000 for one year at $i^{(1)} = 8\%$. The annual inflation rate for that year was 2%.

   a) What was the annual real rate of return on Jack's investment?
   b) What was Jack's annual real after-tax rate of return, if he paid tax at a 40% rate?
   c) Repeat part b) for a 50% tax rate.

Solution a
$$i_{real} = \frac{0.08 - 0.02}{1 + 0.02} = 0.058823529 \doteq 5.88\%$$

What is happening is that Jack has $1080 at the end of the year. However, he cannot buy an additional $80 worth of goods because the price of those goods has increased by 2%. Jack can now buy $1080/1.02 = $1058.82 worth of goods at the end of the year in real terms, or an extra $58.82 worth of goods.

Solution b   With a 40% tax rate, Jack keeps only 60% of his investment return. Thus, Jack's annual real after-tax rate of return was

$$i_{real\ after-tax} = \frac{0.08(0.60) - 0.02}{1 + 0.02} = 0.02745098 \doteq 2.75\%$$

At the end of the year, Jack has an extra $80 in interest. However, 40% of this is taxed as income, so he gets to keep only 60% or $48. Since prices have increased by 2%, Jack can buy only $1048/1.02 = $1027.45 worth of goods at the end of the year. He is still ahead of the game, but both the government and the economy have conspired to eat away at his $80 of extra income.

Solution c   Similarly, with a 50% tax rate, Jack's annual real after-tax rate of return was

$$i_{real\ after-tax} = \frac{0.08(0.5) - 0.02}{1 + 0.02} = 0.019607843 \doteq 1.96\%$$

EXAMPLE 6   a)   Suppose that the forecast for next year's annual inflation rate is $r = 5\%$, and for the annual interest rate it is $i = 4\%$. What will be the corresponding real rate of interest for the next year?

   b)   Using the values of r and i in part a), suppose you borrow $10 000 for a year at $i = 4\%$ and buy 5000 units of a certain item that has a current cost of $2 per unit. If the price of this item is tied to a rate of inflation, $r = 5\%$, and you sell the item one year from now at the inflated price, what will be your net gain on this transaction?

Solution a $i_{real} = \dfrac{0.04 - 0.05}{1.05} \doteq -0.00952381 \doteq -0.95\%$

Solution b

$$
\begin{aligned}
\text{Sell goods} &= \$5000(2)(1.05) = \$10\ 500 \\
\text{Pay back long} &= \$10\ 000(1.04) = \underline{\$10\ 400} \\
\text{Net gain} &= \quad\ \ \$100
\end{aligned}
$$

OBSERVATION:

Example 6 illustrates that during times when inflation rates exceed interest rates there is an incentive to borrow at the negative real rate of interest. Similarly, it can be shown that at low real rates of interest there is an incentive to consume rather than to save.

Exercise 2.3

Part A

1. A city increased in population 4% a year during the period 1999 to 2009. If the population was 40 000 in 1999, what is the estimated population in 2019, assuming the rate of growth remains the same?

2. The population of Happy Town on December 31, 2007, was 15 000. The town is growing at a rate of 2% per annum. What would be the increase in population in the calendar year 2015?

3. At what annual growth rate will the population of a city double in 11 years?

4. If the cost of living rises 8% a year, how long will it take for the purchasing power of \$1 to fall to 60¢?

5. The cost of living rises 2.1% a year for 5 years. Over that period of time, what would be the increase in value of a \$320 000 house due to inflation only?

6. A university graduate starts his new job on his 22nd birthday at an annual salary of \$48 000. If his salary goes up 5% a year (on his birthday), how much will he be making when he retires one day before his 65th birthday?

7. Calculate the real annual rate of return for the following pairs of annual interest rates $i^{(1)} = i$ and annual inflation rates r:
   a) $i = 6\%$ $r = 2\%$
   b) $i = 8\%$ $r = 4\%$
   c) $i = 10\%$ $r = 6\%$
   For a), b), and c), calculate the real after-tax rate of return if the tax rate is 26%.

8. A potentially dangerous oil spill has occurred. It initially covered 0.25 square kilometres, but it is spreading at a rate of 10% per hour. If nothing is done to stop it, how long will it take before it covers an area of 10 square kilometres?

Part B

1. a) The number of fruit-flies in a certain lab increases at the compound rate of 4% every 40 minutes. If there are 100 000 flies at 1 p.m. today, what will be the increase in the number of flies between 7 a.m. and 11 a.m. tomorrow?

   b) At what time will there be 200 000 flies in the lab?

2. The population of a county was 200 000 in 1990 and 250 000 in 2000. Estimate the change in population of the county between 2010 and 2015.

3. You will need $X U.S. one year from now and can invest funds in a U.S.-dollar account for the next year at $i^{(1)} = 3\%$. Alternatively, you can invest in a Canadian-dollar account for the next year at $i^{(1)} = 6\%$. If the current exchange rate* is $0.91 U.S. = $1 Cdn., what is the implied exchange rate one year from now? Assume that both alternatives require the same amount of currency today.

4. Let i be the annual effective interest rate and r be the annual effective inflation rate. Show that the present value of $(1 + r)^n$ due in n years at an annual effective rate i is equal to the present value of $(1 + r)^n$ due in n years at an annual effective rate $\dfrac{i - r}{1 + r}$.

Section 2.4

Treasury Bills

Treasury bills (T-bills) are popular short-term and low-risk securities issued by governments as a way to meet short-term financing needs. They are made available every two weeks for investors to purchase and are issued in denominations (or face values) of $1000, $5000, $25 000, $100 000, and $1 000 000. They have a maturity of a number of days that does not exceed 364 days. In the United States, common maturities are 12, 28, 91, and 182 days. In Canada, maturities are a multiple of 7.

The face value of a T-bill is the amount that government guarantees it will pay on the maturity date. There is no interest rate stated on a T-bill. Instead, to determine the purchase price of a T-bill, you need to discount the face value to the date of sale at an interest rate that is determined by market conditions. Since all T-bills have a term of less than one year, you would use either simple interest or simple discount formulas. (Maturities of greater than one year are government bonds and they would use compound interest.)

There is a difference between Canada and the United States regarding how the price of a T-bill is determined.

Canada

The face value is discounted using simple interest with the value of time, t, being calculated by taking the exact number of days divided by 365.

United States

The face value is discounted using simple discount with the value of time, t, being calculated by taking the exact number of days divided by 360.

*For a current exchange rate, see **www.bankofcanada.ca/en/rates/exchform.htm**

EXAMPLE 1   A T-bill with a face value of $25 000 is purchased on March 25, 2012, by an investor who wishes to yield 3.80%. The maturity date is June 24, 2012. What price is paid if this T-bill was purchased in a) Canada; b) the United States?

Solution   The maturity value (face value) of the T-bill is $S = 25\ 000$. March 25, 2012 to June 24, 2012 is 13 weeks or $13 \times 7 = 91$ days.

Solution a   Price, $P = S[1 + it]^{-1} = 25\ 000\left[1 + (0.038)\left(\frac{91}{365}\right)\right]^{-1} = \$24\ 765.37$

Solution b   Price, $P = S[1 - dt] = 25\ 000\left[1 - (0.038)\left(\frac{91}{360}\right)\right] = \$24\ 759.86$

EXAMPLE 2   A 182-day T-bill with a face value of $100 000 is purchased for $97 250. What rate of simple interest (rate of return) is assumed if the T-bill is purchased in a) Canada; b) the United States?

Solution   We have $P = 97\ 250$ and $S = 100\ 000$.

Solution a $i = \dfrac{I}{Pt} = \left[\dfrac{100\ 000 - 97\ 250}{(97\ 250)\left(\frac{182}{365}\right)}\right] = 0.056710642 = 5.67\%$

Solution b $d = \dfrac{I}{St} = \left[\dfrac{100\ 000 - 97\ 250}{(100\ 000)\left(\frac{182}{360}\right)}\right] = 0.054395604 = 5.44\%$

We need to calculate the equivalent simple interest rate, i, assuming a regular 365-day investment year:

$$(1 + it) = (1 - dt)^{-1}$$
$$\left[1 + i\left(\tfrac{182}{365}\right)\right] = \left[1 - (0.054395604)\left(\tfrac{182}{360}\right)\right]^{-1}$$
$$i = \frac{\left[1 - (0.054395604)\left(\tfrac{182}{360}\right)\right]^{-1} - 1}{\tfrac{182}{365}} = 0.056710641 = 5.67\%$$

Exercise 2.4

1. An investor bought a 13-week Treasury bill to yield 3.45%. In the following questions, assume the T-bill was purchased in the United States and then repeat the questions assuming it was purchased in Canada.
   a) What was the price paid by the investor if the face value was $5000?
   b) The investor sold the T-bill 40 days later to another investor who wishes to yield 3.10%. What price did the T-bill sell for?
   c) What rate of return did the original investor earn on his investment?

2. An investment dealer bought a $25 000 Treasury bill for $24 876.91 on September 9, 2012. The maturity date of the T-bill is October 7, 2012. In the following questions, assume the T-bill was purchased in the United States and then repeat the questions assuming it was purchased in Canada.
   a) What yield rate is implied?
   b) The dealer sold the Treasury bill to another investor on September 20, 2012, for $24 943.65. What yield rate did the other investor wish to earn? What rate of return did the dealer end up earning?

| *Section 2.5* | **Summary and Review Exercises** |

- Equivalence of dated values at compound interest rate $i = \frac{i^{(m)}}{m}$:

  X is due on a given date is equivalent to Y due n periods later, if $Y = X(1 + i)^n$ or $X = Y(1 + i)^{-n}$.

  Note: The above definition of equivalence of dated values at compound interest rate i satisfies the property of transitivity. At compound interest rate i, any choice of a comparison date to set up an equation of value will result in the same answer.

- Given P = present value, S = accumulated value, then

  - solving for the interest rate, $i = \left(\frac{S}{P}\right)^{\frac{1}{n}} - 1$

  - solving for the time, $n = \dfrac{\log\left(\frac{S}{P}\right)}{\log(1 + i)}$

- given i = rate of return (interest rate) and r = rate of inflation, then real rate of return, $i_{\text{real}} = \dfrac{i - r}{1 + r}$

Review Exercise 2.5

1. Determine the total value on June 1, 2011, of $1000 due on December 1, 2006, and $800 due on December 1, 2016, at $i^{(2)} = 6.38\%$.

2. Ahmed buys goods worth $1500. He wants to pay $500 at the end of 3 months, $600 at the end of 6 months, and $300 at the end of 9 months. If the store charges $i^{(12)} = 21\%$ on the unpaid balance, what down payment will be necessary?

3. How long will it take $1000 to accumulate to $2500 at $i^{(365)} = 6\%$?

4. An investment fund advertises that it will triple your money in 10 years. What rate of interest, $i^{(4)}$, is implied?

5. A loan of $10 000, taken on January 1, 2009, is to be repaid with interest at $i^{(2)} = 12\%$ on January 1, 2015. The debtor would like to pay $2000 on January 1, 2012, and make equal payments on January 1, 2014, and January 1, 2015. What will the size of these payments be if money is worth $i^{(4)} = 8\%$?

6. By what date will $1000 deposited on November 20, 2010, at $i^{(365)} = 12\frac{1}{2}\%$ be worth at least $1250?

7. To pay off a loan of $5000 at $i^{(12)} = 9\%$, Mrs. Leung agrees to make three payments in 2, 5, and 10 months respectively. The second payment is to be double the first, and the third payment is to be triple the first. What is the size of the first payment?

8. At what nominal rate compounded a) monthly, b) daily, c) continuously will money triple in value in 10 years?

9. Paul has deposited $1000 in a savings account paying interest at $i^{(1)} = 4.5\%$ and now finds that his deposits have accumulated to $1246.18. If he had been able to invest the $1000 over the same period in a guaranteed investment certificate paying interest at $i^{(1)} = 6\%$, to what sum would his $1000 now have accumulated?

10. A piece of land can be purchased by paying $500 000 cash or $200 000 down and equal payments of $200 000 at the end of two and four years respectively. To pay cash, the buyer would have to withdraw money from an investment earning interest at rate $i^{(2)} = 8\%$. Which option is better and by how much?

11. You borrow $4000 now and agree to pay $X in 3 months, $2X in 7 months, and $2X in 12 months. Determine X, if interest is at 9% compounded a) monthly; b) continuously.

12. How long will it take to double your money at a nominal interest rate of 10% compounded a) daily, b) continuously, c) quarterly, d) semi-annually? Calculate both the exact answers and the answers using the Rule of 70 for a), c), and d).

13. A $1000 T-bill is due in 91 days. The yield is quoted as 2.850%. Calculate the price in Canada.

14. A $2000 T-bill, due in 28 days, has a quoted price of 99.19487 per 100. Determine the yield rate as a simple discount rate for this bond if held to maturity in the United States.

15. A $10 000 T-bill matures in 182 days (26 weeks). Calculate the purchase price today at:
    a) simple discount rate of 4% and using 360 days per year;
    b) simple interest rate of 3.5% and using a 365 days per year.

16. Bing makes deposits of $1000 today and $5000 in five years time. The accumulated value of these amounts in ten years is exactly $7350. Calculate the annual rate of interest, $i^{(1)}$.

17. Lucy has loans due in n and $2n$ years of $10 000 each. If the total present value of these loans at $i = 6.5\%$ per annum is $11 550.17, determine n.

18. Amy deposits $1000 today. Four years later she has an accumulated value of $1275.
    a) Calculate her rate of return per annum.
    b) If the rate of inflation was 2.1% per annum over that four-year period of time, what is her real rate of return per annum?

19. The Weyerhauser Timber Company plants seedlings today that are 3 cm in diameter. They will be cut and turned into lumber when they achieve a diameter of 60 cm. If these trees increase in diameter at a rate of 5.5% per annum, how long will it be before these trees are harvested (to the nearest year)?

CHAPTER *3*

Simple Annuities

Learning Objectives

There are many situations where people make regular deposits into an account, or regular payments on a loan, or regular withdrawals from a fund. If the deposits, payments, or withdrawals are made at equal intervals of time and are the same amount each period, we end up with what is referred to as an annuity.

There are many examples of annuities in the financial world. Mortgage payments on a home, car loan payments, monthly retirement income, interest payments on bonds, payments of rent, deposits to and withdrawals from mutual fund accounts, dividends, payments on instalment purchases, and premiums on insurance policies are but a few examples of annuities.

Upon completing this chapter, you will be able to do the following:

- Understand what an annuity is, what types of annuities are available, the type of notation that is used, how to set up the solution to an annuity problem, and how to distinguish among different types of annuities.
- Calculate the accumulated or future value of an ordinary simple annuity.
- Calculate the present or discounted value of an ordinary simple annuity.
- Calculate the accumulated or present value of an annuity-due.
- Calculate the present value of a deferred annuity.
- Determine the term of an annuity along with the value of the final payment.
- Determine the rate of return (or interest rate) of an annuity.
- Perform some of the calculations using a financial calculator or a computer spreadsheet.

Section 3.1 | Definitions

An **annuity** is a sequence of periodic payments, usually equal, made at equal intervals of time. The time between successive payments of an annuity is called the **payment interval.** The time from the beginning of the first payment interval to the end of the last payment interval is called the **term** of an annuity. When the term of an annuity is fixed, i.e., the dates of the first and the last payments are fixed, the annuity is called an **annuity certain**. When the term of the annuity depends on some uncertain event, the annuity is called a **contingent annuity.** Bond interest payments form an annuity certain; life-insurance premiums form a contingent annuity (they cease with the death of the insured). Unless otherwise specified, the word annuity will refer to an annuity certain.

When the payments are made at the ends of the payment intervals, the annuity is called an **ordinary annuity** (or **immediate annuity**). When the payments are made at the beginning of the payment intervals, the annuity is called an **annuity due**. A **deferred annuity** is an annuity whose first payment is due at some later date.

When the payment interval and interest compounding period coincide, the annuity is called a **simple annuity**; otherwise, it is a **general annuity** (see section 4.1).

We define the **accumulated value** or **future value** of an annuity as the equivalent dated value of the set of payments due at the end of the term. Similarly, the **discounted value** or **present value** of an annuity is defined as the equivalent dated value of the set of payments due at the beginning of the term.

We shall use the following notation (in parentheses are typical symbols used on a financial calculator):

R = the periodic payment of the annuity (PMT).

n = the number of interest compounding periods during the term of an annuity (in the case of a simple annuity, n equals the total number of payments) (N or n).

i = interest rate per conversion period (assume $i > 0$). (I/Y, $\%i$, or i).

S = the accumulated value, or the amount of an annuity (FV).

A = the discounted value, or the present value of an annuity (PV).

Section 3.2

Accumulated Value of an Ordinary Simple Annuity

The accumulated value S of an ordinary simple annuity is defined as the equivalent dated value of the set of payments due at the end of the term, i.e., **we choose a focal date equal to the date of the last payment**. Below we display an ordinary simple annuity on a time diagram with the interest period as the unit of measure.

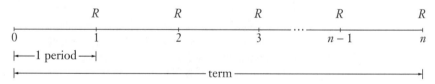

We can calculate the accumulated value S by repeated application of the compound interest formula as shown in the following example.

EXAMPLE 1   Calculate the accumulated value of an ordinary simple annuity consisting of four quarterly payments of $250 each if money is worth 6% per annum compounded quarterly.

Solution   We arrange the data on a time diagram below.

$$i^{(4)} = 6\%; \quad i = \frac{0.06}{4} = 0.015 \text{ per quarter}$$

To obtain S we need to recognize the time value of money. That is, $250 paid at time 4 is not the same as $250 paid at time 1. We must write an equation of value using the end of the term (date of the last payment) as the focal date. This gives

$$
\begin{aligned}
S &= \text{sum of the accumulated value of each \$250 payment} \\
&= 250 + 250(1.015)^1 + 250(1.015)^2 + 250(1.015)^3 \\
&= 250 + 253.75 + 257.56 + 261.42 \\
&= \$1022.73
\end{aligned}
$$

Now we develop a general formula for the accumulated value S of an ordinary simple annuity using the sum of a geometric progression.

Let us consider an ordinary simple annuity of n payments of $1 each as shown on a time diagram below.

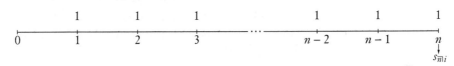

Let us denote the accumulated value of this annuity $s_{\overline{n}|i}$ (read "s angle n at i"). Note that the symbol $s_{\overline{n}|i}$ is the accumulated value of the n payments of $1 using the date of the nth payment as the focal date. To obtain $s_{\overline{n}|i}$ we write an equation of value at the end of the term, accumulating each $1 payment to the date of the last payment.

$$s_{\overline{n}|i} = 1 + 1(1+i)^1 + 1(1+i)^2 + \cdots + 1(1+i)^{n-3} + 1(1+i)^{n-2} + 1(1+i)^{n-1}$$

The expression on the right side of the equal sign in the above equation is a geometric progression of n terms whose first term is $t_1 = 1$ and whose common ratio is $r = (1+i) > 1$. Then, applying the formula for the sum of a geometric progression, we obtain

$$s_{\overline{n}|i} = t_1 \frac{r^n - 1}{r - 1} = 1 \frac{(1+i)^n - 1}{(1+i) - 1} = \frac{(1+i)^n - 1}{i}$$

The factor $s_{\overline{n}|i} = \dfrac{(1+i)^n - 1}{i}$ is called an **accumulation factor for n payments,** or the **accumulated value of $1 per period.**

To obtain the accumulated value S of an ordinary simple annuity of n payments of R each, we simply multiply R by $s_{\overline{n}|i}$. Thus the basic formula for the accumulated value S of an ordinary simple annuity is

$$S = R s_{\overline{n}|i} = \frac{R(1+i)^n - 1}{i} \tag{10}$$

Applying **(10)** in Example 1 above, we calculate

$$S = 250s_{\overline{4}|0.015} = 250\frac{(1.015)^4 - 1}{0.015} = \$1022.73$$

CALCULATION TIP:

In this textbook we calculate the factor $s_{\overline{n}|i} = \frac{(1 + i)^n - 1}{i}$ directly on a calculator using all the digits of the display of the calculator to achieve the highest possible accuracy in our results.

EXAMPLE 2   A couple deposits \$500 every 3 months into a savings account that pays interest at $i^{(4)} = 4\%$. They made the first deposit on March 1, 2010. How much money will they have in the account just after they make their deposit on September 1, 2014?

Solution   We arrange the data on a time diagram below, noting that the first deposit is made on March 1, 2010 (designated as time 1). To assist in calculating the correct value of n, we determine the date that represents time 0, which is one interest period (one quarter-year) before the first deposit, or December 1, 2009.

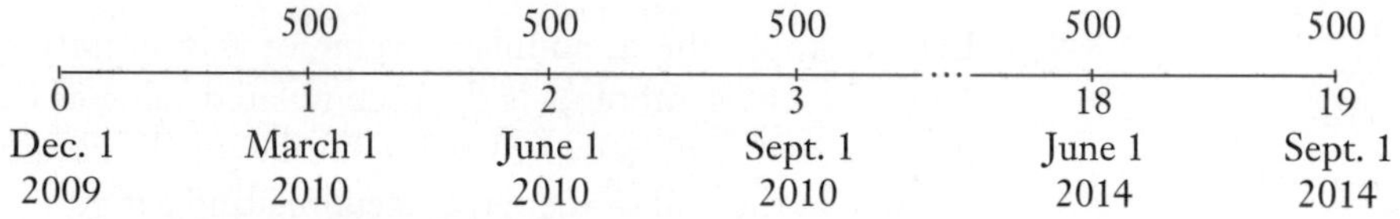

	500	500	500		500	500
0	1	2	3	...	18	19
Dec. 1	March 1	June 1	Sept. 1		June 1	Sept. 1
2009	2010	2010	2010		2014	2014

The time elapsed from December 1, 2009, to September 1, 2014, is exactly 4 years 9 months, or $n = 4.75 \times 4 = 19$ quarters. Thus we calculate the accumulated value S of an ordinary simple annuity of 19 payments of \$500 each at $i^{(4)} = 4\%$ or $i = 0.01$ per quarter as

$$S = 500s_{\overline{19}|0.01} = 500\frac{(1.01)^{19} - 1}{0.01} = \$10\ 405.45$$

EXAMPLE 3   You make deposits of \$1500 every six months starting today into a fund that pays interest at $i^{(2)} = 7\%$. How much do you have in your fund immediately after the 30th deposit?

Solution   We have $R = 1500$, $n = 30$, and $i = 0.07/2 = 0.035$ per half-year. Even though your first deposit is made today, you have been asked to determine the accumulated value on the date of your 30th deposit, which makes this an ordinary annuity. Thus,

$$S = 1500s_{\overline{30}|0.035} = 1500\frac{(1.035)^{30} - 1}{0.035} = \$77\ 434.02$$

EXAMPLE 4   Scott invests $10 000 in a mutual fund. The fund pays interest at $i^{(1)} = 8\%$. Scott takes the interest from his mutual fund and deposits it in his bank account, which pays interest at $i^{(1)} = 4\%$.

a) How much does Scott have in total at the end of 10 years?
b) How much would he have if both interest rates were $i^{(1)} = 5\%$?

Solution a   Each year the mutual fund pays out 8% of $10 000, or $800. Scott deposits the $800 into his bank account at the end of every year. Thus, at the end of 10 years, Scott has his original $10 000 plus the accumulated value of his bank account at $i = 0.04$.

$$S = 10\ 000 + 800 s_{\overline{10}|0.04}$$
$$= 10\ 000 + 800 \frac{(1.04)^{10} - 1}{0.04} = 10\ 000 + 9604.89$$
$$= \$19\ 604.89$$

Solution b   Each year the mutual fund pays out 5% of $10 000 or $500. Thus,

$$S = 10\ 000 + 500 s_{\overline{10}|0.05}$$
$$= 10\ 000 + 6288.95$$
$$= \$16\ 288.95$$

Note that if both the mutual fund and the bank account pay interest at $i^{(1)} = 5\%$, then we have the rather interesting result of the question being a straightforward, chapter 2 compound interest problem:

$$S = 10\ 000(1.05)^{10} = \$16\ 288.95$$

Calculating the Periodic Payment

When equation **(10)** is solved for R, we obtain

$$\boxed{R = \frac{S}{s_{\overline{n}|i}} = \frac{S}{\frac{(1 + i)^n - 1}{i}}}$$

as the periodic payment of an ordinary simple annuity whose accumulated value S is given. This result is particularly useful for determining the deposit needed to achieve a future financial goal, as the next example illustrates.

EXAMPLE 5   A man wants to accumulate a $200 000 retirement fund. He made the first deposit on March 1, 2004, and his plan calls for the last deposit to be made on September 1, 2025. Determine the size of each deposit needed if

a) he makes the deposits semi-annually in a fund that pays 5% per annum compounded semi-annually.
b) he makes the deposits monthly in a fund that pays 5% per annum compounded monthly.

Solution a We have $S = 200\,000$ and $i = 0.05/2 = 0.025$ per half-year. We wish to determine R.

The first deposit is made on March 1, 2004 (designated as time 1). We need a date to represent time 0. It would be one interest period (in this case 6 months) earlier, which is September 1, 2003. We then note September 1, 2003 to September 1, 2025 (date of final deposit) is exactly 22 years or $n = 44$ half-years.

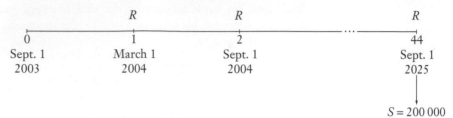

We calculate $R = \dfrac{200\,000}{s_{\overline{44}|0.025}} = \dfrac{200\,000}{\frac{(1.025)^{44} - 1}{0.025}} = \$2546.07.$

Semi-annual deposits of \$2546.07 will accumulate at $i^{(2)} = 5\%$ to \$200 000 by September 1, 2025.

Solution b We have $S = 200\,000$ and $i = 0.05/12 = 0.00416666$ per month.

The date that would represent time 0 is one interest period (in this case 1 month) before March 1, 2004, which is February 1, 2004. We then note February 1, 2004 to September 1, 2025 is exactly 21 years, 7 months. Thus $n = 259$ months.

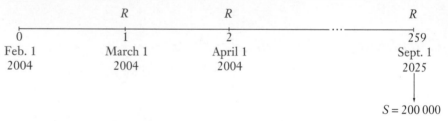

We calculate $R = \dfrac{200\,000}{s_{\overline{259}|i}} = \dfrac{200\,000}{\frac{(1 + i)^{259} - 1}{i}} = \$430.52.$

Monthly deposits of \$430.52 will accumulate at $i^{(12)} = 5\%$ to \$200 000 by September 1, 2025.

For some annuities, the interest rate may change over time. In other annuities, the periodic payment may change after a certain period of time.

To calculate the accumulated value for these types of annuities, we can use the "blocking technique." Every time the interest rate changes, or every time the periodic payment changes, we can consider that to be a "block." We then accumulate that block of payments to the focal date. The final equation of value will be the sum of the accumulated values of each block of payments.

Example 5 illustrates this method in a situation where the interest rate changes over time.

EXAMPLE 6 Mrs. Simpson has deposited $1000 at the end of each year into her Registered Retirement Savings Plan for the last 10 years. Her investments earned $i^{(1)} = 5\%$ for the first 4 years and $i^{(1)} = 4\frac{1}{2}\%$ for the last 6 years. What is the value of her RRSP 5 years after the last deposit, assuming that her RRSP continues to earn $i^{(1)} = 4\frac{1}{2}\%$ for the 5-year period after the last deposit?

Solution We arrange the data on a time diagram below.

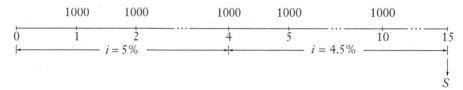

In this example, there are two blocks. The first block consists of the 4 deposits of $1000 while the interest rate is $i = 5\%$. The second block consists of the 6 deposits made while the interest rate is $i = 4.5\%$.

We need to accumulate each block to the focal date, which in this case is the end of 15 years (time 15). Don't forget that the first block of payments is first accumulated to the date of the last payment (time 4) at $i = 5\%$, and then that accumulated value is accumulated to time 15 at $i = 4.5\%$, which is the interest rate in effect for the 11 years from time 4 to time 15.

$$S = \text{accumulated value of block 1} + \text{accumulated value of block 2}$$
$$= 1000 s_{\overline{4}|0.05}(1.045)^{11} + 1000 s_{\overline{6}|0.045}(1.045)^5$$
$$= 1000\frac{(1.05)^4 - 1}{0.05}(1.045)^{11} + 1000\frac{(1.045)^6 - 1}{0.045}(1.045)^5$$
$$= 6994.70 + 8370.47 = 15\,365.17$$

The value of the RRSP 5 years after the last deposit is $15 365.17.

Using a Financial Calculator to Calculate Accumulated Values

We will illustrate the process using the Texas Instruments BA-II Plus calculator.

To calculate the accumulated value of an ordinary simple annuity, you will need to enter the term in interest periods (*N* key), the periodic interest rate as a number not a percentage (*I/Y* key), the periodic payment entered as a negative value (*PMT* key) and a value of 0 for the present value (*PV* key). The latter value is entered as a precaution to avoid incorrect answers. To obtain the accumulated value, hit the *CPT* key followed by the *FV* key.

To calculate the periodic payment of an ordinary simple annuity, you will need to enter the accumulated value as a negative number (*FV* key). Then hit the *CPT* key followed by the *PMT* key.

The following illustrates the proper calculator entries for calculating the accumulated value of the annuity in Example 3 (***Note:*** the values can be entered in any order):

30 $\boxed{N}$ 3.5 $\boxed{I/Y}$ −1500 $\boxed{PMT}$ 0 $\boxed{PV}$ $\boxed{CPT}$ $\boxed{FV}$

77 434.01591

The following illustrates the proper calculator entries for calculating the semi-annual payment in Example 5a):

44 $\boxed{N}$ 2.5 $\boxed{I/Y}$ −200 000 $\boxed{FV}$ 0 $\boxed{PV}$ $\boxed{CPT}$ $\boxed{PMT}$

2546.073651

Exercise 3.2

Part A

1. Determine the accumulated value of an ordinary simple annuity of $2000 per year for 5 years if money is worth a) $i^{(1)} = 9\%$, b) $i^{(1)} = 2\frac{1}{2}\%$.

2. Determine the accumulated value of an annuity of $500 at the end of each month for 4 years at 9% compounded monthly.

3. Lauren deposits $100 every month in a savings account that pays interest at $i^{(12)} = 4.5\%$. If she makes her first deposit on July 1, 2010, how much will she have in her account just after she makes her deposit on January 1, 2013?

4. A man deposits R dollars every 3 months beginning March 17, 2006, to September 17, 2009, after which he deposits $2R$ dollars beginning December 17, 2009, until June 17, 2015, at which time he will have $25 000. If he can earn $i^{(4)} = 6\%$ on his money, what is R?

5. Jason is repaying a debt with payments of $120 a month. If he misses his payments for June, July, August, and September, what payment will be required in October to put him back on schedule if interest is at 6% compounded monthly?

6. Determine the accumulated value of an annuity of $50 a month for 25 years if interest is a) 8% compounded monthly, b) $i^{(12)} = 3\%$.

7. Determine the accumulated value of annual deposits of $1000 each immediately after the 10th deposit if the deposits earned 5% per annum in the first 5 years and 6% per annum in the last 5 years.

8. Michael deposits $1000 at the end of each half-year for 5 years and then $2000 at the end of each half-year for 8 years. Determine the accumulated value of these deposits at the end of 13 years if interest is $i^{(2)} = 7\%$.

9. Ashley deposits $500 into an investment fund each January 1 starting in 2005 and continuing to 2014 inclusive. If the fund has an average annual growth rate of $i^{(1)} = 10\%$, how much will be in her account on January 1, 2019?

10. Mr. Juneau has deposited $800 at the end of each year into an RRSP investment fund for the last 10 years. His investments earned $i^{(1)} = 4\%$ for the first 7 years and $i^{(1)} = 6\%$ for the last 3 years. How much money does he have in his account 10 years after his last deposit if rates of return have remained level at $i^{(1)} = 6\%$?

11. Rebecca has deposited $80 at the end of each month for 7 years. For the first 5 years the deposits earned 6% compounded monthly. After 5 years they earned 4.5% compounded monthly. Determine the value of the annuity after a) 7 years, b) 10 years.

12. What quarterly deposits should be made into a savings account paying $i^{(4)} = 4\%$ to accumulate $10 000 at the end of 10 years?

13. It is estimated that a machine will need replacing 10 years from now at a cost of $80 000. How much must be set aside each year to provide that money if the company's savings earn interest at an 8% annual effective rate?

14. Jack has made semi-annual deposits of $500 for 5 years into an investment fund growing at $i^{(2)} = 3\frac{1}{4}\%$. What semi-annual deposits for the next 2 years will bring the fund up to $10 000?

15. Marie deposited $150 at the end of each month into an account earning $i^{(12)} = 8\%$. She made these deposits for 14 years except that in the fifth year she was unable to make any deposits. Determine the value of the account two years after the last deposit.

16. Ranjini deposits $5000 in a stock fund that pays out dividends at the rate of $i^{(1)} = 7\%$ at the end of each year. These dividends are then deposited in her bank account that pays interest at $i^{(1)} = 5\%$.
   a) How much does Ranjini have in total at the end of 10 years?
   b) If both the stock fund and the bank account paid interest at $i^{(1)} = 6\%$, how much does she have in total at the end of 10 years?

Part B

1. Shawn invests $1 which earns interest at an annual rate i_1 paid at the end of each year. He reinvests this interest into a second account that earns interest at an annual rate i_2.
   a) Show that at the end of n years, Shawn has accumulated a total of $1 + i_1 \, s_{\overline{n}|i_2}$.
   b) Show that if $i_1 = i_2 = i$, then at the end of n years Shawn has accumulated a total of $1(1 + i)^n$.

2. Jane opened an investment account with a deposit of $1000 on January 1, 2003. She then made monthly deposits of $200 for 10 years (first deposit February 1, 2003). She then made monthly withdrawals of $300 for 5 years (first withdrawal February 1, 2013). Determine the balance in this account just after the last $300 withdrawal (i.e., January 1, 2018) if $i^{(12)} = 6\%$.

3. Frank has deposited $1000 at the end of each year into his Registered Retirement Savings Plan for the last 10 years. His deposits earned $i^{(1)} = 9\%$ for the first 3 years, $i^{(1)} = 11\%$ for the next 4 years, and $i^{(1)} = 8\%$ for the last 3 years. What is the value of his plan after his last deposit?

4. Prove
   a) $(1 + i)s_{\overline{n}|i} = s_{\overline{n+1}|i} - 1$.
   b) $s_{\overline{m+n}|i} = s_{\overline{m}|i} + (1 + i)^m s_{\overline{n}|i} = (1 + i)^n \, s_{\overline{m}|i} + s_{\overline{n}|i}$
   c) Illustrate both a) and b) using a time diagram.
   d) $(1 + i)a_{\overline{n}|i} = a_{\overline{n-1}|i} + 1$

5. If $s_{\overline{n}|i} = 10$ and $i = 10\%$, calculate $s_{\overline{n+2}|i}$ and $s_{\overline{2n}|i}$.

6. Beginning June 30, 2010, and continuing every three months until December 31, 2014, Albert deposits $300 into a mutual fund account. Starting September 30, 2015, he makes quarterly withdrawals of $500. What is Albert's balance after the withdrawal on June 30, 2017, if growth of the mutual fund is at $i^{(4)} = 8\%$ until March 31, 2013 and $i^{(4)} = 6\%$ afterward?

7. Deposits of $400 are made every 6 months. After 5 years, the deposits are increased to $800. After another 5 years, the deposits are decreased to $600. If the deposits earn $i^{(2)} = 8\%$, how much has been accumulated just before the 26th deposit?

8. a) Show that $(1 + i)^n = 1 + is_{\overline{n}|i}$.
   b) Verbally interpret this formula.

9. Determine an expression for an accumulation factor for n equal payments of $1 assuming simple interest at rate i per payment period.

10. a) Barbara wants to accumulate $10 000 by the end of 10 years. She starts making quarterly deposits in her investment account, which pays $i^{(4)} = 8\%$. Determine the size of these deposits.
   b) After 4 years, the rate of return changes to $i^{(4)} = 6\%$. Determine the size of the quarterly deposits now required if the $10 000 goal is to be met.

11. George wants to accumulate $7000 in a fund at the end of 10 years. He deposits $300 at the end of each year for the first 5 years and then $(300 + x)$ at the end of each year for the next 5 years. Determine x if $i^{(1)} = 6\frac{1}{4}\%$.

12. You want to accumulate $100 000 at the end of 20 years. You deposit $1000 at the end of each year for the first 10 years and $(1000 + x)$ at the end of each year for the second 10 years. Rate of return is $i^{(1)} = 3\frac{1}{4}\%$.
   a) Determine x.
   b) If the last 4 payments of $1000 (at the end of years 7 through 10) were missed, what would be the value of x?

13. Beginning on June 1, 2009, and continuing until December 1, 2014, a company will need $250 000 semi-annually to retire a series of bonds. What equal semi-annual deposits in a fund paying $i^{(2)} = 10\%$ beginning on June 1, 2004, and continuing until December 1, 2014, are necessary to retire the bonds as they fall due?

Section 3.3

Discounted Value of an Ordinary Simple Annuity

The discounted value A of an ordinary simple annuity is defined as the equivalent dated value of the set of payments due at the beginning of the term, i.e., **we choose a focal date equal to 1 period before the first payment.** Below we display an ordinary simple annuity on a time diagram.

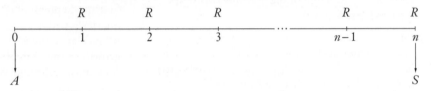

It is possible to derive the discounted value A in at least two different ways. Note first that A is the sum of a series of single discounted payments of R dollars each. That is,

$$A = R(1 + i)^{-1} + R(1 + i)^{-2} + R(1 + i)^{-3} + \cdots + R(1 + i)^{-(n-1)} + R(1 + i)^{-n}$$

The value of A can be found as the sum of a geometric progression of n terms whose first term is $t_1 = R(1 + i)^{-1}$ and whose common ratio is $r = (1 + i)^{-1}$. We obtain:

$$A = t_1\frac{1 - r^n}{1 - r} = R(1 + i)^{-1}\frac{1 - (1 + i)^{-n}}{1 - (1 + i)^{-1}}$$

If we then multiply by $\frac{1+i}{1+i}$, we get:

$$A = R\frac{1 - (1 + i)^{-n}}{(1 + i) - 1} = R\frac{1 - (1 + i)^{-n}}{i}$$

Alternatively, we note that A and S are both dated values of the same set of payments and thus they can be made equivalent to each other using

$$A = S(1 + i)^{-n}$$

Substituting for S from equation **(10)** we have:

$$A = Rs_{\overline{n}|i}(1 + i)^{-n} = R\frac{(1 + i)^n - 1}{i}(1 + i)^{-n} = R\frac{1 - (1 + i)^{-n}}{i}$$

If we set $R = 1$, we can denote the discounted value of this annuity as $a_{\overline{n}|i}$ (read "a angle n at i"). That is,

$$a_{\overline{n}|i} = \frac{1 - (1 + i)^{-n}}{i}$$

Note that this symbol $a_{\overline{n}|i}$ is the discounted, or present value of the n payments of $1 using the date one interest period before the first payment is due as the focal date.

If we wish to determine the discounted value of n payments of R dollars, we simply multiply R by $a_{\overline{n}|i}$. Thus, the basic formula for the discounted value A of an ordinary simple annuity is

$$A = Ra_{\overline{n}|i} = R\frac{1 - (1 + i)^{-n}}{i} \tag{11}$$

The factor $a_{\overline{n}|i} = \dfrac{1 - (1 + i)^{-n}}{i}$ a **discount factor for n payments**, or **the discounted value of $1 per period.**

<u>**CALCULATION TIP:**</u>

We calculate the factor $a_{\overline{n}|i} = \frac{1 - (1+i)^{-n}}{i}$ directly on a calculator and use all the digits of the display of the calculator to achieve the highest possible accuracy in our results.

EXAMPLE 1 On July 10, 2010 Mrs. Luigi buys an annuity that will provide her with payments of $1000 every 3 months, with the first payment October 10, 2010, and the final payment due on April 10, 2019. If the annuity pays interest at $i^{(4)} = 5.2\%$, how much does Mrs. Luigi pay for the annuity?

Solution We have $R = 1000$ and $i = 0.052/4 = 0.013$ per quarter. We note that July 10, 2010 is exactly one interest period (in this case 3 months) before the first payment is due, so we have an ordinary annuity.

To determine n, we count the number of interest periods from July 10, 2010 (designated as time 0), to April 10, 2019. There are exactly 8 years, 9 months between these dates and thus $n = 8.75 \times 4 = 35$ payments. We arrange the data on a time diagram below.

	1000	1000		1000	1000	1000	1000
0	1	2	⋯	32	33	34	35
July 10	Oct. 10	Jan. 10		July 10	Oct. 10	Jan 10	April 10
2010	2010	2011		2018	2018	2019	2019

A

Setting up an equation of value at time 0 and using equation **(11)** we get,

$$A = 1000a_{\overline{35}|0.013} = 1000\frac{1 - (1.013)^{-35}}{0.013} \doteq \$27\,976.08$$

Note that the total value of the 35 payments of $1000 is $35 000, but Mrs. Luigi needs to invest only $27 976.08 on July 10, 2010 in order to receive the 35 quarterly payments. The difference of $7023.92 is due to compound interest.

EXAMPLE 2 Mr. Li buys some equipment and signs a contract that calls for a down payment of $1500 and for the payment of $200 a month for 10 years. The interest rate is 12% compounded monthly.

a) What is the cash value of the contract?
b) If Mr. Li missed the first 8 payments of $200, what must he pay at the time the 9th payment is due to bring himself up to date?
c) If Mr. Li missed the first 8 payments of $200, what must he pay at the time the 9th payment is due to discharge his indebtedness completely?
d) If, at the beginning of the 5th year (just after the 48th payment is made), the contract is sold to a buyer at a price that will yield $i^{(12)} = 15\%$, what does the buyer pay?

Solution a Let C denote the cash value of the contract. Then C is $1500 plus the discounted value of 120 monthly payments of $200 each:

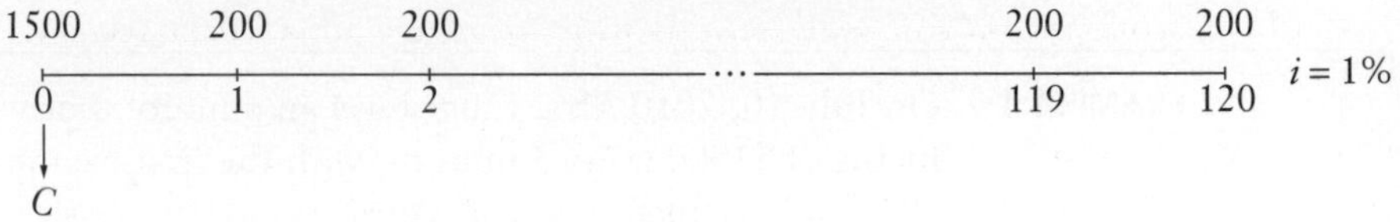

We calculate

$$C = 1500 + 200a_{\overline{120}|0.01} = 1500 + 200\frac{1 - (1.01)^{-120}}{0.01}$$
$$\doteq 1500 + 13\,940.10 = \$15\,440.10$$

Solution b Let X denote the required payment. Mr. Li must pay the accumulated value of the first 9 payments at the time the 9th payment is due.

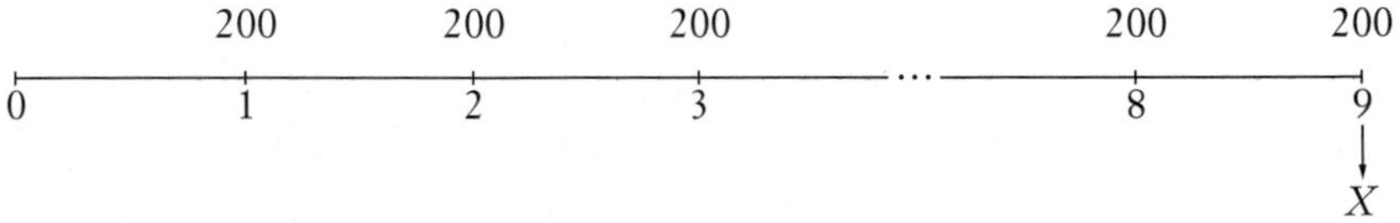

We calculate

$$X = 200s_{\overline{9}|0.01} = 200\frac{(1.01)^9 - 1}{0.01} \doteq \$1873.71$$

Solution c Let Y denote the required payment. Mr. Li must pay the accumulated value of the first 9 payments plus the discounted value of the last $(120 - 9) = 111$ payments at the time the 9th payment is due, in order to discharge his indebtedness completely.

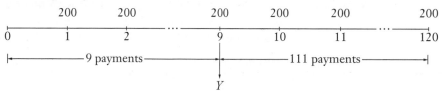

$$Y = 200 s_{\overline{9}|0.01} + 200 a_{\overline{111}|0.01}$$
$$= 200 \frac{(1.01)^9 - 1}{0.01} + 200 \frac{1 - (1.01)^{-111}}{0.01}$$
$$\doteq 1873.71 + 13\,372.38 = \$15\,246.09$$

Alternatively, we can calculate Y by calculating the discounted value of all 120 payments and then accumulating it to the end of the 9th period, i.e.,

$$Y = 200 a_{\overline{120}|0.01}(1.01)^9 = 200 \frac{1 - (1.01)^{-120}}{0.01}(1.01)^9 \doteq \$15\,246.09$$

Solution d Let Z be the price of the contract the buyer must pay. Then Z is the discounted value of the remaining $(120 - 48) = 72$ payments at $i^{(12)} = 15\%$. We calculate

$$Z = 200 a_{\overline{72}|0.0125} = 200 \frac{1 - (1.0125)^{-72}}{0.0125} \doteq \$9458.49$$

OBSERVATION:

The solution to Example 2, part d) illustrates one of the major lessons to be learned in the mathematics of finance: to determine the price to be paid for an investment, the buyer (investor) needs to calculate the discounted value of his/her future cash flows. The interest rate used in the calculation is generally the rate of return the investor wishes to earn.

Calculating the Periodic Payment

When equation **(11)** is solved for R, we obtain

$$\boxed{R = \frac{A}{a_{\overline{n}|i}} = \frac{A}{\frac{1 - (1 + i)^{-n}}{i}}}$$

as the periodic payment of an ordinary simple annuity whose discounted value A is given. This result is particularly useful in determining the periodic payment of an interest-bearing loan. Examples 3 and 4 illustrate this. It is also useful in determining the withdrawal that can be made every period from an initial lump-sum investment. Example 5 illustrates this.

EXAMPLE 3   A bank loan of $5000 is to be repaid with quarterly payments over 4 years. Calculate the payment and the total interest paid on the loan if the bank charges interest at $i^{(4)} = 8\%$.

Solution   The first payment is assumed to be due one period after the loan is taken out, unless otherwise stated.

We have $A = 5000$, $i = 0.08/4 = 0.02$, $n = 4 \times 4 = 16$ and calculate:

$$R = \frac{5000}{a_{\overline{16}|0.02}} = \frac{5000}{\frac{1 - (1.02)^{-16}}{0.02}} \doteq 368.25$$

Total interest paid over life of loan, $I = nR - A$
$$\begin{aligned} &= 16(368.25) - 5000 \\ &= 892.00 \end{aligned}$$

The required loan payment made every 3 months is $368.25 and the total interest paid over the 4-year period is $892.00.

EXAMPLE 4   A car selling for $22 500 may be purchased by paying $2500 down and the balance in equal monthly payments for 5 years. Determine these monthly payments at a) $i^{(12)} = 12\%$; b) $i^{(12)} = 4.9\%$.

Solution a   We have $A = 20\ 000$, $i = \frac{0.12}{12} = 0.01$, $n = 5 \times 12 = 60$, and calculate

$$R = \frac{20\ 000}{a_{\overline{60}|0.01}} = \frac{20\ 000}{\frac{1 - (1.01)^{-60}}{0.01}} \doteq \$444.89.$$

Solution b   Using $A = 20\ 000$, $i = \frac{0.049}{12}$, $n = 60$

$$R = \frac{20\ 000}{a_{\overline{60}|i}} = \frac{20\ 000}{\frac{1 - (1 + i)^{-60}}{i}} \doteq \$376.51.$$

Note the impact of the interest rate on the monthly payment. In a), at $i^{(12)} = 12\%$, total interest on the loan is $60(\$444.89) - \$20\ 000 = \$6693.40$. In b), at $i^{(12)} = 4.9\%$, total interest on the loan is only $60(\$376.51) - \$20\ 000 = \$2590.60$, more than $4100 less.

EXAMPLE 5   With the death of the insured on September 1, 2010, a life insurance policy pays out $80 000 as a death benefit. The beneficiary is to receive monthly payments, with the first payment on October 1, 2010. Determine the size of the monthly payments if interest is earned at $i^{(12)} = 8\%$ and the beneficiary is to receive 120 payments.

Solution   We have $A = 80\ 000$, $i = \frac{0.08}{12}$, $n = 120$ and calculate

$$R = \frac{80\ 000}{a_{\overline{120}|i}} = \frac{80\ 000}{\frac{1 - (1 + i)^{-120}}{i}} \doteq 970.62$$

The size of the monthly payments is $970.62.

The next example deals with determining the discounted value of an ordinary annuity where the interest rate changes over time. In section 3.2 we discussed using the blocking technique to calculate the accumulated value of an annuity where either the interest rates change or the periodic payments change (or both) at some point during the term. The same technique can be used to determine the discounted value.

EXAMPLE 6   Susan has just retired and, as part of her retirement planning, she wishes to buy an annuity that pays her $2000 a month for 20 years (first payment made one month from now). How much will this annuity cost her today if the interest rate is $i^{(12)} = 6\%$ for the first 6 years and $i^{(12)} = 4.2\%$ thereafter?

Solution   We set up a time diagram.

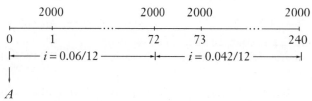

There are two blocks of payments. The first block consists of the 72 payments made while $i = 0.06/12 = 0.005$. The second block consists of the remaining 168 payments made while $i = 0.042/12 = 0.0035$.

Both blocks need to be discounted to the focal date (time 0). Don't forget the second block must first be discounted to time 72 (one period before the first payment of the second block) and then further discounted to time 0 at $i = 0.005$, the interest rate in effect during the first 6 years.

$$A = \text{discounted value of 1st block} + \text{discounted value of 2nd block}$$
$$= 2000a_{\overline{72}|0.005} + 2000a_{\overline{168}|0.0035}(1.005)^{-72}$$
$$\doteq 120\ 679.028 + 253\ 709.9679(1.005)^{-72}$$
$$= 120\ 679.028 + 177\ 166.287$$
$$= \$297\ 845.32$$

Using a Financial Calculator to Calculate Discounted Values

We will demonstrate the calculations using the Texas Instruments BA-II Plus calculator.

To calculate the discounted value of an ordinary simple annuity, you will need to enter the term (N key), the periodic interest rate (I/Y key), the periodic payment entered as a negative value (PMT key), and a value of 0 for the accumulated value (FV key). The latter value is entered as a precaution to avoid incorrect answers. To obtain the discounted value, hit the CPT key followed by the PV key.

To calculate the periodic payment of an ordinary simple annuity, you will need to enter the discounted value as a negative number (PV key). Then hit the CPT key followed by the PMT key.

The following illustrates the proper calculator entries for calculating the discounted value of the annuity in Example 1:

$$35 \quad \boxed{N} \quad 1.3 \quad \boxed{I/Y} \quad -1000 \quad \boxed{PMT} \quad 0 \quad \boxed{FV} \quad \boxed{CPT} \quad \boxed{PV}$$

27 976.07902

The following illustrates the proper calculator entries for calculating the semi-annual payment in Example 4b):

$$60 \quad \boxed{N} \quad 0.408333 \quad \boxed{I/Y} \quad -20\ 000 \quad \boxed{PV} \quad 0 \quad \boxed{FV} \quad \boxed{CPT} \quad \boxed{PMT}$$

376.5090709

Exercise 3.3

Part A

1. Determine the discounted value of an ordinary simple annuity of $1000 per year for 5 years if money is worth a) $i^{(1)} = 8\%$, b) $i^{(1)} = 3\%$, c) $i^{(1)} = 12.79\%$.

2. Determine the discounted value of an annuity of $380 at the end of each half-year for 3 years at a) $i^{(2)} = 8\%$, b) $i^{(2)} = 6\%$, c) $i^{(2)} = 10.38\%$.

3. Mr. Goldberg wants to save enough money to send his two children to university. Since they are three years apart in age, he wants to have a sum of money that will provide $6000 a year for six years. Determine the single sum required one year before the first withdrawal if interest is at $i^{(1)} = 8\%$.

4. Diana has an insurance policy with a cash value at age 65 that will provide payments of $1500 a year for 15 years, first payment at age 66. If the insurance company pays $i^{(1)} = 5\%$ on its funds, what is the cash value at age 65?

5. Alec buys a used car by paying $500 down plus $180 a month for 3 years. What was the price of the car if the interest rate on the loan is $i^{(12)} = 9\%$?

6. An annuity pays R dollars per month starting February 1, 2010, and ending January 1, 2013 (inclusive). If the value of this annuity on January 1, 2013, is $8000 and $i^{(12)} = 7.2\%$, what is its value on January 1, 2010?

7. Maria receives an inheritance of $25 000 on May 14, 2010. If she invests the money in a fund paying $i^{(4)} = 7\%$, how much can she withdraw every 3 months if the first withdrawal is August 14, 2010, and the final withdrawal is August 14, 2025?

8. Determine the discounted value of annual payments of $1000 each over 10 years if interest is $i^{(1)} = 6.5\%$ for the first 4 years and $i^{(1)} = 8\%$ for the last 6 years.

9. An annuity pays $2000 at the end of each half-year for 5 years and then $1000 at the end of each half-year for the next 8 years. Determine the discounted value of these payments if $i^{(2)} = 10\%$.

10. An annuity pays 10 annual payments of $2000 each starting January 1, 2013. Determine the discounted value of these payments on January 1, 2010, if $i^{(1)} = 7\%$.

11. A contract calls for payments of $250 a month for 10 years. At the beginning of the 5th year (just after the 48th payment is made) the contract is sold to a buyer at a price that will yield $i^{(12)} = 9\%$. What does the buyer pay?

12. A used car is purchased for $2000 down and $200 a month for 6 years. Interest is at $i^{(12)} = 10\%$.
    a) Determine the price of the car.
    b) If the first 4 monthly payments are missed, what payment at the time of the 5th payment will update the payments?
    c) Assuming no payments are missed, what single payment at the end of 2 years will completely pay off the debt?
    d) After 27 payments have been made, the contract is sold to a buyer who wishes to yield $i^{(12)} = 12\%$. Determine the sale price.

13. An insurance policy is worth $10 000 at age 65. What monthly annuity payment will this fund provide for 15 years if the insurance company pays interest at $i^{(12)} = 6\%$?

14. On the birth of their first child a couple puts $2000 in an investment account earning $i^{(1)} = 6\%$. This fund is used to pay university fees and allows for three withdrawals corresponding to the 18th through 20th birthdays. What size are these withdrawals?

15. A television set worth $780 may be purchased by paying $80 down and the balance in monthly instalments for 2 years. Calculate the size of the monthly instalments if $i^{(12)} = 15\%$.

16. A family needs to borrow $5000 for some home renovations. The loan is to be repaid with monthly payments over 5 years. If they go to a finance company, the interest rate will be $i^{(12)} = 15\%$; if they use their credit card, the interest rate will be $i^{(12)} = 12\%$; and if they go to the bank, the rate will be $i^{(12)} = 9\%$.

Determine the respective monthly payments and the total interest to be paid for each loan.

17. At age 65 Mrs. Bergeron takes her life savings of $120 000 and buys a 15-year annuity certain with monthly payments. Determine the size of these payments a) at 6% compounded monthly; b) at 9% compounded monthly.

18. A person buys a boat with a cash price of $14 500. She pays $500 down and the balance is financed at $i^{(12)} = 8.64\%$. If she is to make 24 equal monthly payments, what will be the size of each payment?

19. Mr. Sanjani plans to accumulate $600 000 in a retirement fund on the day he turns age 65. He plans to make deposits of R every year starting on the day he turns age 31 with his final deposit made on the day he turns age 60. If the deposits earn $i^{(1)} = 4.25\%$, determine the value of R.

Part B

1. Prove
   a) $(1 + i)a_{\overline{n}|i} = a_{\overline{n-1}|i} + 1$
   b) $\dfrac{1}{s_{\overline{m}|i}} + i = \dfrac{1}{a_{\overline{m}|i}}$
   c) $a_{\overline{m+n}|i}$
      $= a_{\overline{m}|i} + (1 + i)^{-m}a_{\overline{n}|i} = (1 + i)^{-n}\,a_{\overline{m}|i} + a_{\overline{n}|i}$

2. If $a_{\overline{n}|i} = 10$ and $i = 0.08$, determine $s_{\overline{n}|i}$ and $a_{\overline{2n}|i}$.

3. Explain logically why $1 = ia_{\overline{n}|i} + (1 + i)^{-n}$ and illustrate on a time diagram.

4. If $a_{\overline{2n}|i} = 1.6a_{\overline{n}|i}$ and $i = 10\%$, determine $s_{\overline{2n}|i}$.

5. If $a_{\overline{n}|i} = 6$ when $i = \frac{1}{9}$, determine $a_{\overline{n+2}|i}$.

6. Determine an expression for a discounted factor for n equal payments of $1 assuming simple interest at rate i per payment period.

7. If money doubles itself in n years at rate i, show that $a_{\overline{n}|i}$, $a_{\overline{2n}|i}$, and $s_{\overline{n}|i}$ are in arithmetic progression.

8. Prove that $(1 - ia_{\overline{n}|i})$, 1, $(is_{\overline{n}|i} + 1)$ are in geometric progression.

9. If $X(s_{\overline{2n}|i} + a_{\overline{2n}|i}) = (s_{\overline{3n}|i} + a_{\overline{n}|i})$, what is the value of X?

10. Mrs. Cheung signed a contract that calls for payments of $150 a month for 5 years. The interest rate is $i^{(12)} = 6\%$.

a) What is the cash value of the contract?
b) If Mrs. Cheung missed making the first 6 payments, what must she pay at the time of the 7th payment to be fully up to date?
c) If Mrs. Cheung missed the first 6 payments, what must she pay at the time of the 7th payment to fully discharge all indebtedness? (Can you find the answer to c) directly from the answer to a)?)
d) If, at the beginning of the 3rd year (after 24 payments have been made) the contract is sold to a buyer at a price that will yield $i^{(12)} = 9\%$, what does the buyer pay? Is this value larger or smaller than the discounted value of Mrs. Cheung's indebtedness at that time?

11. An annuity pays $200 at the end of each month for 2 years, then $300 at the end of each month for the next year, and then $400 at the end of each month for the next 2 years. How much does it cost to buy this annuity today if $i^{(12)} = 10\%$?

12. The ABC corporation borrows $100 000 on September 10, 2010. The interest rate on the loan is $i^{(2)} = 10\%$ until March 10, 2013, when it changes to $i^{(2)} = 7\%$ until September 10, 2017, upon which it changes to $i^{(2)} = 5\%$ thereafter. To repay the loan, ABC pays R dollars from March 10, 2011, until September 10, 2022. What is R?

13. The Ace Manufacturing Company is considering the purchase of two machines. Machine A costs $200 000 and Machine B costs $400 000. The machines are projected to have a life of 5 years and to yield the following revenues:

| | Cash Revenue | |
End of Year	Machine A	Machine B
1	none	$90 000
2	$100 000	90 000
3	100 000	90 000
4	100 000	90 000
5	100 000	300 000

The company's hoped-for rate of return is 14% per annum compounded yearly. Which machine should the company purchase?

14. A man aged 31 wishes to accumulate a fund for retirement by depositing $1000 each year for the next 35 years (ages 31 to 65 inclusive). Starting on his 66th birthday he will make 15 annual withdrawals of equal amount. Determine the amount of each withdrawal if $i^{(1)} = 4.4\%$ throughout.

15. To prepare for early retirement, a self-employed consultant makes deposits of $5500 into her Registered Retirement Savings Plan each year for 20 years, starting on her 31st birthday. When she is 51 she wishes to draw out 30 equal annual payments. What is the size of each withdrawal if interest is at $i^{(1)} = 6\%$ until the 10th deposit and at $i^{(1)} = 5\%$ for the remaining time?

16. Mr. Horvath has been accumulating a retirement fund at an annual effective rate of 9% that will provide him with an income of $12 000 per year for 20 years, the first payment on his 65th birthday. If he now wishes to reduce the number of retirement payments to 15, what should he receive annually?

17. Today Wilma purchased a cottage and a boat worth a combined present value of $390 000. To purchase the cottage, Wilma agreed to pay $60 000 down and $2100 at the end of each month for 20 years. To buy the boat, Wilma was required to pay $6000 down and R dollars at the end of each month for 4 years. Determine R if $i^{(12)} = 12\%$.

| Section 3.4 | **Other Simple Annuities** |

In this section we introduce other simple annuities that can be treated as minor modifications of ordinary annuities.

Annuities Due

An **annuity due** is an annuity whose periodic payments are due at the beginning of each payment interval. The term of an annuity due starts at the time of the first payment and ends one payment period after the date of the last payment. The diagram below shows the simple case (payment intervals and interest periods coincide) of an annuity due of n payments.

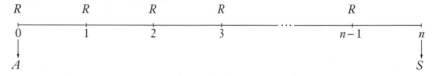

It is easy to recognize an annuity due as a "slipped" ordinary annuity, that is, each of the n payments of R has been moved one period to the left on the time diagram (compare this time diagram to the one on page 80 in section 3.3). Thus we can simply write the formulas for the accumulated value S and discounted value A of an annuity due, by adjusting equations **(10)** and **(11)** from sections 3.2 and 3.3.

Since the accumulated value of an annuity was defined as the equivalent dated value of the payments at the end of the term, it means that the accumulated value S of an annuity due is an equivalent value **due one period after the last payment**.

The accumulated value of the payments on the date of the nth payment (which is time $n - 1$) is $Rs_{\overline{n}|i}$. We then accumulate $Rs_{\overline{n}|i}$ for one interest period, to obtain

$$S = Rs_{\overline{n}|i}(1 + i)$$

To determine A, we recall that the discounted value of an annuity was defined as the equivalent dated value of the payments at the beginning of the term. Thus the discounted value of an annuity due is an equivalent value **due at the time of the first payment**.

The discounted value of the payments 1 period before the 1st payment is $Ra_{\overline{n}|i}$. We then accumulate $Ra_{\overline{n}|i}$ for one interest period to obtain

$$A = Ra_{\overline{n}|i}(1 + i)$$

Actuaries often use the following notation for the accumulated and discounted value of a \$1 annuity due:

1. Accumulated value, $\ddot{s}_{\overline{n}|i} = s_{\overline{n}|i}(1 + i)$.

2. Discounted value, $\ddot{a}_{\overline{n}|i} = a_{\overline{n}|i}(1 + i)$.

EXAMPLE 1   Mary Jones deposits $100 at the beginning of each month for 3 years into an account paying $i^{(12)} = 4.5\%$. How much is in her account at the end of 3 years?

Solution   We arrange the data on a time diagram below.

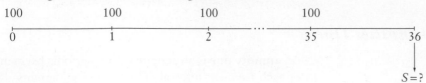

The payments are made from time 0 to time 35 (but there are $n = 3 \times 12 = 36$ payments in total). Note how we wish to determine the accumulated value at the end of 3 years, or time 36, which is one period after the final payment. Thus we have an annuity due situation.

We have $R = 100$, $i = \frac{0.045}{12} = 0.00375$, $n = 36$ and calculate

$$S = 100\ddot{s}_{\overline{36}|0.00375} = 100s_{\overline{36}|0.00375}(1.00375) = \$3861.03$$

EXAMPLE 2   The monthly rent for a townhouse is $1640 payable at the beginning of each month. If money is worth $i^{(12)} = 9\%$,

a) what is the equivalent yearly rent payable in advance,
b) what is the cash equivalent of 5 years of rent?

Solution a   We arrange the data on a time diagram below.

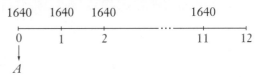

We wish to determine the present value of the 12 payments of $1640 at time 0, which is the same date where the first payment is made. Thus we have an annuity due.

$$A = 1640\ddot{a}_{\overline{12}|0.0075} = 1640a_{\overline{12}|0.0075}(1.0075) = \$18\ 893.91$$

Solution b   We calculate the discounted value A of an annuity due of 60 payments of $1640 each at $i^{(12)} = 9\%$

$$A = 1640\ddot{a}_{\overline{60}|0.0075} = 1640a_{\overline{60}|0.0075}(1.0075) = \$79\ 596.87$$

In Example 1, if there was a deposit made at the end of 3 years (that is, at time 36), there would be $n = 37$ deposits in total and the accumulated value at the end of 3 years would increase by \$100 to \$3961.03. Another way to obtain this answer is to note that the accumulated value would now be calculated at the time of the 37th deposit, making it an ordinary annuity:

$$100s_{\overline{37}|0.00375} = \$3961.03$$

We can generalize this result (with $R = 1$) as follows:

$$\boxed{\ddot{s}_{\overline{n}|i} = s_{\overline{n+1}|i} - 1}$$

In Example 2a), we could consider the payment made at time 0 as a down payment and treat the remaining payments as an ordinary annuity. That is,

$$18\ 893.91 = 1640 + \text{discounted value of other 11 payments}$$
$$= 1640 + 1640a_{\overline{11}|0.0075}$$

We can generalize this result (with $R = 1$) as follows:

$$\boxed{\ddot{a}_{\overline{n}|i} = 1 + a_{\overline{n-1}|i}}$$

EXAMPLE 3   A debt of \$10 000 is due today. However, it is agreed that it can be paid back with 8 quarterly payments, the first due today. If $i^{(4)} = 11\%$, determine the required quarterly payment.

Solution   Arranging the data on a time diagram below:

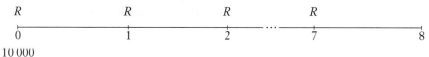

We have $A = 10\ 000$, $i = 0.0275$, $n = 8$ and calculate R one of two ways:

$$10\ 000 = R\ddot{a}_{\overline{8}|0.275} = Ra_{\overline{8}|0.275}(1.0275)$$
$$R = \frac{10\ 000}{a_{\overline{8}|0.0275}(1.0275)} = \$1371.85$$

OR

$$10\ 000 = R\ddot{a}_{\overline{8}|0.275} = R + Ra_{\overline{7}|0.275}$$
$$R = \frac{10\ 000}{1 + a_{\overline{7}|0.0275}} = \$1371.85$$

EXAMPLE 4   You wish to accumulate $20 000 in 5 years time. To do so, you plan to make 10 semi-annual deposits, first deposit made today. If you can earn $i^{(2)} = 6\%$, what deposit is needed?

Solution   We have $S = 20\ 000$, $i = 0.03$, $n = 10$, and the following time diagram:

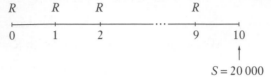

We calculate R one of two ways:

$$20\ 000 = R\ddot{s}_{\overline{10}|0.03} = Rs_{\overline{10}|0.03}(1.03)$$

$$R = \frac{20\ 000}{s_{\overline{10}|0.03}(1.03)} = \$1693.80$$

OR

$$20\ 000 = R\ddot{s}_{\overline{10}|0.03} = Rs_{\overline{11}|0.03} - R$$

$$R = \frac{20\ 000}{s_{\overline{11}|0.03} - 1} = \$1693.80$$

Deferred Annuities

A **deferred annuity** is an annuity with its first payment due some time later than the end of the first interest period. It is customary to analyze all deferred annuities as ordinary deferred annuities. Thus, an ordinary deferred annuity is an ordinary annuity whose term is deferred for (let's say) k periods. The time diagram below shows the simple case of an ordinary deferred annuity.

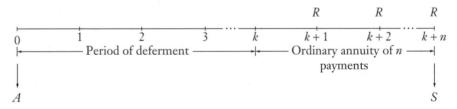

OBSERVATION:

Note that in the above diagram the period of deferment is k periods and the first payment of the ordinary annuity is at time $k + 1$. This is because the term of an ordinary annuity starts one period before its first payment. Thus, the period of deferment is equal to: time of first payment $- 1$.

To determine the discounted value A of an ordinary deferred annuity we calculate the discounted value of n payments one period before the first payment and discount this sum for k periods.

Discounted value one period before first payment (time k) = $Ra_{\overline{n}|i}$
Discount factor for k periods = $(1 + i)^{-k}$

Thus

$$A = Ra_{\overline{n}|i}(1 + i)^{-k}$$

If you now return to Exercise 3.3, Part A, you will see that we have already handled questions of this nature (questions 10 and 14, for example).

EXAMPLE 5 What sum of money should be set aside on a child's birth to provide 8 semi-annual payments of $4000 to cover the expenses for university education if the first payment is to be made on the child's 18th birthday? The fund will earn interest at $i^{(2)} = 7\%$.

Solution We arrange the data on a time diagram below.

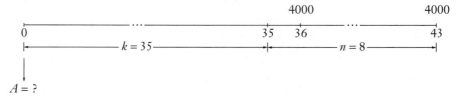

We have $R = 4000$, $i = 0.035$ per half-year, $n = 8$, $k = 35$, and calculate:

$$A = 4000a_{\overline{8}|0.035}(1.035)^{-35}$$
$$= 27\ 495.82215(1.035)^{-35} \doteq \$8248.11$$

EXAMPLE 6 Jaclyn wins $100 000 in a provincial lottery. She takes only $20 000 in cash and invests the balance at $i^{(12)} = 4\%$ with the understanding that she will receive 180 equal monthly payments with the first one to be made in 4 years. Calculate the size of the payments.

Solution The first payment is due in $4 \times 12 = 48$ months, so the deferral period is one less, or $k = 47$.

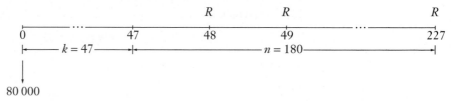

We have $A = 80\ 000$, $i = \frac{0.04}{12}$, $n = 180$, $k = 47$ and calculate R from the equation

$$80\ 000 = Ra_{\overline{180}|i}(1 + i)^{-47}$$
$$R = \frac{80\ 000(1 + i)^{47}}{a_{\overline{180}|i}} = \$691.93$$

CALCULATION TIP:

In general, problems involving any simple annuities can be efficiently solved by applying equations **(10)** and **(11)** for ordinary annuities to find equivalent lump sums and then moving to a requested point in time.

EXAMPLE 7   A couple deposits \$200 a month in a savings account paying interest at $i^{(12)} = 4\frac{1}{2}\%$. The first deposit is made on February 1, 2010 and the last deposit on July 1, 2016.

   a) How much money is in the account on
      i) January 1, 2014 (after the payment is made)
      ii) January 1, 2015 (before the payment is made)
      iii) January 1, 2018?
   b) If they want to draw down their account with equal monthly withdrawals from February 1, 2018 to February 1, 2019, how much will they get each month?

Solution a   We arrange the data on a time diagram below.

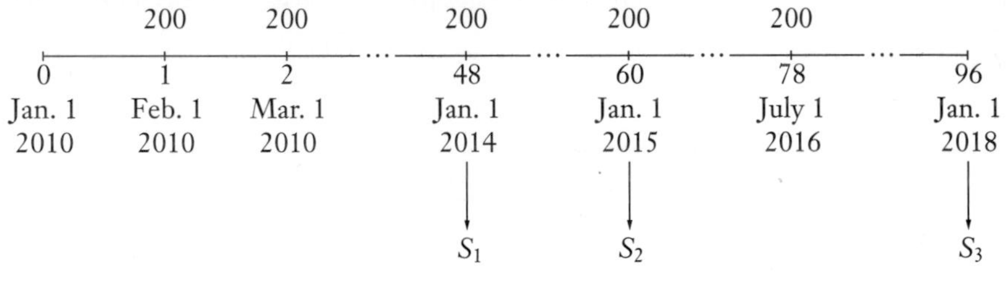

	200	200	200	200	200	
0	1	2	48	60	78	96
Jan. 1	Feb. 1	Mar. 1	Jan. 1	Jan. 1	July 1	Jan. 1
2010	2010	2010	2014	2015	2016	2018
			S_1	S_2		S_3

   i)   We have $R = 200$, $i = \frac{0.045}{12}$, and calculate the accumulated value of 48 payments at the time of the 48th payment (thus we have an ordinary annuity).

$$S_1 = 200s_{\overline{48}|i} = \$10\ 496.77$$

   ii) We have an annuity due and we can calculate the accumulated value of 59 payments.

$$S_2 = 200\ddot{s}_{\overline{59}|i} = 200s_{\overline{59}|i}(1 + i) = \$13\ 229.11$$

      OR

We can calculate the accumulated value of 60 payments of an ordinary annuity and subtract the last payment.

$$S_2 = 200s_{\overline{60}|i} - 200 = \$13\ 229.11$$

iii) We calculate the accumulated value of 78 payments to the time of the 78th payment ($= 200s_{\overline{78}|i}$) and then accumulate this amount for 18 more months.

$$S_3 = 200s_{\overline{78}|i}(1 + i)^{18} = \$19\ 342.37$$

Solution b Using result iii) from solution a) the accumulated value of their deposits on January 1, 2018, becomes the discounted value of their 13 future withdrawals, one month before the first withdrawal. We calculate the monthly withdrawal,

$$19\ 342.37 = Ra_{\overline{13}|i}$$

$$R = \frac{19\ 342.37}{a_{\overline{13}|i}} = \$1527.22$$

Forborne Annuities

Forborne annuities are almost the mirror image of deferred annuities. Whereas a deferred annuity has a period of time before the first payment is made, a forborne annuity has a period of time after the last payment or deposit is made and before the time when the accumulated value is calculated.

In general, the accumulated value of a forborne annuity consisting of n payments of R, calculated m periods after the nth payment, is

$$S = Rs_{\overline{n}|i}(1 + i)^m$$

In Exercise 3.4.B7, you are asked to show that

$$s_{\overline{n}|i}(1 + i)^m = s_{\overline{n+m}|i} - s_{\overline{m}|i}$$

The following is an example of a forborne annuity (as is Exercise 3.3.A19 and Example 7a)iii) above).

EXAMPLE 8 A family establishes a university savings account on the birth of their daughter. They make monthly deposits of $100 one month after her birth, continuing up to her 18th birthday (216 deposits in total).

It so happens that the daughter does not go to university at age 18. Instead, she starts to draw monthly payments from the savings account over 4 years starting on her 23rd birthday. If the savings account earns $i^{(12)} = 6\%$,

a) How much money is in the account on her 23rd birthday?
b) What is the size of the monthly withdrawal starting on her 23rd birthday?

Solution a   The first deposit is made one month after the birth of the child and the final deposit is made at time 18 years × 12 = 216. Thus, $n = 216$.

We want the accumulated value on the daughter's 23rd birthday, or time 23 × 12 = 276, which is $276 - 216 = 60$ months after the final deposit. Thus, $m = 60$.

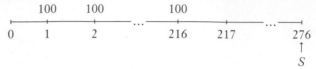

$$S = 100s_{\overline{216}|0.005}(1.005)^{60} = \$52\ 248.14$$

Solution b   The first withdrawal is made on the daughter's 23rd birthday and continues for $n = 48$ months. Thus, we have an annuity due with $A = 52\ 248.14$. If the monthly withdrawal is R, then

$$52\ 248.14 = R\ddot{a}_{\overline{48}|0.005}$$

$$R = \frac{52\ 248.14}{a_{\overline{48}|0.005}(1.005)} = \$1220.94$$

Using a Financial Calculator for Annuities Due

For calculating periodic payments, accumulated or discounted values of an annuity due, you need to make sure your BA-II Plus calculator is in *BGN* mode (*BGN* stands for "payments at the beginning of each period"). To do this, hit the *2ND* key and press *BGN*. If your calculator reads *END*, then hit the *2ND* key and press *SET*. Your calculator should now read *BGN*. Then press the *CE/C* button. You then follow the exact same steps as given in sections 3.2 and 3.3.

The following illustrates the proper calculator entries for calculating the accumulated value of the annuity due in Example 1:

36 $\boxed{N}$ 0.375 $\boxed{I/Y}$ −100 $\boxed{PMT}$ 0 $\boxed{PV}$ $\boxed{CPT}$ $\boxed{FV}$

3861.033641

The following illustrates the proper calculator entries for calculating the discounted value of the annuity due in Example 2a):

12 $\boxed{N}$ 0.75 $\boxed{I/Y}$ −1640 $\boxed{PMT}$ 0 $\boxed{FV}$ $\boxed{CPT}$ $\boxed{PV}$

18 893.390621

The following illustrates the proper calculator entries for calculating the quarterly payment in Example 3:

8 $\boxed{N}$ 2.75 $\boxed{I/Y}$ −10 000 $\boxed{PV}$ 0 $\boxed{FV}$ $\boxed{CPT}$ $\boxed{PMT}$

1371.853506

Using a Financial Calculator for Deferred Annuities

You must first get out of *BGN* mode by pressing the *2ND* key and then pressing *BGN*. If your calculator reads *BGN*, hit the *2ND* key and press *SET*. The calculator should now read *END*. Press the *CE/C* key. You must also have set up your equation of value so that you know the value of *n* (term of the annuity) and *k* (deferral period). The process is to first calculate the discounted value of the annuity and then discount that value *k* periods. The following illustrates the proper calculator entries for calculating the discounted value of the deferred annuity in Example 5:

8 $\boxed{N}$ 3.5 $\boxed{I/Y}$ −4000 $\boxed{PMT}$ 0 $\boxed{FV}$ $\boxed{CPT}$ $\boxed{PV}$

27 495.82215

After this calculation, you add a negative sign to your answer and then push the *FV* key (as −$27 495.82215 represents the future value of your annuity that is supposed to start *k* = 35 periods earlier). The full sequence is:

$\boxed{FV}$ 3.5 $\boxed{N}$ 3.5 $\boxed{I/Y}$ 0 $\boxed{PMT}$ $\boxed{CPT}$ $\boxed{PV}$

8248.110436

Exercise 3.4

Part A

1. Determine the discounted value and the accumulated value of $500 payable semi-annually at the beginning of each half-year over 10 years if interest is 8% per annum payable semi-annually.

2. A couple wants to accumulate $10 000 by December 31, 2015. They make 10 annual deposits starting January 1, 2006. If interest is at $i^{(1)} = 2\%$, what annual deposits are needed?

3. The premium on a life insurance policy can be paid either yearly or at the beginning of each month. If the annual premium is $120, what monthly premium would be equivalent at $i^{(12)} = 5\%$?

4. Deposits of $350 are made every 3 months from June 1, 2010, to June 1, 2013. How much has been accumulated on September 1, 2013, if the deposits earn $i^{(4)} = 6\%$?

5. An insurance policy provides a death benefit of $100 000 or payments at the beginning of each month for 10 years. What size would these monthly payments be if $i^{(12)} = 5.5\%$?

6. A used car sells for $9550. Brent wishes to pay for it in 18 monthly instalments, the first due on the day of purchase. If 12% compounded monthly is charged, determine the size of the monthly payment.

7. A real estate agent rents office space for $5800 every 3 months, payable in advance. He immediately invests half of each payment in a fund paying 9% compounded quarterly. How much is in the fund at the end of 5 years?

8. A refrigerator is bought for $60 down and $60 a month for 15 months. If interest is charged at $i^{(12)} = 8\frac{1}{2}\%$, what is the cash price of the refrigerator?

9. Determine the discounted value of an ordinary annuity deferred 5 years paying $1000 a year for 10 years if interest is at $i^{(1)} = 8\%$.

10. Determine the discounted value of an ordinary annuity deferred 3 years, 6 months that pays $500 semi-annually for 7 years if interest is 7% compounded semi-annually.

11. What sum of money must be set aside at a child's birth to provide for 6 semi-annual payments of $1500 to cover the expenses for a

university education if the first payment is to be made on the child's 19th birthday and interest is at $i^{(2)} = 8\%$?

12. On Mr. Pimentel's 55th birthday, the Pimentels decide to sell their house and move into an apartment. They realize $150 000 on the sale of the house and invest this money in a fund paying $i^{(1)} = 6\%$. On Mr. Pimentel's 65th birthday they make their first of 15 annual withdrawals that will exhaust the fund. What is the dollar size of each withdrawal?

13. Mrs. Howlett changes employers at age 46. She is given $85 000 as her vested benefits in the company's pension plan. She invests this money in an RRSP (Registered Retirement Savings Plan) paying $i^{(1)} = 8\%$ and leaves it there until her ultimate retirement at age 61. She plans on 25 annual withdrawals from this fund, the first withdrawal on her 61st birthday. Determine the size of these withdrawals.

14. Determine the value on January 1, 2011, of quarterly payments of $100 each over 10 years if the first payment is on January 1, 2013, and interest is 7% compounded quarterly.

15. Determine the value on July 1, 2010, of semi-annual payments of $500 each over 6 years if the first payment is on January 1, 2014, and interest is at $5\frac{1}{4}\%$ payable semi-annually.

16. The XYZ Furniture Store sells a chesterfield for $950. It can be purchased for $50 down and no payments for 3 months. At the end of the third month you make your first payment and continue until a total of 18 payments are made. Determine the size of each payment if interest is at $i^{(12)} = 18\%$.

17. An 8-year-old child wins $1 000 000 from a lottery. The law requires that this money be set aside in a trust fund until the child reaches 18. The child's parents decide that the money should be paid out in 20 equal annual payments with the first payment at age 18. Calculate these payments if the trust fund pays interest at $i^{(1)} = 5\%$.

18. The Smiths deposit $500 at the end of each month for 25 years to fund a 20-year retirement annuity, with the first withdrawal made exactly 5 years after the last deposit of $500. Calculate

the monthly retirement withdrawal if
a) the interest rate is $i^{(12)} = 6\%$ throughout.
b) the interest rate is $i^{(12)} = 7.2\%$ for the investment growth period and $i^{(12)} = 4.2\%$ at the time of the first retirement withdrawal.

Part B

1. A man aged 40 deposits $5000 at the beginning of each year for 25 years into an RRSP paying interest at $i^{(1)} = 7\%$. Starting on his 65th birthday he makes 15 annual withdrawals from the fund at the beginning of each year. During this period (i.e., from his 65th birthday on) the fund pays interest at $i^{(1)} = 6\%$. Determine the amount of each withdrawal starting at age 65.

2. Jacques signed a contract that calls for payments of $500 at the beginning of each 6 months for 10 years. If money is worth $i^{(2)} = 13\%$, determine the value of the remaining payments
a) just after he makes the 4th payment;
b) just before he makes the 6th payment. If after making the first 3 payments he failed to make the next 3 payments,
c) what would he have to pay when the next payment is due to bring himself back on schedule?

3. Using a geometric progression, derive the formula for the accumulated value S of an annuity due
$$S = Rs_{\overline{n}|i}(1 + i)$$
Show that it is equivalent to
$$S = R(s_{\overline{n+1}|} - 1)$$

4. Using a geometric progression derive the formula for the discounted value A of an annuity due
$$A = Ra_{\overline{n}|i}(1 + i)$$
Show that it is equivalent to
$$A = R(a_{\overline{n-1}|} + 1)$$

5. A mutual fund promises a rate of growth of 10% a year on funds left with it. How much would an investor who makes deposits of $1000 at the beginning of each year have on deposit by the time the first deposit has grown by 159%? You may assume that the time is approximately an integral number of years and that the investor is about to make, but has not made, an annual deposit at that time.

6. Show that the discounted value A of an ordinary deferred annuity is equivalent to
$$A = R(a_{\overline{k+n}|i} - a_{\overline{k}|i})$$

7. Show that $s_{\overline{n}|i}(1 + i)^m = s_{\overline{n+m}|i} - s_{\overline{m}|i}$.

8. Show that $s_{\overline{n+1}|i} - \ddot{a}_{\overline{n+1}|i} = \ddot{s}_{\overline{n}|i} - a_{\overline{n}|i}$.

9. Starting on his 45th birthday, a man deposits $10 000 a year in an investment account that pays interest at $i^{(1)} = 3\%$. He makes his last deposit on his 64th birthday. On his 65th birthday he transfers his total savings to a special retirement fund that pays $i^{(1)} = 4\frac{1}{2}\%$. From this fund he will receive level payments of $X at the beginning of each year for 15 years (first payment on his 65th birthday). Determine X.

10. Given the following diagram

$1 $1 $1 $1 $1 $1 $1
```
0  1  2  3  4  5  6  7  8  9  10 11 12 13 14 15
```

determine simplified expressions for a single sum equivalent to the seven payments calculated at times 1, 5, 8, 12, and 15, assuming rate i per period.

11. Provide symbolic answers (using $a_{\overline{n}|i}$, $s_{\overline{n}|i}$, i) in simplified form for the value of the following payments at the time indicated, assuming rate i per payment period.

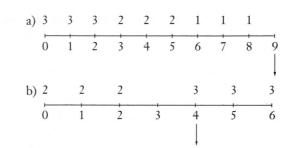

12. Deposits are $100 per month for 3 years, nothing for 2 years, and then $200 per month for 3 years. Interest rates start at $i^{(12)} = 8\%$ and fall to $i^{(12)} = 6\%$ on the date of the first $200 deposit. Determine the accumulated value at the time of the final $200 deposit.

13. The present value of an annuity of $1000 payable for n years commencing one year from now is $6053. The annual effective rate of interest is 12.5%. Determine the present value of an annuity of $1000 commencing one year from now and payable for $(n + 2)$ years.

14. A person deposits $100 at the beginning of each year for 20 years. Simple interest at an annual rate of i is credited to each deposit from the date of deposit to the end of the 20-year period. The total amount thus accumulated is $2840. If, instead, compound interest had been credited at an annual effective rate of i, what would the accumulated value of these deposits have been at the end of 20 years?

Section 3.5   **Determining the Term of an Annuity**

In some problems the accumulated value S or the discounted value A, the periodic payment R, and the rate i are specified. This leaves the number of payments n to be determined. Formulas **(10)** and **(11)** may be solved for n by the use of logarithms. Normally, when given a value of S or A, R, and a rate i, you will not find an integer time period n for the annuity. Algebraically this means that there is usually no integer n such that $S = Rs_{\overline{n}|i}$ or $A = Ra_{\overline{n}|i}$. It is necessary to make the concluding payment different from R in order to have equivalence. One of the following procedures is followed in practice.

Procedure 1: The last regular payment is increased by a sum that will make the payments equivalent to the accumulated value S or the discounted value A. This increase is sometimes referred to as a *balloon* payment.

Procedure 2: A smaller concluding payment is made one period after the last full payment. This smaller concluding payment is sometimes referred to as a *drop* payment. Sometimes, when a certain sum of money is to be accumulated, a smaller concluding payment will not be required because the interest after the last full payment will equal or exceed the balance needed (Example 1).

CALCULATION TIP:

Unless specified otherwise, we shall use Procedure 2 throughout this book. Procedure 2 is more often used in practice.

EXAMPLE 1 A couple wants to accumulate $10 000 by making payments of $800 at the end of each half-year into an investment account that earns interest at $i^{(2)} = 9\%$. Calculate the number of full payments required and the size of the concluding payment using both Procedures 1 and 2.

Solution We have $S = 10\ 000$, $R = 800$, $i = 4\frac{1}{2}\%$, and we want to calculate n. Substituting in equation **(10)** we obtain:

$$800s_{\overline{n}|0.045} = 10\ 000$$
$$s_{\overline{n}|0.045} = 12.5$$
$$\frac{(1.045)^n - 1}{0.045} = 12.5$$
$$(1.045)^n - 1 = (12.5)(0.045)$$
$$(1.045)^n = 1.5625$$
$$n \log 1.045 = \log 1.5625$$
$$n = 10.13899776$$

Thus there will be 10 full deposits of $800, plus a final payment, needed to reach the $10 000 goal.

Procedure 1 Let X be the balloon payment that will be added to the last regular payment to make the payments equivalent to the accumulated value $S = 10\ 000$. We arrange the data on a time diagram below.

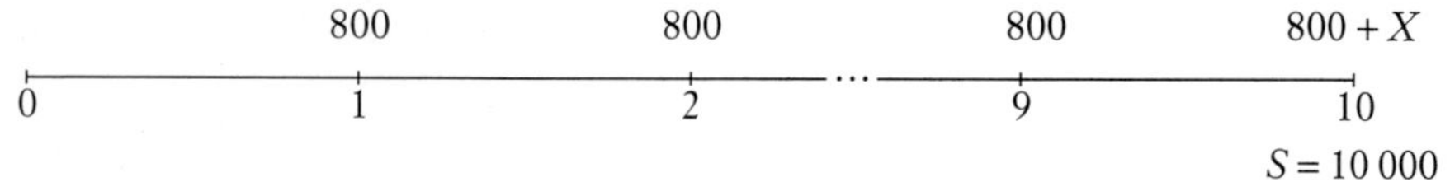

	800	800		800	800 + X
0	1	2	...	9	10

$$S = 10\ 000$$

Using 10 as a focal date, we obtain the equation of value for unknown X:

$$800s_{\overline{10}|0.045} + X = 10\ 000$$
$$X = 10\ 000 - 800s_{\overline{10}|0.045}$$
$$X \doteq 10\ 000 - 9830.57$$
$$X = 169.43$$

Thus the 10th deposit will be $800 + $169.43 = $969.43.

Procedure 2 Let Y be the size of a smaller concluding payment (drop payment) made a half-year after the last full deposit. We arrange the data on a time diagram below.

$$
\begin{array}{ccccccccc}
& & 800 & & 800 & & 800 & & 800 & & Y \\
\hline
0 & & 1 & & 2 & \cdots & 9 & & 10 & & 11
\end{array}
$$

$$S = 10\,000$$

Using time 11 as the focal date we obtain the equation of value for unknown Y:

$$800s_{\overline{10}|0.045}(1.045) + Y = 10\,000$$
$$10\,272.94 + Y \doteq 10\,000$$
$$Y = -272.94$$

The negative value of Y indicates that there is no concluding payment required (that is, $Y = 0$); the interest after the last full payment has increased the accumulated balance past the $10\,000 goal by $272.94.

EXAMPLE 2 A man dies and leaves his wife an estate of $50\,000. The money is invested at $i^{(12)} = 12\%$. How many monthly payments of $750 would the widow receive and what would be the size of the concluding payment?

Solution We have $A = 50\,000$, $R = 750$, $i = 1\%$. Substituting in equation **(11)** we obtain:

$$750a_{\overline{n}|0.01} = 50\,000$$
$$a_{\overline{n}|0.01} = \frac{50\,000}{750}$$
$$\frac{1 - (1.01)^{-n}}{0.01} = \frac{200}{3}$$
$$1 - (1.01)^{-n} = \frac{2}{3}$$
$$(1.01)^{-n} = \frac{1}{3}$$
$$-n \log 1.01 = \log \frac{1}{3}$$
$$n \doteq 110.409624$$

Thus the widow will receive 110 full payments of $750 and one smaller concluding payment, say Y, 1 month after the last full payment. We arrange the data on a time diagram below.

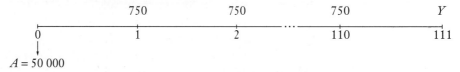

$$
\begin{array}{ccccccc}
& & 750 & & 750 & & 750 & & Y \\
\hline
0 & & 1 & & 2 & \cdots & 110 & & 111
\end{array}
$$

$A = 50\,000$

Using time 111 as the focal date, we obtain the equation of value for unknown Y:

$$750s_{\overline{110}|0.01}(1.01) + Y = 50\ 000(1.01)^{111}$$
$$150\ 575.63 + Y = 150\ 883.76$$
$$Y = 308.12$$

Using time 0 as the focal date, we obtain the equation of value

$$750a_{\overline{110}|0.01} + Y(1.01)^{-111} = 50\ 000$$
$$49\ 897.89 + Y(1.01)^{-111} = 50\ 000$$
$$Y(1.01)^{-111} = 102.11$$
$$Y = 102.11(1.01)^{111}$$
$$Y = 308.12$$

If the widow wanted to withdraw all remaining funds at the time of the last full $750 withdrawal, then let X be the balloon payment, made at time 110. Using time 0 as the focal date, we obtain

$$750a_{\overline{110}|0.01} + X(1.01)^{-110} = 50\ 000$$
$$X(1.01)^{-110} = 102.11$$
$$X = 102.11(1.01)^{110} = 305.08$$

The final withdrawal is $750 + $305.08 = $1055.08.

Using a Financial Calculator to Determine n

We illustrate the required entries for the BA-II Plus calculator.
In Example 1, the steps are as follows:

10 000 $\boxed{FV}$ 0 $\boxed{PV}$ -800 $\boxed{PMT}$ 4.5 $\boxed{I/Y}$ $\boxed{CPT}$ $\boxed{N}$
10.13899776 (half-years)

In Example 2, the steps are as follows:

0   $\boxed{FV}$ 50 000 $\boxed{PV}$ -750 $\boxed{PMT}$ 1 $\boxed{I/Y}$ $\boxed{CPT}$ $\boxed{N}$
110.409624 (months)

Using a Computer Spreadsheet to Determine n

In some instances, a computer spreadsheet has built-in functions that allow you to calculate certain answers more quickly. Calculating the value of n for an annuity is a situation where a financial function can be used.

We will illustrate this using Microsoft's Excel and the financial function **NPER**$(i, -PMT, PV, FV, type)$ where,

i = effective rate per compounding period (typed as a decimal)
$type$ = 0 (ordinary annuity) or 1 (annuity due)

In Example 1, you would type **NPER**(0.045, −800, 0, 10 000, 0), which would result in the answer 10.13899776 half-years.

In Example 2, you would type **NPER**(0.01, −750, 50 000, 0, 0), which would result in the answer 110.409624 months.

Exercise 3.5

Part A

1. A debt of $4000 bears interest at $i^{(2)} = 8\%$. It is to be repaid by semi-annual payments of $400. Determine the number of full payments needed and the final smaller payment after the last full payment.

2. Melissa takes her inheritance of $25 000 and invests it at $i^{(12)} = 6\%$. How many monthly payments of $250 can she expect to receive and what will be the size of the concluding payment? Use both Procedure 1 and Procedure 2.

3. A couple wants to accumulate $10 000. If they deposit $250 at the end of each quarter-year in an account paying $i^{(4)} = 6\%$, how many deposits must they make and what will be the size of the final deposit? Use both Procedure 1 and Procedure 2.

4. A firm buys a machine for $30 000 and pays $5000 down and $5000 at the end of each year. If interest is at $i^{(1)} = 10\%$, how many full payments must the firm make and what will be the size of the concluding smaller payment?

5. A fund of $20 000 is to be accumulated by n annual payments of $2500 plus a final smaller payment made one year after the last regular payment. If interest is at $i^{(1)} = 4\%$, determine n and the final irregular payment.

6. A loan of $10 000 is to be repaid by monthly payments of $400, the first payment due in one year's time. If $i^{(12)} = 12\%$, determine the number of regular monthly payments needed and the size of the final smaller payment.

7. A fund of $8000 is to be accumulated by semi-annual payments of $2000. If $i^{(2)} = 5\%$, determine the number of full deposits required and the final smaller payment.

8. On July 1, 2010, Shannon has $10 000 in an account paying interest at $i^{(4)} = 6\frac{1}{2}\%$. She plans to withdraw $500 every three months with the first withdrawal on October 1, 2010. How many full withdrawals can she make and what will be the size and the date of the concluding withdrawal?

9. A parcel of land, valued at $350 000, is sold for $150 000 down. The buyer agrees to pay the balance with interest at $i^{(12)} = 9\%$ by paying $5000 monthly as long as necessary, the first payment due 2 years from now.
   a) Determine the number of full payments needed and the size of the concluding payment one month after the last $5000 payment.
   b) Determine the monthly payment needed to pay off the balance by 36 equal payments, if the first payment is 1 year from now and interest is at $i^{(12)} = 12\%$.

10. From July 1, 2002, to January 1, 2007, a couple made semi-annual deposits of $500 into an investment account paying $i^{(2)} = 7\%$. Starting July 1, 2011, they start making semi-annual withdrawals of $800.
    a) How many withdrawals can they make and what is the size and date of the last withdrawal?
    b) If the couple decided to exhaust their savings with equal semi-annual withdrawals from July 1, 2011, to July 1, 2021, inclusive, how much will they get each half-year?

11. In October 2007, an industrialist gave your school $30 000 to be used for future scholarships of $4000 at each fall convocation starting the year the industrialist dies. If the industrialist died May 2010, and the money earns interest at $i^{(1)} = 8\%$, for how many years will full scholarships be awarded?

12. A debt of $18 000 is to be repaid in annual instalments of $3000 with the first instalment due at the end of the second year and a final instalment of less than $3000. Interest is 9% per year compounded annually. Calculate the final payment.

Part B

1. Antonio is accumulating a $10 000 fund by depositing $100 each month, starting September 1, 2010. If the interest rate on the fund is $i^{(12)} = 4\%$ until May 1, 2013, and then it drops to $i^{(12)} = 3\%$, determine the time and amount of the reduced final deposit.

2. A widow, as beneficiary of a $100 000 insurance policy, will receive $20 000 immediately and $1800 every 3 months thereafter. The company pays interest at $i^{(4)} = 6\%$; after 3 years, the rate is increased to $i^{(4)} = 7\%$.
   a) How many full payments of $1800 will she receive?
   b) What additional sum paid with the last full payment will exhaust her benefits?
   c) What payment 3 months after the last full payment will exhaust her benefits?

3. On his 25th birthday, Yves deposited $4000 in a fund paying $i^{(1)} = 5\%$ and continued to make such deposits each year, the last on his 49th birthday. Beginning on his 50th birthday, Yves plans to make equal annual withdrawals of $20 000.
   a) How many such withdrawals can be made?
   b) What additional sum paid with the last withdrawal will exhaust the fund?
   c) What sum paid one year after the last full withdrawal will exhaust the fund?

4. A couple bought land worth $300 000. They paid $50 000 down and signed a contract agreeing to repay the balance with interest at $i^{(1)} = 12\%$ by annual payments of $50 000 for as long as necessary and a smaller concluding payment one year later. The contract was sold just after the 4th annual payment to an investor who wants to realize a yield of $i^{(1)} = 13\%$. Determine the selling price.

5. A loan of $20 000 is to be repaid by annual payments of $4000 per year for the first 5 years and payments of $4500 per year thereafter for as long as necessary. Determine the total number of payments and the amount of the smaller final payment made one year after the last regular payment. Assume an annual effective rate of 7.5%.

6. Solve the equation $S = Rs_{\overline{n}|i}$ for n.

7. Solve the equation $A = Ra_{\overline{n}|i}$ for n.

8. A friend agrees to lend you $2000 on September 1 each year for 4 years to help with education costs. One year after the last payment you are expected to start annual repayments of $800 for as long as necessary. Interest on the loan is $i^{(1)} = 6\frac{1}{2}\%$. Determine the number of repayments needed, and the amount of the final payment.

9. A car loan of $10 000 at $i^{(12)} = 12\%$ is being paid off by n payments. The first $(n - 1)$ payments are $263.34 per month. The final monthly payment is $263.24. Determine n.

Section 3.6   # Determining the Interest Rate

A very practical application of equations **(10)** and **(11)** is determining the interest rate. In many business transactions the true interest rate is concealed in one way or another. In order to compare different propositions (options, investments), it is necessary to determine the true interest rate of each proposition and make the decision based on true interest rates.

When R, n, and either S or A are given, the interest rate i may be determined approximately by linear interpolation. For most practical purposes, linear interpolation gives sufficient accuracy and will be used throughout this textbook.

CALCULATION TIP:

To obtain a starting value to solve the equation $s_{\overline{n}|i} = k$ by linear interpolation, we may use the formula $i \doteq \frac{(\frac{k}{n})^2 - 1}{k}$. To obtain a starting value to solve the equation $a_{\overline{n}|i} = k$ by linear interpolation, we may use the formula $i \doteq \frac{1 - (\frac{k}{n})^2}{k}$.

EXAMPLE 1   Determine the interest rate $i^{(4)}$ at which deposits of \$275 at the end of every 3 months will accumulate to \$5000 in 4 years.

Solution   We have $S = 5000$, $R = 275$, $n = 16$, and using equation **(10)** we obtain:

$$275 s_{\overline{16}|i} = 5000$$
$$s_{\overline{16}|i} = 18.1818$$

We want to determine the rate $i^{(4)} = 4i$ such that $s_{\overline{16}|i} = \frac{(1 + i)^{16} - 1}{i} = 18.1818$.

A starting value to solve $s_{\overline{16}|i} = 18.1818$ is $i = \frac{(\frac{18.1818}{16})^2 - 1}{18.1818} = 0.0160227$

or $i^{(4)} = 4i = 6.41\%$. We suspect $6\% <$ true $i^{(4)} < 7\%$.

By successive trials we find two factors $s_{\overline{16}|i}$, one greater than 18.1818 and one less than 18.1818. The corresponding rates $i^{(4)} = 4i$ will provide an upper and lower bound on the unknown rate $i^{(4)}$, which is then approximated by a linear interpolation.

CALCULATION TIP:

The values of factors $s_{\overline{n}|i}$ and $a_{\overline{n}|i}$ will be rounded off to 4 decimal places, since additional places do not really increase the accuracy. For fixed n, factors $s_{\overline{n}|i}$ increase when i increases, whereas factors $a_{\overline{n}|i}$ decrease when i increases. Closer bounds on the nominal rate $i^{(m)}$ generally provide better approximations of the unknown rate $i^{(m)}$ by linear interpolation. In this textbook we will interpolate between two nominal rates that are 1% apart.

For $i^{(4)} = 6\%$, we calculate $s_{\overline{16}|i} = 17.9324$

For $i^{(4)} = 7\%$, we calculate $s_{\overline{16}|i} = 18.2817$

Now we have two rates, $i^{(4)} = 6\%$ and $i^{(4)} = 7\%$, 1% apart, that provide upper and lower bounds for interpolation.

Arranging our data in an interpolation table we have:

	$s_{\overline{16}|i}$	$i^{(4)}$
	17.9324	6%
	18.1818	$i^{(4)}$
	18.2817	7%

$0.3493 \begin{bmatrix} 0.2494 \begin{bmatrix} 17.9324 & 6\% \\ 18.1818 & i^{(4)} \end{bmatrix} d \\ 18.2817 & 7\% \end{bmatrix} 1\%$

$$\frac{d}{1\%} = \frac{0.2494}{0.3493}$$
$$d = 0.7140$$
$$\text{and } i^{(4)} = 6.7140 \doteq 6.71\%$$

We may check the accuracy of this answer by substituting $R = 275$, $n = 16$, and $i = \frac{0.0671}{4}$ into equation (10) and calculate the accumulated value:

$$S = \frac{275(1 + i)^{16} - 1}{i} \doteq \$4999.37$$

Linear interpolation between two nominal rates, 1% apart, gave us a very good approximation of the unknown rate $i^{(4)}$.

OBSERVATION:

The interest rates i and $i^{(m)} = mi$ may be computed directly using either a financial calculator or a spreadsheet.

Using a Financial Calculator to Determine i

Using the BA-II Plus calculator, we enter

5000 $\boxed{FV}$ 0 $\boxed{PV}$ −275 $\boxed{PMT}$ 16 $\boxed{N}$ $\boxed{CPT}$ $\boxed{I/Y}$

Which solves for $i = 1.679127782$
and thus $i^{(4)} = 4i = 6.716511129 \doteq 6.72\%$.

Using a Computer Spreadsheet to Determine i

We use Excel's financial function wizard **RATE**(n, −PMT, PV, FV, type), where type = 0 for an ordinary annuity and type = 1 for an annuity due.

We type in **RATE**(16, −275, 0, 5000, 0)*4
and obtain $i^{(4)} = 6.71651113 \doteq 6.72\%$.

EXAMPLE 2   A used car sells for $24 000 cash or $4000 down and $3600 a month for 6 months. Determine the interest rate, $i^{(12)}$, if the purchaser buys the car on the instalment plan.

Solution   For any instalment plan, the following equation of value must hold to have the cash option equivalent to the instalment option.

$$\boxed{\text{cash price} = \text{down payment} + \text{discounted value of instalments}}$$

We have

$$24\,000 = 4000 + 3600a_{\overline{6}|i}$$
$$a_{\overline{6}|i} = \frac{20\,000}{3600}$$
$$a_{\overline{6}|i} = 5.5556$$

We want to determine the rate $i^{(12)} = 12i$ such that

$$a_{\overline{6}|i} = \frac{1 - (1 + i)^{-6}}{i} = 5.5556 = k.$$

A starting value to solve the equation $a_{\overline{6}|i} = 5.5556$ is $i = \frac{1 - (\frac{5.5556}{6})^2}{5.5556} = $
0.025676338 or $i^{(12)} = 12i = 30.81\%$. We suspect $30\% < $ true $i^{(12)} < 31\%$.

By successive trials we find two factors $a_{\overline{6}|i}$, one greater than 5.5556 and one less than 5.5556, such that the corresponding rates $i^{(12)}$ are 1% apart.

For $i^{(12)} = 26\%$, we calculate $a_{\overline{6}|i} = 5.5701$.

For $i^{(12)} = 27\%$, we calculate $a_{\overline{6}|i} = 5.5545$.

Recall that the starting point formula provides only an approximation to the value of $i^{(m)}$. In this example it provided a poor approximation for the value of $i^{(12)}$. The formula led us to suspect that $30\% < $ true $i^{(12)} < 31\%$. However, at $i^{(12)} = 30\%$, $a_{\overline{6}|0.025} = 5.5081$, which is too low. To raise the value of $a_{\overline{6}|0.025}$ we needed to lower the value of $i^{(12)}$, ultimately to between 26% and 27%.

Arranging our data in an interpolation table we have:

		$a_{\overline{6}|i}$	$i^{(12)}$		
		5.5701	26%		
	0.0145			d	
0.0156		5.5556	$i^{(12)}$		1%
		5.5545	27%		

$$\frac{d}{1\%} = \frac{0.0145}{0.0156}$$
$$d = 0.93\%$$
$$\text{and } i^{(12)} = 26.93\%$$

Checking the accuracy of our answer we calculate the discounted value of the instalment plan at $i^{(12)} = 26.93\%$

$$4000 + 3600a_{\overline{6}|i} = 24\,000.04$$

Note: Using the BA-II Plus calculator, we enter

0 $\boxed{FV}$ $20\,000$ $\boxed{PV}$ -3600 $\boxed{PMT}$ 6 $\boxed{N}$ $\boxed{CPT}$ $\boxed{I/Y}$

Which solves for $i = 2.244219895$
and thus $i^{(12)} = 12i = 26.9306371 \doteq 26.93\%$.

Using Excel's financial function wizard = **RATE**(6, −3600, 20 000, 0, 0)*12 gives $i^{(12)} = 26.93\%$.

EXAMPLE 3   Deposits of $6000 are made every 6 months into a fund starting today and continuing until 10 deposits have been made. Six months after the last deposit, there is $70 630 in the fund. What nominal rate of interest, $i^{(2)}$, do the deposits earn?

Solution   We have $S = 70\ 630$, $R = 6000$, $n = 10$, and an annuity due as shown on the time diagram below.

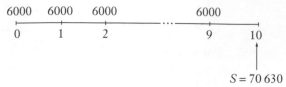

Our equation of value is

$$70\ 630 = 6000\ddot{s}_{\overline{10}|i} \text{ where } i = i^{(2)}/2$$

To use the starting point formula, we need to use the ordinary annuity symbol $s_{\overline{n}|i}$. We recall from section 3.4, $\ddot{s}_{\overline{n}|i} = s_{\overline{n+1}|i} - 1$.

Thus,

$$70\ 630 = 6000\ddot{s}_{\overline{10}|i} = 6000(s_{\overline{11}|i} - 1)$$
$$76\ 630 = 6000s_{\overline{11}|i}$$

$$s_{\overline{11}|i} = \frac{76\ 630}{6000} = 12.7717 = k \text{ (and } n \text{ is now 11)}$$

Using the starting point formula, $i = \dfrac{\left(\frac{12.7717}{11}\right)^2 - 1}{12.7717} = 0.02725$, which gives $i^{(2)} \doteq 5.45\%$. We suspect $5\% <$ true $i^{(2)} < 6\%$.

For $i^{(2)} = 5\%$, $s_{\overline{11}|i} = 12.4835$
For $i^{(2)} = 6\%$, $s_{\overline{11}|i} = 12.8078$
Arranging our data in an interpolation table, we have:

	$s_{\overline{11}|i}$	$i^{(2)}$	
$0.3243\begin{cases}0.2882\begin{cases} & 12.4835 & 5\% \\ & 12.7717 & i^{(2)} \\ & 12.8078 & 6\%\end{cases}d\end{cases}$			1%

$$\frac{d}{1\%} = \frac{0.2882}{0.3243}$$
$$d = 0.8887\%$$
$$\text{and } i^{(2)} \doteq 5.89\%$$

To check,

$$6000\ddot{s}_{\overline{10}|0.02945} = 6000s_{\overline{10}|0.02945}(1.02945) = \$70\ 629.85$$

Note: Using the BA-II Plus calculator (make sure you are in *BGN* mode since this is an annuity due):

70630 ⬚FV⬚   0 ⬚PV⬚   −6000 ⬚PMT⬚   10 ⬚N⬚   ⬚CPT⬚   ⬚I/Y⬚

Which gives $i = 2.945037944$ and thus $i^{(2)} = 2i = 5.890075888 \doteq 5.89\%$.
Using Excel's financial function wizard = **RATE**(10, −6000, 0, 70630, 1)*2 gives $i^{(2)} = 5.89\%$.

Exercise 3.6

Part A

(Use linear interpolation; you can then use a financial calculator or spreadsheet to confirm your answers.)

1. Determine the interest rate $i^{(2)}$ at which semi-annual deposits of $500 will accumulate to $6000 in 5 years.

2. What rate of interest $i^{(1)}$ must be earned for deposits of $500 at the end of each year to accumulate to $12 000 in 10 years?

3. An insurance company will pay $80 000 to a beneficiary or monthly payments of $1000 for 10 years. What rate $i^{(12)}$ is the insurance company using?

4. A television set sells for $1400. Sales tax of 7% is added to that. The TV may be purchased for $200 down and monthly payments of $120 for one year. What is the interest rate $i^{(12)}$? What is the annual effective interest rate?

5. You borrow $1600 from a licensed small loan company and agree to pay $160 a month for 12 months. What nominal rate $i^{(12)}$ is the company charging?

6. A store offers to sell a watch for $55 cash or $5 a month for 12 months. What nominal rate $i^{(12)}$ is the store actually charging on the instalment plan, if the first payment is made immediately?

7. On February 1, 1994, Andreas made the first of a sequence of regular annual deposits of $1000 into an investment account. The last deposit was made February 1, 2010. If the account earned $i^{(1)} = 5\%$, the balance 1 year after the last deposit would have been $27 132.38, while it would have been $28 481.20 at $i^{(1)} = 5.5\%$. In fact, the balance in the account one year after the last deposit was $27 500. What annual effective rate of interest did the account earn?

Part B

The following problems are examples of situations that could arise if there were no government legislation concerning disclosure of interest rates.

Many countries have "truth in lending" laws setting down regulations on the disclosure of the rate of interest involved in financial transactions. It is very important to check out all loan clauses fully.

1. The "Fly By Night" Used Car Lot uses the following to illustrate its 12% finance plan on a car paid for over 3 years.

Cost of car	$12 000.00
12% finance charge	4 320.00 $\left(\begin{smallmatrix}12\% \text{ of } 12\,000\\ \times\ 3 \text{ years}\end{smallmatrix}\right)$
Total cost	$16 320.00

   Monthly payment $= \frac{\$16\,320}{36} = \$453.33$

   What is the true interest rate $i^{(12)}$ being charged?

2. A dealer sells an article for $6000. He will allow a customer to buy it by paying $2400 down and the balance by paying $300 a month for a year. If the customer pays cash for the item he will give a 10% discount. Determine the interest rate $i^{(12)}$ paid by the purchaser who uses the instalment plan described above.

3. Goods worth $1000 are purchased using the following carrying-charge plan: A down payment of $100 is required after which 9% of the unpaid balance is added on and the amount is then divided into 12 equal monthly instalments. What rate of interest $i^{(12)}$ does the plan include?

4. A finance company charges 10% "interest in advance" and allows the client to repay the loan in 12 equal monthly payments. The monthly payment is calculated as one-12th of the total of principal and interest (10% of principal). Determine the nominal rate compounded monthly and the annual effective rate charged.

5. To buy a car costing $27 200 you can pay $3200 down and the balance in 36 monthly payments of $900 each. You can also borrow the money from a loan company and repay $27 200 by making quarterly payments of $2120 over 5 years, first payment in 3 months. Compare the annual effective rates of interest charged and determine which option is better.

6. A TV rental company uses the following illustration to prove that renting a big-screen TV at $45 a month is cheaper than buying.

Cost of TV	$1200
Sales Tax	84
Total	$1284

Therefore monthly payments over 3 years at 12% are $\frac{1284 + (0.12)(1284)(3)}{36} = \$48.51$. Redo this illustration properly at $i^{(12)} = 12\%$ and comment.

7. You are offered a loan of $10 000 with no payments for 6 months, then $600 per month for 1 year, and $500 per month for the following year. What annual effective rate of interest does this loan charge?

8. On July 1, 2009, $8500 is deposited in Fund X. On July 1, 2009, the first of 10 consecutive semi-annual payments of $1000 each is deposited in Fund Y. Both funds earn interest at a nominal rate $i^{(2)}$. The balances in the two funds are equal on July 1, 2014. Calculate $i^{(2)}$.

Section 3.7   Summary and Review Exercises

● **Summary** — n payments of R at i per period

Annuity Type	Discounted Value	Focal Date	Accumulated Value	Focal Date
Ordinary	$Ra_{\overline{n}|i}$	One period before the first payment	$Rs_{\overline{n}|i}$	At time of nth payment
Due	$R\ddot{a}_{\overline{n}|i} =$ $Ra_{\overline{n}|i}(1 + i) =$ $R(1 + a_{\overline{n-1}|i})$	At time of first payment	$R\ddot{s}_{\overline{n}|i} =$ $Rs_{\overline{n}|i}(1 + i) =$ $R(s_{\overline{n+1}|i} - 1)$	One period after nth payment
Deferred	$Ra_{\overline{n}|i}(1 + i)^{-k}$	$k + 1$ periods before the first payment		
Forborne			$Rs_{\overline{n}|i}(1 + i)^{m}$	m periods after the nth payment

where

$a_{\overline{n}|i} = \dfrac{1 - (1 + i)^{-n}}{i}$ is called a discount factor for n payments.

$s_{\overline{n}|i} = \dfrac{(1 + i)^{n} - 1}{i}$ is called an accumulation factor for n payments.

● When calculating factors $s_{\overline{n}|i}$ and $a_{\overline{n}|i}$, do not round off the value of i. Use all digits provided by your calculator and, when necessary, store the value of i in the memory of your calculator. Note that for $i > 0$, $s_{\overline{n}|i} > n$, and $a_{\overline{n}|i} < n$.

Review Exercises 3.7

1. Determine the accumulated and the discounted value of an annuity of $500 at the end of each month at $i^{(12)} = 9\%$ for a) 10 years, b) 20 years.

2. At age 65 Mrs. Papadopoulos takes her life savings of $100 000 and buys a 20-year annuity certain with quarterly payments. Determine the size of these payments
   a) at 5% compounded quarterly,
   b) at 7% compounded quarterly.

3. An annuity provides $600 at the end of each month for 3 years and $800 at the end of each month for the following 2 years. If $i^{(12)} = 5\%$, calculate the present value of the annuity.

4. To finance the purchase of a car, Wendy agrees to pay $400 at the end of each month for 4 years. The interest rate is $i^{(12)} = 15\%$.
   a) If Wendy misses the first 4 payments, what must she pay at the time of the 5th payment to be fully up to date?
   b) Assuming Wendy has missed no payments, what single payment at the end of 2 years would completely discharge her of her indebtedness?

5. A couple needs a loan of $60 000 to buy a boat. One lender will charge $i^{(12)} = 9\%$ while a second lender charges $i^{(12)} = 7\%$. What will be the monthly savings in interest using the lower rate if the monthly payments are to run for 5 years?

6. Determine the accumulated and the discounted value of semi-annual payments of $500 at the end of every half-year over 10 years if interest is $i^{(2)} = 6\%$ for the first four years and $i^{(2)} = 8\%$ for the last six years.

7. Instead of paying $900 rent at the beginning of each month for the next 10 years, a couple decides to buy a townhouse. What is the cash equivalent of the 10 years of rent at $i^{(12)} = 9\%$?

8. A company sets aside $15 000 at the beginning of each year to accumulate a fund for future expansion. What is the amount in the fund at the end of 5 years if the fund earns $i^{(1)} = 8.5\%$?

9. According to Mr. Peterson's will, the $100 000 life insurance benefit is invested at $i^{(1)} = 8\%$ and from this fund his widow will receive $15 000 each year, the first payment immediately, so long as she lives. On the payment date following the death of his wife, the balance of the fund is to be donated to a local charity. If his wife died 4 years, 3 months later, how much did the charity receive?

10. Five years from now a company will need $150 000 to replace worn-out equipment. Starting now, what monthly deposits must be made in a fund paying $i^{(12)} = 9\%$ for 5 years to accumulate this sum?

11. Doreen bought a car on September 1, 2010, by paying $8000 down and agreeing to make 36 monthly payments of $700, the first due on December 1, 2010. If interest is at 12% compounded monthly, determine the equivalent cash price.

12. An office space is renting for $30 000 a year payable in advance. Determine the equivalent monthly rental payable in advance if money is worth 6% compounded monthly.

13. A farmer borrowed $80 000 to buy some farm equipment. He plans to pay off the loan with interest at $i^{(1)} = 13\frac{3}{4}\%$ in 8 equal annual payments, the first to be made 5 years from now. Determine the annual payment.

14. Charlie wants to accumulate $100 000 by making monthly deposits of $1000 into a fund that accumulates interest at $i^{(12)} = 6\%$. Determine the number of full deposits required and the size of the concluding deposit using both procedures 1 and 2.

15. Lise borrows $10 000 at $i^{(4)} = 10\%$. How many $800 quarterly payments will she pay and what will be the size of the drop payment, 3 months after the last $800 payment?

16. On June 1, 2010, Ms. Kaminski purchased furniture for $2200. She paid $400 down and agreed to pay the balance by monthly payments of $100 plus a smaller final payment, the first payment due on July 1, 2010. If interest is at $i^{(12)} = 9\%$, when is the final payment made and what is the amount of the final payment?

17. A used car sells for $5000 cash or $1000 down and $800 a month for 6 months. Calculate the interest rate $i^{(12)}$ if the purchaser buys the car on the instalment plan.

18. Determine the rate $i^{(12)}$ at which deposits of $200 at the end of each month will accumulate to $10 000 in 3 years.

19. The XYZ Finance Company charges 10% "interest in advance" and allows the client to repay the loan in 12 equal monthly payments. Thus for a loan of $6000, they would charge $600 interest and have 12 monthly repayments of $550 each. What is the corresponding rate of interest convertible monthly?

20. A refrigerator is listed at $650. If a customer pays $200 down, the balance plus a carrying charge of $50 can be paid in 12 equal monthly payments. If the customer pays cash, he can get a discount of 15% off the list price. What is the nominal rate compounded monthly if the refrigerator is bought on time?

21. Paul wants to accumulate $5000 by depositing $300 every 3 months into an account paying 8% per annum converted quarterly. He makes the first deposit on July 1, 2010. How many full deposits should he make and what will be the size and the date of the concluding deposit?

22. How much a month for 5 years at $i^{(12)} = 6\%$ would you have to save in order to receive $800 a month for 3 years afterward?

23. A bank account paying $i^{(12)} = 5\frac{1}{2}\%$ contains $5680 on March 1, 2010. Beginning April 1, 2010, the first of a sequence of monthly withdrawals of $400 is made. What is the date of the last $400 withdrawal? By what date (first of the month) will the balance again exceed $400?

24. Jones agrees to pay Smith $800 at the end of each quarter for 5 years, but is unable to do so until the end of the 15th month when he wins $100 000 in a lottery. Assuming money is worth $i^{(4)} = 6\%$, what single payment at the end of 15 months liquidates his debt?

25. A deposit of $1000 is made to open an account on March 1, 2010. Monthly deposits of $300 are then made for 5 years, starting April 1, 2010. Starting April 1, 2015, the first of a sequence of 20 monthly withdrawals of $800 is made. Determine the balance in the account on December 1, 2017, assuming $i^{(12)} = 3\%$.

26. Fred needs a loan of $15 000 to buy a new car. The dealer offers him the loan at $i^{(12)} = 10\%$. Fred can get the loan at his bank at $i^{(12)} = 9\%$.
   a) What will be the monthly savings using the lower rate at his bank if the monthly payments are to run for 3 years?
   b) What will be the total interest on the loan at his bank?
   c) Assume that Fred takes the loan of $15 000 at his bank and decides to pay $600 at the end of each month. How many months will it take him to repay the loan, assuming a drop payment 1 month after the last $600 payment? Determine the drop payment.

27. On November 10, 2010, I.M. Broke obtained a bank loan of $4000 at 10% compounded monthly. I.M. Broke will repay the loan by making monthly payments of $250 beginning on December 10, 2010. Determine the number of full payments, the date, and the size of the smaller concluding payment required.

28. The Sound Warehouse advertises a "no interest for 1 year" option. For example, you can buy a $1200 stereo by paying $100 at the end of each month for 1 year. However, if you pay in full at the time of the purchase, you get a 10% cash discount. What rate of interest, $i^{(12)}$, is the Sound Warehouse actually charging?

29. a) Elsa wants to accumulate $20 000 by the end of 6 years by making quarterly deposits in a fund that pays interest at 10% compounded quarterly. Determine the size of these deposits.
   b) After 4 years the fund rate changes to $i^{(4)} = 8\%$. Determine the size of the quarterly deposits now required if the $20 000 goal is to be met.
   c) What is the total interest earned on the fund over 6 years?

30. Today, Walt purchased a cottage and a boat worth a combined present value of $600 000. To purchase the cottage, Walt agreed to pay $100 000 down and $4000 at the end of each month for 15 years. To buy the boat, he was required to pay $20 000 down and $R at the end

of each month for 5 years. Determine R if $i^{(12)} = 12\%$.

31. Erika deposited $100 monthly in a fund earning $i^{(12)} = 6\%$. The first deposit was made on June 1, 2000, and the last deposit on November 1, 2010.

   a) Determine the value of the fund on
      i) September 1, 2005 (after the payment is made);
      ii) December 1, 2012.
   b) From May 1, 2015, she plans to draw down the fund with monthly withdrawals of $1000. Determine the date and the size of the smaller concluding withdrawal one month after the last $1000 withdrawal.

32. Home appliances are on sale with the following payment terms: either pay cash and receive a 5% discount, or pay monthly for 15 months with no money down. To calculate the monthly payments, add a $50 finance charge per $1000 to the purchase price, then divide this amount into 15 equal payments. What annual effective rate of interest is being charged for buying on time?

33. Peter wants to invest in a mutual fund. His goal is to accumulate enough money over the next 20 years so that he can withdraw $30 000 annually for 25 years afterward. From www.globefund.com he found out that the Trimark Fund earned $i^{(1)} = 10.84\%$ over the past 15 years (as of December 31, 2005). What annual deposits for 20 years would provide him with an annuity of $30 000 per year if he invests in the Trimark Fund, assuming that the first withdrawal will be 1 year after the last deposit and the fund will keep earning $i^{(1)} = 10.84\%$ over the next 45 years?

CASE STUDY 1   *Car Loans*

You are interested in buying a brand-new car for a total of $22 535.60. You have the option of paying cash for the car or you can finance the purchase through the car dealership, which offers a 4-year loan at 7.45% with monthly payments.

The car dealership suggests that you would be better off taking out the car loan and investing the $22 536.60 in a guaranteed investment certificate (GIC). The best interest rate on a 4-year GIC is currently 4.40%. The dealership claims that you could actually earn more on your investment than you would pay in interest on the car loan.

The dealership states that 48 months of interest on a 7.45% loan of $22 536.60 would be $3593.68, while the same principal invested at 4.40% per year would earn interest of $4235.80 — a profit of $642.12. The reason given by the dealership for this non-intuitive result is that the 7.45% is applied to a declining balance, while the 4.40% is applied to an increasing balance.

   a) Verify the figures given in the third paragraph.
   b) Is the dealership correct in recommending the car loan as a better option than the cash purchase? Justify your answer.

CASE STUDY 2   *Car Insurance Premiums*

Charlie changed car insurance companies and received an insurance policy covering two vehicles for 6 months for a premium of $650 plus $32.50 sales tax (total $682.50). The new policy takes effect on December 1. Charlie was given three options in which to pay this amount. The first option was to simply pay the $682.50 on December 1. The other two options consisted of paying the premium in instalments as follows:

a) Option 2 allows Charlie to pay the premium over the next 6 months. The insurance company levels a financing charge of 3% on the premium (not including the tax). The total premium ($650, plus $19.50 finance charge, plus $32.50 tax = $702) is then divided by 6 to get a monthly payment of $117. However, the company requires the first *two* months' payments up front (i.e. on December 1), with the four remaining payments made at the start of each of the next four months (Jan. 1, Feb. 1, Mar. 1, Apr. 1). The insurance company claims it is charging Charlie an annual rate of interest of only 3% (better than you could get at a bank!). However, what is the actual rate, $i^{(1)}$, being charged? (Use interpolation to calculate $i^{(12)}$ and then calculate equivalent $i^{(1)}$.)

b) Charlie is buying the insurance through a broker and the broker provides a third option, which he claims avoids the 3% financing charge. For a $15 service fee, Charlie can pay the premium in 3 equal monthly instalments, with the first payment paid on December 1. The monthly payment would be $232.50 (i.e. $650 plus $32.50 tax plus $15 service fee all divided by 3). Is this really a better deal? To determine, calculate the actual rate, $i^{(1)}$, being charged. (Again, use interpolation to calculate $i^{(12)}$ and then calculate equivalent $i^{(1)}$.)

CASE STUDY 3   *Lease or Buy?*

Many people lease their vehicle rather than buying it. The main reason is to avoid tying up so much of one's money in an automobile.

You determine that you can buy a new vehicle for a total cost of $27 000, or you can lease the same vehicle by paying $4000 down plus lease payments of $400 at the end of each month for 36 months. At the end of the lease agreement, you return the car to the dealer and walk away.

If you buy the car, best estimates are that in 3 years you will be able to sell it for $16 000.

Ignoring all other factors, at what interest rate $i^{(12)}$ are these options equivalent?

CHAPTER *4*

General and Other Types of Annuities

Learning Objectives

In chapter 3, we discussed simple annuities where level payments were made with the same frequency that interest was compounded. For example, an annuity with interest compounded semi-annually and payments made semi-annually is a simple annuity. However, it is common for annuities to have payments that are made at different times than when interest is paid. An example would be an annuity where the payments are made quarterly, but interest is compounded annually. Such annuities are called general annuities.

There are also other types of simple annuities that we are interested in, such as annuities where level payments start at some point and continue forever, and annuities where the payments are not level but instead vary over time. Lastly, we introduce the concept of continuous annuities. While these are not used for "real-world" transactions, they constitute an important building block in actuarial science.

Upon completing this chapter, you will be able to do the following:

- Calculate the accumulated and present value of a general annuity where the payment period and the interest period are not the same.
- Calculate the periodic payment of a mortgage.
- Calculate the present value or periodic payment of a perpetuity, where payments begin on a certain date and continue forever.
- Calculate the accumulated and present value of an annuity where the payments change each period by a constant percentage.
- Calculate the accumulated and present value of an annuity where the payments change each period by a constant amount.
- Calculate the accumulated value of an investment that pays interest at one rate but where the interest is reinvested at another rate.
- Calculate the accumulated and present value where payments are made continuously.

Section 4.1

General Annuities

So far, we have assumed that periodic payments have been made at the same dates as the interest is compounded. This is not always the case. In this section we will consider annuities for which payments are made more or less frequently than interest is compounded. Such a series of payments is called a **general annuity.**

One way to solve general annuity problems is to **replace the given interest rate** by an equivalent rate for which the interest compounding period is the same as the payment period. (A review of section 1.7 will reacquaint you with this process.) In effect, the general annuity problems are transformed into simple annuity problems and the methods outlined in chapter 3 can be directly used; thus no new theory is required.

The second, and historical, approach used in solving general annuity problems is to **replace the given payments** by equivalent payments made on the stated interest conversion dates.

OBSERVATION:

In this textbook we follow the "change of rate" approach, which is the preferred method of solution when calculators are used. The "change of payment" approach is illustrated in problems 2 through 5 of Part B of Exercise 4.1.

In order to solve a general annuity problem, we use the following two-step procedure:

> **1.** Convert the general annuity into an equivalent ordinary simple annuity by replacing the given interest rate with an equivalent rate compounded with the same frequency that payments are made (see section 1.7).
>
> **2.** Solve a simple annuity problem using the methods outlined in chapter 3.

EXAMPLE 1   Jackie makes deposits of $100 at the end of every month into an account earning $i^{(2)} = 5\%$. Determine the value of her account at the end of 6 years.

Solution   First, determine the rate i per month equivalent to 2.5% per half-year, such that

$$(1 + i)^{12} = (1.025)^2$$
$$i = (1.025)^{\frac{1}{6}} - 1$$
$$i = 0.004123915$$

Second, calculate the accumulated value S of an ordinary simple annuity with $R = 100, n = 6 \times 12 = 72, i = 0.004123915$.

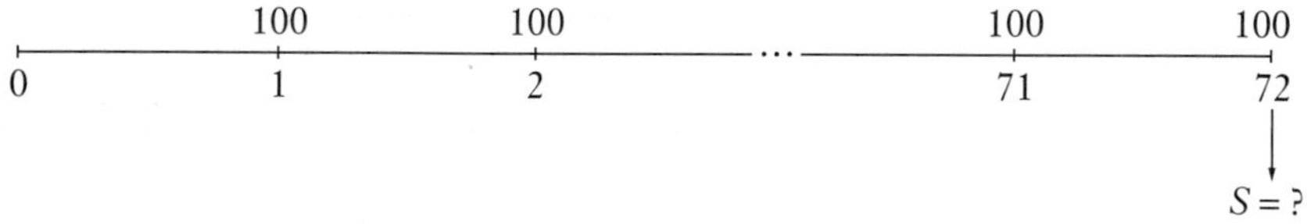

$$S = 100s_{\overline{72}|i} = \$8363.14$$

CALCULATION TIP:

Do not round off the value of i but use all digits provided by your calculator. Store the value of i in the memory of your calculator.

EXAMPLE 2   A contract calls for payments of $300 at the end of every 3-month period for 5 years and an additional payment of $2000 at the end of 5 years. What is the present worth of the contract at a) 6% compounded monthly b) 8% compounded continuously?

Solution a   First, determine the rate i per quarter equivalent to $\frac{0.06}{12} = 0.005$ per month, such that

$$(1 + i)^4 = (1.005)^{12}$$
$$1 + i = (1.005)^3$$
$$i = (1.005)^3 - 1$$
$$i = 0.015075125$$

Second, determine the discounted value A of an ordinary simple annuity and of the additional payment of $2000.

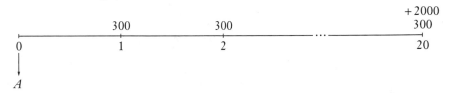

$$A = 300a_{\overline{20}|i} + 2000(1 + i)^{-20} \doteq 5146.78 + 1482.74 = 6629.52$$

The present value of the contract is $6629.52.

Solution b   First, determine the rate i per quarter equivalent to $\delta = 8\%$, such that

$$(1 + i)^4 = e^{0.08}$$
$$i = e^{0.08/4} - 1$$
$$i = 0.02020134$$

Second, calculate the discounted value A of an ordinary simple annuity and of the additional payment of $2000.

$$A = 300a_{\overline{20}|i} + 2000(1 + i)^{-20} \doteq 4895.91 + 1340.64 = 6236.55$$

The present value of the contract is $6236.55.

EXAMPLE 3   What equal monthly payments for 10 years will pay off a loan of $20 000 with interest at 10% compounded daily, if the first payment is made 6 months from now?

Solution   First, determine the rate i per month equivalent to $\frac{0.10}{365}$ per day, such that

$$(1 + i)^{12} = (1 + \tfrac{0.10}{365})^{365}$$
$$i = (1 + \tfrac{0.10}{365})^{365/12} - 1$$
$$i = 0.008367001$$

The monthly payment R of a simple deferred annuity with $A = 20\,000$, $n = 120$, $k = 5$, $i = 0.008367001$ is obtained from the time diagram:

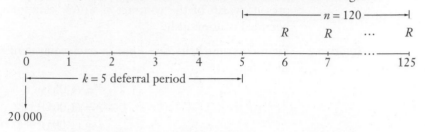

From an equation of value, we solve for R.

$$Ra_{\overline{120}|i}(1 + i)^{-5} = 20\,000$$
$$R = \frac{20\,000}{a_{\overline{120}|i}(1 + i)^{-5}} = \$276.01$$

EXAMPLE 4 A couple would like to accumulate $\$20\,000$ in 3 years as a down payment on a house, by making deposits at the beginning of each week in an account paying interest at $i^{(12)} = 4.2\%$. Determine the size of the weekly deposit.

Solution First, determine the rate i per week equivalent to $\frac{0.042}{12} = 0.0035$ per month, such that

$$(1 + i)^{52} = (1.0035)^{12}$$
$$1 + i = (1.0035)^{12/52}$$
$$i = (1.0035)^{12/52} - 1$$
$$i = 0.000806607$$

Second, determine the weekly deposit R of a simple annuity *due* with $S = 20\,000$, $n = 3 \times 52 = 156$, and $i = 0.000806607$.

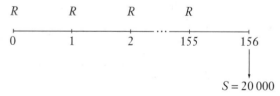

$$20\,000 = R\ddot{s}_{\overline{156}|i}$$
$$R = \frac{20\,000}{s_{\overline{156}|i}(1 + i)} = \$120.26$$

EXAMPLE 5 A loan of $\$25\,000$ is repaid with eight quarterly payments of $\$3500$. What nominal rate compounded monthly is being charged?

Solution First, we calculate the nominal rate $i^{(4)}$ by solving

$$3500a_{\overline{8}|i} = 25\ 000$$
$$a_{\overline{8}|i} = 7.1429$$

A starting value to solve $a_{\overline{8}|i} = 7.1429$ is

$$i = \frac{1 - (\frac{7.1429}{8})^2}{7.1429} = 0.028391347$$

or $i^{(4)} = 4i = 11.36\%$. Using linear interpolation (as in chapter 3, section 3.6) we have

	$a_{\overline{8}|i}$	$i^{(4)}$
	7.1701	10%
0.0758 $\begin{Bmatrix} 0.0272 \begin{Bmatrix} \\ \end{Bmatrix} \end{Bmatrix}$	7.1429	$i^{(4)}$ $\end{Bmatrix} d$
	7.0943	11%

$$\frac{d}{1\%} = \frac{0.0272}{0.0758}$$
$$d = 0.3588\%$$
and $i^{(4)} \doteq 10.36\%$

Check: $3500\ a_{\overline{8}|0.1036/4} = \$24\ 999.45$

Second, we calculate the nominal rate $i^{(12)}$ equivalent to $i^{(4)} = 10.36\%$.

$$(1 + i)^{12} = (1 + \tfrac{0.1036}{4})^4$$
$$1 + i = (1 + \tfrac{0.1036}{4})^{1/3}$$
$$i = (1 + \tfrac{0.1036}{4})^{1/3} - 1$$
$$\text{and } i^{(12)} = 12i = 12[(1 + \tfrac{0.1036}{4})^{1/3} - 1] \doteq 10.27\%$$

Note: Using the BA-II Plus calculator, we first calculate the quarterly rate of interest, $i = i^{(4)}/4$,

25 000 $\boxed{PV}$ 0 $\boxed{FV}$ −3500 $\boxed{PMT}$ 8 $\boxed{N}$ $\boxed{CPT}$ $\boxed{I/Y}$

2.589486866

The equivalent nominal rate compounded monthly is,
$$i^{(12)} = 12[(1.02589486866)^{4/12} - 1] \doteq 10.27\%$$

Situations Where Payments Are Made More Frequently Than Interest Is Compounded

Examples 1 and 4 were examples where payments were made more frequently than interest was compounded. In these situations, financial institutions use different methods for calculating interest for parts of an interest period. The two most common procedures are as follows:

1. *Simple interest* is given for part of an interest period. In these situations you cannot use the "change of rate" method. Instead, you must use the **"change of payment"** method where the given payments are accumulated

to the end of the interest period by using simple interest. This will result in an equivalent payment made with the same frequency that interest is compounded (see Example 6 below).

2. *Compound interest* is given for part of an interest period. (This situation is, by far, the most common.) In these situations you can use the "**change of rate**" method. This is how Examples 1 and 4 were solved.

EXAMPLE 6   Payments of $200 are made at the end of each month in an account paying $i^{(4)} = 8\%$. How much money will be accumulated in the account at the end of 5 years if a) simple interest is paid for the fractional part of a period? b) compound interest is paid for the fractional part of a period?

Solution a   First we determine an **equivalent payment R per quarter** by accumulating the monthly payments to the end of a 3-month period at a simple interest rate of 8%.

$$R = 200[1 + (0.08)(\tfrac{2}{12})] + 200[1 + (0.08)(\tfrac{1}{12})] + 200$$
$$= 600 + 200(0.08)(\tfrac{3}{12}) = \$604.00$$

We now have quarterly payments of $604.00, $n = 5 \times 4 = 20$ quarters, $i = \tfrac{0.08}{4} = 0.02$ per quarter.

The accumulated value S equals

$$S = 604 s_{\overline{20}|0.02} = \$14\ 675.61$$

Solution b   First, determine the rate i per month equivalent to 2% per quarter-year, such that

$$(1 + i)^{12} = (1.02)^4$$
$$1 + i = (1.02)^{1/3}$$
$$i = (1.02)^{1/3} - 1$$
$$i = 0.00662271$$

Second, determine the accumulated value S of an ordinary simple annuity with $R = 200$, $n = 60$, $i = 0.00662271$.

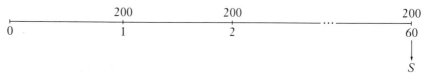

$$S = 200 s_{\overline{60}|i} \doteq \$14\ 675.18$$

EXAMPLE 7   Redo Example 1 assuming simple interest is paid for the fractional part of an interest period.

Solution   First we need to determine a semi-annual payment, R, that is equivalent to $100 per month using simple interest.

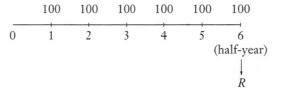

$$R = 100[1 + (0.05)(\tfrac{5}{12})] + 100[1 + (0.05)(\tfrac{4}{12})] + 100[1 + (0.05)(\tfrac{3}{12})] +$$
$$100[1 + (0.05)(\tfrac{2}{12})] + 100[1 + (0.05)(\tfrac{1}{12})] + 100$$
$$= 600 + 100(0.05)(\tfrac{15}{12})$$
$$= 606.25$$

We now have semi-annual payments of 606.25, $n = 6\,\text{yrs} \times 2 = 12$, $i = \frac{0.05}{2} = 0.025$ per half-year.

$$S = 606.25 s_{\overline{12}|0.025} = \$8363.55$$

OBSERVATION:

Not many people are aware of the fact that simple interest brings more money for a part of a conversion period than compound interest. The difference is not large; however, it is important to know the rules that apply to the particular transaction.

Exercise 4.1

Part A

1. George deposits $200 at the beginning of each year in a bank account that earns interest at $i^{(4)} = 6\%$. How much money will be in his bank account at the end of 5 years?

2. A car is purchased by paying $4000 down and then $600 each quarter-year for 3 years. If the interest on the loan was $i^{(2)} = 9.2\%$, what did the car sell for?

3. An insurance policy requires premium payments of $15 at the beginning of each month for 20 years. Determine the discounted value of these payments at $i^{(4)} = 5\%$.

4. Payments of $1000 are to be made at the end of each half-year for the next 10 years. Determine their discounted value if the interest rate is 12% per annum compounded a) half-yearly; b) quarterly; c) annually; d) continuously.

5. Deposits of $100 are made at the end of each quarter to a bank account for 5 years. Determine the accumulated value of these payments if a) $i^{(12)} = 6\%$; b) $i^{(4)} = 6\%$; c) $i^{(1)} = 6\%$; d) $\delta = 6\%$.

6. Determine the monthly payment on a $30\,000 loan for 4 years at a) $i^{(4)} = 9\%$; b) $\delta = 9\%$.

7. Determine the discounted value at $i^{(2)} = 10\%$ of 20 annual payments of $200 each, the first payment due in 5 years.

8. Julia borrows $10 000. The loan is to be repaid with equal payments at the end of each month for the next 5 years. Determine the size of these payments if a) $i^{(4)} = 12\%$; b) $i^{(1)} = 12\%$.

9. Upon graduation, Scott determines that he has borrowed $8000 from the provincial loan plan over his three years of university. This loan must be repaid with monthly payments (first payment at the end of the first month) over the next 5 years. If $i^{(2)} = 8\%$, determine the monthly payment.

10. How much must be deposited in a bank account at the end of each quarter for 4 years to accumulate $4000 if a) $i^{(12)} = 3.6\%$; b) $i^{(2)} = 3.6\%$; c) $i^{(365)} = 3.6\%$?

11. Upon her husband's death, a widow finds that her husband had a $30 000 life insurance policy. One option available to her is a monthly annuity over a 10-year period. If the insurance company pays 6% per annum, what monthly income (at the end of each month) would this provide?

12. A city wants to accumulate $500 000 over the next 20 years to redeem an issue of bonds. What payment will be required at the end of each 6 months to accumulate this amount if interest is earned at 7% compounded monthly?

13. Loan payments of $200 are made at the end of each month for 5 years. The interest rate is $i^{(4)} = 4\%$. Determine the loan amount if
   a) simple interest is paid for part of a period;
   b) compound interest is paid for part of a period.

14. Determine the accumulated value of $100 deposits made at the end of each month for 5 years at $i^{(1)} = 5\%$ if a) compound interest; b) simple interest is paid for part of an interest period.

15. A loan of $15 000 is taken out at $i^{(1)} = 8\%$ and is to be repaid over 5 years with semi-annual payments, the first payment 6 months from now. If simple interest is charged for the fractional part of an interest period, what semi-annual payment is needed?

16. Which is cheaper?
   a) Buy a car for $28 000 and after 3 years trade it in for $8000.
   b) Rent a car for $750 a month payable at the end of each month for 3 years. Assume maintenance and licence costs are identical and $i^{(1)} = 7.9\%$.

17. An insurance company pays 5% per annum on money left with it. What would be the cost of an annuity certain paying $250 at the end of each month for 10 years?

18. What rate of interest $i^{(4)}$ must be earned for deposits of $100 at the end of each month to accumulate to $2000 in 18 months?

19. A furniture suite listing for $2100 may be purchased for $300 down and 18 monthly payments of $100. If cash is paid, a 10% discount is given. Calculate the highest interest rate $i^{(2)}$ at which the buyer can borrow money in order to take advantage of the cash discount.

20. Amanda's New Year's resolution is to make regular weekly deposits of $50 into her savings account earning $i^{(12)} = 3\%$. Determine the number of full deposits and the size of the smaller concluding deposit necessary to accumulate $3000.

21. Jack has made deposits of $250 at the end of each month for 2 years into an investment fund paying interest at $i^{(4)} = 8\%$. What monthly deposits for the next 12 months will bring the fund up to $10 000?

22. An annuity consists of 40 payments of $300 each made at intervals of 3 months. Interest is at $i^{(1)} = 12\%$. Determine the value of this annuity at each of the following times:
   a) 3 months before the time of the first payment;
   b) at the time of the last payment;
   c) at the time of the first payment;
   d) 3 months after the last payment;
   e) 4 years and 3 months before the first payment.

23. A couple made monthly deposits of $400 into an account paying interest at 5.25% compounded quarterly. The first deposit was made on August 1, 2010; the last deposit was made on December 1, 2013.

a) How much money will be in the account on January 1, 2014?

b) How much money will they be able to withdraw monthly, starting on February 1, 2014, and ending February 1, 2015, to pay for their expenses during their planned trip around the world?

24. Melvin borrows $1000 today at 10% compounded semi-annually. The loan is to be repaid with 10 equal monthly payments, the first due one year from today. Determine the size of the payments.

25. A university graduate must repay the government $12 600 for outstanding student loans. The graduate can afford to pay $450 monthly. If the first payment is made at the end of the first year and money is worth 8% compounded quarterly, determine the number of full payments required and the size of the smaller concluding payment.

26. At age 65 a man takes his life savings of $96 000 and buys a 20-year annuity with monthly payments. Determine the size of these payments if interest is at 4% per annum compounded a) daily; b) continuously.

Part B

1. Using the "change of rate" method, fill in the table below to show the accumulated value of an ordinary annuity of $1, p times per year, for 10 years at $i^{(m)} = 12\%$.

	$m = 2$	$m = 4$	$m = 12$
$p = 2$			
$p = 4$			
$p = 12$	$i = (1.06)^{1/6} - 1$ $s_{\overline{120}\mid i}$		

2. Develop the replacement formula $R = \dfrac{W}{s_{\overline{m/p}\mid i}}$ to replace an ordinary general annuity with payments of W made p times a year by an equivalent ordinary simple annuity with payments of R made m times a year.

3. Using the "change of payment" method, fill in the table below to show the discounted value of an ordinary annuity of $1, p times per year, for 10 years at $i^{(m)} = 12\%$.

	$m = 2$	$m = 4$	$m = 12$
$p = 2$			$\dfrac{a_{\overline{120}\mid 0.01}}{s_{\overline{6}\mid 0.01}}$
$p = 4$			
$p = 12$			

4. Convert an annuity with semi-annual payments of $500 into an equivalent annuity with
a) annual payments if money is worth $i^{(1)} = 8\%$;
b) quarterly payments if money is worth $i^{(2)} = 10\%$.

5. Convert an annuity with quarterly payments of $1000 into an equivalent annuity with
a) monthly payments if money is worth $i^{(12)} = 9\%$;
b) annual payments if money is worth $i^{(4)} = 7\%$.

6. Develop the following formulas for the accumulated value S and the discounted value A of an ordinary general annuity with payments W, p times per year, for k years at rate $i^{(m)}$.

$$S = W \frac{(1 + i)^{km} - 1}{(1 + i)^{m/p} - 1}$$

$$A = W \frac{1 - (1 + i)^{-km}}{(1 + i)^{m/p} - 1} \quad \text{where } i = \frac{i^{(m)}}{m}$$

7. Develop the following formulas for the accumulated value S and the discounted value A of a general annuity due with payments W, p times per year, for k years at rate $i^{(m)}$.

$$S = W \frac{s_{\overline{km}\mid i}}{s_{\overline{m/p}\mid i}} (1 + i)^{m/p}$$

$$A = W \frac{a_{\overline{km}\mid i}}{s_{\overline{m/p}\mid i}} (1 + i)^{m/p} \quad \text{where } i = \frac{i^{(m)}}{m}$$

8. A father has saved money in a fund that was set up to help his son to pay for his 4-year university program. The fund will pay $300 at the beginning of each month for 8 months (September through April) plus an extra $2000 each September 1st for 4 years. If $i^{(4)} = 8\%$, what is the value of the fund on the first day of university (before any withdrawals)?

9. A used car may be purchased for $7600 cash or $600 down and 20 monthly payments of $400 each, the first payment to be made in 6 months. What annual effective rate of interest does the instalment plan use?

10. A $5000 loan is repaid by 24 monthly payments of $175 each, followed by 24 monthly payments of $160 each. What interest rate $i^{(1)}$ is being charged?

11. Three years from now, a condominium owners' association will need $100\,000$ to be used for major renovations. For the last 2 years they made deposits of $4000 at the end of each quarter into a fund that earns interest at $i^{(365)} = 6\%$. What quarterly deposits to the fund will be needed to reach the goal of $100\,000$, 3 years from now?

12. In a recent court case, the ABC Development Company sued the XYZ Trust Company. The ABC Development Company had borrowed $8.2 million from the XYZ Trust Company at 5%. The loan was paid off over 3 years with monthly payments. The ABC Development Company thought the rate of interest was $i^{(1)} = 5\%$. The XYZ Trust Company was using $i^{(365)} = 5\%$. The court sided with the Development Company and awarded them the total dollar difference (without interest). Determine the size of the award.

13. To prepare for early retirement, a self-employed businesswoman makes RRSP deposits of $11\,500$ each year for 20 years, starting on her 32nd birthday. When she is 55, she plans to make the first of 30 equal annual withdrawals. What will be the size of each withdrawal if interest is at 7% compounded a) semi-annually; b) continuously?

14. A deposit of $2000 is made to open an account on April 1, 2010. Quarterly deposits of $300 are then made for 5 years, starting July 1, 2010. Starting October 1, 2016, the first of a sequence of $1000 quarterly withdrawals is made. Assuming an interest rate of 10% compounded continuously, determine the balance in the account a) on October 1, 2013; b) on October 1, 2019.

15. Show that the accumulated value S of an ordinary annuity of n payments of R dollars each, p payments per year over t years, at rate δ is

$$S = Rs_{\overline{n}|\delta} = R\frac{e^{\delta t} - 1}{e^{\delta/p} - 1}$$

16. Show that the discounted value A of an ordinary annuity of n payments of R dollars each, p payments per year over t years, at rate δ is

$$A = Ra_{\overline{n}|\delta} = R\frac{1 - e^{-\delta t}}{e^{\delta/p} - 1}$$

Section 4.2 — **Mortgages**

During a lifetime, individuals or households may borrow money for a range of purposes, including cars, education, holidays, and personal equipment. However, the biggest loan that most individuals take out is to enable them to buy their home. These housing loans are called mortgages. The institution lending the money (say, the bank) normally requires the borrower to deliver the title of the property as security for the loan. That is, should the individual be unable to repay the loan, the lender has the right to sell the property and use the proceeds to repay the loan. It is also worth noting that many housing loans are initially set for a term of 20 to 25 years, as individuals expect to repay them throughout their working lifetime.

In the United States, mortgage interest rates are, by law, nominal rates compounded monthly. U. S. mortgages are complicated by their use of "points". Purchasing points is equivalent to lowering your interest rate. The purchase of each point generally lowers the interest rate on your mortgage by 0.25%. Most lenders provide the opportunity to purchase anywhere from zero to three discount points. Discount points are tax deductible. A discount point costs 1% of the mortgage amount.

Canadian mortgage regulations require that the interest can be compounded, at most, semi-annually, whereas mortgage payments are usually made monthly. Thus mortgage repayments in Canada are, in effect, general annuities. There are no legal ceilings on mortgage interest rates in Canada; the rates fluctuate with the price of money on the open market.* Unlike in the United States, mortgage payments are not tax deductible in Canada.

While the monthly payment on a mortgage is usually determined using a repayment period of 20, 25, or 30 years, the interest rate stated in the mortgage is not guaranteed for that length of time. Rather, the interest rate will change after (usually) one, three, or five years depending on the mortgage chosen. At the time the interest rate is renegotiated, the mortgage is open and can be repaid in full. Refinancing of a mortgage will be discussed in chapter 5.

EXAMPLE 1   You are buying a $200 000 house in the United States and can pay $100 000 down, meaning that you require a $100 000 mortgage. You decide on a 30-year amortization schedule. The lender offers you an interest rate of 6% compounded monthly. It costs $1000 for every discount point offered by the lender and each discount point lowers the given interest rate by 0.25%. Thus, if you buy 3 discount points, it will cost you $3000, but you can obtain a mortgage interest rate of 5.25%.

Calculate the monthly payment under these two options and determine the length of time you would have to hold the mortgage to break even if the $3000 could earn interest at 6% compounded monthly.

Solution   The original mortgage rate is $i^{(12)} = 6\%$, which is $\frac{1}{2}\%$ per month.

Given a 30-year $100 000 mortgage at $i^{(12)} = 6\%$, then the term is $n = 30 \times 12 = 360$ and the monthly payment is R, such that:

$$100\ 000 = Ra_{\overline{360}|.005}$$
$$R = \$599.55$$

Taking advantage of the discounts, the mortgage rate becomes $i^{(12)} = 5.25$, which is $i = 0.4375\%$ per month.

$$100\ 000 = Ra_{\overline{360}|.004375}$$
$$R = \$552.20$$

We thus save $47.35 per month.

The break-even period is n (months) where:

$$3000 = 47.35a_{\overline{n}|.005}$$
$$a_{\overline{n}|.005} = 63.358$$

$$\frac{1 - (1.005)^{-n}}{.005} = 63.358$$

$$(1.005)^n = 1.464$$

---

*For the current mortgage rates offered by major Canadian banks, see **www.rbc.com**, **www.bmo.ca**, **www.td.com**, **www.scotiabank.com**, **www.cibc.com**.

Solving:

$$n = \frac{\log 1.464}{\log 1.005} = 76.38$$

Thus, you would have to live in your house a minimum 6 years 5 months for this alternative to be advantageous.

EXAMPLE 2   In July 1990, mortgage rates in Canada averaged around $i^{(2)} = 11\%$. In 2009, mortgage rates averaged around $i^{(2)} = 5.50\%$. Given a \$100 000 mortgage to be repaid over 25 years, determine the required monthly payment at the two different rates of interest.

Solution a   At $i^{(2)} = 11\%$, first determine the rate i per month equivalent to $5\frac{1}{2}\%$ per half-year, such that

$$(1 + i)^{12} = (1.055)^2$$
$$1 + i = (1.055)^{1/6}$$
$$i = (1.055)^{1/6} - 1$$
$$i = 0.008963394$$

Second, determine the monthly payment R of an ordinary simple annuity with $A = 100\,000$, $n = 300$, $i = 0.008963394$.

$$R = \frac{100\,000}{a_{\overline{300}|i}} = 962.53$$

At $i^{(2)} = 11\%$ the monthly mortgage payment required is \$962.53.

Solution b   At $i^{(2)} = 5.50\%$, first determine the rate i per month equivalent to 2.75% per half-year such that

$$(1 + i)^{12} = (1.0275)^2$$
$$1 + i = (1.0275)^{1/6}$$
$$i = (1.0275)^{1/6} - 1$$
$$i = 0.004531682$$

Second, determine the monthly payment R of an ordinary simple annuity with $A = 100\,000$, $n = 300$, and $i = 0.004531682$.

$$R = \frac{100\,000}{a_{\overline{300}|i}} = \$610.39$$

At $i^{(2)} = 5.50\%$ the monthly mortgage payment required is \$610.39. Notice the significant effect the rate of interest has on a mortgage payment.

The total interest paid over the life of the mortgage can be calculated as follows:
a)   At $i^{(2)} = 11\%$, total interest $= 300(\$962.53) - \$100\,000 = \$188\,759$.
b)   At $i^{(2)} = 5.50\%$, total interest $= 300(\$610.39) - \$100\,000 = \$83\,117$.

Again, notice the significant effect the rate of interest has on the total interest paid over the life of a mortgage.

EXAMPLE 3   A Canadian couple is buying a home for $300 000. They make a down payment of 20% and finance the rest through a mortgage loan at 6.5% compounded semi-annually.

   a) Calculate the couple's monthly mortgage payment based on the following repayment periods: 25 years, 20 years, 15 years.
   b) If the couple can afford to pay $2000 monthly on their mortgage loan, how many full payments will be required and what will be the smaller concluding payment 1 month after the last full payment?

Solution a   First, calculate the down payment = $300 000 (0.20) = $60 000. The size of the mortgage loan is $300 000 − $60 000 = $240 000.

Next, determine the rate i per month equivalent to 3.25% per half-year, such that

$$(1 + i)^{12} = (1.0325)^2$$
$$1 + i = (1.0325)^{1/6}$$
$$i = (1.0325)^{1/6} - 1$$
$$i = 0.00534474$$

Then calculate the monthly payment of an ordinary simple annuity with $A = 240\,000$, $i = 0.00534474$.

For $n = 300$ (25-year period): $R = \dfrac{240\,000}{a_{\overline{300}|i}} = \$1607.58$

For $n = 240$ (20-year period): $R = \dfrac{240\,000}{a_{\overline{240}|i}} = \$1777.20$

For $n = 180$ (15-year period): $R = \dfrac{240\,000}{a_{\overline{180}|i}} = \$2079.29$

Note that the longer the amortization period, the lower the mortgage payment. However, it is also true that the longer the amortization period, the more interest is paid over the life of the mortgage:*
   For $n = 300$, total interest = 300($1607.58) − $240 000 = $242 274.00
   For $n = 240$, total interest = 240($1777.20) − $240 000 = $186 528.00
   For $n = 180$, total interest = 180($2079.29) − $240 000 = $134 272.20

OBSERVATION:

Borrowers are advised to choose the term of the loan best suited to their particular situation.

Sub-Prime Mortgage Problem In 2007 and 2008, the United States was hit by the sub-prime mortgage crisis. This was basically a situation in which low-interest-rate mortgages were being offered — many to people who could not afford them, especially after the interest rates rose substantially on the first renewal. Canadian mortgage lenders did not offer these types of mortgages. However, for a short period of time Canadian lenders did offer mortgages with a 40-year term. To see what impact this has, calculate $R = \dfrac{240\,000}{a_{\overline{480}|i}} = \$1390.37$ and calculate the total interest paid over the 40 years = 480(1390.37) − 240 000 = $427 377.60. When compared to the standard 25-year term, the borrower ends up paying in excess of $185 000 more in interest over the life of the mortgage.

Solution b We have an ordinary simple annuity with $A = 240\,000$, $R = 2000$, $i = 0.00534474$ and we calculate n as follows:

$$2000\,a_{\overline{n}|\,i} = 240\,000$$
$$a_{\overline{n}|\,i} = 120$$
$$\frac{1 - (1.00534474)^{-n}}{0.00534474} = 120$$
$$1 - (1.00534474)^{-n} = 0.6413688$$
$$(1.00534474)^{-n} = 0.3586312$$
$$-n \log 1.00534474 = \log 0.3586312$$
$$n = 192.3758$$

Thus there will be 192 full monthly payments and a smaller concluding (drop) payment, X dollars, 1 month after the last full payment.

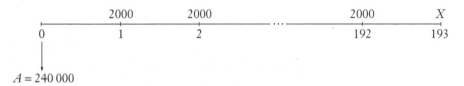

$A = 240\,000$

Using time 193 (16 years, 1 month) as a focal date, we obtain the equation of value for unknown X at rate $i = 0.00534474$.

$$2000 s_{\overline{192}|\,i}(1 + i) + X = 240\,000(1 + i)^{193}$$
$$670\,688.63 + X = 671\,441.50$$
$$X = \$752.87$$

EXAMPLE 4 A home costs \$350 000. A down payment of 10% is made with the remainder financed through a mortgage loan, to be repaid over 25 years. If the interest rate is $i^{(2)} = 6\%$, what is the mortgage payment made a) once every two weeks; b) twice a month; c) weekly?

Solution a Mortgage loan $= \$350\,000 - (0.10)\$350\,000 = \$350\,000 - \$35\,000 = \$315\,000$. Determine the rate i per 2-week period equivalent to 3% per half-year, such that

$$(1 + i)^{26} = (1.03)^2$$
$$i = (1.03)^{2/26} - 1$$
$$i = 0.00227634$$

Then determine the payment R made every 2 weeks with $A = 315\,000$, $n = 25$ years $\times 26 = 650$, $i = 0.00227634$.

$$R = \frac{315\,000}{a_{\overline{650}|\,i}} = \$928.95$$

The payment made every 2 weeks is \$928.95.

Solution b Determine the rate i per twice a month equivalent to 3% per half-year, such that

$$(1 + i)^{24} = (1.03)^2$$
$$i = (1.03)^{2/24} - 1$$
$$i = 0.00246627$$

Then determine the payment R made twice a month with $A = 315\,000$, $n = 25 \times 24 = 600$, $i = 0.00246627$:

$$R = \frac{315\,000}{a_{\overline{600}|i}} = \$1006.45$$

The payment made twice a month is $1006.45.

Solution c Determine the rate i per week equivalent to 3% per half-year, such that

$$(1 + i)^{52} = (1.03)^2$$
$$i = (1.03)^{2/52} - 1$$
$$i = 0.001137523$$

Then determine the payment R made every week with $A = 315\,000$, $n = 25 \times 52 = 1300$, $i = 0.001137523$:

$$R = \frac{315\,000}{a_{\overline{1300}|i}} = \$464.21$$

The payment made every week is $464.21.

Exercise 4.2

Part A

In each question listed below, calculate the monthly mortgage payment.

No.	Mortgage Loan	Interest Rate	Repayment Period
1.	$105\,000	$i^{(2)} = 6.25\%$	25 years
2.	$465\,000	$i^{(2)} = 14.75\%$	20 years
3.	$200\,000	$i^{(2)} = 7.50\%$	22 years
4.	$135\,000	$i^{(2)} = 9.75\%$	12 years

5. A home selling for $375\,000 is to be purchased with a 20% down payment and the remainder financed through a mortgage with monthly payments over 25 years. Determine the monthly payment if a) $i^{(2)} = 5\%$; b) $i^{(2)} = 7\%$; c) $i^{(2)} = 9\%$.

6. A $150\,000 mortgage is obtained at a rate $i^{(2)} = 10\frac{1}{4}\%$. The mortgage can be paid over 20, 25, or 30 years. Determine the monthly payments necessary under each of these three options. Calculate the total interest paid over each of the three terms.

7. A $300\,000 mortgage is being obtained. The mortgage will be repaid over 30 years. Determine the monthly payment if:
a) $i^{(2)} = 7\%$
b) $i^{(12)} = 7\%$

8. Politicians have sometimes suggested putting a ceiling on mortgage interest rates. Mr. and Mrs. Gordon want to buy a house that would require a $160\,000 mortgage to be paid off in 25 years. Interest is at rate $i^{(12)} = 9\%$. If the government guaranteed lower mortgage interest rates, then we would expect the demand for housing to increase, thus forcing house prices upward

(given a constant supply). Would Mr. and Mrs. Gordon be better off if they could get a government mortgage at $i^{(12)} = 6\%$ but the price of the house rose such that it required a $180 000 mortgage?

9. A couple is looking at buying one of two houses. The smaller house would require a $130 000 mortgage, the larger house a $160 000 mortgage. If $i^{(2)} = 7.5\%$, what difference would there be in their monthly payments between these two houses (assume a 25-year repayment period is used in both cases)?

10. Mr. and Mrs. Battiston are considering the purchase of a house. They would require a mortgage loan of $120 000 at rate $i^{(2)} = 6.75\%$. If they can afford to pay $900 monthly, how many full payments will be required and what will be the smaller concluding payment?

11. The Belangers can buy a certain house listed at $400 000 and pay $70 000 down. They can get a mortgage for $330 000 at $i^{(12)} = 7\%$ payable monthly over 25 years. The seller of the house offers them the house for $420 000 and he will give them a $350 000 mortgage at $i^{(12)} = 6\%$ with a 25-year repayment period. If these interest rates are guaranteed for 25 years, what should they do?

12. A couple requires a $280 000 mortgage loan at $i^{(2)} = 7.6\%$ to buy a new house.
    a) Determine the couple's mortgage payment made every 2 weeks based on the following repayment periods: 25 years, 20 years, and 15 years.
    b) If the couple can afford to pay $1000 every 2 weeks on their mortgage loan, what repayment period (in years) should they request?

13. To purchase a house for $215 000, you make a 15% down payment and finance the rest with a mortgage at $i^{(12)} = 6.90\%$ over 25 years. Calculate the required mortgage payment made a) weekly; b) twice a month.

14. In an effort to advertise low rates of interest, but still achieve high rates of return, lenders sometimes charge *points*. Each point is a 1% discount from the face value of the loan. Suppose that a cottage is being sold for $550 000 and that the buyer pays $150 000 down and gets a $400 000, 15-year mortgage at

$i^{(12)} = 9\%$ from a lender who charges three points. What is the true interest rate on the loan?

15. The Sanjanis have agreed to buy the Chans' house for $400 000. The Sanjanis can pay $50 000 down and can get a mortgage from the bank for $300 000. The Chans agree to take a second mortgage for the remaining $50 000. If the bank rate is $i^{(12)} = 6\%$, the Chans want $i^{(12)} = 9\%$, and both loans are amortized over 20 years, what will be the Sanjanis' monthly payment?

Part B

In each question listed below, determine the unknown part.

No.	Mortgage Loan	Interest Rate	Repayment Period	Monthly Payment
1.	?	$i^{(2)} = 6.75\%$	25 years	$920
2.	$100 000	$i^{(2)} = ?$	20 years	$828
3.	$ 89 000	$i^{(12)} = 6.45\%$	?	$750
4.	$ 400 000	$i^{(12)} = 5.62\%$	17 years	?

5. The Friedmans have a $135 000 mortgage with monthly payments over 25 years at $i^{(2)} = 7\%$. Because they each get paid weekly, they decide to switch to weekly payments (still at $i^{(2)} = 7\%$ and paid over 25 years). Compare their weekly payments to their monthly payments.

6. A couple must decide between a red house and a blue house. To purchase the red house they must take a $155 000 mortgage to be repaid over 20 years at 7.8% compounded monthly. To purchase the blue house, they must take a mortgage to be repaid over 25 years at 7.1% compounded monthly. If the monthly mortgage payments are equal, determine the value of the mortgage on the blue house.

7. You want to take a $105 000 mortgage at $i^{(12)} = 9\%$ and can afford to pay up to $300 per week. What repayment period in years should you request and what will be your weekly payment?

| *Section 4.3* | # Perpetuities |

A **perpetuity** is an annuity whose payments begin on a fixed date and continue forever.

Illustration: Let us consider a person who invests $10 000 at rate $i^{(2)} = 10\%$, keeps the original investment intact and collects $500 interest at the end of each half-year. As long as the interest rate does not change and the original principal of $10 000 is kept intact, interest payments of $500 can be collected forever. We say the interest payments of $500 form a perpetuity.

The present value or discounted value of this infinite series of payments is $10 000, as shown on the diagram below.

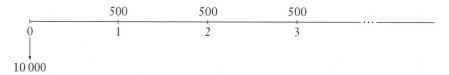

Examples of perpetuities are the series of interest payments from a sum of money invested permanently at a certain interest rate, a scholarship paid from an endowment on a perpetual basis, and the dividends on a share of preferred stock.

It is meaningless to speak about the accumulated value of a perpetuity, since there is no end to the term of a perpetuity. The discounted value, however, is well defined as the equivalent dated value of the set of payments at the beginning of the term of the perpetuity.

The terminology defined for annuities applies to a perpetuity as well. First we shall discuss an **ordinary simple perpetuity**, that is, a lump sum is invested and a series of level periodic payments are made, with the first payment made at the end of the first interest period and payments continuing forever. The other simple perpetuities, i.e., **perpetuities due** and **deferred perpetuities** may be handled using the concept of an equation of value.

Let A be the discounted value of an ordinary simple perpetuity; let $i > 0$ be the interest rate per period; and let R be the periodic payment of the perpetuity.

Then A must be equivalent to the set of payments R as shown on the diagram below.

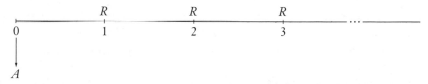

From first principles,

$$A = R(1 + i)^{-1} + R(1 + i)^{-2} + R(1 + i)^{-3} + \cdots$$

We know that the sum of an infinite geometric progression can be expressed as

$$\frac{t_1}{1 - r} \text{ if } -1 < r < 1$$

In our infinite geometric progression $t_1 = R(1 + i)^{-1}$ and $r = (1 + i)^{-1}$. Obviously, $0 < (1 + i)^{-1} < 1$ for $i > 0$. Therefore,

$$A = \frac{R(1 + i)^{-1}}{1 - (1 + i)^{-1}} = \frac{R}{(1 + i) - 1} = \frac{R}{i}$$

Alternatively, it is evident that A will perpetually provide $R = Ai$ as interest payments on the invested capital A at the end of each interest period as long as it remains invested at rate i.

From $R = Ai$ we obtain the discounted value A of an ordinary simple perpetuity

$$\boxed{A = \frac{R}{i}} \tag{12}$$

OBSERVATION:

Formula **(12)** for the discounted value A of an ordinary simple perpetuity can also be obtained as the limit of the discounted value of an ordinary simple annuity

$$A = \lim_{n \to \infty} R a_{\overline{n}|i} = \lim_{n \to \infty} R \frac{1 - (1 + i)^{-n}}{i} = \frac{R}{i}$$

Actuaries use the notation $a_{\overline{\infty}|i} = \lim_{n \to \infty} a_{\overline{n}|i} = \frac{1}{i}$ when referring to the discounted value of a \$1 ordinary simple perpetuity.

EXAMPLE 1 How much money is needed to establish a scholarship fund paying scholarships of \$1000 each half-year if the endowment can be invested at $i^{(2)} = 5\%$ and if the first scholarships will be provided

a) a half-year from now;
b) immediately;
c) 4 years from now?

Solution a The payments form an ordinary simple perpetuity and we have $R = 1000$ and $i = 0.025$; using **(12)** we calculate

$$A = \frac{1000}{0.025} = \$40\,000$$

Solution b We have a perpetuity due, since the first payment is due at the time the lump-sum deposit is made. Thus, the endowment is the sum of the above perpetuity and \$1000, i.e.

$$A = 1000 + \frac{1000}{0.025}$$
$$= 1000 + 40\,000$$
$$= \$41\,000$$

Solution c   We have a deferred perpetuity. The first scholarship is due 4 years from now, or at time 8; thus the deferral period is 7 half-years. The amount needed today is

$$A = \frac{1000}{0.025}(1.025)^{-7}$$
$$= 40\,000(1.025)^{-7}$$
$$= \$33\,650.61$$

OBSERVATION:

Since a perpetuity is an annuity with $n \to \infty$, we may develop formulas for the discounted value A of other simple perpetuities as in section 3.4:

$$A = \frac{R}{i}(1 + i) = \frac{R}{i} + R \text{ for a simple perpetuity due}$$

$$A = \frac{R}{i}(1 + i)^{-k} \text{ for an ordinary simple perpetuity deferred } k \text{ periods.}$$

EXAMPLE 2   A company is expected to pay \$0.90 every 3 months on a share of its preferred stock. What should a share of the stock be selling for, if money is worth a) $i^{(4)} = 6\%$; b) $i^{(4)} = 8\%$?

Solution a   We have $R = 0.90$ and $i = 0.015$; and using **(12)** we calculate

$$A = \frac{0.90}{0.015} = \$60$$

Solution b   Using $i = 0.02$, we calculate $A = \frac{0.90}{0.02} = \$45$.

Note the effect of interest rates on preferred stock values.

When the payment interval and the interest period do not coincide, we have a **general perpetuity**. The simplest way to solve a general perpetuity problem is to calculate the equivalent rate of interest per payment interval and then use formula **(12)**.

EXAMPLE 3   What should a share of the stock in Example 2 be selling for if the money is worth a) $i^{(12)} = 6\%$; b) $i^{(1)} = 6\%$?

Solution a   First we calculate the rate i per quarter-year equivalent to $\frac{0.06}{12} = 0.005$ per month, such that

$$(1 + i)^4 = (1 + 0.005)^{12}$$
$$1 + i = (1.005)^3$$
$$i = (1.005)^3 - 1$$
$$i = 0.015075125$$

We now have an ordinary simple perpetuity with $R = 0.90$ and $i = 0.015075125$; and using **(12)** we calculate

$$A = \frac{0.90}{i} = \$59.70$$

Solution b   First we determine the rate i per quarter-year equivalent to 0.06 per year, such that

$$(1 + i)^4 = 1.06$$
$$1 + i = (1.06)^{1/4}$$
$$i = (1.06)^{1/4} - 1$$
$$i = 0.014673846$$

We now have an ordinary simple perpetuity with $R = 0.90$ and $i = 0.014673846$; using **(12)** we calculate

$$A = \frac{0.90}{i} = \$61.33$$

EXAMPLE 4   An alumna gives a cash donation of \$100 000 to her former university. The donation is invested in an endowment fund at $i^{(1)} = 7\%$. An annual scholarship is to be paid from this fund of \$$R$ for the first 10 years, followed by \$$1.5R$ thereafter. What is R?

Solution   The time diagram looks like:

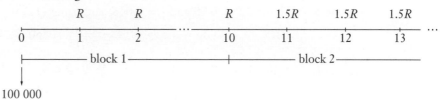

We use the blocking technique to solve:

$$100\,000 = \text{p.v. of block 1} + \text{p.v. of block 2}$$
$$= Ra_{\overline{10}|0.07} + \left(\frac{1.5R}{0.07}\right)(1.07)^{-10}$$
$$= 7.02358154R + 10.89319912R$$
$$R = \frac{100\,000}{17.91678066} = \$5581.36$$

Exercise 4.3

Part A

1. Determine the discounted value of an ordinary simple perpetuity paying \$50 a month if
   a) $i^{(12)} = 6\%$; b) $i^{(12)} = 7.2\%$; c) $i^{(12)} = 9\%$.

2. Determine the discounted value of an ordinary simple perpetuity paying \$400 a year if interest is a) $i^{(1)} = 8\%$; b) $i^{(1)} = 12.48\%$.

3. How much money is needed to establish a scholarship fund paying \$1500 annually if the fund will earn interest at $i^{(1)} = 6\%$ and the first

payment will be made a) at the end of the first year; b) immediately; c) 5 years from now?

4. On September 1, 2010, a philanthropist gives a university a fund of $50 000, which is invested at $i^{(2)} = 6\%$. If semi-annual scholarships are awarded for 20 years from this grant, what is the size of each scholarship if the first one is awarded on a) September 1, 2010; b) September 1, 2012?

5. If the semi-annual scholarships in question 4 were to be awarded indefinitely, what would be the size of the payments for the two starting dates listed above?

6. It costs the Railroad company $100 at the end of each month to maintain a level-crossing gate system. How much can the company contribute toward the cost of an underpass that will eliminate the level-crossing system if money is worth 9% payable monthly?

7. How much money is needed to establish a research fund paying $2000 semi-annually forever (first payment at the end of six months) if money is worth a) $i^{(1)} = 7\%$; b) $i^{(2)} = 7\%$; c) $i^{(12)} = 9\%$?

8. A family is considering putting aluminum siding on their house as it needs painting immediately. Painting the house costs $4200 and must be done every four years. What price can the family afford for the aluminum siding if they earn interest at $i^{(1)} = 5.75\%$ on their savings?

9. The XYZ company has a stock that pays a semi-annual dividend of $4. If the stock sells for $64, what yield $i^{(2)}$ did the investor desire? What is the equivalent rate $i^{(1)}$?

10. The discounted value of a perpetuity is $20 000 and the yield on the fund is $i^{(2)} = 8\%$. What payment will this fund provide a) at the end of each month; b) at the beginning of each year?

11. Deposits of $1000 are placed into a fund at the beginning of each year for the next 20 years. At the end of the 20th year, annual payments from the fund commence and continue forever. If $i^{(1)} = 6\frac{1}{2}\%$, determine the value of these payments.

12. On the basis of an unspecified interest rate, i per

annum, a perpetuity paying $330 at the end of each year forever may be purchased for $3000. Determine i.

13. If money is worth $i^{(1)} = 4\%$, determine the present value of a deferred perpetuity of $1000 per year if the first payment is due at the end of 6 years.

14. What annual deposits are needed for 15 years to provide for a perpetuity of $2000 per year, with the first payment due 10 years after the final deposit? Assume interest is at $i^{(1)} = 8\%$.

Part B

1. Use an infinite geometric progression to derive the formula for the discounted value of a simple perpetuity due.

2. Derive $a_{\overline{n}|i} = \frac{1 - (1 + i)^{-n}}{i}$ as the difference between the discounted value of an ordinary simple perpetuity of $1 per period and the discounted value of an ordinary simple perpetuity of $1 per period deferred for n periods.

3. In 2010, a research foundation was established by a fund of $2 000 000 invested at a rate that would provide $240 000 payments at the end of each year, forever.
   a) What interest rate was being earned in the fund?
   b) After the payment in 2015, the foundation learned that the rate of interest earned on the fund was being changed to $i^{(1)} = 10\%$. If the foundation wants to continue annual payments forever, what size will the new payments be?
   c) If the foundation continues with the $240 000 payments annually, how many full payments can be made at the new rate?

4. A university estimates that its new campus centre will require $30 000 for upkeep at the end of each year for the next 5 years and $50 000 at the end of each year thereafter indefinitely. If money is worth $i^{(1)} = 8\%$, how large an endowment is necessary for the future upkeep of the campus centre?

5. You take out a loan for L at $i^{(12)} = 18\%$ and repay $300 at the end of each month for as long as necessary. This loan is invested at $i^{(1)} = 10\%$ and provides for a *perpetuity due* that pays the prize in the annual "Liar's Contest." The prize

is $200 for the 1st year and increases by $150 each year until it reaches $500. From then on the prize remains $500. Determine the time and amount of the final repayment on the loan.

6. A university receives a certain sum as a bequest and invests it to earn $i^{(1)} = 8\%$. The fund can be used to pay for a lecturer at $60 000 payable at the end of each year forever, or the money can be used to pay for a new building that the university is planning to erect. The building will be paid for with 25 equal annual payments, the first of which is due 4 years from today when the building will be occupied. Calculate the amount of each building payment.

7. How much must you deposit at the end of each year for 10 years to fund a perpetuity of $2500 per year with the 1st payment due 5 years after the last deposit? Interest rate is $i^{(1)} = 6\%$ for 15 years, then $i^{(12)} = 9\%$.

8. A perpetuity paying $1000 at the end of each year is replaced with an annuity paying $X at the end of each month for 10 years. Calculate X if $i^{(4)} = 7\%$ in both cases.

9. If, in question 8, the annuity paid $250 at the end of each month, how long would the annuity last and what would be the size of the final smaller payment?

10. On September 1, 2010, a wealthy industrialist gives a university a fund of $100 000 that is invested at 8% compounded daily. If semi-annual scholarships are awarded for 20 years from this grant, what is the size of each scholarship if the first one is awarded on a) September 1, 2010; b) September 1, 2012?

11. If the semi-annual scholarships in question 10 were awarded indefinitely, what would be the size of the payments for the two starting dates listed above?

12. Determine the present value of a perpetuity of $362.99 payable every 4 years, the first payment 3 years hence, at the annual effective rate of 4%.

13. Determine the monthly deposit needed for 5 years to provide for a perpetuity of $400 per month. The 1st perpetuity payment is made 2 years after the last deposit, and interest changes from $i^{(12)} = 8\%$ to $i^{(12)} = 9\%$ on that date.

14. You deposit $1000 per year for 10 years at $i^{(1)} = 8\%$. This fund then provides for a perpetuity of $3000 per year, with the first payment made n years after the final deposit. At the time of the first perpetuity payment, interest rates fall to $i^{(4)} = 7\%$. Calculate n.

15. A perpetuity pays $4000 per year, as follows:
    a) in odd-numbered years, a payment of $4000 is made at the end of the year;
    b) in even-numbered years, a payment of $1000 is made at the end of each quarter.
    Interest is at an annual effective rate of 8%. At the beginning of an odd-numbered year, this perpetuity is exchanged for another of equal value which provides semi-annual payments, the first payment due 6 months hence. What is the semi-annual payment of the new perpetuity?

Section 4.4   Continuous Annuities

A continuous annuity is a special case of an annuity in which payments are made more frequently than interest is compounded. In this case, payments are made every second of every day. In other words, they are made continuously throughout an interest period. Continuous annuities are very important for mathematical analysis but do not actually exist in the marketplace.

Present Value of a Continuous Annuity

The present value of a continuous annuity, denoted $\bar{a}_{\overline{n}|i}$, represents the present value of $1 payable continuously over each interest period for a total of n periods. We will derive the value of $\bar{a}_{\overline{n}|i}$ in an intuitive manner.

EXAMPLE 1   Determine the present value of payments of $1 at the end of each year for 5 years if the interest rate is $i = 6\%$ per year.

Solution

This is simply $a_{\overline{5}|.06} = 4.212364$.

EXAMPLE 2   Continue this analysis if payments are $0.50 each $\frac{1}{2}$ year, $0.25 each $\frac{1}{4}$ year, as far as $\$\frac{1}{365}$ daily (so that the total payment over each year is $1), but all calculated at $i = 6\%$ per year.

Solution   We invite the reader to verify the following values:

m	$\frac{1}{m}a_{\overline{5m}|.06}$	Equivalent "i"
1	4.212364	0.06 per year
2	4.274629	0.029563014 per $\frac{1}{2}$ year
4	4.305992	0.014673846 per $\frac{1}{4}$ year
365	4.337161	0.000159654 per day

We can extend the calculation in Example 2 by letting the value of m approach infinity. This will allow us to calculate $\bar{a}_{\overline{n}|i}$ by taking the limit:

$$\lim_{m \to \infty} \sum_{t=1}^{mn} \frac{1}{m}(1+i)^{-\frac{t}{m}} = \int_0^n (1+i)^{-t}dt$$

$$= \frac{-(1+i)^{-t}}{\ln(1+i)}\Big|_0^n$$

$$= \frac{1-(1+i)^{-n}}{\delta}$$

Thus,

$$\boxed{\bar{a}_{\overline{n}|i} = \frac{1-(1+i)^{-n}}{\delta}}$$

If $i = 6\%$ per year, then $\bar{a}_{\overline{5}|.06} = \frac{1-(1.06)^{-5}}{\delta}$, where $\delta = \ln(1.06) = 0.058268908$.

This says that the present value of an annuity that has payments of $1 every year, where the payments are made continuously throughout each year, for a total of 5 years, is

$$\bar{a}_{\overline{5}|.06} = 4.337508$$

Accumulated Value of a Continuous Annuity

In a similar manner we can show that:

$$\bar{s}_{\overline{n}|i} = \int_0^n (1 + i)^{n-t} dt$$

$$= \frac{(1 + i)^{n-t}}{-\ln(1 + i)} \Big|_0^n$$

$$= \frac{1 - (1 + i)^n}{-\ln(1 + i)}$$

$$= \frac{(1 + i)^n - 1}{\delta}$$

Thus,

$$\boxed{\bar{s}_{\overline{n}|i} = \frac{(1 + i)^n - 1}{\delta}}$$

Continuous Annuities With Continuously Compounded Interest

These types of annuities exist in theory, and are a special type of ordinary annuity (interest period = payment interval = continuous). If the question states that interest is compounded continuously at force of interest, δ, then we have:

$$\bar{a}_{\overline{n}|\delta} = \frac{1 - e^{-\delta n}}{\delta}$$

and

$$\bar{s}_{\overline{n}|\delta} = \frac{e^{\delta n} - 1}{\delta}$$

Note 1: If the payment is $R per period, payable continuously, then $A = R\bar{a}_{\overline{n}|i}$ and $S = R\bar{s}_{\overline{n}|i}$.

Note 2: $\bar{a}_{\overline{n}|i} = \frac{i}{\delta} a_{\overline{n}|i}$ and $\bar{s}_{\overline{n}|i} = \frac{i}{\delta} s_{\overline{n}|i}$.

EXAMPLE 3   There is a $100 000 fund which is accumulating interest at rate $\delta = 5\%$. If money is withdrawn continuously at the rate of $6000 per annum, how long will the fund last?

Solution   We have $100\ 000 = 6000\bar{a}_{\overline{n}|\delta}$, with $\delta = 0.05$.

$$\bar{a}_{\overline{n}|\delta} = 16.666667$$

$$\frac{1 - e^{-0.05n}}{0.05} = 16.666667$$

$$n = \frac{\ln(0.1666667)}{-0.05}$$

$$= 35.8 \text{ years}$$

EXAMPLE 4   Money is deposited into a fund at a continuous rate of $500 every year for 20 years, paying interest at $i = 8\%$. At the end of 20 years, the amount in the fund is used to buy a 10-year continuous annuity paying interest at $\delta = 6\%$. What is the annual payment of the second annuity?

Solution   We will set up an equation of value at the time that the first annuity ends and the second annuity begins:

$$\text{a.v. of deposits} = \text{p.v. of withdrawals}$$

$$500\bar{s}_{\overline{20}|0.08} = R\bar{a}_{\overline{10}|\delta=0.06}$$

$$500\frac{(1.08)^{20} - 1}{\ln(1.08)} = R\frac{1 - e^{-(0.06)(10)}}{0.06}$$

Which solves for $R = \$3162.91$.

Exercise 4.4

Part A

1. For $i = 10\%$ and $n = 5$ years, calculate $a_{\overline{n}|i}$ and $\bar{a}_{\overline{n}|i}$. Are the outcomes what you expected in relative size?

2. There is a $160\,000$ fund accumulating interest at $\delta = 0.05$. If money is withdrawn continuously at the rate of $10\,000$ per annum, how long will the fund last?

3. If $\bar{a}_{\overline{n}|\delta} = 3$ and $\bar{s}_{\overline{n}|\delta} = 9$, determine δ.

4. Calculate $\bar{a}_{\overline{20}|\delta}$ if $\delta = 0.06$.

5. Qinshi and her husband, Yick, have a joint savings account that earns $\delta = 3\%$. The current balance is $50\,000$. Yick wishes to withdraw money continuously at an annual rate of 4000. Qinshi wants the account to last 25 years and will make deposits of X payable continuously into the account. Calculate X.

6. In 2011, Ray deposits $10 a day (at the end of each day) into a bank account. In 2012, he increases his deposits to $12 a day. The rates of these accounts are $i^{(365)} = 4\%$ in 2011 and $i^{(365)} = 4.5\%$ in 2012. Determine the amount in the account at the end of 2012:
   a) using daily deposits and $i^{(365)}$.
   b) using continuous deposits and δ.

Part B

1. A level annuity pays $100 per annum continuously for 20 years. If $\delta_t = \dfrac{1}{1 + t}$, calculate the present value of this annuity.

2. A level continuous annuity pays $1000 a month for 10 years. If the force of interest is $\delta_t = \dfrac{5}{3 + 2t}$, calculate the present value of this annuity.

3. Determine the time, t, $0 < t < 1$, such that $1 paid at time t is equivalent to $1 paid continuously over the interval $(0, 1)$.

4. Kim deposits P into a fund at time $t = 0$. The fund earns interest at $\delta = 5\%$. Over the period from $(6, 20)$ Kim withdraws $100 a year payable continuously. At time $t = 20$, the fund balance is zero. Determine P.

5. You are given $\bar{a}_{\overline{10}|\delta} = 7.52$ and $\dfrac{d}{d\delta}a_{\overline{10}|i} = -33.865$. Determine d.

Section 4.5 Annuities Where Payments Vary

Thus far, all the annuities considered have had level payments. Unfortunately, this is not always the case in real life. Thus, it is necessary to be able to handle situations where the size of the payments may vary.

First, we consider situations where the annuity **payments vary in terms of a common ratio**. That is, each succeeding payment of an annuity increases or decreases by a constant percentage over the preceding payment. This is commonly the case when benefits are indexed to inflation. As a result, the payments will form a geometric progression. To calculate the present or accumulated value of the payments, we will make use of the formula for the sum of a geometric progression.

EXAMPLE 1 Mr. Fung wants to buy an annuity of $20 000 a year for 10 years that is protected against inflation. The XYZ Trust Company offers to sell him an annuity where payments increase each year by exactly 5%. Determine the cost of this annuity if a) $i^{(1)} = 6\%$; b) $i^{(1)} = 4\%$. (Assume the payments are at the end of each year and the first payment is $20 000.)

Solution a We arrange the data on a time diagram below.

Using 0 as a focal date, we write the equation of value for the discounted value A of these payments at $i^{(1)} = 6\%$.

$$A = 20\,000(1.06)^{-1} + 20\,000(1.05)(1.06)^{-2} + \cdots + 20\,000(1.05)^9(1.06)^{-10}$$

The expression on the right-hand side of the equal sign of the above equation is the sum of 10 terms of a geometric progression with first term $t_1 = 20\,000(1.06)^{-1}$ and common ratio $r = (1.05)(1.06)^{-1} < 1$. Thus, applying the formula for the sum of n terms of a geometric progression $S_n = t_1 \dfrac{1 - r^n}{1 - r}$ we obtain

$$A = 20\,000(1.06)^{-1}\left[\frac{1 - (1.05)^{10}(1.06)^{-10}}{1 - (1.05)(1.06)^{-1}}\right] = 180\,867.50$$

The cost of the annuity is $180 867.50.

It is worth noting that a 10-year $20 000 annuity purchased at $i^{(1)} = 6\%$ with no inflation factor would cost only $20\,000a_{\overline{10}|6\%} = \$147\,201.74$.

Solution b Using 0 as a focal date, we write the equation of value for the discounted value A of these payments at $i^{(1)} = 4\%$.

$$A = 20\,000(1.04)^{-1} + 20\,000(1.05)(1.04)^{-2} + \cdots + 20\,000(1.05)^9(1.04)^{-10}$$

The expression on the right-hand side has $n = 10$ terms, $t_1 = 20\,000\,(1.04)^{-1}$ and common ratio $r = (1.05)(1.04)^{-1} > 1$. Thus,

$$A = 20\,000(1.04)^{-1}\left[\frac{(1.05)^{10}\,(1.04)^{-10} - 1}{(1.05)(1.04)^{-1} - 1}\right] = 200\,845.69$$

The cost of this annuity is \$200\,845.69.

It is worth noting that with no inflation factor, this annuity would cost only $20\,000a_{\overline{10}|4\%} = \$162\,217.92$.

EXAMPLE 2   Nicholas deposits \$2500 in a savings account today. He plans to continue making deposits every 3 months, each succeeding deposit being 2% lower than the preceding deposit. If the fund earns $i^{(4)} = 6\%$, how much has he accumulated at the end of 8 years, 3 months after his last deposit?

Solution   We arrange the data on a time diagram below.

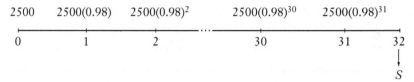

$$\begin{array}{cccccc} 2500 & 2500(0.98) & 2500(0.98)^2 & 2500(0.98)^{30} & 2500(0.98)^{31} \end{array}$$

Using time 32 as the focal date, we write the equation of value for the accumulated value S of these payments at $i^{(4)} = 6\%$.

$$S = 2500(1.015)^{32} + 2500(0.98)(1.015)^{31} + \cdots + 2500(0.98)^{31}(1.015)$$

The right-hand side of the equation is the sum of 32 terms of a geometric progression with $t_1 = 2500(1.015)^{32}$ and $r = (0.98)(1.015)^{-1} < 1$. Thus,

$$S = 2500(1.015)^{32}\left[\frac{1 - (0.98)^{32}(1.015)^{-32}}{1 - (0.98)(1.015)^{-1}}\right] \doteq 78\,766.99$$

Nicholas has \$78\,766.99 in his account at the end of 8 years.

EXAMPLE 3   Mr. Peloski is looking at investing in shares of XYZ Corporation. Yesterday XYZ paid out an annual dividend of \$8 per share. The XYZ Corporation is expected to grow in production and profits (and in dividends) at a rate of 5% per year. How much should Mr. Peloski pay for one share of XYZ Corporation if his desired rate of return is 7% per year?

Solution   Let P = price of one share.

Future annual dividends of XYZ are shown on the time diagram:

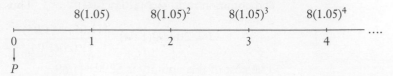

Using time 0 as the focal date,

$$P = 8(1.05)(1.07)^{-1} + 8(1.05)^2(1.07)^{-2} + 8(1.05)^3(1.07)^{-3} + \cdots$$

The right-hand side of the above is an infinite geometric series. The sum of an infinite geometric series is $\dfrac{t_1}{1-r}$ (as long as $r < 1$).

Here we have $t_1 = 8(1.05)(1.07)^{-1}$, $r = 1.05/1.07 < 1$, and thus,

$$P = \frac{8(1.05)(1.07)^{-1}}{1 - (1.05)(1.07)^{-1}} = \$42.00$$

Second, we consider situations where **payments vary in arithmetic progression**, that is, annuities where payments increase or decrease every period by a constant amount (as opposed to a constant percentage). We illustrate a popular method of solution in the following two examples.

EXAMPLE 4   Mrs. Soros has a job that pays \$25 000 a year. Each year she gets a \$1000 raise. What is the discounted value of her income for the next 15 years at $i^{(1)} = 7\%$? (Assume payments are at the end of each year with a first payment of \$25 000.)

Solution   We arrange the data on a time diagram below.

	25 000	26 000	27 000		38 000	39 000
0	1	2	3	...	14	15

A

Using 0 as the focal date we write the equation of value for the discounted value A of her income.

$$A = 25\,000(1.07)^{-1} + 26\,000(1.07)^{-2} + 27\,000(1.07)^{-3} + \cdots + 38\,000(1.07)^{-14} + 39\,000(1.07)^{-15}$$

If we multiply A by (1.07) we obtain

$$(1.07)A = 25\,000 + 26\,000(1.07)^{-1} + 27\,000(1.07)^{-2} + \cdots + 38\,000(1.07)^{-13} + 39\,000(1.07)^{-14}$$

Subtracting the first equation from the second gives

$$0.07A = 25\,000 + 1000[(1.07)^{-1} + (1.07)^{-2} + \cdots + (1.07)^{-14}] - 39\,000(1.07)^{-15}$$

$$0.07A = 25\,000 + 1000a_{\overline{14}|0.07} - 39\,000(1.07)^{-15}$$

$$A = \frac{1}{0.07}[25\,000 + 1000a_{\overline{14}|0.07} - 39\,000(1.07)^{-15}]$$

$$A = \$280\,143.90$$

EXAMPLE 5 Consider an annuity with a term of n periods in which payments begin at P at the end of the first period and change by Q each period thereafter. Assuming an interest rate i per period, $P > 0$, and $P + (n - 1)Q > 0$ (to avoid negative payments if $Q < 0$), show that

a) the discounted value of the annuity is given by

$$A = Pa_{\overline{n}|i} + Q\frac{a_{\overline{n}|i} - n(1 + i)^{-n}}{i}$$

b) the accumulated value of the annuity is given by

$$S = Ps_{\overline{n}|i} + Q\frac{s_{\overline{n}|i} - n}{i}$$

Solution a We arrange the data on a time diagram below.

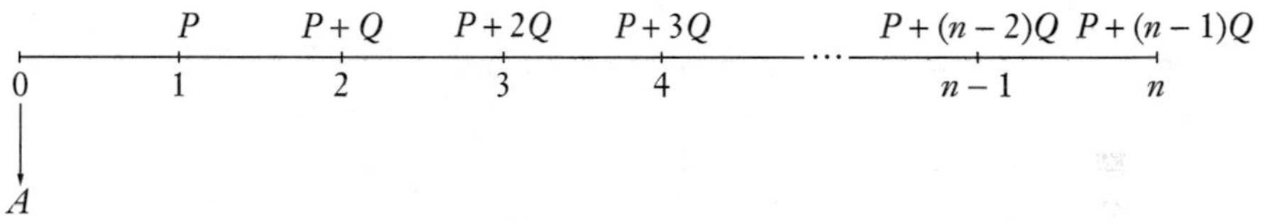

Using 0 as the focal date, we write the equation of value for the discounted value A of the annuity:

$$A = P(1 + i)^{-1} + (P + Q)(1 + i)^{-2} + (P + 2Q)(1 + i)^{-3} + \cdots +$$
$$[P + (n - 2)Q](1 + i)^{-(n-1)} + [P + (n - 1)Q](1 + i)^{-n}$$

If we multiply A by $(1 + i)$, we obtain:

$$(1 + i)A = P + (P + Q)(1 + i)^{-1} + (P + 2Q)(1 + i)^{-2} + (P + 3Q)(1 + i)^{-3} + \cdots +$$
$$[P + (n - 2)Q](1 + i)^{-(n-2)} + [P + (n - 1)Q](1 + i)^{-(n-1)}$$

Subtracting the first equation from the second we obtain:

$$iA = P + Q[(1+i)^{-1} + (1+i)^{-2} + \cdots + (1+i)^{-(n-1)}] - P(1+i)^{-n} - (n-1)Q(1+i)^{-n}$$
$$= P[1 - (1+i)^{-n}] + Q[(1+i)^{-1} + (1+i)^{-2} + \cdots + (1+i)^{-n}] - nQ(1+i)^{-n}$$
$$= P[1 - (1+i)^{-n}] + Qa_{\overline{n}|i} - nQ(1+i)^{-n}$$

Thus

$$A = P\frac{1 - (1 + i)^{-n}}{i} + Q\frac{a_{\overline{n}|i} - n(1 + i)^{-n}}{i} = Pa_{\overline{n}|i} + Q\frac{a_{\overline{n}|i} - n(1 + i)^{-n}}{i}$$

In the actuarial literature, if $P = 1$ and $Q = 1$, we denote the present value by $(Ia)_{\overline{n}|i}$, which represents the present value of an increasing annuity where payments are 1, 2, 3, ...

Thus,

$$(Ia)_{\overline{n}|i} = a_{\overline{n}|i} + \frac{a_{\overline{n}|i} - n(1+i)^{-n}}{i}$$

$$= \frac{ia_{\overline{n}|i}}{i} + \frac{a_{\overline{n}|i} - n(1+i)^{-n}}{i}$$

$$= \frac{a_{\overline{n}|i}(1+i) - n(1+i)^{-n}}{i}$$

$$= \frac{\ddot{a}_{\overline{n}|i} - n(1+i)^{-n}}{i}$$

Solution b The accumulated value

$$S = A(1+i)^n = \left[Pa_{\overline{n}|i} + Q\frac{a_{\overline{n}|i} - n(1+i)^{-n}}{i} \right](1+i)^n = Ps_{\overline{n}|i} + Q\frac{s_{\overline{n}|i} - n}{i}$$

If $P = 1$ and $Q = 1$, then we can denote the accumulated value by $(Is)_{\overline{n}|i}$ and the formula becomes:

$$(Is)_{\overline{n}|i} = s_{\overline{n}|i} + \frac{s_{\overline{n}|i} - n}{i}$$

$$= \frac{is_{\overline{n}|i}}{i} + \frac{s_{\overline{n}|i} - n}{i}$$

$$= \frac{s_{\overline{n}|i}(1+i) - n}{i}$$

$$= \frac{\ddot{s}_{\overline{n}|i} - n}{i}$$

$$= \frac{s_{\overline{n+1}|} - (n+1)}{i}$$

OBSERVATION:

Using the formula of Example 5 (part a) to solve Example 4, we substitute $P = 25\,000$, $Q = 1000$, $n = 15$, $i = 0.07$ to obtain

$$A = 25\,000a_{\overline{15}|0.07} + 1000\frac{a_{\overline{15}|0.07} - 15(1.07)^{-15}}{0.07} = \$280\,143.90$$

EXAMPLE 6 Mr. Smith, who just turned age 45, wishes to save money for his retirement. He decides to make monthly deposits, with his first deposit being $1500 (made today) and each succeeding deposit being $5 less. He makes deposits for 20 years. If his deposits earn $i^{(12)} = 6\%$, how much will he have accumulated at age 65?

Solution We arrange the data on a time diagram below and note that we have an annuity due.

$$
\begin{array}{ccccccc}
1500 & 1495 & 1490 & & 310 & 305 & \\
\vdash & \vdash & \vdash & \cdots & \vdash & \vdash & \dashv \\
0 & 1 & 2 & & 238 & 239 & 240 \\
& & & & & & \downarrow \\
& & & & & & S
\end{array}
$$

Using the "P & Q" formula (Example 5 b) with $P = 1500$, $Q = -5$, $n = 240$, and $i = 0.005$, we obtain the accumulated value of an ordinary annuity at the time of the 240th deposit (time 239).

$$1500 s_{\overline{240}|0.005} - 5\left[\frac{s_{\overline{240}|0.005} - 240}{0.005}\right] = \$471\ 020.45$$

To obtain the accumulated value at time 240 (one month after the last deposit), we accumulate the above value for one more month:

$$S = \$471\ 020.45(1.005) = \$473\ 375.56$$

Mr. Smith will have \$473 375.56 when he turns age 65.

A common example of annuities where payments vary in arithmetic progression is a situation where a primary investment pays out interest at rate i_1, after which the interest payments must be reinvested in another account paying interest at i_2. The next example illustrates this.

EXAMPLE 7 Miss Wirjanio deposits \$1000 at the beginning of each year in a fund that pays interest at rate $i^{(1)} = i_1 = 8\%$. Deposits must be in units of \$1000 for this fund. Miss Wirjanio reinvests the interest payments from this fund into a bank account paying interest at $i^{(1)} = i_2 = 5\%$.

a) How much does she have in total at the end of 10 years?
b) How much would she have in total at the end of 10 years if $i_1 = i_2 = 6\%$?

Solution a Future annual dividends are shown on the time diagram:
Original fund:

$$
\begin{array}{cccccc}
1000 & 1000 & 1000 & 1000 & 1000 & \\
\vdash & \vdash & \vdash & \vdash & \cdots & \vdash & \dashv \\
0 & 1 & 2 & 3 & 9 & 10 \\
\downarrow & \downarrow & \downarrow & \downarrow & \downarrow & \downarrow \\
\text{Interest:} & 80 & 160 & 240 & 720 & 800
\end{array}
$$

Accumulated value of the original fund $= 10(1000) = 10\,000$.

Accumulated value of the interest fund $= 80 (Is)_{\overline{10}|.05} = 80\left[\frac{s_{\overline{11}|0.05} - 11}{0.05}\right] = 5130.86$.

The total amount Miss Wirjanio has at the end of
10 years $= 10\,000 + 5130.86 = \$15\,130.86$.

Solution b Things that change in part b) are that the interest fund starts at $60 and increases by $60 per year and earns 6% per year:

Accumulated value of the interest fund $= 60(Is)_{\overline{10}|.06} = 60\left[\frac{s_{\overline{11}|.06} - 11}{0.06}\right] = 3971.64.$

The total amount Miss Wirjanio has at the end of
10 years $= 10\,000 + 3971.64 = \$13\,971.64.$

Note: Since $i_1 = i_2 = 6\%$, we could have obtained the answer as follows:

$$\text{Total amount at the end of 10 years} = 1000\ddot{s}_{\overline{10}|0.06}$$
$$= 1000s_{\overline{10}|0.06}(1.06) = \$13\,971.64$$

EXAMPLE 8 An investor deposits $1000 at the beginning of each year in a special fund paying interest at $i = 10\%$ per annum effective. These interest payments are then deposited in a bank account paying interest at $i^{(365)} = 6\%$. How much does the investor have in total at the end of year 10?

Solution

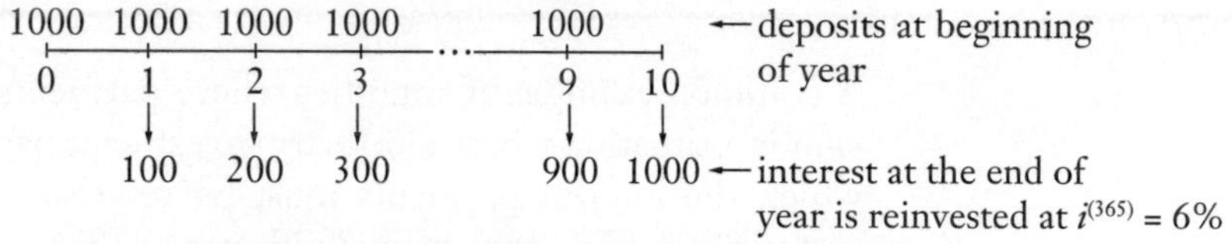

$$S = \text{a.v. of deposits} + \text{a.v. of interest}$$
$$= 10\,000 + 100\,(Is)_{\overline{10}|i}$$

where i is the equivalent annual rate:

$$(1 + i) = \left(1 + \frac{0.06}{365}\right)^{365} = 1.0618313$$

$$\text{or} \quad i = 6.18313\%$$

Thus, using the formula for $(Is)_{\overline{n}|i}$, as given above, we calculate:

$$S = 10\,000 + 100\left[\frac{s_{\overline{11}|i} - 11}{i}\right] = 10\,000 + 6658.01 = \$16\,658.01$$

EXAMPLE 9   Derive a formula for $(Ia)_{\overline{\infty}|i}$, an increasing perpetuity.

Solution   We take the limit of $(Ia)_{\overline{n}|i}$:

$$(Ia)_{\overline{\infty}|i} = \lim_{n \to \infty} (Ia)_{\overline{n}|i}$$

$$= \lim_{n \to \infty} \frac{\ddot{a}_{\overline{n}|} - n(1+i)^{-n}}{i}$$

$$= \frac{\ddot{a}_{\overline{\infty}|}}{i}$$

$$= \left(\frac{1}{i}\right)\left(\frac{1}{d}\right)$$

$$= \left(\frac{1}{i}\right)\left(\frac{1+i}{i}\right)$$

$$= \frac{1+i}{i^2}$$

EXAMPLE 10   Determine the present value of an annuity that pays \$1 at the end of the 3rd year, \$2 at the end of the 6th year, \$3 at the end of the 9th year and so on, for ever.

Solution
$$A = (1+i)^{-3} + 2(1+i)^{-6} + 3(1+i)^{-9} + \cdots$$
$$(1+i)^3 A = 1 + 2(1+i)^{-3} + 3(1+i)^{-6} + 4(1+i)^{-9} + \cdots$$
$$[(1+i)^3 - 1]A = 1 + (1+i)^{-3} + (1+i)^{-6} + (1+i)^{-9} + \cdots$$

The right-hand-side is an infinite geometric progression with $|r| < 1$ and whose sum is:

$$\frac{a}{1-r}$$

So

$$[(1+i)^3 - 1]A = \frac{1}{1 - (1+i)^{-3}}$$

$$A = \left[\frac{1}{1 - (1+i)^{-3}}\right]\left[\frac{1}{(1+i)^3 - 1}\right]$$

$$= \frac{(1+i)^{-3}}{[1 - (1+i)^{-3}]^2}$$

EXAMPLE 11   Derive an expression for $(Da)_{\overline{n}|i}$, a decreasing annuity, where the payments are $n, n-1, n-2, \ldots, 3, 2, 1$.

Solution

	n	$n-1$	$n-2$		2	1
0	1	2	3	$\cdots$	$n-1$	n

$$A = n(1+i)^{-1} + (n-1)(1+i)^{-2} + (n-2)(1+i)^{-3} + \cdots + (1+i)^{-(n)}$$
$$(1+i)A = n + (n-1)(1+i)^{-1} + (n-2)(1+i)^{-2} + \cdots + (1+i)^{-(n-1)}$$
$$iA = n - [(1+i)^{-1} + (1+i)^{-2} + \cdots + (1+i)^{-n}]$$
$$A = \frac{n - a_{\overline{n}|i}}{i}$$

You can use a similar method to determine the accumulated value of the above set of payments, or in other words, calculate the accumulated value of a decreasing annuity:

$$(Ds)_{\overline{n}|i} = \frac{n(1+i)^n - s_{\overline{n}|i}}{i}$$

Exercise 4.5

Part A

1. Determine the discounted value of a series of 20 annual payments of $500 if $i^{(1)} = 5\%$ and we want to allow for an inflation factor of $i^{(1)} = 2\%$. (Assume the payments are at the end of each year and the first payment is $500.)

2. A court is trying to determine the discounted value of the future income of a man paralyzed in a car accident. At the time of the accident the man was earning $45 000 a year and anticipated getting a 4% raise each year. He is 30 years away from retirement. If money is worth $i^{(1)} = 5\%$, what is the discounted value of his future income? (Assume payments are at the end of each year and the first payment is $45 000(1.04) = $46 800.)

3. Determine the discounted value of a series of 15 payments made at the end of each year at $i^{(1)} = 6\%$ if the first payment is $300, the second payment is $600, the third $900, and so on.

4. Mrs. Tong makes semi-annual deposits into a fund earning interest at $i^{(2)} = 8\%$. Her first deposit is $2000 and each succeeding deposit is 6% higher than the preceding deposit. What is the accumulated value of her fund immediately after her 15th deposit?

5. An investor deposits $1000 at the beginning of each year in a special fund paying interest at $i^{(1)} = 10\%$. These interest payments are then deposited in a bank account paying interest at $i^{(1)} = 6\%$. How much money has been accumulated at the end of 6 years?

6. A certain site is returning an annual rent of $5000 per year payable at the beginning of the year. It is expected that the rent will increase, on the average, 6% per year. Calculate the present value of the site at $i^{(1)} = 10\%$.

7. Mr. Martin needs to have his house painted immediately. Painting the house will cost $1200, so he is trying to decide if he should put on aluminum siding. If we assume the house must be painted every 5th year (forever) and that the cost of painting will rise by 3% per year (forever), how much should Mr. Martin be willing to pay for aluminum siding if he can earn $i^{(1)} = 6\%$ on his money?

8. Calculate the accumulated value of quarterly payments of $100, $110, $120, ... for 20 years if interest is at $i^{(12)} = 12\%$ and payments are at the end of each quarter.

9. What is the present value of quarterly payments of $100, $110, $120, $130, ... for 20 years, if $i^{(2)} = 8\%$ and payments are at the beginning of each quarter?

10. An annuity provides for 30 annual payments. The first payment of $100 is made immediately and the remaining payments increase by 8% per annum. Interest is calculated at $i^{(1)} = 9.4\%$. Calculate the present value of this annuity.

11. Determine the discounted value one year before the first payment of a series of 20 annual payments, the first of which is $500. The payments increase by 6% per year and interest is at $i^{(1)} = 8\%$.

12. What is the accumulated value of quarterly payments of $100, $115, $130, ... for 15 years if interest is $i^{(4)} = 10\%$ and payments are at the beginning of each quarter?

13. A decreasing annuity will pay $800 at the end of 6 months, $750 at the end of 1 year, etc., until a final payment of $350 is made at the end of 5 years. Determine the present value of the payments if money is worth 8% compounded monthly.

14. Determine the present value of monthly payments of $20, $25, $30, $35, ... for 100 months if interest is $\delta = 10\%$ and payments are at the end of each month.

15. How much would you pay per share for the ABC Company, which just paid out an annual dividend of $1.75, if this company is expected to grow in profits and dividends at 4% per year and your desired rate of return is 9% per year?

16. It is desired to accumulate a fund of $18 000 at the end of 3 years by equal deposits at the beginning of each month. If the deposits earn interest at $i^{(12)} = 9\%$ but the interest can be reinvested only at $i^{(12)} = 6\%$, determine the size of the necessary deposit.

Part B

1. An investor deposits $1 at the beginning of each year in a fund that pays interest at rate i_1. The interest payments are reinvested into another account that pays interest at rate i_2.
   a) How much does the investor have in total at the end of n years?
   b) If $i_1 = i_2 = i$, show that the total accumulated value at the end of n years is $\ddot{s}_{\overline{n}|i}$.

2. Consider a perpetuity in which payments begin at P at the end of the first period and increase by Q per period thereafter. Assuming the interest rate i per period and $P > 0$, $Q > 0$ (to avoid negative payments), show that the discounted value of this perpetuity is given by
$$\frac{P}{i} + \frac{Q}{i^2}$$
(*Hint:* take the limit of the formulas in Example 5a as n approaches infinity.)

3. Using the result of problem 2,
   a) show that the discounted value of a $1 increasing perpetuity, denoted by $(Ia)_{\overline{\infty}|i}$, is
$$(Ia)_{\overline{\infty}|i} = \frac{1}{i} + \frac{1}{i^2}$$
   b) calculate the present value of a perpetuity whose payments start at $100 at the end of the first month and increase by $2 per month thereafter, assuming $i^{(12)} = 6\%$.

4. Determine the discounted value of payments made at the beginning of each year indefinitely at $i^{(2)} = 7\%$ if the first payment is $100; the second is $200; the third is $300; and so on.

5. Calculate the accumulated value of deposits of $1, $2, $3, ... , $98, $99, $100, $99, $98, ..., $3, $2, $1 if interest is 2% per period and deposits are at the end of periods.

6. Consider an annuity where payments vary as represented in the following diagram ($0 < i_1 < 1$):

$R(1 + i_1)$	$R(1 + i_1)^2$	$R(1 + i_1)^3$	...	$R(1 + i_1)^n$
0	1	2	3	n

Further, assume the interest rate is i_2 per interest period. Let i be the rate such that
$$(1 + i) = \frac{1 + i_2}{1 + i_1}$$
Show that the discounted value A of the above annuity at rate i_2 is
$$A = Ra_{\overline{n}|i}$$

7. Derive an algebraic proof of the following identities and interpret by means of time diagrams.
   a) $a_{\overline{1}|i} + a_{\overline{2}|i} + a_{\overline{3}|i} + \cdots + a_{\overline{n}|i} = \dfrac{n - a_{\overline{n}|i}}{i}$
   b) $s_{\overline{1}|i} + s_{\overline{2}|i} + s_{\overline{3}|i} + \cdots + s_{\overline{n-1}|i} = \dfrac{\ddot{s}_{\overline{n}|i} - n}{i}$

8. Show that the discounted value A of a decreasing annuity whose n payments at the end of each year are nR, $(n - 1)R$, $(n - 2)R$, ..., $2R$, R is $A = \frac{R}{i}(n - a_{\overline{n}|i})$ at rate i per year.

9. The principal on a loan of $5000 is to be repaid in equal annual instalments of $1000 each at the end of each of the next 5 years. Interest will be paid at the end of each year at $i^{(1)} = 4\frac{1}{2}\%$ on the entire outstanding balance, including the $1000 payment then due. Determine the purchase price of the loan to yield $i^{(1)} = 5\%$.

10. Determine the present value of an annuity where payments are $200 per month at the end of each month during the first year; $195 per month during the second year; $190 per month in the third year; etc., with monthly payments decreasing by $5 after the end of each year. Five dollars will be paid at the end of each month during the 40th year and nothing thereafter. Interest is at $i^{(12)} = 12\%$.

11. Mrs. Rider has just retired and is trying to decide between two retirement income options as to where she should place her life savings. Fund A will pay her quarterly payments for

25 years starting at $3000 at the end of the first quarter. Fund A will increase her payments each quarter thereafter using an inflation factor equivalent to 4% compounded quarterly. Fund B pays $4500 at the end of each quarter for 25 years with no inflation factor. Which fund should Mrs. Rider choose if she compares the funds using 6% compounded quarterly?

12. Determine the present value of a perpetuity under which an amount p is paid at the end of the second year, $p + q$ at the end of the fourth year, $p + 2q$ at the end of the sixth year, $p + 3q$ at the end of the eighth year, etc., if interest is at rate i per year.

13. Consider the perpetuity whose payments at the end of each year are $R, R + p, R + 2p, ..., R + (n − 1)p, R + np, R + np, ...$. The payments increase by a constant amount p until they reach $R + np$, after which they continue without change. Show that the discounted value A of such a perpetuity at rate i per annum is given by

$$A = \frac{R + pa_{\overline{n}|i}}{i}$$

14. A man deposits $100 at the beginning of each year into a fund paying interest to him in cash at $i^{(1)} = 6\%$ each year on the principal in the fund. At the end of each year he deposits the interest payments into a second fund earning interest at $i^{(1)} = 4\%$. At the end of which year will the interest fund first exceed the principal fund?

15. For the same lump-sum payment, an insurance company will provide a choice of
   a) an ordinary annuity of $1000 per year for 20 years; or
   b) an ordinary increasing annuity of X per year initially, inflating at 10% per year, for 20 years.
   Determine X if interest is at $i^{(1)} = 8\%$. What is the final payment of the increasing annuity?

16. Jeanne has won a lottery that pays $1000 per month in the first year, $1100 per month in the second year, $1200 per month in the third year, etc. Payments are made at the end of each month for 10 years. Using an annual effective interest rate of 3%, calculate the present value of this prize.

| Section 4.6 | **Continuous Varying Annuities** |

A continuous varying annuity is a theoretical concept in which an annuity has payments that are made continuously at a continuously varying rate.

Let $h(t)\, dt$ = payment made at exact time t, $t > 0$.

Then the present value is $\int_0^n h(t)(1 + i)^{-t}dt$ and the accumulated value is

$$\int_0^n h(t)(1 + i)^t dt.$$

The most common type of continuous varying annuity is the case where $h(t) = t$. The notation for the present value is $(\bar{I}\bar{a})_{\overline{n}|i}$.

$$(\bar{I}\bar{a})_{\overline{n}|i} = \int_0^n t(1 + i)^{-t}dt$$

Using integration by parts with $u = t$, $du = dt$, $dv = (1 + i)^{-t}\, dt$,

$v = \dfrac{(1 + i)^{-t}}{-\ln(1 + i)}$, we get:

$$(\bar{I}\bar{a})_{\overline{n}|i} = \int_0^n t(1 + i)^{-t}dt$$

$$= t\frac{(1 + i)^{-t}}{-\ln(1 + i)}\Big|_{t=0}^{t=n} - \int_0^n \frac{(1 + i)^{-t}}{-\ln(1 + i)}dt$$

$$= \frac{n(1 + i)^{-n}}{-\ln(1 + i)} - \frac{(1 + i)^{-t}}{(-\ln(1 + i))^2}\Big|_{t=0}^{t=n}$$

$$= \frac{n(1 + i)^{-n}}{-\delta} - \frac{(1 + i)^{-n} - 1}{(-\delta)^2}$$

$$= \frac{1 - (1 + i)^{-n}}{(\delta)\delta} - \frac{n(1 + i)^{-n}}{\delta}$$

$$= \frac{\bar{a}_{\overline{n}|i}}{\delta} - \frac{n(1 + i)^{-n}}{\delta}$$

Thus, for the present value of a continuously increasing annuity:

$$(\bar{I}\bar{a})_{\overline{n}|i} = \frac{\bar{a}_{\overline{n}|i} - n(1 + i)^{-n}}{\delta} \quad \text{(Similar to: } (Ia)_{\overline{n}|i} = \frac{\ddot{a}_{\overline{n}|i} - n(1 + i)^{-n}}{i})$$

Similarly, for the accumulated value of a continuously increasing annuity:

$$(\bar{I}\bar{s})_{\overline{n}|i} = \frac{\bar{s}_{\overline{n}|i} - n}{\delta} \quad \text{(Similar to: } (Is)_{\overline{n}|i} = \frac{\ddot{s}_{\overline{n}|i} - n}{i})$$

For the present value of a continuously increasing perpetuity,

$$(\bar{I}\bar{a})_{\overline{\infty}|i} = \frac{1}{\delta^2}$$

EXAMPLE 1 Show that a) $\frac{d}{di}a_{\overline{n}|i} = -(1 + i)^{-1}(Ia)_{\overline{n}|i}$ and b) $\frac{d}{d\delta}\bar{a}_{\overline{n}|\delta} = -(\bar{I}\bar{a})_{\overline{n}|\delta}$.

Solution a

$$\frac{d}{di}a_{\overline{n}|i} = \frac{d}{di}\sum_{t=1}^n (1 + i)^{-t}$$

$$= -\sum_{t=1}^n t(1 + i)^{-(t+1)}$$

$$= -(1 + i)^{-1}\sum_{t=1}^n t(1 + i)^{-t}$$

$$= -(1 + i)^{-1}(Ia)_{\overline{n}|i}$$

Solution b

$$\frac{d}{d\delta}\bar{a}_{\overline{n}|\delta} = \frac{d}{d\delta}\int_0^n e^{-\delta t}dt$$

$$= \int_0^n \frac{d}{d\delta}e^{-\delta t}dt$$

$$= \int_0^n -te^{-\delta t}dt$$

$$= -(\bar{I}\bar{a})_{\overline{n}|\delta}$$

These relationships are important because they confirm that as interest rates rise, the present value of annuities falls. They will prove even more important in advanced topics in actuarial science.

EXAMPLE 2

Determine the value of $a_{\overline{5}|i}$ if $i = 10.1\%$.

Solution

Today, it is easy to solve this problem: we just determine the value of:

$$\frac{1 - (1.101)^{-5}}{0.101} = 3.781122431$$

But a generation ago, there were no pocket calculators or laptop computers. All you had were published interest rate table values, but only at discrete rates and certainly not at 10.1%.

So, assume we have the value of $a_{\overline{5}|i}$ at $i = 10\%$, which is 3.790786769.

We also know from example 1 above, that

$$\frac{d}{di}a_{\overline{n}|i} = -(1 + i)^{-1}(Ia)_{\overline{n}|i}$$

We can calculate $(Ia)_{\overline{5}|.1}$ by using $\dfrac{\ddot{a}_{\overline{5}|i} - 5(1 + i)^{-5}}{i}$ and get $(Ia)_{\overline{5}|.1} = 10.65258831$.

And, $-(1 + i)^{-1}(Ia)_{\overline{5}|.1} = -9.684171191$.

Thus, the value of $a_{\overline{5}|i}$ will decrease by 0.09684171191 for every unit change of $i\%$, and decrease by 0.009684171191 for every rate change of $+0.001 = +0.1\%$. This results in:

$$\begin{aligned}
a_{\overline{5}|.101} &\doteq a_{\overline{5}|.10} - 0.009684171191 \\
&= 3.790786769 - 0.009684171191 \\
&= 3.781102598
\end{aligned}$$

which is correct to 4 decimal places!

Note 1: If interest is compounded continuously at δ, then the present value is $\int_0^n h(t)e^{-\delta t}dt$.

Note 2: If interest is compounded continuously at a varying rate δ_t, then the present value is $\int_0^n h(t)e^{-\int_0^t \delta_r dr}dt$.

EXAMPLE 3

Calculate the present value of a continuously increasing annuity with a term of 10 years with interest compounded continuously at $\delta = 7\%$ and with the payment at exact time t is $h(t) = 1000t$.

Solution

$$\text{p.v.} = \int_0^n 1000te^{-\delta t}dt$$

$$= 1000\left[-t\frac{e^{-\delta t}}{\delta}\Big|_{t=0}^{t=n} - \int_0^n \frac{e^{-\delta t}}{-\delta}dt\right]$$

$$= 1000\left[\frac{-ne^{-n\delta}}{\delta} - \frac{e^{-\delta t}}{\delta^2}\Big|_{t=0}^{t=n}\right]$$

$$= 1000\left[\frac{-ne^{-n\delta}}{\delta} - \frac{e^{-\delta n}-1}{\delta^2}\right]$$

$$= 1000\left[\frac{1}{\delta^2} - \left(\frac{e^{-n\delta}}{\delta}\right)\left(n + \frac{1}{\delta}\right)\right]$$

$$- 1000\left[\frac{1}{(0.07)^2} - \left(\frac{e^{-10(0.07)}}{0.07}\right)\left(10 + \frac{1}{0.07}\right)\right]$$

$$= \$31\ 796.94$$

Exercise 4.6

Part A

1. Show that $(\bar{I}\bar{s})_{\overline{n}|i} = \dfrac{\bar{s}_{\overline{n}|i} - n}{\delta}$.

2. Determine the ratio of the total payments made under $(\bar{I}\bar{a})_{\overline{10}|i}$ during the second half of the term of the annuity to those made in the first half.

3. Calculate $(\bar{I}\bar{a})_{\overline{\infty}|\delta}$ if $\delta = 0.05$.

4. Calculate $(\bar{D}\bar{a})_{\overline{10}|\delta}$ if $\delta = 0.06$.

5. Calculate the accumulated value at $t = 10$ years of a continuous payment stream paid at rate $1000e^{-0.04t}$. The force of interest is $\delta_t = 0.04$.

6. Determine the present value of a perpetuity that pays at rate $5t$ at time t with interest at $i^{(1)} = 4\%$.

7. Determine the present value of a payment stream that pays at rate $(10 - t)$ at time t. The payments start at $t = 0$ and continue to $t = 10$, with interest at $\delta = 5\%$.

8. Redo Question 7, but determine the accumulated value.

9. Deposits are made into an account at rate $(7k + tk)$. Interest is paid at a force of interest $\delta_t = \dfrac{1}{7 + t}$. After 10 years the account is worth $\$20\ 000$. Determine k.

Part B

1. Calculate the present value of a continuously increasing annuity $(\bar{I}\bar{a})_{\overline{10}|i}$ with a term of 10 years if the force of interest is $\delta = 0.5$ and the rate of pay is t^2 at time t.

2. Payments under a continuous perpetuity are made at rate $(1 + k)^t$ at time t. If $0 < k < i$, determine the present value of this perpetuity.

3. Determine an expression for:

   a) $\dfrac{d}{di}a_{\overline{n}|i}$

   b) $\dfrac{d}{d\delta}\bar{a}_{\overline{n}|\delta}$

4. Determine an expression for:

   a) $\dfrac{d}{dn}\bar{a}_{\overline{n}|i}$

   b) $\dfrac{d}{dn}\bar{s}_{\overline{n}|i}$

5. Determine the accumulated value at time $t = 10$ of payments payable continuously. The payment rate is $\$100$ in year 1, $\$105$ in year 2, and so on, up to $\$145$ in year 10. The effective rate of interest is $i = 4\%$.

| Section 4.7 | **Summary and Review Exercises** |

- Change of rate approach to general annuity problems: Calculate the equivalent interest rate per payment period and then solve a simple annuity problem using the methods of chapter 3.

- For general annuities where it is stated that simple interest is paid for part of an interest period you must use the "change of payment" approach, which requires using simple interest to calculate an equivalent payment made with the same frequency as interest is compounded and then solve a simple annuity problem using the methods of chapter 3.

- Discounted value of a simple perpetuity is given by

$$A = \frac{R}{i} \quad \text{for an ordinary perpetuity}$$

$$A = \frac{R}{i}(1 + i) \quad \text{for a perpetuity due}$$

$$A = \frac{R}{i}(1 + i)^{-k} \quad \text{for a deferred perpetuity}$$

- The present value of a continuous annuity of \$1 per annum payable continuously is

$$\bar{a}_{\overline{n}|i} = \frac{1 - (1 + i)^{-n}}{\delta}.$$

- The accumulated value of a continuous annuity of \$1 per annum payable continuously is

$$\bar{s}_{\overline{n}|i} = \frac{(1 + i)^n - 1}{\delta}.$$

- To calculate the discounted value A (or the accumulated value S) of an annuity with payments varying in a constant ratio, we write A as a sum of discounted values of individual payments (or S as a sum of accumulated values of individual payments) and then determine the sum of n terms of the resulting geometric progression.

- For an annuity with a term of n periods in which payments begin at P at the end of the first period and change by Q each period thereafter (assuming $i > 0, P > 0$, $P + (n - 1)Q > 0$), the discounted value A is given by

$$A = Pa_{\overline{n}|i} + Q\frac{a_{\overline{n}|i} - n(1 + i)^{-n}}{i}$$

and the accumulated value S is given by

$$S = Ps_{\overline{n}|i} + Q\frac{s_{\overline{n}|i} - n}{i}$$

- For a perpetuity in which payments begin at P at the end of the first period and increase by $Q > 0$ each period thereafter, the discounted value A is given by

$$A = \frac{P}{i} + \frac{Q}{i^2}$$

- Special case where $P = Q = 1$:

$$(Ia)_{\overline{n}|i} = \frac{\ddot{a}_{\overline{n}|i} - n(1 + i)^{-n}}{i}$$

$$(Is)_{\overline{n}|i} = \frac{\ddot{s}_{\overline{n}|i} - n}{i}$$

- Special cases where $P = n$, $Q = -1$:

$$(Da)_{\overline{n}|} = \frac{n - a_{\overline{n}|i}}{i}$$

$$(Ds)_{\overline{n}|} = \frac{n(1 + i)^n - s_{\overline{n}|i}}{i}$$

- Continuously increasing annuities:

$$(\overline{I}\overline{a})_{\overline{n}|} = \frac{\overline{a}_{\overline{n}|i} - n(1 + i)^{-n}}{i}$$

$$(\overline{I}\overline{s})_{\overline{n}|} = \frac{\overline{s}_{\overline{n}|i} - n}{i}$$

- Continuously decreasing annuities:

$$(\overline{D}\overline{a})_{\overline{n}|} = \frac{n - \overline{a}_{\overline{n}|i}}{i}$$

$$(\overline{D}\overline{s})_{\overline{n}|} = \frac{n(1 + i)^n - \overline{s}_{\overline{n}|i}}{i}$$

Review Exercise 4.7

1. Replace an annuity with quarterly payments of $300 by an equivalent annuity with
   a) semi-annual payments if money is worth 5% compounded semi-annually;
   b) monthly payments if money is worth 7% compounded quarterly.

2. Determine the accumulated and the discounted value of payments of $100 at the end of each quarter-year for 10 years at $i^{(12)} = 4\%$.

3. Deposits of $100 are made at the end of each month to an account paying interest at 8% compounded semi-annually. How much money will be accumulated in the account at the end of 3 years if
   a) simple interest is paid for part of a conversion period;
   b) compounded interest is paid for part of a conversion period?

4. How many monthly deposits of $100 each and what final deposit one month later will be necessary to accumulate $3000 if interest is
   a) $6\frac{1}{2}\%$ compounded semi-annually;
   b) 9% compounded quarterly?

5. A company wishes to have $150 000 in a fund at the end of 8 years. What deposit at the end of each month must it make if the fund pays interest at 5% compounded daily?

6. Steve buys a car worth $15 000. He pays $3000 down and agrees to pay $500 at the end of each month as long as necessary. Determine the number of full payments and the final payment one month later if interest is at $i^{(1)} = 14.2\%$.

7. If it takes $50 per month for 18 months to repay a loan of $800, what nominal rate compounded semi-annually is being charged? What annual effective rate is being charged?

8. A used car is sold for $8000 down and 6 semi-annual payments of $3000, the first due at the end of 2 years. Calculate the cash value of the car if money is worth 6% compounded daily.

9. Determine the accumulated and discounted value of payments of $100 made at the beginning of each month for 5 years at $i^{(4)} = 6\%$.

10. An annuity consists of 60 payments of $200 at the end of each month. Interest is at $i^{(1)} = 11.05\%$. Determine the value of this annuity at each of the following times:
    a) at the time of the first payment;
    b) two years before the first payment;
    c) at the time of the last payment.

11. Which is cheaper?
    a) Buy a car for $27 200 and after 3 years trade it in for $7200.
    b) Lease a car for $636 a month payable at the beginning of each month for 3 years.

Assume maintenance costs are identical and that money is worth $i^{(1)} = 8\%$.

12. On November 1, 2010, a research fund of $300 000 was established to provide for equal annual grants for 10 years. What will be the size of each grant if
a) the fund earns interest at 8% compounded daily and the first grant is awarded on November 1, 2010;
b) the fund earns interest at 10% compounded monthly and the first grant is awarded on November 1, 2013?

13. A couple requires a $190 000 mortgage loan at $i^{(2)} = 6\frac{3}{4}\%$ to buy a new house.
a) Calculate the couple's monthly mortgage payment based on the following repayment periods: 30 years, 20 years, and 10 years.
b) If the couple can afford to pay up to $1700 monthly on their mortgage loan, what repayment period in years should they request? What will be their monthly payment?

14. An annuity paying $200 at the end of each year for 20 years is replaced by another annuity paying $X at the end of every 6 months for 12 years. Determine X if $i^{(12)} = 9\%$ in both cases.

15. Starting on her 36th birthday, Ms. Gagnon deposits $2000 a year into an investment account. Her last deposit is at age 65. Starting one month later, she makes monthly withdrawals for 15 years. If $i^{(4)} = 8\%$ throughout, determine the size of the monthly withdrawals.

16. Danielle and Sue would like to open their own business in 3 years. They estimate they will need $40 000 at that time. How much should they deposit at the end of each month into their account if they have $5000 in the account now and interest is at $i^{(4)} = 7\%$?

17. What sum of money should be set aside to provide an income of $500 a month for a period of 3 years if money earns interest at $i^{(12)} = 6\%$ and the first payment is to be received a) one month from now; b) immediately; c) two years from now?

18. The proceeds of a $100 000 death benefit are left on deposit with an insurance company for 7 years at an annual effective interest rate of 5%. The balance at the end of 7 years is paid to the beneficiary in 120 equal monthly payments of $X, with the first payment made immediately. During the payout period, interest is credited at an annual effective interest rate of 3%. Calculate X.

19. A certain stock is expected to pay a dividend of $4 at the end of each quarter for an indefinite period in the future. If an investor wishes to realize an annual effective yield of 10%, how much should he pay for the stock?

20. How much money is needed to establish a scholarship fund paying $1000 a year indefinitely if
a) the fund earns interest at $i^{(1)} = 8\%$ and the first scholarship is provided at the end of 3 years?
b) the fund earns interest at $i^{(12)} = 8\%$ and the first scholarship is provided immediately?

21. On the assumption that a farm will net $60 000 annually indefinitely, what is a fair price for it if money is worth a) $i^{(1)} = 8\%$, b) $i^{(12)} = 7.2\%$?

22. Mr. Jenkins invests $1000 at the end of each year for 10 years in an investment fund which pays $i^{(1)} = 8\%$. The fund pays the interest out in check form at the end of each year and does not allow deposits of less than $1000. Mr. Jenkins deposits his annual interest payment from the fund into his bank account, which pays interest at $i^{(1)} = 4\%$. How much money does he have at the end of 10 years?

23. Show that in question 22, if both rates of interest had been equal to $i\%$, the answer would have been $1000s_{\overline{10}|i}$.

24. Calculate the discounted and the accumulated value of a decreasing annuity of 20 payments at the end of each year at $i^{(1)} = 12\%$, if the first payment is $2000, the second $1900, and so on, the last payment being $100.

25. Calculate the discounted value of a series of payments that start at $18 000 at the end of year one and then increase by $2000 each year forever if interest is at $i^{(1)} = 10\%$.

26. Mrs. Zheng deposits $R today into a fund earning interest at $i^{(1)} = 7\%$. Each succeeding deposit is 10% lower than the preceding deposit. One year after her 20th deposit, she has $150 000 in her fund. What is R?

27. Under the terms of a contract, the following payments are guaranteed:
    a) $100 000 payable immediately.
    b) $75 000 per year for 5 years, payable in equal monthly instalments of $6250 at the end of each month.
    c) $50 000 per year, payable annually at the end of the 6th through the 10th years.

    If interest is at 5% compounded annually, determine the discounted value at the beginning of the 4th year of the remaining payments due under the contract.

28. Every 2 years Mrs. Furtado deposits $1000 into a fund that pays interest at $i^{(2)} = 10\%$. The first deposit is on her 53rd birthday and the last deposit is on her 65th birthday. Beginning 3 months after her 65th birthday and continuing every 3 months thereafter, she withdraws equal amounts of X dollars, which will exactly exhaust the fund on her 79th birthday. Determine X.

29. Determine the present value of an ordinary annuity paid annually for 25 years if payments are $1000 per year for the first 7 years, $5000 for the following 8 years, and $2000 in the final 10 years. Interest is $i^{(12)} = 6\%$ throughout this period.

30. A $5000 loan at $i^{(1)} = 9.2\%$ is repaid by 10 quarterly payments, as shown. Calculate X.

	X	X	X	2X	2X	2X		2X
0	1	2	3	4	5	6	⋯	10

31. $100 is deposited in an account paying $i^{(12)} = 6\%$ every month for 20 years. Exactly 6 months after the last deposit the rate changes to $i^{(4)} = 5\%$. On this date the first withdrawal is made in a series of quarterly withdrawals for 15 years. Determine the amount of each withdrawal.

32. Determine the present value of future contributions to a pension plan, for a person aged 35 earning $90 000 per year and expecting to retire at age 65. The pension plan requires contributions of 5% of salary and the employee expects to receive average annual salary increases of 3%. Use an annual effective rate of interest of 7% and assume contributions are at the end of each year.

33. Alice has $100 000 in her retirement account earning $i^{(1)} = 4.9\%$ per year. If she wishes to withdraw $15 000 per year, payable continuously, how long will the fund last?

34. Calculate $\bar{s}_{\overline{10}|}$ at:
    a) $i = 7\%$
    b) $\delta = 7\%$

35. Determine an approximate value of $a_{\overline{20}|.071}$ if $a_{\overline{20}|.07} = 10.59401425$ using the fact that
    $$\frac{d}{di}a_{\overline{n}|i} = -(1+i)^{-1}(Ia)_{\overline{n}|i}.$$
    Afterward, use your calculator to calculate a more accurate answer.

36. Show that $(\bar{I}\bar{a})_{\overline{n}|i} + (\overline{D}\bar{a})_{\overline{n}|i} = n - \bar{a}_{\overline{n}|i}$.

CASE STUDY 1 **Canadian Mortgages**

Consider a purchase of a $480 000 house with a down payment of $80 000 and a $400 000 mortgage at $i^{(2)} = 7\%$.

a) Determine the monthly payment based on the following repayment periods: 25 years, 20 years, and 15 years.

b) Using a 20-year repayment period, calculate the concluding payment, the total cost of financing, and the interest and principal parts of the first payment.

c) If you can afford to pay up to $4000 a month on the mortgage, what repayment period (in full years) should you request?

d) Compare the total payouts using monthly payments of $2000 with weekly payments of $1000.

CASE STUDY 2 **Lottery Winnings**

Charlie, who is just 16 years old, won a lottery. However, the lottery does not pay out any money until a person is at least age 25. Charlie hires a financial consultant and this consultant suggests that Charlie invest the money and then begin receiving monthly payments of $2500 once he reaches age 25.

The consultant also suggests that Charlie should protect himself from inflation by having his payments increase by 2.3% each year. Thus, the 12 monthly payments in year 1 will be $2500 (age 25 to age 25, 11 months), the 12 monthly payments for year 2 will be $2500(1.023) (age 26 to age 26, 11 months), the 12 monthly payments for year 3 will be $2500(1.023)^2$ (age 27 to age 27, 11 months), and so on. (**Note:** This is a situation where the payments are monthly, but the percentage increase is annually.)

It turns out that Charlie has won enough money for this payment scheme to last for a total of 25 years after he turns 25. If Charlie can earn $i^{(1)} = 8\%$ on his lottery winnings and if the consultant charges 1.5% of the winnings as a fee (payable up front when Charlie is 16), how much did Charlie win in the lottery?

CASE STUDY 3 **Scholarships**

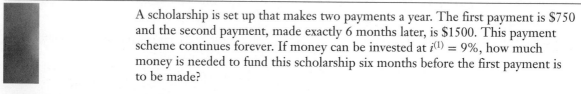

A scholarship is set up that makes two payments a year. The first payment is $750 and the second payment, made exactly 6 months later, is $1500. This payment scheme continues forever. If money can be invested at $i^{(1)} = 9\%$, how much money is needed to fund this scholarship six months before the first payment is to be made?

CASE STUDY 4 **Scholarships**

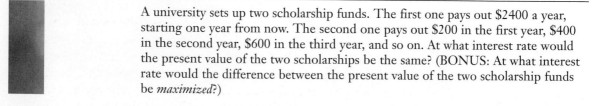

A university sets up two scholarship funds. The first one pays out $2400 a year, starting one year from now. The second one pays out $200 in the first year, $400 in the second year, $600 in the third year, and so on. At what interest rate would the present value of the two scholarships be the same? (BONUS: At what interest rate would the difference between the present value of the two scholarship funds be *maximized*?)

CHAPTER 5

REPAYMENT OF DEBTS

Learning Objectives

Many businesses and consumers will take out at least one loan in their lifetime. For many people, the largest loan they will ever see will be the mortgage on their home. As a result, it is useful to spend a bit more time taking a closer mathematical look at how loans are repaid. This chapter will cover in some detail the two main methods used to repay a loan.

Upon completing this chapter, you will be able to do the following:

- Use the amortization method to determine the periodic payment and outstanding balance of a loan at any time, along with determining how much of each periodic payment goes toward interest and how much goes toward reducing the outstanding balance.
- Create complete or partial amortization schedules either by hand or using a computer spreadsheet.
- Calculate the new periodic payment on a refinanced loan.
- Determine whether or not you should refinance a loan when there is a penalty involved
- Understand the concept of a sinking fund and how it can be used to pay back a loan.
- Perform a comparison between the amortization and sinking-fund methods of repaying a loan.

Section 5.1   ## Amortization of a Debt

In this chapter we shall discuss different methods of repaying interest-bearing loans, which is one of the most important applications of annuities in business transactions.

The first and most common method is the **amortization method**. When this method is used to liquidate an interest-bearing debt, a series of periodic payments, usually equal, is made. Each payment pays the interest on the unpaid balance and also repays a part of the outstanding principal. As time goes on, the outstanding principal is gradually reduced and interest on the unpaid balance decreases.

When a debt is amortized by equal payments at equal payment intervals, the debt becomes the discounted value of an annuity. The size of the payment is determined by the methods used in the annuity problems of the preceding chapters.

The common commercial practice is to round the payment up to the next cent. This practice will be used in this textbook unless specified otherwise. Instead of rounding up to the next cent, the lender may round up to the next dime or dollar. In any case the rounding of the payment up to the cent, to the dime, or to the dollar will result in a smaller concluding payment. An equation of value at the time of the last payment will give the size of the smaller concluding payment.

EXAMPLE 1 A loan of $20 000 is to be amortized with equal monthly payments over a period of 10 years at $i^{(12)} = 12\%$. Determine the concluding payment if the monthly payment is rounded up to a) the cent; b) the dime.

Solution First we calculate the monthly payment R, given $A = 20\ 000$, $n = 120$, and $i = 0.01$. Using equation **(11)** of section 3.3 we calculate

$$R = \frac{20\ 000}{a_{\overline{120}|0.01}} = 286.9418968$$

and set up an equation of value for X at 120:

$$X = 20\ 000(1.01)^{120} - Rs_{\overline{119}|}(1.01)$$

Solution a If the monthly payment is rounded up to the next cent, we have $R = \$286.95$ and calculate

$$X = 20\ 000(1.01)^{120} - 286.95s_{\overline{119}|0.01}(1.01)$$
$$\doteq 66\ 007.74 - 65\ 722.65$$
$$= \$285.09$$

Solution b If the monthly payment is rounded up to the next dime, we have $R = \$287$ and calculate

$$X = 20\ 000(1.01)^{120} - 287s_{\overline{119}|0.01}(1.01)$$
$$\doteq 66\ 007.74 - 65\ 734.10$$
$$= \$273.64$$

When interest-bearing debts are amortized by means of a series of equal payments at equal intervals, it is important to know how much of each payment goes toward interest and how much goes toward the reduction of principal. This might be a necessary part of determining one's taxable income or tax deductions. For example, the interest paid on some loans can be deducted for income tax purposes. Thus it is necessary to know how much interest is paid during each year of the loan. We can construct an **amortization schedule** to show how much of each loan payment goes toward interest and how much goes toward reducing the principal. It will also show the outstanding balance of the loan after each loan payment.

> **CALCULATION TIP:**
>
> The common commercial practice for loans that are amortized by equal payments is to round the payment up to the next cent (sometimes up to the next nickel, dime, or dollar if so specified). For each loan you should calculate the reduced final payment. For all other calculations (other than the regular amortization payment), use the normal round-off procedure. Do not round off the interest rate per conversion period. Use all the digits provided by your calculator (store the rate in the memory of the calculator) to avoid significant round-off errors.

EXAMPLE 2 A debt of $22 000 with interest at $i^{(4)} = 10\%$ is to be amortized by payments of $5000 at the end of each quarter for as long as necessary. Construct an amortization schedule showing the distribution of the payments as to interest and the repayment of principal.

Solution The following amortization schedule is obtained.

Payment Number	Monthly Payment	Interest Payment	Principal Payment	Outstanding Balance
0				$22 000.00
1	5000.00	550.00	4450.00	17 550.00
2	5000.00	438.75	4561.25	12 988.75
3	5000.00	324.72	4675.28	8313.47
4	5000.00	207.84	4792.16	3521.31
5	3609.34	88.03	3521.31	0
Totals	23 609.34	1609.34	22 000.00	

1. A payment number 0 is needed to set up the original amount of the loan.

2. The interest due at the end of the first quarter is 2.5% of $22 000, or $22 000(0.025) = $550.

3. The payment of $5000 made at the end of the first quarter (payment 1) will first pay the interest owed. This leaves $5000 − $550 = $4450 which will go toward reducing the loan balance.

4. The **outstanding principal balance*** after the first payment is $5000 − $4450 = $17 550.

5. For the next line of the table (payment 2), the interest due at the end of the second quarter is 2.5% of the current outstanding balance of $17 550, or $17 550(0.025) = $438.75. The remainder, $5000 − $438.75 = $4561.25, goes toward reducing the loan balance, which becomes $17 550 − $4561.25 = $12 988.75.

---

*__Outstanding principal balance__ is also referred to as outstanding principal or outstanding balance.

6. The next two lines are calculated using the same methodology.

7. It should be noted that the 5th and final payment is only $3609.34, which is the sum of the outstanding balance at the end of the 4th quarter ($3521.31) plus the interest due at 2.5% (3521.31(0.025) = 88.03).

The totals at the bottom of the schedule are for checking purposes. The total amount of principal repaid (the sum of the principal payment column) must equal the original debt. Also, the total of the periodic payments must equal the total interest plus the total principal repaid. Note that the entries in the principal repaid column (except the final payment) are in the ratio $(1 + i)$. That is,

$$\frac{4561.25}{4450.00} \doteq \frac{4675.28}{4561.25} \doteq \frac{4792.16}{4675.28} \doteq 1.025.$$

EXAMPLE 3   Consider a $6000 loan that is to be repaid over 5 years with monthly payments at $i^{(12)} = 6\%$. Show the first three lines of the amortization schedule.

Solution   First, we calculate the monthly payment R given $A = 6000$, $n = 60$, and $i = 0.005$.

$$R = \frac{6000}{a_{\overline{60}|0.005}} = \$116.00$$

To create the amortization schedule for the first three months, we follow the method outlined in Example 2 with $i = 0.005$.

Payment Number	Monthly Payment	Interest Payment	Principal Payment	Outstanding Balance
0				$6000.00
1	116.00	30.00	86.00	5914.00
2	116.00	29.57	86.43	5827.57
3	116.00	29.14	86.86	5740.71

As before, the entries in the principal repaid column are in the ratio $1 + i$. That is,

$$\frac{86.43}{86.00} \doteq \frac{86.86}{86.43} \doteq 1.005.$$

EXAMPLE 4   Prepare a spreadsheet and show the first 3 months and the last 3 months of a complete amortization schedule for the loan of Example 3 above. Also show total payments, total interest, and total principal paid.

Solution   In any amortization schedule we reserve cells A1 through E1 for headings. The same headings will be used in all future Excel spreadsheets showing amortization schedules.

Type the loan amount in cell E2, 6000. In cell F3 type the interest rate, =0.06/12. In cell F2 type the appropriate formula to calculate the periodic payment. You would type =ROUNDUP(E2/((1−(1+F3)^−60)/F3),2). The ROUNDUP function will round the periodic payment up to the next cent.

We summarize the rest of the entries in an Excel spreadsheet and their interpretation in the table below.

	CELL	ENTER	INTERPRETATION
Headings	A1	Pmt #	'Payment number'
	B1	Payment	'Monthly payment'
	C1	Interest	'Interest payment'
	D1	Principal	'Principal payment'
	E1	Balance	'Outstanding principal balance'
Line 0	A2	0	Time starts
	E2	6000	Loan amount
Line 1	A3	=A2+1	End of month 1
	B3	F2	Monthly payment (up to the next cent)
	C3	=E2*F3	Interest 1=(Balance 0) (0.005)
	D3	=B3−C3	Principal 1=Payment−Interest 1
	E3	=E2−D3	Balance 1=Balance 0−Principal 1

To generate the complete schedule copy A3.E3 to A4.E62

To get the last payment adjust B62=E61+C62

To get totals apply Σ to B3.D62

Below are the first 3 months and the last 3 months of a complete amortization schedule together with the required totals.

	A	B	C	D	E
1	Pmt#	Payment	Interest	Principal	Balance
2	0				6,000.00
3	1	116.00	30.00	86.00	5,914.00
4	2	116.00	29.57	86.43	5,827.57
5	3	116.00	29.14	86.86	5,740.71
⋮	⋮	⋮	⋮	⋮	⋮
60	58	116.00	1.72	114.28	230.05
61	59	116.00	1.15	114.85	115.20
62	60	115.78	0.58	115.20	0.00
63		6,959.78	959.78	6,000.00	

If you want to see the amortization schedule for a loan amount of \$15 000 at $i^{(12)} = 8\%$ (but still a 5-year loan), all you have to do is type 15 000 in E2 and =0.08/12 into F3. Your periodic payment becomes \$304.15 and all other values in the amortization table will automatically change.

EXAMPLE 5   A couple purchases a home and signs a mortgage contract for $315 000 to be paid in equal monthly payments over 25 years with interest at $i^{(2)} = 6.60\%$. Determine the monthly payment and make out a partial amortization schedule showing the distribution of the first six payments as to interest and repayment of principal.

Solution   Since the interest is compounded semi-annually and the payments are paid monthly we have a general annuity problem. First we calculate rate i per month equivalent to 3.3% per half-year and store it in the memory of the calculator.

$$(1 + i)^{12} = (1.033)^2$$
$$(1 + i) = (1.033)^{\frac{1}{6}}$$
$$i = (1.033)^{\frac{1}{6}} - 1$$
$$i = 0.005425865$$

The monthly payment $R = \dfrac{315\ 000}{a_{\overline{300}|i}} \doteq \$2129.08$.

To make out the amortization schedule for the first 6 months, we follow the same method as in the previous two examples with $i = 0.005425865$.

Payment Number	Monthly Payment	Interest Payment	Principal Payment	Outstanding Balance
0				$315 000.00
1	2129.08	1709.15	419.93	314 580.07
2	2129.08	1706.87	422.21	314 157.86
3	2129.08	1704.58	424.50	313 733.35
4	2129.08	1702.27	426.81	313 306.55
5	2129.08	1699.96	429.12	312 877.43
6	2129.08	1697.63	431.45	312 445.98
Totals	12 774.48	10 220.46	2554.02	

During the first 6 months only $2554.02 of the original $315 000 debt is repaid. It should be noted that about 80% of the first six payments goes for interest and only 20% for the reduction of the outstanding balance.

Again, the entries in the principal repaid column are in the ratio of $(1 + i)$. That is:

$$\frac{422.21}{419.93} \doteq \frac{424.50}{422.21} \doteq \ldots \doteq \frac{431.45}{429.12} \doteq 1 + i$$

EXAMPLE 6   Prepare an Excel spreadsheet and show the first 6 months and the last 6 months of a complete amortization schedule for the mortgage loan of Example 5 above. Also show total payments, total interest, and total principal paid.

Solution   Type the loan amount in cell E2, 315 000. In cell F3 type the given semi-annual interest rate, =0.066/2. In cell F4 calculate the equivalent monthly interest rate by typing =(1+F3)^(1/6)−1. In cell F2 calculate the monthly payment by typing in =ROUNDUP(E2/((1−(1+F4)^−300)/F4),2). We summarize the entries for line 0 and line 1 of an Excel spreadsheet.

CELL	ENTER
A2	0
E2	315 000
A3	=A2+1
B3	F2
C3	=E2*F4
D3	=B3−C3
E3	=E2−D3

To generate the complete schedule copy A3.E3 to 4.E302

To get the last payment adjust B302=E301+C302

To get the totals apply Σ to B3.D302

Below are the first 6 months and the last 6 months of a complete amortization schedule together with the required totals.

	A	B	C	D	E	F
1	Pmt#	Payment	Interest	Principal	Balance	
2	0				315,000.00	2,129.08
3	1	2,129.08	1,709.15	419.93	314,580.07	0.033
4	2	2,129.08	1,706.87	422.21	314,157.86	0.0054259
5	3	2,129.08	1,704.58	424.50	313,733.35	
6	4	2,129.08	1,702.27	426.81	313,306.55	
7	5	2,129.08	1,699.96	429.12	312,877.43	
8	6	2,129.08	1,697.63	431.45	312,445.98	
⋮	⋮	⋮	⋮	⋮	⋮	
299	297	2,129.08	45.57	2,083.51	6,315.44	
300	298	2,129.08	34.27	2,094.81	4,220.62	
301	299	2,129.08	22.90	2,106.18	2,114.44	
302	300	2,125.92	11.47	2,114.44	0.00	
303		638,720.84	323,720.84	315,000.00		

EXAMPLE 7   **General amortization schedule**

Consider a loan of A to be repaid with level payments of R at the end of each period for n periods, at rate i per period. Show that in the kth line of the amortization schedule ($1 \le k \le n$)

a) Interest payment $I_k = iRa_{\overline{n-k+1}|i} = R[1 - (1 + i)^{-(n-k+1)}]$

b) Principal payment $P_k = R(1 + i)^{-(n-k+1)}$

c) Outstanding balance $B_k = Ra_{\overline{n-k}|i}$

Verify that

d) Sum of principal repaid column = original loan amount = $A = Ra_{\overline{n}|i}$
e) Sum of interest payments column = total interest paid = $nR - A$
f) Principal payments are in the ratio of $(1 + i)$:

$$\frac{P_{k+1}}{P_k} = (1 + i)$$

Solution a   The outstanding balance after the $(k - 1)$st payment is the discounted value of the remaining $n - (k - 1) = n - k + 1$ payments, that is

$$B_{k-1} = Ra_{\overline{n-k+1}|i}$$

Interest paid in the kth payment is

$$I_k = iB_{k-1} = iRa_{\overline{n-k+1}|i} = iR\frac{1 - (1 + i)^{-(n-k+1)}}{i} = R[1 - (1 + i)^{-(n-k+1)}]$$

Solution b   Principal repaid in the kth payment is

$$P_k = R - I_k = R - R[1 - (1 + i)^{-(n-k+1)}] = R(1 + i)^{-(n-k+1)}$$

Solution c   The outstanding balance after the kth payment is the discounted value of the remaining $(n - k)$ payments, that is

$$B_k = Ra_{\overline{n-k}|i}$$

Solution d   The sum of the principal payments is

$$\sum_{k=1}^{n} P_k = \sum_{k=1}^{n} R(1 + i)^{-(n-k+1)} = R[(1 + i)^{-n} + \cdots + (1 + i)^{-1}] = Ra_{\overline{n}|i} = A$$

Solution e   The sum of the interest payment is

$$\sum_{k=1}^{n} I_k = \sum_{k=1}^{n} R[1 - (1 + i)^{-(n-k+1)}] = nR - Ra_{\overline{n}|i} = nR - A$$

Solution f

$$\frac{P_{k+1}}{P_k} = \frac{R(1 + i)^{-[n-(k+1)+1]}}{R(1 + i)^{-(n-k+1)}} = (1 + i)^{(-n+k)+(n-k+1)} = (1 + i)$$

EXAMPLE 8   A loan of $10 000 at $i^{(2)} = 6.5\%$ is to be repaid over 10 years with semi-annual payments.

a) How much interest is paid in the 14th payment?
b) How much principal is repaid as part of the 5th payment?
c) What is the outstanding balance of the loan after 13 payments?

Solution a   First we need to calculate the semi-annual payment as

$$R = \frac{10\ 000}{a_{\overline{20}|0.0325}} = \$687.79$$

The interest portion of the 14th payment is

$$I_{14} = 687.79[1 - (1.0325)^{-(20-14+1)}]$$
$$= 687.79[1 - (1.0325)^{-7}]$$
$$\doteq \$137.96$$

Solution b   The principal portion of the 5th payment is

$$P_5 = 687.79(1.0325)^{-(20-5+1)}$$
$$= 687.79(1.0325)^{-16}$$
$$\doteq \$412.30$$

Solution c   The outstanding balance immediately after the 13th payment is

$$B_{13} = 687.79a_{\overline{20-13}|0.0325} = \$4245.04$$

Note: From this value you can calculate the outstanding balance after the 14th payment as follows. From **a)**, we can calculate $P_{14} = \$687.79 - \$137.96 = \$549.83$. Thus

$$B_{14} = B_{13} - P_{14} = \$4245.04 - \$549.83 = \$3695.21$$

EXAMPLE 9   A loan of $\$A$ is to be repaid with 20 payments. The principal repaid in the 9th and 10th payments is $278.00 and $282.17 respectively. What is A?

Solution   We calculate the periodic interest rate by taking the ratio of the principal repaid values

$$\frac{P_{10}}{P_9} = \frac{282.17}{278.00} = 1.015$$

Thus, $i = 0.015$

Note: we do not know at what frequency this interest rate is compounded, but we do not need this information.

We calculate the periodic payment,

$$P_9 = R(1 + i)^{-(20-9+1)}$$
$$278.00 = R(1.015)^{-12}$$
$$R = 278.00(1.015)^{12} \doteq \$332.38$$

From this we calculate the loan amount,

$$A = 332.38a_{\overline{20}|0.015} \doteq \$5706.51$$

Exercise 5.1

Part A

1. A loan of $5000 is to be amortized with equal quarterly payments over a period of 5 years at $i^{(4)} = 12\%$. Determine the concluding payment if the quarterly payment is rounded up to a) the cent; b) the dime.

2. A loan of $20 000 is to be amortized with equal monthly payments over a 3-year period at $i^{(12)} = 8\%$. Determine the concluding payment if the monthly payment is rounded up to a) the cent; b) the dime.

3. A $5000 loan is to be amortized with 8 equal semi-annual payments. If interest is at $i^{(2)} = 9\%$, determine the semi-annual payment and construct an amortization schedule.

4. A loan of $900 is to be amortized with 6 equal monthly payments at $i^{(12)} = 12\%$. Determine the monthly payment and construct an amortization schedule.

5. A debt of $50 000 with interest at $i^{(4)} = 8\%$ is to be amortized by payments of $10 000 at the end of each quarter for as long as necessary. Create an amortization schedule.

6. A $10 000 loan is to be repaid with semi-annual payments of $2500 for as long as necessary. If interest is at $i^{(12)} = 12\%$, create a complete amortization schedule.

7. A $16 000 car is purchased by paying $1000 down and then equal monthly payments for 3 years at $i^{(12)} = 8.4\%$. Determine the size of the monthly payments and complete the first three lines of the amortization schedule.

8. A mobile home worth $46 000 is purchased with a down payment of $6000 and monthly payments for 15 years. If interest is $i^{(2)} = 10\%$, determine the monthly payment and complete the first 6 lines of the amortization schedule.

9. A couple purchases a home worth $256 000 by paying $86 000 down and then taking out a mortgage at $i^{(2)} = 7\%$. The mortgage will be amortized over 25 years with equal monthly payments. Determine the monthly payment and create a partial amortization schedule showing the distribution of the first 6 payments as to interest and principal. How much of the principal is repaid during the first 6 months?

10. In September 1981, mortgage interest rates peaked at $i^{(2)} = 21\frac{1}{2}\%$. Redo question 12 using $i^{(2)} = 21\frac{1}{2}\%$.

11. On a loan with $i^{(12)} = 12\%$ and monthly payments, the amount of principal in the 6th payment is $40.
   a) Determine the amount of principal in the 15th payment.
   b) If there are 36 equal payments in all, determine the amount of the loan.

12. A loan is being repaid over 10 years with equal annual payments. Interest is at $i^{(1)} = 7\%$. If the amount of principal repaid in the third payment is $100, determine the amount of principal repaid in the 7th payment.

13. A loan is being repaid by monthly instalments of $100 at $i^{(12)} = 18\%$. If the loan balance after the fourth month is $1200, determine the original loan value.

14. A loan is being repaid with 10 annual instalments. The principal portion of the 7th payment is $110.25 and the interest portion is $39.75. What annual effective rate of interest is being charged?

15. Below is part of a mortgage amortization schedule.

Payment	Interest	Principal	Balance
	243.07	31.68	
	242.81	31.94	

Determine
   a) the monthly payment;
   b) the effective rate of interest per month;
   c) the nominal rate of interest $i^{(2)}$, rounded to the nearest $\frac{1}{8}\%$ (*Note:* Use this rounded nominal rate from here on);
   d) the outstanding balance just after the first payment shown above;
   e) the remaining period of the mortgage if interest rates don't change.

16. Part of an amortization schedule shows

Payment	Interest	Principal	Balance
	440.31	160.07	
	438.71	161.67	

Complete the next two lines of this schedule.

Part B

1. A debt of $2000 will be repaid by monthly payments of $500 for as long as necessary, the first payment to be made at the end of 6 months. If interest is at $i^{(12)} = 9\%$, calculate the size of the debt at the end of 5 months and create the complete schedule starting at that time.

2. A couple buys some furniture for $1500. They pay off the debt at $i^{(12)} = 15\%$ by paying $200 a month for as long as necessary. The first payment is at the end of 3 months. Do a complete amortization schedule for this loan.

3. The ABC Bank develops a special scheme to help its customers pay their loans off quickly. Instead of making payments of X dollars once a month, mortgage borrowers are asked to pay $\frac{X}{4}$ dollars once a week (52 times a year).

The Gibsons are buying a house and need a $180 000 mortgage. If $i^{(2)} = 8\%$, determine
a) the monthly payment required to amortize the debt over 25 years;
b) the weekly payment $\frac{X}{4}$ suggested in the scheme;
c) the number of weeks it will take to pay off the debt using the suggested scheme.
Compare these results and comment.

4. A loan is being repaid with 20 annual instalments at $i^{(1)} = 15\%$. In which instalment are the principal and interest portions most nearly equal to each other?

5. A loan at $i^{(1)} = 9\%$ is being repaid by monthly payments of $750 each. The total principal repaid in the 12 monthly instalments of the 8th year is $400. What is the total interest paid in the 12 instalments of the 10th year?

6. On mortgages repaid by equal annual payments covering both principal and interest, a mortgage company pays as a commission to its agents 10% of the portion of each scheduled instalment, which represents interest. What is the total commission paid per $1000 of original mortgage loan if it is repaid with n annual payments at rate i per year?

7. Fred buys a personal computer from a company whose head office is in the United States. The computer includes software designed to calculate mortgage amortization schedules. Fred has a $75 000 mortgage with 20-year amortization at $i^{(2)} = 6\frac{1}{2}\%$. According to his bank statement, his monthly payment is $555.38. When Fred uses his software, he enters his original principal balance of $75 000, the amortization period of 20 years, and the nominal annual rate of interest of $6\frac{1}{2}\%$. The computer produces output that says the monthly payment should be $559.18. Which answer is correct? Can you explain the difference?

8. As part of the purchase of a home on January 1, 2010, you have just negotiated a mortgage in the amount of $150 000. The amortization period for calculation of the level monthly payments (principal and interest) has been set at 25 years and the interest rate is 5.5% per annum compounded semi-annually.
a) What level monthly payment is required, assuming the first one is to be made at February 1, 2010?
b) It has been suggested that if you multiply the monthly payment [calculated in a)] by 12, divide by 52, then pay the resulting amount each week, with the first payment at January 8, 2010, then the amortization period will be shortened. If the lender agrees to this, at what time in the future will the mortgage be fully paid?
c) What will be the size of the smaller, final weekly payment, made 1 week after the last regular payment [as calculated for part b)]?

9. You lend a friend $15 000 to be amortized by semi-annual payments for 8 years, with interest at $i^{(2)} = 9\%$. You deposit each payment in an account paying $i^{(12)} = 7\%$. What annual effective rate of interest have you earned over the entire 8-year period?

10. A loan of $10 000 is being repaid by 10 semi-annual principal payments of $1000.

Interest on the outstanding balance at $i^{(2)}$ is paid in addition to the principal repayments. The total of all payments is $12 200. Determine $i^{(2)}$.

11. A loan of A dollars is to be repaid by 16 equal semi-annual instalments, including principal and interest, at rate i per half-year. The principal in the first instalment (six months hence) is $30.83. The principal in the last is $100. Determine the annual effective rate of interest.

12. A loan is to be repaid by 16 quarterly payments of $50, $100, $150, …, $800, the first payment due 3 months after the loan is made. Interest is at 8% compounded quarterly. Calculate the total amount of interest contained in the payments.

13. A loan of $20 000 with interest at $i^{(12)} = 6\%$ is amortized by equal monthly payments over 15 years. In which payment will the interest portion be less than the principal portion for the first time?

14. You are choosing between two mortgages for $160 000 with a 20-year amortization period. Both charge $i^{(2)} = 7\%$ and permit the mortgage to be paid off in less than 20 years. Mortgage A allows you to make weekly payments, with each payment being $\frac{1}{4}$ of the normal monthly payment. Mortgage B allows you to make double the usual monthly payment every 6 months. Assuming that you will take advantage of the mortgage provisions, calculate the total interest charges over the life of each mortgage to determine which mortgage costs less.

15. In the United States, in an effort to advertise low rates of interest but still achieve high rates of return, lenders sometimes charge *points*. Each point is a 1% discount from the face value of the loan. Suppose a home is being sold for $220 000 and that the buyer pays $60 000 down and gets a $160 000 15-year mortgage at $i^{(12)} = 8\%$. The lender charges 5 points, that is 5% of $160 000 = $8000, so the loan is $152 000, but $160 000 is repaid. What is the true interest rate, $i^{(12)}$, on the loan?

Section 5.2 **Outstanding Balance**

It is quite important to know the amount of principal remaining to be paid at a certain time. The borrower may want to pay off the outstanding balance of the debt in a lump sum, the borrower or lender may want to refinance the loan, or the lender may wish to sell the contract.

One could determine the outstanding balance by making out an amortization schedule. This becomes rather tedious without a spreadsheet when a large number of payments are involved. In this section we shall calculate the outstanding balance directly from an appropriate equation of value.

Let B_k denote the outstanding balance immediately after the kth payment has been made.

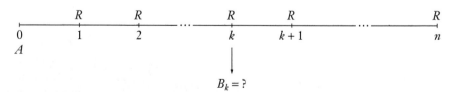

Two methods for finding B_k are available.

The Retrospective Method: This method uses the past history of the debt — the payments that have been made already. The outstanding balance B_k is calculated as

B_k = Accumulated value of original debt
  − Accumulated value of payments made to date

$$B_k = A(1 + i)^k - Rs_{\overline{k}|i}$$ **(13)**

Equation **(13)** always gives the correct value of the outstanding balance B_k and can be used in all cases, but is particularly useful when the number of payments is not known or the last payment is an irregular one.

The Prospective Method: This method uses the future prospects of the debt — the payments yet to be made. The outstanding balance B_k is calculated as

B_k = Discounted value of the remaining $(n - k)$ payments

If all the payments, including the last one, are equal, we obtain

$$B_k = Ra_{\overline{n-k}|i}$$ **(14)**

While equations **(13)** and **(14)** are algebraically equivalent (see problem B8 in Exercise 5.2), equation **(14)** cannot be used when the concluding payment is an irregular one. However, it is useful if you don't know the original value of the loan or if there have been several interest rate changes in the past. When the concluding payment is an irregular one, equation **(14)** is still applicable if suitably modified, but it is usually simpler to use the retrospective method than to discount the $(n - k)$ payments yet to be made.

EXAMPLE 1   A loan of $2000 with interest at $i^{(12)} = 12\%$ is to be amortized by equal payments at the end of each month over a period of 18 months. Determine the outstanding balance at the end of 8 months.

Solution   First we calculate the monthly payment R, given $A = 2000$, $n = 18$, $i = 0.01$,

$$R = \frac{2000}{a_{\overline{18}|0.01}} \doteq \$121.97$$

$$B_8 = ?$$

The retrospective method We have $A = 2000$, $R = 121.97$, $k = 8$, $i = 0.01$, and calculate B_8 using equation **(13)**

$$B_8 = 2000(1.01)^8 - 121.97s_{\overline{8}|0.01}$$
$$\doteq 2165.71 - 1010.60 = \$1155.11$$

The prospective method We have $R = 121.97$, $n - k = 10$, $i = 0.01$, and calculate B_8 using equation **(14)**

$$B_8 = 121.97 a_{\overline{10}|0.01} = \$1155.21$$

The difference of 10 cents is due to rounding the monthly payment R up to the next cent. The concluding payment is, in fact, slightly smaller than the regular payment $R = 121.97$, so the value of B_8 under the prospective method is not accurate.

EXAMPLE 2

On July 15, 2010, a couple borrowed \$10 000 at $i^{(12)} = 7.2\%$ to start a business. They plan to repay the debt in equal monthly payments over 8 years with the first payment on August 15, 2010. a) How much principal did they repay during 2010? b) How much interest can they claim as a tax deduction during 2010?

Solution

We arrange our data on a time diagram below.

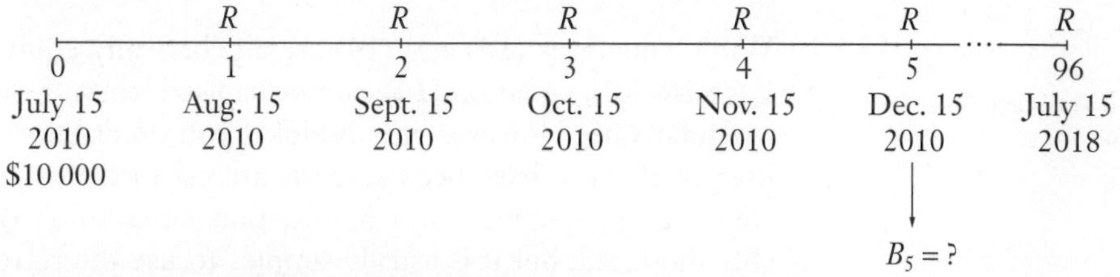

	R	R	R	R	R	R
0	1	2	3	4	5	96
July 15	Aug. 15	Sept. 15	Oct. 15	Nov. 15	Dec. 15	July 15
2010	2010	2010	2010	2010	2010	2018
\$10 000						

$$B_5 = ?$$

First we calculate the monthly payment R, given $A = 10\,000$, $n = 96$, $i = 0.006$

$$R = \frac{10\,000}{a_{\overline{96}|0.006}} \doteq 137.34$$

Then we calculate the outstanding balance B_5 on December 15, 2010, after the 5th payment has been made. We have $A = 10\,000$, $R = 137.34$, $k = 5$, $i = 0.006$, and using equation **(13)** we calculate

$$B_5 = 10\,000(1.006)^5 - 137.34 s_{\overline{5}|0.006}$$
$$= 10\,303.62 - 694.99$$
$$= \$9608.63$$

The total reduction in principal in 2010 is the difference between the outstanding balance on December 15, 2010, after the 5th payment has been made, and the original debt of \$10 000. Thus, they repaid \$10 000 − \$9608.63 = \$391.37 of principal during 2010.

To get the total interest paid in 2010, we subtract the amount they repaid on principal from the total of the 5 payments, i.e., total interest = 5 × \$137.34 − \$391.37 = \$295.33. They can deduct \$295.33 as an expense on their 2010 income tax return.

This method of amortization is quite often used to pay off loans incurred in purchasing a property. In such cases, the outstanding balance is called the **seller's equity**. The amount of principal that has been paid already plus the down payment is called the **buyer's equity**, or **owner's equity**. At any point in time we have the following relation:

> **Buyer's equity + Seller's equity = Original selling price**

The buyer's equity starts with the down payment and is gradually increased with each periodic payment by the part of the payment which is applied to reduce the outstanding balance. It should be noted that the buyer's equity, as defined above, does not make any allowance for increases or decreases in the value of the property.

EXAMPLE 3   The Mancinis buy a cottage worth $178 000 by paying $38 000 down and the balance, with interest at $i^{(2)} = 6.75\%$, in monthly instalments of $2000 for as long as necessary. Determine the Mancinis' equity at the end of 5 years.

Solution   The monthly payments form a general annuity. First, we calculate a monthly rate of interest i equivalent to $3\frac{3}{8}\%$ each half-year.

$$(1 + i)^{12} = (1.03375)^2$$
$$(1 + i) = (1.03375)^{\frac{1}{6}}$$
$$i = (1.03375)^{\frac{1}{6}} - 1$$
$$i = 0.005547491$$

Using the retrospective method, we calculate the seller's equity as the outstanding balance at the end of 60 months.

$$B_{60} = 140\,000(1 + i)^{60} - 2000s_{\overline{60}|i}$$
$$= 195\,111.68 - 141\,921.73$$
$$= \$53\,189.95$$

The Mancinis' equity is then

$$\text{Buyer's equity} \doteq 178\,000 - 53\,189.95 = \$124\,810.05$$

Exercise 5.2

Part A

1. To pay off the purchase of a car, Chantal got a $15 000, 3-year bank loan at $i^{(12)} = 12\%$. She makes monthly payments. How much does she still owe on the loan at the end of 2 years (24 payments)? Use both the retrospective and prospective methods.

2. A debt of $10 000 will be amortized by payments at the end of each quarter of a year for 10 years. Interest is at $i^{(4)} = 10\%$. Determine the outstanding balance at the end of 6 years.

3. On July 1, 2010, Brian borrowed $30 000 to be repaid with monthly payments (first payment August 1, 2010) over 3 years at $i^{(12)} = 8\%$. How much principal did he repay in 2010? How much interest?

4. A couple buys a house worth $468 000 by paying $138 000 down and taking out a mortgage for $330 000. The mortgage is at $i^{(2)} = 5.5\%$ and will be repaid over 25 years with monthly payments. How much of the principal does the couple pay off in the first year?

5. On May 1, 2010, the Morins borrow $4000 to be repaid with monthly payments over 3 years at $i^{(12)} = 9\%$. The 12 payments made during 2011 will reduce the principal by how much? What was the total interest paid in 2011?

6. To pay off the purchase of home furnishings, a couple takes out a bank loan of $2000 to be repaid with monthly payments over 2 years at $i^{(12)} = 9\%$. What is the outstanding debt just after the 10th payment? What is the principal portion of the 11th payment?

7. A couple buys a piece of land worth $200 000 by paying $50 000 down and then taking a loan out for $150 000. The loan will be repaid with quarterly payments over 15 years at $i^{(4)} = 8\%$. Determine the couple's equity at the end of 8 years.

8. A family buys a house worth $326 000. They pay $110 000 down and then take out a mortgage for the balance at $i^{(2)} = 6\frac{1}{2}\%$ to be amortized over 20 years. Payments will be made monthly. Determine the outstanding balance at the end of 5 years and the owners' equity at that time.

9. Land worth $80 000 is purchased by a down payment of $12 000 and the balance in equal monthly instalments for 15 years. If interest is at $i^{(12)} = 9\%$, determine the buyer's and seller's equity in the land at the end of 9 years.

10. A loan of $10 000 is being repaid by instalments of $200 at the end of each month for as long as necessary. If interest is at $i^{(4)} = 8\%$, determine the outstanding balance at the end of 1 year.

11. A debt is being amortized at an annual effective rate of interest of 10% by payments of $5000 made at the end of each year for 11 years.

Determine the outstanding balance just after the 7th payment.

12. A loan is to be amortized by semi-annual payments of $802 at 8% compounded semi-annually. What is the original amount of the loan if the outstanding balance is reduced to $17 630 at the end of 3 years?

13. A loan is being repaid with semi-annual instalments of $1000 for 10 years at 10% compounded semi-annually. Determine the amount of principal in the 6th instalment.

14. Jones purchased a cottage, paying $10 000 down and agreeing to pay $500 at the end of every month for the next 10 years. The rate of interest is $i^{(2)} = 5\%$. Jones discharges the remaining indebtedness without penalty by making a single payment at the end of 5 years. Determine the extra amount that Jones pays in addition to the regular payment then due.

Part B

1. With mortgage rates at $i^{(2)} = 11\%$, the XYZ Trust Company makes a special offer to its customers. It will lend mortgage money and determine the monthly payment as if $i^{(2)} = 9\%$. The mortgage will be carried at $i^{(2)} = 11\%$ and any deficiency that results will be added to the outstanding balance. If the Moras are taking out a $100 000 mortgage to be repaid over 25 years under this scheme, what will their outstanding balance be at the end of 5 years?

2. The Hwangs can buy a home for $380 000. To do so would require taking out a $250 000 mortgage from a bank at $i^{(2)} = 7.25\%$. The loan will be repaid over 25 years with the rate of interest fixed for 5 years.

   The seller of the home is willing to give the Hwangs a mortgage at $i^{(2)} = 6.25\%$. The monthly payment will be determined using a 25-year repayment schedule. The seller will guarantee the rate of interest for 5 years at which time the Hwangs will have to pay off the seller and get a mortgage from a bank. If the Hwangs accept this offer, the seller wants $390 000 for the house, forcing the Hwangs to borrow $260 000. If the Hwangs can earn $i^{(12)} = 4\%$ on their money, what should they do?

3. The Smiths buy a home and take out a $160 000 mortgage on which the interest rate is allowed to float freely. At the time the mortgage is issued, interest rates are $i^{(2)} = 6\%$ and the Smiths choose a 25-year amortization schedule. Six months into the mortgage, interest rates rise to $i^{(2)} = 8\%$. Three years into the mortgage (after 36 payments) interest rates drop to $i^{(2)} = 7\%$, and four years into the mortgage interest rates drop to $i^{(2)} = 5\frac{1}{2}\%$. Determine the outstanding balance of the mortgage after 5 years. (The monthly payment is set at issue and does not change.)

4. A young couple buys a house and assumes a $180 000 mortgage to be amortized over 25 years. The interest rate is guaranteed at $i^{(2)} = 8\%$. The mortgage allows the couple to make extra payments against the outstanding principal each month. By saving carefully the couple manages to pay off an extra $200 each month. Because of these extra payments, how long will it take to pay off the mortgage and what will be the size of the final smaller monthly payment?

5. A loan is made on January 1, 2010, and is to be repaid by 25 level annual instalments. These instalments are in the amount of $3000 each and are payable on December 31 of the years 2010 through 2034. However, just after the December 31, 2014, instalment has been paid, it is agreed that, instead of continuing the annual instalments on the basis just described, henceforth instalments will be payable quarterly with the first such quarterly instalment being payable on March 31, 2015, and the last one on December 31, 2034. Interest is at an annual effective rate of 10%. By changing from the old repayment schedule to the new one, the borrower will reduce the total amount of payments made over the 25-year period. Determine the amount of this reduction.

6. The ABC Trust Company issues loans where the monthly payments are determined by the rate of interest that prevails on the day the loan is made. After that, the rate of interest varies according to market forces but the monthly payments do not change in dollar size. Instead, the length of time to full repayment is either lengthened (if interest rates rise) or shortened (if interest rates fall).

Medhaf takes out a 10-year, $20 000 loan at $i^{(2)} = 8\%$. After exactly 2 years (24 payments) interest rates change. Determine the duration of the remaining loan and the final smaller payment if the new interest rate is a) $i^{(2)} = 9\%$; b) $i^{(2)} = 7\%$.

7. Big Corporation built a new plant in 2008 at a cost of $1 700 000. It paid $200 000 cash and assumed a mortgage for $1 500 000 to be repaid over 10 years by equal semi-annual payments due each June 30 and December 31, the first payment being due on December 31, 2008. The mortgage interest rate is 5.5% per annum compounded semi-annually and the original date of the loan was July 1, 2008.
   a) What will be the total of the payments made in 2010 on this mortgage?
   b) Mortgage interest paid in any year (for this mortgage) is an income tax deduction for that year. What will be the interest deduction on Big Corporation's 2010 tax form?
   c) Suppose the plant is sold on January 1, 2012. The buyer pays $700 000 cash and assumes the outstanding mortgage. What is Big Corporation's capital gain (amount realized less original price) on the investment in the building?

8. Given a loan L to be repaid at rate i per period with equal payments R at the end of each period for n periods, give the retrospective and prospective expressions for the outstanding balance of the loan at time k (after the kth payment is made) and prove that the two expressions are equal.

9. A 5-year loan is being repaid with level monthly instalments at the end of each month, beginning with January 2010 and continuing through December 2014. A 12% interest rate compounded monthly was used to determine the amount of each monthly instalment. On which date will the outstanding balance of this loan first fall below one-half of the original amount of the loan?

10. A debt is amortized at $i^{(4)} = 10\%$ by payments of $300 per quarter. If the outstanding principal is $2853.17 just after the kth payment, what was it just after the $(k - 1)$st payment?

11. A loan of $3000 is to be repaid by annual payments of $400 per annum for the first 5 years and payments of $450 per year thereafter for as long as necessary. Determine the total number of payments and the amount of the smaller final payment made one year after the last regular payment. Assume an annual effective rate of 7%.

12. Five years ago, Justin deposited $1000 into a fund out of which he draws $100 at the end of each year. The fund guarantees interest at 5% on the principal on deposit during the year. If the fund actually earns interest at a rate in excess of 5%, the excess interest earned during the year is paid to Justin at the end of the year in addition to the regular $100 payment. The fund has been earning 8% each year for the past 5 years. What is the total payment Justin now receives?

13. An advertisement by Royal Trust said:

Our new Double-Up mortgage can be paid off faster and that dramatically reduces the interest you pay. You can double your payment any or every month, with no penalty. Then your payment reverts automatically to its normal amount the next month. What this means to you is simple. You will pay your mortgage off sooner. And that's good news because you can save thousands of dollars in interest as a result.

Consider a $120 000 mortgage at 8% compounded semi-annually, amortized over 25 years with no anniversary prepayments.

a) Determine the required monthly payment for the above mortgage.

b) What is the total amount of interest paid over the full amortization period (assuming $i^{(2)} = 8\%$)?

c) Suppose that payments were "Doubled-Up," according to the advertisement, every 6th and 12th month.

   i) How many years and months would be required to pay off the mortgage?

   ii) What would be the total amount of interest paid over the full amortization period?

   iii) How much of the loan would still be outstanding at the end of 3 years, just after the Doubled-Up payment then due?

   iv) How much principal is repaid in the payment due in 37 months?

| *Section 5.3* | **Refinancing a Loan — The Amortization Method** |

It is common to want to renegotiate a long-term loan after it has been partially paid off. In this section, we are interested in two situations:

1. At the end of the guaranteed interest rate period, a loan is often refinanced; that is, the loan is renewed at whatever interest rates are in effect in the market at that time. We will calculate the revised loan payment based on the new interest rate (which may have gone up or down).

2. Sometimes loans are refinanced *before* the maturity date of the loan or before the end of the guaranteed interest rate period. This is generally initiated by the borrower if interest rates have fallen. However, there is often a penalty involved in refinancing a loan early in these situations. We need to take this penalty into account when determining whether or not the borrower should refinance.

EXAMPLE 1   Mr. Bouchard buys $5000 worth of home furnishings from the ABC Furniture Mart. He pays $500 down and agrees to pay the balance with monthly payments over 5 years at $i^{(12)} = 12\%$. The contract he signs stipulates that if he pays off the contract early there is a penalty equal to 3 months payments. After 2 years (24 payments) Mr. Bouchard realizes that he could borrow the money from the bank at $i^{(12)} = 8.4\%$. He realizes that to do so means he will have to pay the 3-month penalty on the ABC Furniture Mart contract. Should he refinance?

Solution   First, calculate the monthly payments required under the original contract.

$$R_1 = \frac{4500}{a_{\overline{60}|0.01}} \doteq \$100.10$$

Now, calculate the outstanding balance B_{24} on the original contract at the end of 2 years.

$$B_{24} = 4500(1.01)^{24} - 100.10 s_{\overline{24}|0.01} \doteq \$3013.76$$

If Mr. Bouchard repays the loan he will also pay a penalty equal to $3 \times R = \$300.30$. Therefore, the amount he must borrow from the bank is

$$\$3013.76 + \$300.30 = \$3314.06$$

To calculate the new monthly payment, we take the outstanding balance after 24 payments (including the penalty) and treat it like a brand-new loan. That is, we use $A = B_{24} = 3314.06$, $n = 36$, and $i = 0.084/12 = 0.007$.

Thus, the new monthly payments on the bank loan are

$$R_2 = \frac{3314.06}{a_{\overline{36}|0.007}} \doteq \$104.46$$

Therefore, he should not refinance since $104.46 is larger than $100.10.

The largest single loan the average person is likely to take will be the mortgage on one's home. At one time, interest rates on mortgages were guaranteed for the life of the repayment schedule, which could be as long as 25 or 30 years. Now, the longest period of guaranteed interest rates available is usually 5 years, although homeowners may choose mortgages where the interest rate is adjusted every three years, every year, or even daily to current interest rates.

A homeowner who wishes to repay the mortgage in full before the defined renegotiation date may sometimes have to pay a penalty (although in cases where you refinance your mortgage early with the same institution, there may not be a penalty). In some cases, this penalty is defined as three months of interest on the outstanding balance. In other cases the penalty varies according to market conditions and can be determined by the lender at the time of prepayment (the formula that the lender must use may be defined in the mortgage contract, however). This situation is illustrated in Example 3.

Today, many new and different mortgages are being offered to the prospective borrower. It is important that students are capable of analyzing these contracts fully. Several examples are illustrated in the exercises contained in this chapter.

EXAMPLE 2 A couple purchased a home and signed a mortgage contract for $180 000 to be paid with monthly payments calculated over a 25-year period at $i^{(2)} = 10\%$. The interest rate is guaranteed for 5 years. After 5 years, they renegotiate the interest rate and refinance the loan at $i^{(2)} = 6\frac{1}{2}\%$. There is no penalty if a mortgage is refinanced at the end of an interest rate guarantee period. Calculate

a) the monthly payment for the initial 5-year period;
b) the new monthly payments after 5 years;
c) the accumulated value of the savings for the second 5-year period (at the end of that period) at $i^{(12)} = 4\frac{1}{2}\%$; and
d) the outstanding balance at the end of 10 years.

Solution a First we calculate a monthly rate of interest i equivalent to $i^{(2)} = 10\%$:

$$(1 + i)^{12} = (1.05)^2$$
$$(1 + i) = (1.05)^{\frac{1}{6}}$$
$$i = (1.05)^{\frac{1}{6}} - 1$$
$$i = 0.008164846$$

Now $A = 180\ 000$, $n = 300$, $i = 0.008164846$, and we calculate the monthly payment R_1 for the initial 5-year period.

$$R_1 = \frac{180\ 000}{a_{\overline{300}|i}} \doteq \$1610.08$$

Solution b First we calculate the outstanding balance of the loan after 5 years.

$$180\ 000(1 + i)^{60} - 1610.08 s_{\overline{60}|i}$$
$$= 293\ 201.03 - 124\ 015.89 = \$169\ 185.14$$

This outstanding balance is refinanced at $i^{(2)} = 6\frac{1}{2}\%$ over a 20-year period. First, calculate the rate i per month equivalent to $i^{(2)} = 6\frac{1}{2}\%$.

$$(1 + i)^{12} = (1.0325)^2$$
$$(1 + i) = (1.0325)^{\frac{1}{6}}$$
$$i = (1.0325)^{\frac{1}{6}} - 1$$
$$i = 0.00534474$$

Now $A = 169\ 185.14$, $n = 240$, $i = 0.00534474$ and we calculate the new monthly payment R_2.

$$R_2 = \frac{169\ 185.14}{a_{\overline{240}|i}} = \$1252.82$$

Solution c   The monthly savings after the loan is renegotiated after 5 years at $i^{(2)} = 6\frac{1}{2}\%$ is

$$1610.08 - 1252.82 = \$357.26$$

If these savings are deposited in an account paying $i^{(12)} = 4\frac{1}{2}\%$, the accumulated value of the savings at the end of the 5-year period is:

$$357.26s_{\overline{60}|0.00375} \doteq \$23\ 988.42$$

Solution d   The outstanding balance of the loan at the end of 10 years at $i = 0.00534474$ is

$$169\ 185.14(1 + i)^{60} - 1252.82s_{\overline{60}|i}$$
$$= 232\ 950.05 - 88\ 344.94 = \$144\ 605.11$$

The outstanding balance at the end of 10 years is \$144 605.11. That means that only \$180 000 − \$144 605.11 = \$35 394.89 of the loan was repaid during the first 10 years (they still owe 80.3% of the original \$180 000 loan). This is despite the fact that payments in the first 10 years totalled (60 × \$1610.08 + 60 × \$1252.82) or \$171 774.

EXAMPLE 3   The Knapps buy a house and borrow \$145 000 from the ABC Insurance Company. The loan is to be repaid with monthly payments over 30 years at $i^{(2)} = 9\%$. The interest rate is guaranteed for 5 years. After exactly 2 years of making payments, the Knapps see that interest rates have dropped to $i^{(2)} = 7\%$ in the market place. They ask to be allowed to repay the loan in full so they can refinance. The Insurance Company agrees to renegotiate but sets a penalty exactly equal to the money the company will lose over the next 3 years. Calculate the value of the penalty.

Solution   First, calculate the monthly payments R required on the original loan at $i^{(2)} = 9\%$. Determine i such that

$$(1 + i)^{12} = (1.045)^2$$
$$(1 + i) = (1.045)^{\frac{1}{6}}$$
$$i = (1.045)^{\frac{1}{6}} - 1$$
$$i = 0.007363123$$

Now $A = 145\ 000$, $n = 360$, $i = 0.007363123$, and

$$R = \frac{145\ 000}{a_{\overline{360}|i}} = \$1149.61$$

Next we calculate the outstanding balance after 2 years:

$$= 145\ 000(1 + i)^{24} - 1149.61s_{\overline{24}|i}$$
$$= 172\ 915.20 - 30\ 058.08 = \$142\ 857.12$$

Also, we determine the outstanding balance after 5 years if the loan is not renegotiated.

$$145\ 000(1 + i)^{60} - 1149.61s_{\overline{60}|i}$$
$$= 225\ 180.57 - 86\ 335.54 = \$138\ 845.03$$

If the insurance company renegotiates, it will receive \$142 857.12 plus the penalty of X dollars now. If they do not renegotiate, they will receive \$1149.61 a month for 3 years plus \$138 845.03 at the end of 3 years. These two options should be equivalent at the current interest rate $i^{(2)} = 7\%$.

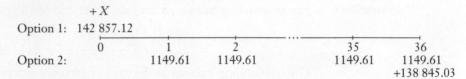

Option 1:   142 857.12 $+X$

Option 2:   0   1   2   35   36
                         1149.61   1149.61   1149.61   1149.61
                                                                         +138 845.03

Determine the monthly rate i equivalent to $i^{(2)} = 7\%$.

$$(1 + i)^{12} = (1.035)^2$$
$$(1 + i) = (1.035)^{\frac{1}{6}}$$
$$i = (1.035)^{\frac{1}{6}} - 1$$
$$i = 0.00575004$$

Using 0 as the focal date we solve an equation of value for X.

$$X + 142\ 857.12 = 1149.61a_{\overline{36}|i} + 138\ 845.03(1 + i)^{-36}$$
$$X + 142\ 857.12 = 37\ 286.97 + 112\ 950.52$$
$$X = 7380.37$$

Thus the penalty at the end of 2 years is \$7380.37.

Should the Knapps refinance? Using $A = 142\ 857.12 + 7380.37 = 150\ 237.49$, $i = 0.00575004$, and $n = 336$ we calculate the revised monthly payment:

$$R_2 = \frac{150\ 237.49}{a_{\overline{336}|0.00575004}} \doteq \$1011.16$$

If the only goal of the Knapps is lower monthly payments, then they should refinance. However, it is not clear whether they should actually refinance. Let's calculate the outstanding balance of the loan after 5 years and assume that the loan is refinanced at that time at $i^{(2)} = 6\%$ (equivalent monthly rate = 0.004938622).

i)   If they do not refinance,

$$B_{60} = 145\ 000(1.007363123)^{60} - 1149.61s_{\overline{60}|i} \doteq \$138\ 845.03$$

and the new monthly payment will be,

$$R = \frac{138\ 845.03}{a_{\overline{300}|0.004938622}} \doteq \$888.34$$

Total payments over mortgage $= 60(\$1149.61) + 300(\$888.34)$
$$= \$335\ 478.60.$$

ii) If they refinance and pay the penalty,

$$B_{60} = 150\,237.49(1.00575004)^{36} - 1011.16s_{\overline{36}|i} \doteq \$144\,365.07$$

and the new monthly payment will be,

$$R = \frac{144\,365.07}{a_{\overline{300}|0.004938622}} \doteq \$923.66$$

Total payments over mortgage $= 24(\$1149.61) + 36(\$1011.16) + 300(\$923.66)$
$= \$341\,090.40$.

The Knapps would end up paying $\$5611.80$ more in interest over the 30 years of the life of the mortgage if they refinanced after the first 2 years and paid the penalty. This will not always be the case. Sometimes it will be better to refinance and pay the penalty. It depends on the size of the penalty and how low is the refinanced interest rate.

Before deciding whether or not to refinance early and pay a penalty, you need to carry out calculations similar to those given above.

Note: Another common penalty is three times the monthly interest due on the outstanding balance at the time of refinancing. In this example, the penalty would have been

$$3 \times \$142\,857.12 \times 0.007363123 = \$3155.62.$$

EXAMPLE 4 The Wongs borrow $\$10\,000$ from a bank to buy some home furnishings. Interest is $i^{(12)} = 9\%$ and the term of the loan is 3 years. After making 15 monthly payments, the Wongs miss the next 2 monthly payments. The bank forces them to renegotiate the loan at a new, higher interest rate $i^{(12)} = 10\frac{1}{2}\%$. Determine

a) the original monthly payments R_1;
b) the outstanding balance of the loan at the time the 17th monthly payment would normally have been made.
c) the new monthly payments R_2 if the original length of the loan term is not extended.

Solution a Using $A = 10\,000$, $n = 36$, $i = \frac{0.09}{12} = 0.0075$ we calculate the original monthly payment

$$R_1 = \frac{10\,000}{a_{\overline{36}|i}} \doteq \$318.00$$

Solution b The first 15 monthly payments of $\$318$ were made. Therefore at the end of 15 months the outstanding balance was

$$10\,000(1+i)^{15} - 318s_{\overline{15}|i}$$
$$= 11\,186.03 - 5028.75 = \$6157.28$$

Then no payments were made for 2 months. Therefore the outstanding balance grows with interest and at the end of 17 months is

$$\$6157.28(1 + i)^2 = \$6249.99$$

Solution c We have $A = 6249.99$, $n = 19$, $i = \frac{0.105}{12} = 0.00875$ and we calculate the new monthly payment

$$R_2 = \frac{6249.99}{a_{\overline{19}|i}} = \$358.49$$

Exercise 5.3

Part A

1. A borrower is repaying a $5000 loan at $i^{(12)} = 9\%$ with monthly payments over 3 years. Just after the 12th payment (at the end of 1 year) he has the loan refinanced at $i^{(12)} = 6\%$. If the number of payments remains unchanged, what will be the new monthly payment and what will be the monthly savings in interest?

2. A 5-year, $6000 loan is being amortized with monthly payments at $i^{(12)} = 10\%$. Just after making the 30th payment, the borrower has the loan refinanced at $i^{(12)} = 8\%$ with the number of payments to remain unchanged. What will be the monthly savings in interest?

3. A borrower has a $5000 loan with the "Easy-Credit" Finance Company. The loan is to be repaid over 4 years at $i^{(12)} = 18\%$. The contract stipulates an early repayment penalty equal to 3 months payments. Just after the 20th payment, the borrower determines that his local bank would lend him money at $i^{(12)} = 12\%$. Should he refinance?

4. The Jones family buys a fridge and stove totalling $1400 from their local appliance store. They agree to pay off the total amount with monthly payments over 3 years at $i^{(12)} = 9\%$. If they wish to pay off the contract early they will experience a penalty equal to 3 months interest on the outstanding balance. After 12 payments they see that interest rates at their local bank are $i^{(12)} = 6\%$. Should they refinance?

5. Consider a couple who bought a house in 1976. Assume they needed a $60 000 mortgage, which was to be repaid with monthly payments over 25 years. In 1976, interest rates were $i^{(2)} = 10\frac{1}{2}\%$. What was their monthly payment? In 1981 (on the 5th anniversary of their mortgage) their mortgage was renegotiated to reflect current market rates. The repayment schedule was to cover the remaining 20 years and interest rates were now $i^{(2)} = 22\%$. What was the new monthly payment? What effect might this have on homeowners?

6. The Steins buy a house and take out a $255 000 mortgage. The mortgage is amortized over 25 years with monthly payments at $i^{(2)} = 9\%$. After $3\frac{1}{2}$ years, the Steins sell their house and the buyer wants to set up a new mortgage better tailored to his needs. The Steins find out that in addition to repaying the principal balance on their mortgage, they must pay a penalty equal to three months interest on the outstanding balance. What total amount must they repay?

7. A couple borrows $15 000 to be repaid with monthly payments over 48 months at $i^{(4)} = 10\%$. They make the first 14 payments and miss the next three. What new monthly payments over 31 months would repay the loan on schedule?

8. A loan of $20 000 is to be repaid in 13 equal annual payments, each payable at year-end. Interest is at $i^{(1)} = 8\%$. Because the borrower is having financial difficulties, the lender agrees that the borrower may skip the 5th and 6th

payments. Immediately after the 6th payment would have been paid, the loan is renegotiated to yield $i^{(1)} = 10\%$ for the remaining 7 years. Determine the new level annual payment for each of the remaining 7 years.

9. A loan of $50 000 is repaid by monthly level instalments over 20 years at $i^{(12)} = 9\%$. After 10 years, the loan is refinanced at $i^{(2)} = 10\frac{1}{2}\%$. What is the new monthly payment?

10. The Mosers buy a camper trailer and take out a $15 000 loan. The loan is amortized over 10 years with monthly payments at $i^{(2)} = 9\%$.
   a) Determine the monthly payment needed to amortize this loan.
   b) Determine the amount of interest paid by the first 36 payments.
   c) After 3 years (36 payments) the Mosers could refinance their loan at $i^{(2)} = 7\%$ provided they pay a penalty equal to three months' interest on the outstanding balance. Should they refinance? (Show the difference in their monthly payments.)

Part B

1. A couple buys a home and signs a mortgage contract for $120 000 to be paid with monthly payments over a 25-year period at $i^{(2)} = 10\frac{1}{2}\%$. After 5 years, they renegotiate the interest rate and refinance the loan at $i^{(2)} = 7\%$. Determine:
   a) the monthly payment for the initial 5-year period;
   b) the new monthly payment after 5 years;
   c) the accumulated value of the savings for the second 5-year period at $i^{(12)} = 3\%$ valued at the end of the second 5-year period;
   d) the outstanding balance at the end of 10 years.

2. Mrs. McDonald is repaying a debt with monthly payments of $100 over 5 years. Interest is at $i^{(12)} = 12\%$. At the end of the second year she makes an extra payment of $350. She then shortens her payment period by 1 year and renegotiates the loan without penalty and without an interest change. What are her new monthly payments over the remaining 2 years? How much interest does she save by doing this?

3. Mr. Fisher is repaying a loan at $i^{(12)} = 12\%$ with monthly payments of $1500 over 3 years. Due to temporary unemployment, Mr. Fisher missed

making the 13th through the 18th payments inclusive. Determine the value of the revised monthly payments needed starting in the 19th month if the loan is still to be repaid at $i^{(12)} = 12\%$ by the end of the original 3 years.

4. Mrs. Metcalf purchased property several years ago (but she cannot remember exactly when). She has a statement in her possession from the mortgage company which shows that the outstanding loan amount on January 1, 2010, is $28 416.60 and that the current interest rate is 11% compounded semi-annually. It further shows that monthly payments are $442.65.

   Assuming continuation of the interest rate until maturity and that monthly payments are due on the 1st of every month:
   a) What is the final maturity date of the mortgage?
   b) What will be the amount of the final payment?
   c) Show the amortization schedule entries for January 1 and February 1, 2010.
   d) Calculate the new monthly payment required (effective after December 31, 2009) if the interest rate is changed to 8% compounded semi-annually and the other terms of the mortgage remain the same.
   e) Calculate the new monthly payment if Mrs. Metcalf decides that she would like to have the mortgage completely repaid by December 31, 2019 (i.e., last payment at December 1, 2019). Assume the 11% compounded semi-annually interest rate, and that new payments will start on February 1, 2010.

5. A loan effective January 1, 2010, is being amortized by equal monthly instalments over 5 years using interest at a nominal annual rate of 12% compounded monthly. The first such instalment was due February 1, 2010, and the last such instalment was to be due January 1, 2015. Immediately after the 24th instalment was made on January 1, 2012, a new level monthly instalment is determined (using the same rate of interest) in order to shorten the total amortization period to $3\frac{1}{2}$ years, so the final instalment will fall due on July 1, 2013. Determine the ratio of the new monthly instalment to the original monthly instalment.

6. A $150 000 mortgage is to be amortized by monthly payments for 25 years. Interest is $i^{(2)} = 9\frac{1}{2}\%$ for 5 years and could change at that time. No penalty is charged for full or partial payment of the mortgage after 5 years.
   a) Calculate the regular monthly payment and the reduced final mortgage payment assuming the $9\frac{1}{2}\%$ rate continues for the entire 25 years.
   b) What is the outstanding balance after
      i) 2 years; ii) 5 years?
   c) During the 5-year period, there is a penalty of 6 months interest on any principal repaid early. After 2 years, interest rates fall to $i^{(2)} = 8\%$ for 3-year mortgages. Calculate the new monthly payment if the loan is refinanced and set up to have the same outstanding balance at the end of the initial 5-year period. Would it pay to refinance? (Exclude consideration of any possible refinancing costs other than the penalty provided in the question.)

7. A $200 000 mortgage is taken out at $i^{(2)} = 6\frac{1}{2}\%$, to be amortized over 25 years by monthly payments. Assume that the $6\frac{1}{2}\%$ rate continues for the entire life of the mortgage.
   a) Calculate the regular monthly payment and the reduced final payment.
   b) Calculate the accumulated value of all the interest payments on the mortgage, at the time of the final payment.
   c) Calculate the outstanding principal after 5 years.
   d) If an extra $5000 is paid off in 5 years (no penalty) and the monthly payments continue as before, how much less will have to be paid over the life of the mortgage?

8. Two years ago the Tongs took out a $175 000 mortgage that was to be amortized over a 25-year period with monthly payments. The initial interest rate was set at $i^{(2)} = 11\frac{1}{4}\%$ and guaranteed for 5 years. After exactly 2 years of payments, the Tongs see that mortgage interest rates for a 3-year term are $i^{(2)} = 7\frac{1}{2}\%$. They ask the bank to let them pay off the old mortgage in full and take out a new mortgage with a 23-year amortization schedule with $i^{(2)} = 7\frac{1}{2}\%$ guaranteed for 3 years. The bank replies that the Tongs must pay a penalty equal to the total dollar difference in the interest payments over the next 3 years. The mortgage allows the Tongs to make a 10% lump-sum principal repayment at any time (i.e., 10% of the remaining outstanding balance). The Tongs argue that they should be allowed to make this 10% lump-sum payment first and then determine the interest penalty. How many dollars will they save with respect to the interest penalty if they are allowed to make the 10% lump-sum repayment?

9. Mr. Adams has just moved to Waterloo. He has been told by his employer that he will be transferred out of Waterloo again in exactly 3 years. Mr. Adams is going to buy a house and requires a $300 000 mortgage. He has his choice of two mortgages, both with monthly payments and a 25-year amortization period.
   Mortgage A is at $i^{(2)} = 7\%$. This mortgage stipulates, however, that if you pay off the mortgage any time before the fifth anniversary, you will have to pay a penalty equal to 3 months interest on the outstanding balance at the time of repayment.
   Mortgage B is at $i^{(2)} = 7.50\%$ but can be paid off at any time without penalty. Given that Mr. Adams will have to repay the mortgage in 3 years and that he can save money at $i^{(1)} = 3\%$, which mortgage should he choose?

10. A house sells for $450 000. The buyer makes a down payment of $150 000 and finances the rest with a $300 000 mortgage. He is offered a 30-year mortgage at $i^{(12)} = 6\%$ from a lender who charges three points.
    a) What is the true interest rate on the loan?
    b) If the buyer moves after 3 years, what is the true interest rate on the loan?

11. In the U.S., mortgage interest is tax deductible. The Guos buy a condominium unit in the U. S. on August 1, 2012, for $420 000. They pay $100 000 down and get a 3-year mortgage for the balance at $i^{(12)} = 7\%$. The loan payment will be rounded up to the nearest dime. The first repayment is on October 1, 2012.
    a) Show the first and last three lines of the amortization schedule. Assume the mortgage is not re-negotiated.
    b) How much mortgage interest can the Guos deduct on their 2012 U.S. income tax return?

Section 5.4   The Sinking-Fund Method of Retiring a Debt

Sinking Funds

When a specified amount of money is needed at a specified future date, it is a good practice to accumulate systematically a fund by means of equal periodic deposits. Such a fund is called a **sinking fund**. Sinking funds are used to pay off debts, to redeem bond issues, to replace worn-out equipment, or to buy new equipment.

Because the amount needed in the sinking fund, the time when the amount is needed, and the interest rate that the fund earns are known, we have an annuity problem in which the size of the payment, the sinking-fund deposit, is to be determined. A schedule showing how a sinking fund accumulates to the desired amount is called a **sinking-fund schedule**.

EXAMPLE 1   An eight-storey condominium apartment building consists of 146 two-bedroom apartment units of equal size. The board of directors of the Homeowners' Association estimated that the building will need new carpeting in the halls at a cost of $78 000 in 5 years.

Assuming that the association can invest its money at $i^{(12)} = 5.4\%$, what should be the monthly sinking-fund assessment per unit?

Solution   The sinking-fund deposits form an ordinary simple annuity with $S = 78\,000$, $i = 0.0045$, $n = 60$.

$$
\begin{array}{ccccccc}
& R & R & & R & R & R \\
\hline
0 & 1 & 2 & \cdots & 58 & 59 & 60 \\
& & & & & & \uparrow \\
& & & & & & S = 78\,000
\end{array}
$$

We calculate the total monthly sinking-fund deposit

$$R = \frac{78\,000}{s_{\overline{60}|0.0045}} = \$1135.30 \text{ (rounded off)}$$

Per-unit assessment should be

$$\frac{1135.30}{146} = \$7.78$$

EXAMPLE 2   Show the first three lines and the last two lines of the sinking-fund schedule, explaining the growth of the fund in Example 1.

Solution   At the end of the first month, a deposit of $1135.30 is made and the fund contains $1135.30. This amount earns interest at 0.45% for 1 month, i.e., $1135.30(0.0045) = \$5.11$. Thus the total increase at the end of the second month is the second payment plus interest on the amount in the fund, i.e.,

$1135.30 + $5.11 = $1140.41, and the fund will contain $2275.71. This procedure may be repeated to complete the entire schedule.

In order to complete the last two lines of the sinking-fund schedule without running the complete schedule, we may calculate the amount in the fund at the end of the 58th month as the accumulated value of 58 payments, i.e.,

$$1135.30 s_{\overline{58}|0.0045} = \$75\ 047.82$$

and complete the schedule from that point. The calculations are tabulated below.

End of the Month	Interest on Fund at $\frac{2}{3}$%	Deposit	Increase in Fund	Amount in Fund
1	—	1135.30	1135.30	1135.30
2	5.11	1135.30	1140.41	2275.71
3	10.24	1135.30	1145.54	3421.25
⋮	⋮	⋮	⋮	⋮
58				75 047.82
59	337.72	1135.30	1473.02	76 520.84
60	344.34	1134.82*	1479.16	78 000.00

*The last deposit is adjusted to have the final amount in the fund equal $78 000.

In General — Sinking-Fund Schedules

Consider an amount S dollars to be accumulated with level deposits of R dollars into a sinking fund at the end of each period for n periods, at rate i per period. The kth line of the sinking-fund schedule ($1 \leq k < n$) is:

a) Interest on fund $= iRs_{\overline{k-1}|i} = R[(1 + i)^{k-1} - 1]$
b) Increase in fund $= R + R[(1 + i)^{k-1} - 1] = R(1 + i)^{k-1}$
c) Amount in fund $= Rs_{\overline{k}|i}$

In Example 2, the 3rd line of the sinking-fund schedule can be calculated as:

Interest on fund $= \$1135.30[(1.0045)^2 - 1] = \$10.24$
Increase in fund $= \$1135.30(1.0045)^2 = \$1145.54$
Amount in fund $= \$1135.30 s_{\overline{3}|.0045} = \$3421.25$

EXAMPLE 3 Prepare an Excel spreadsheet and show the first 3 months and the last 3 months of the sinking-fund schedule of Example 2 above.

Solution We reserve cells A1 through E1 for headings. In cell F3, enter the final amount, 78 000. In cell F2, enter the interest rate earned by the sinking fund by typing =0.054/12. In cell F4, calculate the sinking-fund deposit by typing

=ROUNDUP(F3/(((1+F2)^60−1)/F2),2). The entries are summarized in the table below.

	CELL	ENTER	INTERPRETATION
Headings	A1	Deposit #	'Deposit number' or 'End of the month #'
	B1	Interest	'Interest on fund'
	C1	Deposit	'Monthly deposit'
	D1	Increase	'Increase in fund'
	E1	Amount	'Amount in fund'
Line 0	A2	0	Time starts
	E2	0	Amount in fund at the beginning of month 1
Line 1	A3	=A2+1	End of month 1
	B3	=E2*F2	Interest on fund at the end of month 1
	C3	F4	Monthly deposit
	D3	=B3+C3	Increase in fund at the end of month 1
	E3	=E2+D3	Amount in fund at the end of month 1

To generate the complete schedule copy A3.E3 to A4.E62
To get the last deposit adjust C62=E62−E61−B62

Below are the first 3 months and the last 3 months of the sinking-fund schedule.

	A	B	C	D	E
1	Deposit#	Interest	Deposit	Increase	Amount
2	0				0
3	1	0	1,135.30	1,135.30	1,135.30
4	2	5.11	1,135.30	1,140.41	2,275.71
5	3	10.24	1,135.30	1,145.54	3,421.25
:	:	:	:	:	:
60	58	331.12	1,135.30	1,466.42	75,047.82
61	59	337.72	1,135.30	1,473.02	76,520.83
62	60	344.34	1,134.82	1,479.17	78,000.00

Sinking-Fund Method of Retiring a Debt

An alternative method of paying off a loan is to pay the interest on the loan at the end of each interest period and to pay back the principal in one lump sum at the end of the term of the loan. To ensure that the borrower has enough money at the end of the term to repay the original principal in one lump sum, a sinking fund is often set up to accumulate the required amount. At the end of the term of the loan, the borrower returns the whole principal by transferring the accumulated value of the sinking fund to the lender.

This type of loan is often referred to as a **sinking-fund loan**. Sinking-fund loans are not commonly used for consumer loans, but are reasonably common for long-term corporate or government loans. The sinking-fund method of retiring a debt is also used by corporations and governments that raise money by issuing bonds and is discussed in chapter 6.

Under a sinking-fund loan, the borrower is making two series of payments. One is the interest payments to the lender and the other is the deposits into the sinking fund. Usually, the deposits into the sinking fund are made at the same times as the interest payments on the debt are made to the lender. This leads to one of the two main values that we are interested in calculating in this section:

> **Periodic cost of the debt = Interest payment to lender + Sinking-fund deposit**

The periodic cost of the debt (also referred to as the periodic expense of the debt) represents the total cash outlay the borrower must make each period.

Borrowers are also interested in how much of the loan remains to be repaid at any time. Technically, the outstanding balance of the loan is always equal to the original principal because the borrower is not making any payments toward reducing the principal (as is done for an amortized loan). However, the borrower is accumulating money in a sinking fund. In theory, the accumulated value of the sinking fund can be used to partially pay off the principal at any time. This leads to the following definition:

> **Book value of the debt = Original principal − Accumulated value of the sinking fund**

The book value of the debt can be thought of as the outstanding balance of the loan. It should also be noted that there are two interest rates associated with sinking-fund loans and you need to fully understand which rate is for what use. One interest rate is associated with paying interest on the loan and can be thought of as the lending rate that is paid by the borrower. The other interest rate is the rate that the sinking fund earns and can be thought of as a savings rate that is earned by the borrower.

A sinking-fund schedule can be set up using the same method and headings as shown earlier in this section. The only difference is that you would usually add an extra column to show the book value of the debt.

EXAMPLE 4   A city issues $1 000 000 of bonds paying interest at $i^{(2)} = 6\frac{1}{8}\%$, and by law it is required to create a sinking fund to redeem the bonds at the end of 8 years. If the fund is invested at $i^{(2)} = 5\%$, calculate a) the semi-annual expense of the debt; b) the book value of the city's indebtedness at the beginning of the 7th year.

Solution a   Semi-annual interest payment on the debt: $1 000 000 $\left(\dfrac{0.06125}{2}\right) = \$30\ 625.00$

Semi-anuual deposit into the sinking fund: $R = \dfrac{\$1\ 000\ 000}{s_{\overline{16}|0.025}} \doteq \underline{\$51\ 598.99}$

Semi-annual expense of the debt: $= \$82\ 223.99$

Solution b   The amount in the sinking fund at the end of the 6th year is the accumulated value of the deposits; i.e.,

$$\$51\ 598.99 s_{\overline{12}|0.025} = \$711\ 836.60$$

The book value of the city's indebtedness at the beginning of the 7th year is then

$$\$1\ 000\ 000 - \$711\ 836.60 = \$288\ 163.40$$

EXAMPLE 5   A loan of \$15 000 is taken out. Interest payments are due every 3 months. A sinking fund is set up to pay back the \$15 000 in one lump sum at the end of 6 years. The sinking fund earns $i^{(4)} = 4\%$ and deposits are made quarterly. The quarterly expense of the debt is \$867.35. Calculate a) the interest rate on the loan, $i^{(4)}$; b) the book value of the debt after 2 years.

Solution a   The quarterly sinking-fund deposit is

$$\frac{15\ 000}{s_{\overline{24}|0.01}} \doteq \$556.10$$

Let the quarterly loan interest rate be i. The quarterly expense of the debt is

$$867.35 = 15\ 000i + 556.10$$

which when solved for i gives

$$i = (867.35 - 556.10)/15\ 000 = 0.02075$$

Hence, for $i^{(4)}$:

$$i^{(4)} = 4i = 8.30\%$$

The interest rate on the sinking-fund loan is 8.30% compounded quarterly.

Solution b   The book value of the debt after 2 years (8 payments) is

$$\$15\ 000 - \$556.10 s_{\overline{8}|0.01} = \$15\ 000 - \$4607.66 = \$10\ 392.34$$

Exercise 5.4

Part A

1. A couple is saving a down payment for a home. They want to have $15 000 at the end of 4 years in an account paying interest at $i^{(1)} = 6\%$. How much must be deposited in the fund at the end of each year? Make out a schedule showing the growth of the fund.

2. A company wants to save $100 000 over the next 5 years so it can expand its plant facility. How much must be deposited at the end of each year if the money earns interest at $i^{(1)} = 8\%$? Make out a schedule for this problem.

3. Determine the quarterly deposits necessary to accumulate $10 000 over 10 years in a sinking fund earning interest at $i^{(4)} = 6\%$. Determine the amount in the fund at the end of 9 years and complete the rest of the schedule.

4. A city needs to have $2 000 000 at the end of 15 years to retire a bond issue. What annual deposits will be necessary if the money earns interest at $i^{(1)} = 7\%$? How much interest does the fund earn in the 4th year? What is the increase in the fund in the 9th year? How much is in the fund at the end of 11 years?

5. In its manufacturing process, a company uses a machine that costs $75 000 and is scrapped at the end of 15 years with a value of $5000. The company sets up a sinking fund to finance the replacement of the machine, assuming no change in price, with level payments at the end of each year. Money can be invested at an annual effective interest rate of 4%. Determine the value of the sinking fund at the end of the 10th year.

6. A borrower of $5000 agrees to pay interest semi-annually at $i^{(2)} = 10\%$ on the loan and to build up a sinking fund, which will repay the loan at the end of 5 years. If the sinking fund accumulates at $i^{(2)} = 4\%$, determine his total semi-annual expense. How much is in the sinking fund at the end of 4 years?

7. A city borrows $1 250 000, paying interest annually on this sum at $i^{(1)} = 6.25\%$. What

annual deposits must be made into a sinking fund earning interest at $i^{(1)} = 3\frac{1}{2}\%$ in order to pay off the entire principal at the end of 15 years? What is the total annual expense of the debt?

8. A company issues $500 000 worth of bonds, paying interest at $i^{(2)} = 8\%$. A sinking fund with semi-annual deposits accumulating at $i^{(2)} = 4\%$ is established to redeem the bonds at the end of 20 years. Determine
   a) the semi-annual expense of the debt;
   b) the book value of the company's indebtedness at the end of the 15th year.

9. A city borrows $2 000 000 to build a sewage treatment plant. The debt requires interest at $i^{(2)} = 10\%$. At the same time, a sinking fund is established, which earns interest at $i^{(2)} = 4\frac{1}{2}\%$ to repay the debt in 25 years. Determine
   a) the semi-annual expense of the debt;
   b) the book value of the city's indebtedness at the beginning of the 16th year.

10. On a debt of $4000, interest is paid monthly at $i^{(12)} = 12\%$ and monthly deposits are made into a sinking fund to retire the debt at the end of 5 years. If the sinking fund earns interest at $i^{(4)} = 3.6\%$, what is the monthly expense of the debt?

11. On a debt of $10 000, interest is paid semi-annually at $i^{(2)} = 10\%$ and semi-annual deposits are made into a sinking fund to retire the debt at the end of 5 years. If the sinking fund earns interest at $i^{(12)} = 6\%$, what is the semi-annual expense of the debt?

12. Interest at $i^{(2)} = 12\%$ on a loan of $3000 must be paid semi-annually as it falls due. A sinking fund accumulating at $i^{(4)} = 8\%$ is established to enable the debtor to repay the loan at the end of 4 years.
   a) Determine the semi-annual sinking-fund deposit and construct the last two lines of the sinking-fund schedule, based on semi-annual deposits.
   b) Determine the semi-annual expense of the loan.

c) What is the outstanding principal (book value of the loan) at the end of 2 years?

13. A 10-year loan of $10 000 at $i^{(1)} = 11\%$ is to be repaid by the sinking-fund method, with interest and sinking-fund payments made at the end of each year. The rate of interest earned in the sinking fund is $i^{(1)} = 5\%$. Immediately after the 5th year's payment, the lender requests that the outstanding principal be repaid in one lump sum. Calculate the amount of extra cash the borrower has to raise in order to extinguish the debt.

Part B

1. A sinking fund is being accumulated at $i^{(12)} = 6\%$ by deposits of $200 per month. If the fund contains $5394.69 just after the kth deposit, what did it contain just after the $(k - 1)$st deposit?

2. You borrow $L to be repaid in n years. If you amortize the loan, the interest rate is i_1 per annum. If you repay the loan using a sinking fund, you will pay interest on the $L loan at rate i_2 per annum and you will accumulate $L in a sinking fund at rate i_3 per annum.
   a) Determine the annual cost of the loan under the amortization method and under the sinking-fund method.
   b) If $i_1 = i_2 = i_3 = i$ per annum, show that the two methods of repaying the loan are equivalent in cost.

3. A company issues $2 000 000 worth of bonds paying interest at $i^{(12)} = 10\frac{1}{2}\%$. A sinking fund accumulating at $i^{(4)} = 6\%$ with monthly deposits is established to redeem the bonds at the end of 15 years. Determine
   a) the monthly expense of the debt;
   b) the book value of the company's indebtedness at the beginning of the 6th year.

4. A man is repaying a $10 000 loan by the sinking-fund method. His total monthly expense is $300. Out of this $300, interest is paid to the lender at $i^{(12)} = 12\%$ and a deposit is made to a sinking fund earning $i^{(12)} = 9\%$. Determine the duration of the loan and the final smaller payment.

5. A $100 000 loan is to be repaid in 15 years, with a sinking fund accumulated to repay principal *plus interest*. The loan charges $i^{(2)} = 12\%$, while the sinking fund earns $i^{(2)} = 5\%$. What semi-annual sinking fund deposit is required?

6. A loan of $20 000 bears interest on the amount outstanding at $i^{(1)} = 10\%$. A deposit is to be made in a sinking fund earning interest at $i^{(1)} = 4\%$, which will accumulate enough to pay one-half of the principal at the end of 10 years. In addition, the debtor will make level payments to the creditor, which will pay interest at $i^{(1)} = 10\%$ on the outstanding balance first and the remainder will repay the principal. What is the total annual payment, including that made to the creditor and that deposited in the sinking fund, if the loan is to be completely retired at the end of 10 years?

7. John borrows $10 000 for 10 years and uses a sinking fund to repay the principal. The sinking-fund deposits earn an annual effective interest rate of 5%. The total required payment for both the interest and the sinking-fund deposit made at the end of each year is $1445.05. Calculate the annual effective interest rate charged on the loan.

8. A company borrows $10 000 for 5 years. Interest of $600 is paid semi-annually. To repay the principal of the loan at the end of 5 years, equal semi-annual deposits are made into a sinking fund that credits interest at a nominal rate of 8% compounded quarterly. The first payment is due in 6 months. Calculate the annual effective rate of interest that the company is paying to service and retire the debt.

9. On August 1, 2010, Mrs. Chan borrows $20 000 for 10 years. Interest at 11% compounded semi-annually must be paid as it falls due. The principal is replaced by means of level deposits on February 1 and August 1 in years 2011 to 2020 (inclusive) into a sinking fund earning $i^{(1)} = 7\%$ in 2011 through December 31, 2015, and $i^{(1)} = 6\%$ January 1, 2016, through 2020.
   a) Calculate the semi-annual expense of the loan.
   b) How much is in the sinking fund just after the August 1, 2019, deposit?

c) Show the sinking-fund schedule entries at February 1, 2020, and August 1, 2020.

10. Mr. White borrows $15 000 for 10 years. He makes total payments, annually, of $2000. The lender receives $i^{(1)} = 10\%$ on his investment each year for the first 5 years and $i^{(1)} = 8\%$ for the second 5 years. The balance of each payment is invested in a sinking fund earning $i^{(1)} = 7\%$.

a) Determine the amount by which the sinking fund is short of repaying the loan at the end of 10 years.

b) By how much would the sinking-fund deposit (in each of the first 5 years only) need to be increased so that the sinking fund at the end of 10 years will be just sufficient to repay the loan?

Section 5.5   Comparison of Amortization and Sinking-Fund Methods

We have discussed the two most common methods of paying off long-term loans: the amortization method and the sinking-fund method. When there are several sources available from which to borrow money, it is important to know how to compare the available loans and choose the cheapest one. The borrower should choose that source for which the periodic expense of the debt is the lowest. When the amortization method is used, the periodic expense of the debt is equal to the periodic amortization payment. When the sinking-fund method is used, the periodic expense of the debt is the sum of the interest payment and the sinking-fund deposit.

To study the relationship between the amortization and sinking-fund methods, we define the following:

A = principal of the loan
n = number of interest periods during the term of the loan
i_1 = loan rate per interest period using amortization
i_2 = loan rate per interest period using the sinking fund
i_3 = sinking-fund rate per interest period
R_A = periodic expense using amortization = $\dfrac{A}{a_{\overline{n}|i_1}} = A\left(\dfrac{1}{s_{\overline{n}|i_1}} + i_1\right)$

(See Exercise 3.3 Part B question 1b)

R_S = periodic expense using sinking fund = $\dfrac{A}{s_{\overline{n}|i_3}} + Ai_2 = A\left(\dfrac{1}{s_{\overline{n}|i_3}} + i_2\right)$

We shall examine the relationship between R_A and R_S for different levels of rates i_1, i_2, i_3.

Case I: $i_1 = i_2$ (Interest rate on amortized loan = Interest rate on sinking-fund loan)

a) Let $i_1 = i_2 = i_3 = i$, then $R_A = R_S$

b) Let $i_3 > i_1 = i_2$, then $i_3 > i_1$ implies

$$s_{\overline{n}|i_3} > s_{\overline{n}|i_1}$$

$$\frac{1}{s_{\overline{n}|i_1}} > \frac{1}{s_{\overline{n}|i_3}}$$

$$\frac{1}{s_{\overline{n}|i_1}} + i_1 > \frac{1}{s_{\overline{n}|i_3}} + i_2$$

$$R_A > R_S$$

c) Let $i_3 < i_1 = i_2$, then $i_3 < i_1$ implies

$$s_{\overline{n}|i_3} < s_{\overline{n}|i_1}$$

$$\frac{1}{s_{\overline{n}|i_1}} < \frac{1}{s_{\overline{n}|i_3}}$$

$$\frac{1}{s_{\overline{n}|i_1}} + i_1 < \frac{1}{s_{\overline{n}|i_3}} + i_2$$

$$R_A < R_S$$

Case c) is the most common situation, where savings rate < lending rate. This means the amortized loan will always be cheaper. So, why would anyone take out a loan and pay it back using the sinking-fund method? There are two potential reasons:

1. Under a sinking-fund loan, the sinking-fund deposit usually remains under the control of the borrower. That means the borrower can miss making a sinking-fund deposit (as long as they make it up later). Also, the borrower can take some risk in investing the deposits and perhaps earn a higher rate of return on the sinking fund.

2. The borrower can usually negotiate a lower rate of interest on a sinking-fund loan. This situation is covered in *Case II* below.

Case II: $i_1 > i_2$ (*Interest rate on amortized loan > Interest rate on sinking-fund loan*)

Let $i_3 < i_2 < i_1$. In this case, which is the most common, we can't tell which method is cheaper. We must calculate the actual periodic costs to determine the cheaper source of money, i.e., the source with the smallest periodic expense.

EXAMPLE 1   A company wishes to borrow $500\ 000$ for 5 years. One source will lend the money at $i^{(2)} = 10\%$ if it is amortized by semi-annual payments. A second source will lend the money at $i^{(2)} = 8\%$ if only the interest is paid semi-annually and the principal is returned in a lump sum at the end of 5 years. If the second source is used, a sinking fund will be established by semi-annual deposits that accumulate at $i^{(12)} = 4.2\%$. How much can the company save semi-annually by using the better plan?

Solution   When the first source is used, the semi-annual expense of the debt is

$$R_A = \frac{\$500\ 000}{a_{\overline{10}|0.05}} \doteq \$64\ 752.29$$

When the second source is used, the interest on the debt paid semi-annually is 4% of $500 000 = $20 000.

To calculate the semi-annual deposit into the sinking fund, we must first calculate the semi-annual rate i equivalent to $i^{(12)} = 4.2\%$

$$(1 + i)^2 = (1.0035)^{12}$$
$$i = (1.0035)^6 - 1$$
$$i = 0.021184609$$

Now we calculate the semi-annual deposit R into the sinking fund

$$R = \frac{\$500\ 000}{s_{\overline{10}|i}} = \$45\ 416.52$$

The semi-annual expense of the debt using the second source is

$$R_S = \$20\ 000 + \$45\ 416.52 = \$65\ 416.52$$

Thus, the first source, using amortization, is cheaper and the company can save

$$\$65\ 416.52 - \$64\ 752.29 \text{ or } \$664.23 \text{ semi-annually.}$$

EXAMPLE 2   A firm wants to borrow $500 000. One source will lend the money at $i^{(4)} = 10\%$ if interest is paid quarterly and the principal is returned in a lump sum at the end of 10 years. The firm can set up a sinking fund at $i^{(4)} = 7\%$. At what rate $i^{(4)}$ would it be less expensive to amortize the debt over 10 years?

Solution   We calculate the quarterly expense of the debt.

Interest payment:	$\$500\ 000 \times 0.025 = \$12\ 500.00$
Sinking-fund deposit:	$\dfrac{\$500\ 000}{s_{\overline{40}|0.0175}} \doteq \$\ 8\ 736.05$
Quarterly expense:	$= \$21\ 236.05$

The amortization method will be as expensive if the quarterly amortization payment is equal to $21 236.05. Thus, we want to determine the interest rate i per quarter (and then $i^{(4)}$) given $A = 500\ 000$, $R = 21\ 236.05$, $n = 40$.

We have

$$500\ 000 = 21\ 236.05 a_{\overline{40}|i}$$
$$a_{\overline{40}|i} = 23.544868$$

We want to determine the rate $i^{(4)} = 4i$ such that $a_{\overline{40}|i} = 23.5449$. A starting value to solve $a_{\overline{40}|i} = 23.5449$ is

$$i = \frac{1 - (\frac{23.5449}{40})^2}{23.5449}$$

or $i^{(4)} = 4i = 11.10\%$. Using linear interpolation, we calculate

		$a_{\overline{40}|i}$	$i^{(4)}$		
		24.0781	11%		
0.9633	0.5332	23.5449	$i^{(4)}$	d	1%
		23.1148	12%		

$$\frac{d}{1\%} = \frac{0.5332}{0.9663}$$
$$d \doteq 0.55\%$$
and $i^{(4)} = 11.55\%$

If the firm can borrow the money and amortize the debt at less than $i^{(4)} = 11.55\%$, then it will be less expensive than a straight loan at $i^{(4)} = 10\%$ with a sinking fund at $i^{(4)} = 7\%$.

Exercise 5.5

Part A

1. A company borrows $50 000 to be repaid in equal annual instalments at the end of each year for 10 years. Determine the total annual cost under the following conditions:
   a) the debt is amortized at $i^{(1)} = 9\%$;
   b) interest at 9% is paid on the debt and a sinking fund is set up at $i^{(1)} = 9\%$;
   c) interest at 9% is paid on the debt and a sinking fund is set up at $i^{(1)} = 6\%$.

2. A company can borrow $180 000 for 15 years. They can amortize the debt at $i^{(1)} = 10\%$, or they can pay interest on the loan at $i^{(1)} = 9\%$ and set up a sinking fund at $i^{(1)} = 7\%$ to repay the loan. Which plan is cheaper and by how much per annum?

3. A firm wants to borrow $60 000 to be repaid over 5 years. One source will lend the money at $i^{(2)} = 10\%$ if it is amortized by semi-annual payments. A second source will lend the money at $i^{(2)} = 9\frac{1}{2}\%$ if only the interest is paid semi-annually and the principal is returned in a lump sum at the end of 5 years. The firm can earn $i^{(2)} = 4\%$ on its savings. Which source should be used for the loan and how much will be saved each half-year?

4. A company can borrow $100 000 for 10 years by paying the interest as it falls due at $i^{(2)} = 9\%$ and setting up a sinking fund at $i^{(2)} = 7\%$ to repay the debt. At what rate, $i^{(2)}$, would an amortization plan have the same semi-annual cost?

5. A city can borrow $500 000 for 20 years by issuing bonds on which interest will be paid semi-annually at $i^{(2)} = 9\frac{1}{8}\%$. The principal will be paid off by a sinking fund consisting of semi-annual deposits invested at $i^{(2)} = 8\%$. Determine the nominal rate, $i^{(2)}$, at which the loan could be amortized at the same semi-annual cost.

6. A firm can borrow $200 000 at $i^{(1)} = 9\%$ and amortize the debt for 10 years. From a second source, the money can be borrowed at $i^{(1)} = 8\frac{1}{2}\%$ if the interest is paid annually and the principal is repaid in a lump sum at the end of 10 years. What yearly rate, $i^{(1)}$, must the sinking fund earn for the annual expense to be the same under the two options?

7. A company wants to borrow $500 000. One source of funds will agree to lend the money at $i^{(4)} = 8\%$ if interest is paid quarterly and the principal is paid in a lump sum at the end of 15 years. The firm can set up a sinking fund at $i^{(4)} = 6\%$ and will make quarterly deposits.
   a) What is the total quarterly cost of the loan?
   b) At what rate, $i^{(4)}$, would it be less expensive to amortize the debt over 15 years?

8. You are able to repay an $80 000 loan by either
   a) amortization at $i^{(12)} = 7\%$ with 12 monthly payments; or b) at $i^{(12)} = 6\frac{1}{2}\%$ using a sinking fund earning $i^{(12)} = 4\%$, and paid off in 1 year. Which method is cheaper?

Part B

1. A company needs to borrow $200 000 for 6 years. One source will lend the money at $i^{(2)} = 10\%$ if it is amortized by monthly payments. A second source will lend the money at $i^{(4)} = 9\%$ if only the interest is paid monthly and the principal is returned in a lump sum at the end of 6 years. The company can earn interest at $i^{(365)} = 6\%$ on the sinking fund. Which source should be used for the loan and how much will be saved monthly?

2. Tanya can borrow $10 000 by paying the interest on a loan as it falls due at $i^{(2)} = 12\%$ and by setting up a sinking fund with semi-annual deposits that accumulate at $i^{(12)} = 9\%$ over 10 years to repay the debt. At what rate, $i^{(4)}$, would an amortization scheme have the same semi-annual cost?

3. A loan of $100 000 at 8% per annum is to be repaid over 10 years; $20 000 by the

amortization method and $80 000 by the sinking-fund method, where the sinking fund can be accumulated with annual deposits at $i^{(4)} = 5\%$. What extra annual payment does the above arrangement require as compared to repayment of the whole loan by the amortization method?

4. A company wants to borrow a large amount of money for 15 years. One source would lend the money at $i^{(2)} = 9\%$, provided it is amortized over 15 years by monthly payments. The company could also raise the money by issuing bonds paying interest semi-annually at $i^{(2)} = 8\frac{1}{2}\%$ and redeemable at par in 15 years. In this case, the company would set up a sinking fund to accumulate the money needed for the redemption of the bonds at the end of 15 years. What rate, $i^{(12)}$, on the sinking fund would make the monthly expense the same under the two options?

5. A $10 000 loan is being repaid by the sinking-fund method. Total annual outlay (each year) is $1400 for as long as necessary, plus a smaller final payment made 1 year after the last regular payment. If the lender receives $i^{(1)} = 8\%$ and the sinking fund accumulates at $i^{(1)} = 6\%$, determine the time and amount of the irregular final payment.

6. A $5000 loan can be repaid quarterly for 5 years using amortization and an interest rate of $i^{(12)} = 10\%$ or by a sinking fund to repay both principal and accumulated interest. If paid by a sinking fund, the interest on the loan will be $i^{(12)} = 9\%$. What annual effective rate must the sinking fund earn to make the quarterly cost the same for both methods?

Section 5.6 **Summary and Review Exercises**

● Outstanding balance B_k (immediately after the kth payment has been made) by the retrospective method (looking back)

$$B_k = A(1 + i)^k - Rs_{\overline{k}|i}$$

by the prospective method (looking ahead) assuming all payments equal

$$B_k = Ra_{\overline{n-k}|i}$$

- Total interest = Total payments − Amount of loan

- For a loan of A dollars to be amortized with level payments of R dollars at the end of each period for n periods, at rate i per period, in the kth line of the amortization schedule ($1 \le k \le n$):

  Interest payment $I_k = R[1 - (1 + i)^{-(n-k+1)}]$
  Principal payment $P_k = R(1 + i)^{-(n-k+1)}$
  Outstanding balance $B_k = Ra_{\overline{n-k}|i}$
  Successive principal payments are in the ratio $1 + i$, that is $\dfrac{P_{k+1}}{P_k} = (1 + i)$.

- For a sinking fund designed to accumulate a specified amount of S dollars by equal deposits of R dollars at the end of each period for n periods, at rate i per period, in the kth line of the sinking-fund schedule ($1 \le k \le n$):

  $$\text{Interest on fund} = iRs_{\overline{k-1}|i} = R[(1 + i)^{k-1} - 1]$$
  $$\text{Increase in fund} = R + R[(1 + i)^{k-1} - 1] = R(1 + i)^{k-1}$$
  $$\text{Amount in fund} = Rs_{\overline{k-1}|i}$$

- When a loan A is paid off by the sinking-fund method, the borrower pays interest at i on the loan at the end of each period and accumulates the principal of the loan in a sinking fund earning r. The principal of the loan is repaid at the end of the term of the loan as a lump sum from the sinking fund.

  Periodic expense of the loan = Interest payment + Sinking-fund deposit
  $$= Ai + \frac{A}{s_{\overline{n}|r}}.$$

  Book value of the loan after k periods
  = Principal of the loan − Amount in the sinking fund
  $$= A - \left(\frac{A}{s_{\overline{n}|r}}\right)s_{\overline{k}|r}.$$

Review Exercises 5.6

1. Mr. Roberts borrows $15 000 to be repaid with monthly payments over 10 years at $i^{(12)} = 9\%$.
   a) Determine the monthly payment required.
   b) Determine the outstanding balance of the loan after 3 years (36 payments) and split the 37th payment into principal and interest under the amortization method.

2. A loan of $20 000 is to be amortized by 20 quarterly payments over 5 years at $i^{(12)} = 7\frac{1}{2}\%$. Split the 9th payment into principal and interest.

3. A loan of $10 000 is repaid by 5 equal annual payments at $i^{(2)} = 14\%$. What is the total amount of interest paid?

4. A company wants to borrow a large sum of money to be repaid over 10 years. The company can issue bonds paying interest at $i^{(2)} = 8\frac{1}{2}\%$ redeemable at par in 10 years. A sinking fund earning $i^{(12)} = 7\frac{1}{2}\%$ can be used to accumulate the amount needed in 10 years to redeem the bonds. At what rate, $i^{(12)}$, would the semi-annual cost be the same if the debt were amortized over 10 years?

5. Interest at $i^{(2)} = 10\%$ on a debt of $3000 must be paid as it falls due. A sinking fund accumulating at $i^{(4)} = 4\%$ is established to enable the debtor to repay the loan at the end of 4 years. Calculate the semi-annual sinking-fund deposit and construct the last two lines of the sinking-fund schedule.

6. For a $240\ 000 mortgage at $i^{(2)} = 10\%$ amortized over 25 years, determine
   a) the level monthly payment required;
   b) the outstanding balance just after the 48th payment;
   c) the principal portion of the 49th payment; and
   d) the total interest paid in the first 48 payments.

7. As part of the purchase of a home on January 1, 2010, you negotiated a mortgage in the amount of $220\ 000. The amortization period for calculation of the level payments (principal and interest) was 25 years and the initial interest rate was 6% compounded monthly.
   a) What was the initial monthly payment?
   b) During 2012–2016 inclusive (and January 1, 2017) all monthly mortgage payments were made as they became due. What was the balance of the loan owing just after the payment made January 1, 2017?
   c) At January 1, 2017 (just after the payment then due) the loan was renegotiated at 8% compounded semi-annually (with the end date of the amortization period unchanged). What was the new monthly payment?
   d) All payments, as above, have been faithfully made. How much of the September 1, 2017, payment will be principal and how much represents interest?

8. A couple has a $150\ 000, 5-year mortgage at $i^{(2)} = 9\%$ with a 20-year amortization period. After exactly 3 years (36 payments) they could renegotiate a new mortgage at $i^{(2)} = 7\%$. If the bank charges an interest penalty of three times the monthly interest due on the outstanding balance at the time of renegotiation, what will their new monthly payment be?

9. Janet wants to borrow $10\ 000 to be repaid over 10 years. From one source, money can be borrowed at $i^{(1)} = 10\%$ and amortized by annual payments. From a second source, money can be borrowed at $i^{(1)} = 9\%$ if only the interest is paid annually and the principal repaid at the end of 10 years. If the second source is used, a sinking fund will be established by annual deposits that accumulate at $i^{(4)} = 7\%$. How much can Janet save annually by using the better plan?

10. Given the following information, calculate the original value of the loan.

Payment #	Interest	Principal
1		10.00
2	389.00	
3		
4		13.31

11. The XYZ Mortgage Company lends you $100\ 000 at 9% compounded semi-annually. The loan is to be repaid by monthly payments at the end of each month for 20 years and the rate is guaranteed for 5 years.
    a) Determine the monthly payment.
    b) Determine the total amount of interest paid over the first 5 years.
    c) Split the first monthly payment into principal and interest portions based on the amortization method.
    d) If after 5 years of payments interest rates have increased to 11% compounded semi-annually, determine the new monthly payment at time of mortgage renegotiation exactly 5 years after the original loan agreement based on the amortization method.

12. A loan of $2000 is being repaid by equal monthly payments for an unspecified length of time. Interest on the loan is $i^{(12)} = 15\%$.
    a) If the amount of principal in the 4th payment is $40, what amount of the 18th payment will be principal?
    b) Determine the regular monthly payment.

13. On a loan at $i^{(12)} = 12\%$ with monthly payments, the amount of principal in the 8th payment is $62.
    a) Find the amount of principal in the 14th payment.
    b) If there are 48 equal payments in all, calculate the amount of the loan.

14. Given the following part of an amortization schedule, determine X.

Payment #	Interest	Principal	Balance
1	50 000	180 975	819 025
2			
3			X

15. A couple purchases a home worth $450 000 by paying $90 000 down and taking out a mortgage for $360 000 at a 5-year rate of $i^{(2)} = 7.25\%$. The mortgage will be amortized over 25 years with equal monthly payments. How much of the principal is repaid during the first year?

16. You take out an $80 000 mortgage at $i^{(2)} = 9\%$ with a 25-year amortization period.
   a) Determine the monthly payment required, rounded up to the next dime.
   b) Determine the reduced final payment.
   c) Determine the total interest paid during the 4th year.
   d) At the end of 4 years, you pay down an additional $2500 (no penalty).
      i) How much sooner will the mortgage be paid off?
      ii) What would be the difference in total payments over the life of the mortgage?

17. A company decides to borrow $100 000 at $i^{(1)} = 12\%$ in order to finance a new equipment purchase. One of the conditions of the loan is that the company must make annual payments into a sinking fund (the sinking fund will be used to pay off the loan at the end of 20 years). The sinking-fund investment will earn $i^{(1)} = 6\%$.
   a) What is the amount of each sinking-fund payment if they are all to be equal?
   b) What is the total annual cost of the loan?
   c) What overall annual effective compound interest rate is the company paying to borrow the $100 000 when account is taken of the sinking-fund requirement?

18. A $50 000 loan at $i^{(1)} = 7\%$ is to be amortized over 15 years by annual payments.
   a) Determine the regular payment and the reduced final payment.
   b) The borrower accumulates the money for each annual payment by making 12 monthly deposits into a sinking fund earning $i^{(12)} = 6\%$. Determine the size of each deposit for the first 14 years.

19. A home is being sold for $550 000. The buyer pays $150 000 down and gets a $400 000 25-year mortgage at $i^{(12)} = 7\%$ from a lender who charges 3 points:
   a) What is the true interest rate of the loan?
   b) If the buyer moves after four years, what is the true interest rate of the loan?

20. A couple buys a condominium in the U. S. on May 1, 2012 for $650 000. They make a 20% down payment and get a 29-year mortgage loan at $i^{(12)} = 10\%$ for the balance; the loan is to be amortized by equal monthly payments rounded up to the nearest dime. If they make the first payment on June 1, 2012, how much interest can they deduct when they prepare their U.S. income tax return for 2012? Show the first and last three lines of the amortization schedule.

21. With mortgage rates at $i^{(12)} = 8\%$, the ABC Savings and Loans Company makes a special offer to its customers. It will lend mortgage money and determine the monthly payment for the next five years as if $i^{(12)} = 7\%$. Over the five-year period, the mortgage will be carried at $i^{(12)} = 8\%$ and any deficiency that results will be added to the outstanding balance to be refinanced in five years time. If the Browns are taking out a $180 000 mortgage to be repaid over 25 years under this scheme, calculate their outstanding balance at the end of five years.

22. XYZ Savings and Loans issues mortgages in which payments are determined by the rate of interest that prevails on the day the loan is made. After that, the rate of interest varies according to market forces but the monthly payments do not change in dollar size. Instead, the length of time to full repayment is either lengthened (if interest rates rise) or shortened (if interest rates fall). Mr. Adams takes out a 20-year, $700 000 mortgage at $i^{(12)} = 4\frac{1}{2}\%$. After exactly two years (24 payments) interest rates change. Determine the duration of the loan and the final smaller payment if the new interest rate stays fixed at (a) $i^{(12)} = 5\%$, (b) $i^{(12)} = 4\%$.

CASE STUDY 1   *Comparison of Amortization and Sinking-Fund Methods*

A \$10 000 loan at $i^{(12)} = 12\%$ is to be paid off by monthly payments for 5 years. Using

a) the amortization method,
b) the sinking-fund method, with $i^{(365)} = 6\frac{1}{2}\%$ on the sinking fund, calculate and compare
   i) the monthly expense of the loan;
   ii) the outstanding balance of the loan at the end of 2 years; and
   iii) the interest and principal payment at the end of the 1st month and at the end of 2 years.

CASE STUDY 2   *Increasing Extra Annual Payments*

A \$100 000 mortgage is taken out at $i^{(12)} = 7\%$, to be amortized over 25 years by monthly payments. Payments are rounded up to the *next dime* and the final payment is reduced accordingly.

a) Calculate the regular monthly payment and the reduced final payment.
b) Suppose extra payments are made at the end of every year to get the mortgage paid off sooner. Determine the time and amount of the last payment on the mortgage if these extra payments are: \$300 at the end of year 1, \$350 at the end of year 2, \$400 at the end of year 3, \$450 at the end of year 4, ... (increasing by \$50 each year).

CASE STUDY 3   *Mortgage Amortization*

A \$90 000 mortgage at $i^{(2)} = 9\%$ is amortized over 25 years by monthly payments.

a) Determine the regular monthly payment and the smaller final payment.
b) Determine the total interest (total cost of financing).
c) Show the first three lines of the amortization schedule.
d) Determine the outstanding balance after 2 years.
e) Determine the total principal and the total interest paid in the first 2 years.
f) Suppose you paid an extra \$1000 after 2 years. How much interest would this save over the life of the mortgage?
g) How much less interest would be paid if the mortgage could be amortized over 20 years rather than 25 years?
h) In the 25-year mortgage, after 2 years interest rates drop to $i^{(2)} = 8.5\%$. There is a penalty of 3 months interest on the outstanding balance for early repayment. Does it pay to refinance?

CASE STUDY 4   *Accelerated Mortgage Payments*

"Invest" that extra money back into your mortgage.

Does it pay to accelerate mortgage payments in a low-interest-rate environment?

Interest rates have dropped so low, relative to what they were a few years ago, that you have to wonder if there is any merit to stepping up the mortgage payments on your home. After all, there's a temptation to invest—or spend—the difference between today's payments and the ones you made a few years ago.

Forget it. Your humble, terribly dull mortgage is a far better investment.

The reason: Our tax system will force you to pay tax on any earnings from your investment. If you pay down your mortgage, there's no tax on the interest you save.

Most lenders offer a number of strategies to save you money.

- Provided you can afford it, consider a shorter amortization period when your mortgage comes up for renewal. For instance, if you had an $i^{(12)} = 10\%$ mortgage and renewed at $i^{(12)} = 7\%$, continue to pay at the old rate, instead of the reduced new one. It will shorten the amortization because the difference will be applied to the principal.

  Assuming you had a 25-year $100 000 mortgage at $i^{(12)} = 10\%$, calculate your monthly payment. If the rate drops to $i^{(12)} = 7\%$, calculate the new monthly payment.

  What difference is another couple of hundred bucks going to make? Plenty. If you continue to make the old monthly payments, find the new amortization period.

- Another strategy is to take advantage of any opportunity to make larger monthly payments. For instance, some banks allow a "10 plus 10" plan, in which you can increase your monthly payments by up to 10%. Some banks go a bit further and allow borrowers to "double up" their monthly mortgage payments—that is, pay up to an additional 100% of the payment any or every month of the year. How much interest would you save over the life of the mortgage under each option?

- Finally, consider an accelerated weekly mortgage. Divide your monthly payment by 4, and pay that amount on a weekly basis. That means that you will be painlessly paying the equivalent of 13 months in the space of a year. If you do that, then you'll make larger payments, but knock several years of payments off a 25-year mortgage. For a 25-year mortgage at $i^{(12)} = 6\%$ how many years of payments can you save?

CASE STUDY 5   *Sub-Prime Mortgages*

In the period 2001 to 2008 many lenders extended mortgages to borrowers who previously would not have qualified. They also made first-time home ownership easier by offering very low initial interest rates that often later rose to more ordinary levels. Concerns about mortgage defaults were muted by the assumption that house values could only go up (as they had for many years). Let's look at an example.

The Chens wish to buy a \$400 000 home. The bank is willing to lend them the full \$400 000. The monthly payment will be calculated using $i^{(2)} = 4\%$ with a 40-year repayment period. However, after 3 years payments will be recalculated at $i^{(2)} = 7\%$ (with 37 years left on the mortgage).

Note: The sub-prime mortgage problem was more of a crisis in the United States, where banks often lent money without regard to whether the borrower had income or a job; in Canada this was less of a problem. However, there was still a short period of time when Canadian banks offered mortgages with an initial low interest rate and a 40-year repayment period.

a) Calculate the initial monthly payment.
b) Calculate the monthly payment starting in year 4.
c) If house prices had dropped during that 3-year period, what might the Chens be tempted to do?

CHAPTER 6

BONDS

Learning Objectives

One of the primary ways for governments and publicly listed corporations to raise capital is to issue bonds. Bonds are a method used to borrow money from a large number of investors to help raise funds to finance long-term debt. From the investor's point of view, bonds provide steady periodic interest payments along with returning the amount borrowed at some point in the future.

Upon completing this chapter, you will be able to do the following:

- Understand bond terminology.
- Determine the purchase price of bonds, redeemable at par or otherwise, bought on coupon dates.
- Calculate the premium or discount on the purchase of a bond.
- Set up a bond schedule showing either the amortization of a premium or the accumulation of a discount.
- Calculate the price of a callable bond, where the redemption date is not guaranteed.
- Determine the purchase price of bonds bought between coupon dates.
- Determine the rate of return on a bond using either the method of averages or linear interpolation.
- Discuss other types of bonds, including zero-coupon bonds and strip bonds.

Section 6.1 ## Introduction and Terminology

When a corporation, municipality, or government needs a large sum of money for a long period of time, they issue **bonds**, sometimes called debentures, which are sold to a number of investors. Thus bonds are a form of debt.

A bond is a written contract between the issuer (borrower) and the investor (lender) that specifies:

- The **face value**, or the **denomination**, of the bond, which is stated on the front of the bond. This is usually a multiple of 100 such as $100, $500, $1000, $5000, or $10 000.
- The **redemption date**, or **maturity date**; that is, the date on which the loan (bond) will be repaid.

- The **bond rate**, or **coupon rate**; that is, the rate at which the bond pays interest on its face value at equal time intervals until the maturity date. In most cases this rate is compounded semi-annually.

The amount of money that will be paid on the redemption date is called the **redemption value**. In most cases it is the same as the face value, and in such cases we say the bond is **redeemed at par**. Bonds can be redeemed at values other than par. On rare occasions, bonds are redeemable at a premium (redemption value > face value). In these situations the redemption value is often stated in units of 100. For example, a $500 bond redeemable at 105 would have a redemption value that is 105% of the face value, or 1.05($500) = $525. A $2000 bond redeemable at 101.5 would have a redemption value that is 101.5% of the face value, or 1.015($2000) = $2030.

Some bonds are **callable**; they contain a clause that allows the issuer to pay off the loan at a date earlier than the redemption date. Most callable bonds are called at a premium and the redemption value of a bond called before maturity is a previously specified percentage of the face value. Callable bonds are discussed in section 6.4.

A distinction should be made between savings bonds and marketable bonds. Savings bonds can be cashed in at any time before the redemption date and you will receive the full face value plus accrued interest. Marketable bonds (such as corporate bonds or government bonds) do not allow the bond owner to cash the bond in before maturity. If you no longer wish to own the bond, you must sell the bond on the open "bond market," where the price you receive will be influenced by current interest rates. It is marketable bonds that we will be dealing with in this chapter.

Bonds (as a contract) may be transferred from one investor to another. Bonds may be bought or sold on the bond market at any time. The buyer of the bond, as an investor, wants to realize a certain return on his investment, specified by the **investment** or **yield rate**. This desired rate of return will vary with the financial climate and will affect the price at which bonds are traded.

As an illustration, consider a $1000 bond redeemable at par in 5 years, paying interest at bond rate or coupon rate $i^{(2)} = 8\%$. If the buyer paid $1000 for the bond, then he receives $40 every half-year in interest and we say his yield rate is $i^{(2)} = 8\%$, that is, the same as the bond rate (coupon rate). If the buyer paid less than the face value, his yield rate will be higher than the bond rate $i^{(2)} = 8\%$ because he receives $40 every half-year in interest and on the redemption date he receives the face value of $1000, i.e., more than he invested. Similarly, if the buyer paid more than the face value, his yield rate will be lower than the bond rate. In the latter case, his interest payments at $i^{(2)} = 8\%$ will be partially offset by the loss incurred when the bond is redeemed.

In this chapter we shall use the following notation:

F = the face value or par value of the bond.
C = the redemption value of the bond.
r = the bond rate per interest period (coupon rate).

i = the yield rate per interest period (assume $i > 0$).

n = the number of interest periods until the redemption date.

P = the purchase price of the bond to yield rate i.

Fr = the bond interest payment or coupon, received at the end of each interest period.

The two fundamental problems relating to bonds, which will be discussed in this chapter, are

1. to determine the purchase price P of a bond to yield a given investment (yield) rate i to maturity;

2. to determine the investment rate i that a bond will yield when bought for a given price P.

OBSERVATION:

In this chapter, the yield rate means the yield rate to maturity unless specified otherwise.

Section 6.2 ## Purchase Price of a Bond

We want to determine the purchase price of a bond on a bond interest date n interest periods before maturity so that it earns interest at a specified yield rate i. We shall assume that the bond rate and the yield rate have the same conversion period.

A bond is a financial asset. When purchasing any financial asset, you pay a lump sum of money at the time of purchase and in return you receive future payments, or cash flows, from the asset. As we have seen before, to determine the price paid to buy an asset, you discount each future cash flow to the date of sale at some rate of interest. That is, the price of any financial asset is equal to the discounted value of future payments.

For a bond, the buyer will receive two types of payments or cash flows:

1. a bond interest payment, or coupon Fr, at the end of each interest period;

2. the redemption value C on the redemption date.

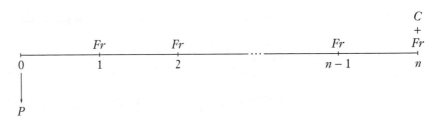

The buyer of a bond who wishes to realize a yield rate i on the investment should pay a price equal to the discounted value of the above payments at rate i. Thus,

P = discounted value of coupons + discounted value of redemption value

$$P = Fra_{\overline{n}|i} + C(1+i)^{-n} \qquad (15)$$

Often financial traders and commercial indices will express the price of a bond as a price per \$100 face value, even when the face value is not \$100.

EXAMPLE 1   A \$2500 bond that pays interest at $i^{(2)} = 8\%$ is redeemable at par at the end of 5 years. Determine the purchase price to yield an investor

a) 10% compounded semi-annually;
b) 6% compounded semi-annually.

Solution   We have $F = C = 2500$, $r = 0.08/2 = 0.04$, $Fr = 100$, $n = 5 \text{ years} \times 2 = 10$.

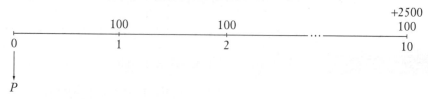

The purchase price P to yield $i^{(2)} = 10\%$ is the discounted value of the above payments at $i = 0.05$.

$$P = 100a_{\overline{10}|0.05} + 2500(1.05)^{-10} \doteq \$772.17 + \$1534.78 = \$2306.96$$

The purchase price of \$2306.96 will yield the buyer a return of $i^{(2)} = 10\%$ on the investment. Since the buyer is buying the bond for less than the redemption value, that is $P < C$, we say the bond is purchased at a **discount**. In the financial pages of your newspaper, the price will be listed as

$$\frac{2306.96}{2500} \times 100 = 92.2784.$$

b) The purchase price P to yield $i^{(2)} = 6\%$ is

$$P = 100a_{\overline{10}|0.03} + 2500(1.03)^{-10} \doteq \$853.02 + \$1860.24 = \$2713.26$$

The purchase price of \$2713.25 will yield the buyer a return of $i^{(2)} = 6\%$ on the investment. Since the buyer is buying the bond for more than the redemption value, that is $P > C$, we say the bond is purchased at a **premium**. In the financial pages of your newspaper, the price will be listed as

$$\frac{2713.25}{2500} \times 100 = 108.53.$$

Using a Financial Calculator to Determine the Price

Using the Texas Instruments BA-II Plus calculator,

PMT = coupon, Fr
    FV = redemption value, C
    N = time to redemption (in bond interest periods)
    I/Y = yield rate per bond interest period (typed as a number, not a decimal)
    PV = price of bond

In Example 1a), the steps are as follows (make sure your calculator has been set to the FIN mode):

$$100 \quad \boxed{PMT} \quad 2500 \quad \boxed{FV} \quad 10 \quad \boxed{N} \quad 5 \quad \boxed{I/Y} \quad \boxed{CPT} \quad \boxed{PV}$$
$$-2306.956627$$

Notice how the final price is negative. Taking the absolute value gives the final price of the bond, \$2306.96.

To obtain the price in Example 1b), all the steps and values are the same except that the yield rate is 3%, which means you key in the value 3 for I/Y.

EXAMPLE 2 A \$5000 bond maturing at 105 on September 1, 2031, has semi-annual coupons at 7%. Determine the purchase price on March 1, 2010, to guarantee a yield of $i^{(2)} = 6.8\%$.

Solution We have $F = 5000$, $r = 0.07/2 = 0.035$, $Fr = 5000 \times 0.035 = 175$, $C = 1.05(5000) = 5250$, and $i = 0.068/2 = 0.034$. To determine n, we know from March 1, 2010 to March 1, 2031 is 21 years, or 42 interest periods. Since the redemption date is one period later, September 1, 2031, $n = 43$.

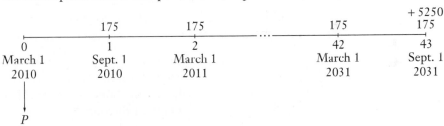

The purchaser receives 43 coupons plus the maturity value. The purchase price P on March 1, 2010, to guarantee a yield of $i^{(2)} = 6.8\%$ is

$$P = 175.00a_{\overline{43}|0.034} + 5250(1.034)^{-43}$$
$$\doteq \$3924.76 + \$1246.74 = \$5171.50$$

or $\frac{5171.50}{5000} \times 100 = \$103.43$ per \$100 unit.

In this example, the buyer is content with a yield rate smaller than the coupon rate on the bond and yet, since the price is less than the redemption value, the bond has been purchased at a discount. This apparent contradiction can be explained by remembering that while the bond is redeemed for \$5250, which affects the price of the bond, the coupons are determined by taking $3\frac{1}{2}\%$ of

$5000, not $3\frac{1}{2}$% of $5250. In fact, if we determine the bond interest rate per unit of redemption, we get $\frac{175}{5250} = 3.3\%$ It is because 3.3% is less than the desired yield rate of 3.4% each half-year that results in the purchase of the bond at a discount.

We will study the concepts of premium and discount in more detail in section 6.3.

The above two examples illustrate that in the bond investment market the price of a bond depends on the bond rate, the yield rate acceptable to investors, the time to maturity, and the redemption value.

OBSERVATION:

Note that unless it is specified otherwise, we assume that bonds are redeemed at par.

An Alternative Purchase-Price Formula

We shall develop an alternative formula for the purchase price of a bond sold on a bond interest date, which is somewhat simpler than formula **(15)**. Using the identity $a_{\overline{n}|i} = \frac{1 - (1 + i)^{-n}}{i}$ from chapter 3, we can get the factor $(1 + i)^{-n}$ as $(1 + i)^{-n} = 1 - ia_{\overline{n}|i}$ and eliminate it in formula **(15)**. Thus,

$$P = Fra_{\overline{n}|i} + C(1 + i)^{-n} = Fra_{\overline{n}|i} + C(1 - ia_{\overline{n}|i})$$

or

$$\boxed{P = C + (Fr - Ci)a_{\overline{n}|i}} \tag{16}$$

Formula **(16)** is often more efficient than formula **(15)** since it requires only one calculation, $a_{\overline{n}|i}$, whereas formula **(15)** requires two: $a_{\overline{n}|i}$ and $(1 + i)^{-n}$. It also tells us immediately whether the bond is purchased at a premium or a discount and the size of the premium or discount.

EXAMPLE 3   A corporation decides to issue 15-year bonds in the amount of $10 000 000. Under the contract, interest payments will be made at the rate $i^{(2)} = 6\%$. The bonds are priced to yield $i^{(2)} = 5\%$ to maturity. What is the issue price of the bond? What is the price of a $1000 bond to yield $i^{(2)} = 5\%$?

Solution   We have $F = C = 10\ 000\ 000$, $r = 0.06/2 = 0.03$, $Fr = 300\ 000$, $n = 30$, $i = 0.05/2 = 0.025$, $Ci = 250\ 000$.

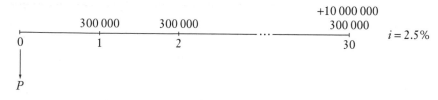

The alternative purchase-price formula will give us

$$P = 10\,000\,000 + (300\,000 - 250\,000)a_{\overline{30}|0.025} \doteq \$11\,046\,514.63$$

The issue price of the bonds to the public is \$11 046 514.63. The bonds will provide the investor with a yield $i^{(2)} = 5\%$ if held to maturity. The price of a \$1000 bond is

$$\frac{\$11\,046\,514.63}{10\,000\,000} \times 1000 = \$1104.65$$

In all examples so far we have considered the case where the bond interest payments, Fr, form an ordinary simple annuity, that is, where the bond interest period coincides with the period the yield rate is compounded. In cases when these periods are different, the bond interest payments form a general annuity and the interest yield rate is recalculated to coincide with the bond coupon period. The following example will illustrate the procedure.

EXAMPLE 4   Determine the issue price of the bonds in Example 3 to yield a) 5% per annum compounded monthly; b) 5% per annum compounded annually.

Solution a   Calculate rate i per half-year such that

$$(1 + i)^2 = (1 + \tfrac{0.05}{12})^{12}$$
$$1 + i = (1 + \tfrac{0.05}{12})^6$$
$$i = (1 + \tfrac{0.05}{12})^6 - 1$$
$$i = 0.025261868$$

Now

$$P = 10\,000\,000 + (300\,000 - 252\,618.68)a_{\overline{30}|i} \doteq \$10\,988\,251.07$$

The issue price of the bonds to the public is \$10 988 251.07. The purchase price of a \$1000 bond is then \$1098.83.

Solution b   Calculate rate i per half-year such that

$$(1 + i)^2 = 1.05$$
$$(1 + i) = (1.05)^{1/2}$$
$$i = (1.05)^{1/2} - 1$$
$$i = 0.024695077$$

Now

$$P = 10\,000\,000 + (300\,000 - 246\,950.77)a_{\overline{30}|i} \doteq \$11\,114\,863.64$$

The issue price of the bonds to the public is \$11 114 863.64. The purchase price of a \$1000 bond is then \$1111.49.

EXAMPLE 5   A 10-year $2000 bond pays semi-annual coupons at $i^{(2)} = 6\%$ and is purchased to yield $i^{(2)} = 6\%$. What is the purchase price if the bond is redeemable at a) par; b) 101.5?

Solution   We have $F = 2000$, $r = 0.03$, $Fr = 60$, $n = 20$. This is a situation where the bond rate is the same as the yield rate, $i = 0.03$.

Solution a   We have $C = 2000$ and $Ci = 60$. From formula **(16)**, we obtain

$$P = 2000 + (60 - 60)a_{\overline{20}|0.03} = 2000$$

Note that when the yield rate is equal to the bond rate and the bond is redeemable at par, the price is equal to the redemption value, $P = C$.

Solution b   We have $C = 2000(1.015) = 2030$ and $Ci = 60.90$. From formula **(16)**, we obtain

$$P = 2030 + (60 - 60.90)a_{\overline{20}|0.03} \doteq 2016.61$$

When the yield rate is equal to the bond rate, but $F \neq C$, then the price is not equal to the redemption value, that is $P \neq C$. In this case, since $P < C$, the bond is said to be purchased at a discount.

EXAMPLE 6   To see the impact the yield rate has on the purchase price of a bond, take the bond given in Example 5a) and calculate the price for nominal yield rates compounded semi-annually starting at 2% and increasing by 1% to 12%. Graph the results.

Solution   The prices are given in the table below.

Yield Rate, $i^{(2)}$	Price
2%	$2721.82
3%	$2515.06
4%	$2327.03
5%	$2155.89
6%	$2000.00
7%	$1857.88
8%	$1728.19
9%	$1609.76
10%	$1501.51
11%	$1402.48
12%	$1311.80

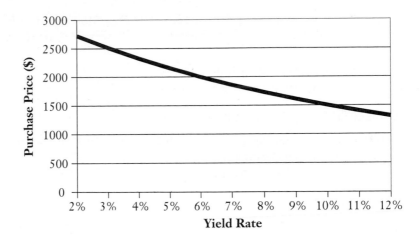

Exercise 6.2

Part A

Problems 1 to 7 use the information in the table below. Using either formula **(15)** or formula **(16)**, determine the purchase price of the bond.

No.	Face Value	Redemption	Bond Interest Rate	Years to Redemption	Yield Rate
1.	$ 500	at par	$i^{(2)} = 9\%$	20	$i^{(2)} = 8\%$
2.	$ 1 000	at par	$i^{(2)} = 9\%$	15	$i^{(2)} = 10\%$
3.	$ 2 000	at par	$i^{(2)} = 6\frac{1}{2}\%$	15	$i^{(4)} = 7\%$
4.	$ 5 000	at par	$i^{(2)} = 12\%$	20	$i^{(2)} = 10\%$
5.	$ 1 000	at 110	$i^{(2)} = 9\%$	18	$i^{(7)} = 12\%$
6.	$ 2 000	at 105	$i^{(2)} = 7\%$	20	$i^{(2)} = 5\%$
7.	$10 000	at 102.5	$i^{(2)} = 10\frac{1}{2}\%$	15	$i^{(12)} = 7\%$

8. A $4000 bond is redeemable at 103 on November 10, 2025. It pays semi-annual coupons at $i^{(2)} = 5\%$. Determine the price of the bond on May 10, 2010, to yield $i^{(2)} = 4\%$.

9. The XYZ Corporation needs to raise some funds to pay for new equipment. They issue $1 000 000 worth of 20-year bonds with semi-annual coupons at $i^{(2)} = 6\%$. These bonds are redeemable at 105. At the time of issue, interest rates in the market place are $i^{(12)} = 6\frac{1}{2}\%$. How much money did they raise?

10. Mr. Simpson buys a $1000 bond paying bond interest at $i^{(2)} = 6\frac{1}{2}\%$ and redeemable at par in 20 years. Mr. Simpson's desired yield rate is $i^{(4)} = 7\%$. How much did he pay for the bond? After exactly five years he sells the bond.

Interest rates have dropped and the bond is sold to yield a buyer $i^{(1)} = 5\%$. Determine the sale price.

11. A corporation issues $600 000 worth of 12-year bonds with semi-annual coupons at $i^{(2)} = 10\%$. The bonds are priced to yield $i^{(2)} = 9\%$. Determine the issue price per $100 unit.

12. A $5000 bond is redeemable at par on March 15, 2022. It pays semi-annual coupons at $i^{(2)} = 6\%$. Determine the price of the bond on the following dates with the following yield rates:
    a) September 15, 2010, and $i^{(2)} = 7\%$
    b) March 15, 2011, and $i^{(2)} = 5.5\%$

Part B

1. Show that if a bond is redeemable at par and $i = r$, then $P = C$.

2. Prove the following formula for a *par value* bond
   $$P = F(1 + i)^{-n} + \frac{r}{i}[F - F(1 + i)^{-n}]$$
   This purchase-price formula is known as Makeham's formula and requires the use of only $(1 + i)^{-n}$ factors.

3. An $\$X$ bond quoted as redeemable at 105 in 10 years is purchased to yield $i^{(2)} = 10\%$. If this same bond was redeemable at par, the actual purchase price would be $113.07 less. Determine the value of X.

4. The XYZ Corporation issues a special 20-year bond issue that has no coupons. Rather, interest will accumulate on the bond at rate $i^{(2)} = 6.5\%$ for the life of the bond. At the time of maturity, the total value of the loan will be paid off, including all accumulated interest. Determine the price of a $1000 bond of this issue to yield $i^{(2)} = 5.5\%$. This type of bond is sometimes referred to as an **accumulation bond**.

5. A $1000 bond bearing coupons at $i^{(2)} = 6\frac{1}{2}\%$ and redeemable at par is bought to yield $i^{(2)} = 6\%$. If the present value of the redemption value at this yield is $412, what is the purchase price? (Do not calculate n.)

6. Two $1000 bonds redeemable at par at the end of n years are bought to yield $i^{(2)} = 10\%$. One bond costs $1153.72 and has semi-annual coupons at $i^{(2)} = 12\%$. The other bond has semi-annual coupons at $i^{(2)} = 8\%$. Determine the price of the second bond.

7. A $1000 bond with semi-annual coupons at $i^{(2)} = 6\%$ and redeemable at the end of n years at $1050 sells at $980 to yield $i^{(2)} = 7\frac{1}{2}\%$. Determine the price of a $1000 bond with semi-annual coupons at $i^{(2)} = 5\%$ redeemable at the end of $2n$ years at $1040 to yield $i^{(2)} = 7\frac{1}{2}\%$. (Do not calculate n.)

8. A bond with a par value of $100 000 has coupons at the rate $i^{(2)} = 6\frac{1}{2}\%$. It will be redeemed at par when it matures a certain number of years hence. It is purchased for a price of $96 446.90. At this price, the purchaser who holds the bond to maturity will realize a yield rate $i^{(2)} = 7\%$. Determine the number of years to maturity.

9. A $1000 bond with annual coupons at $8\frac{1}{2}\%$ and maturing in 20 years at par is purchased to yield an annual effective rate of interest of 9% if held to maturity. The book value of the bond at any time is the discounted value of all remaining payments, using the 9% rate. Ten years later, just after a coupon payment, the bond is sold to yield the new purchaser a 10% annual effective rate of interest if held to maturity. Calculate the excess of the book value over the second sale price.

10. A corporation has an issue of bonds with annual coupons at $i^{(1)} = 5\%$ maturing in five years at par that are quoted at a price that yields $i^{(1)} = 6\%$.
    a) What is the price of a $1000 bond?
    b) It is proposed to replace this issue of bonds with an issue of bonds with annual coupons at $i^{(1)} = 5\frac{1}{2}\%$. How long must the new issue run so that the bond holders will still yield $i^{(1)} = 6\%$? Express your answer to the nearest year.

11. A $1000 bond bearing semi-annual coupons at $i^{(2)} = 10\%$ is redeemable at par. What is the minimum number of whole years that the bond should run so that a person paying $1100 for it would earn at least $i^{(2)} = 8\%$?

12. If the coupon rate on a bond is $1\frac{1}{2}$ times the yield rate when it sells for a premium of $10 per $100, determine the price per $100 for a bond with the same number of coupons and the same yield with coupons equal to $\frac{3}{4}$ of the yield rate.

| Section 6.3 | **Premium and Discount** |

A bond is just a loan agreement between the bond issuer (the borrower) and the investor (the lender). The bond issuer sets a bond interest rate (the coupon rate) and the redemption value and date, and the investor determines the amount of the loan (the purchase price of the bond).

Bond Purchased at a Premium

We have seen that if $P > C$ (the purchase price of a bond exceeds its redemption value), the bond is said to have been purchased **at a premium**. In fact, from the alternative purchase price formula, the size of the premium must be

$$\boxed{\textbf{Premium} = \textbf{\textit{P}} - \textbf{\textit{C}} = \textbf{\textit{(Fr}} - \textbf{\textit{Ci)}}\textbf{\textit{a}}_{\overline{m}|i}}$$

A premium occurs when $Fr > Ci$. In other words, each coupon Fr exceeds the interest desired by the investor Ci, which allows the price P to exceed the redemption value C. For par value bonds (i.e., $C = F$) the bond is purchased at a premium when $r > i$.

When the bond is purchased at a premium, then only C of the original principal is returned on the redemption date. There will be a loss, equal to the premium, at the redemption date.

This loss can be applied against an investor's income at the time of redemption which would result in less tax being owed at that time. However, it would be more efficient, from a tax point of view, if an investor could take the tax savings which occurs at redemption and allocate it over each bond interest period. Bond interest payments are considered taxable income to the investor, so this would lead to paying less tax each period (paying tax on approximately Ci instead of Fr), instead of getting the tax break at redemption.

The government allows bond investors to do this if they so choose. In these cases the premium (or loss at redemption), $P - C$, is amortized over the term of the bond. That is, small "pieces" of the premium are allocated to each bond coupon.

Each coupon payment, in addition to paying interest on the investment (at a yield rate), provides a partial return of the principal P. These payments of principal will continually reduce the value of the bond from the price on the purchase date to the redemption value on the redemption date. These adjusted values of the bond are called the **book values** of the bond and are used by many investors in reporting the asset values of bonds for financial statements. The process of gradually decreasing the value of the bond from the purchase price to the redemption value is called **amortization of a premium** or **writing down a bond**. A **bond amortization schedule** is a table that shows the division of each interest payment into the interest paid on the book value (at a yield rate) and the decrease in the book value of the bond (or the book value adjustment) along with the book value after each bond interest payment is paid.

EXAMPLE 1 A \$1000 bond, redeemable at par on December 1, 2012, pays interest at $i^{(2)} = 6\frac{1}{2}\%$. The bond is bought on June 1, 2010, to yield $i^{(2)} = 5\frac{1}{2}\%$ Determine the purchase price and construct the bond schedule.

Solution The purchase price P on June 1, 2010 can be determined using the alternative purchase-price formula **(16)**.

$$P = 1000 + (32.50 - 27.50)a_{\overline{5}|0.0275} \doteq \$1000 + \$23.06 = \$1023.06$$

The premium is \$23.06 and this is the amount of the loss that occurs on December 1, 2012. This amount could be applied against the investor's income for 2012 and would result in less tax being owed. (We will ignore the fact that the tax savings would be very small in this case due to this being a relatively small bond.) Instead, we will amortize this premium and allocate small "pieces" of it to each of the 5 coupons.

To construct the amortization schedule for this bond, we shall calculate how much of each coupon is used as return on the investment at the desired yield rate and how much is used to adjust the book value or the principal (i.e., amortize the premium).

At the end of the first half-year, on December 1, 2010, the investor's yield should be $\$1023.06 \times 0.0275 = \$28.13$. Since he actually receives \$32.50, the difference of \$4.37 can be regarded as part of the original principal being returned and is used to adjust (reduce) the principal, or amortize the premium. The adjusted value, or book value, after the coupon payment is $\$1023.06 - \$4.37 = \$1018.69$. This book value can be computed independently by the alternative purchase-price formula using $F = C = 1000$, $r = 3\frac{1}{4}\%$, $i = 2\frac{3}{4}\%$, and $n = 4$. The above procedure is continued until the bond matures.

The following is a complete bond schedule with $F = C = 1000$, $r = 0.0325$, $i = 0.0275$, and $n = 5$.

Schedule for a Bond Purchased at a Premium

Date (1)	Time t (2)	Coupon $F \cdot r$ (3)	Interest on Book Value $I_t = B_{t-1} \cdot i$ (4) = (6)$_{t-1} \cdot i$	Book Value Adjustment (5) = (3) − (4)	Book Value B_t (6) = B_{t-1} − (5)
June 1, 2010	0	—	—	—	1023.06
Dec. 1, 2010	1	32.50	28.13	4.37	1018.69
June 1, 2011	2	32.50	28.01	4.49	1014.20
Dec. 1, 2011	3	32.50	27.89	4.61	1009.59
June 1, 2012	4	32.50	27.76	4.74	1004.85
Dec. 1, 2012	5	32.50	27.63	4.87	999.98*
Totals		162.50	139.42*	23.08*	

*The 2¢ error is from the accumulation of round-off.

> **OBSERVATION:**
>
> 1. All the book values can be reproduced using either of the purchase price formulas with n = term remaining.
> 2. The sum of the book value adjustments is equal to the original amount of the premium.
> 3. The book value is gradually adjusted from the original purchase price down to the redemption value.
> 4. Successive book value adjustments are in the ratio $(1 + i)$,
>   i.e., $\frac{4.49}{4.37} \doteq \frac{4.61}{4.49} \doteq \frac{4.74}{4.61} \doteq \frac{4.87}{4.74} \doteq 1.0275$.
> 5. The investor would end up claiming the values "Interest on Book Value" as interest income over the term of the bond. That is, he/she would pay income tax on $139.42 in total as opposed to paying tax on the actual amount received, $162.50. However, he/she would not be allowed to claim the premium of $23.06 against his/her income at the time of redemption.

Bond Purchased at a Discount

Similarly, if $P < C$ (the purchase price is less than the redemption value) the bond is said to have been purchased **at a discount**. From the alternative purchase-price formula, the size of the discount is

$$\boxed{\textbf{Discount} = \textbf{\textit{C}} - \textbf{\textit{P}} = (\textbf{\textit{Ci}} - \textbf{\textit{Fr}})\textbf{\textit{a}}_{\overline{m}|i}}$$

A discount occurs when $Fr < Ci$. In other words, each coupon, Fr, is less than the interest desired by the investor Ci. For a par value bond (i.e., $C = F$) the bond is purchased at a discount when $i > r$.

When the bond is purchased at a discount, the investor's return is more than just the bond interest payment. There will be a gain, equal to the discount, at the redemption date. This gain must be reported as income in the year it occurs, which would result in increased income taxes being owed. But, similar to when a bond is purchased at a premium, it would be more efficient, from a tax point of view, if an investor could take the gain which occurs at redemption and allocate part of it over each bond interest period. This would lead to paying more tax each period (paying tax on approximately Ci instead of Fr), but not having a higher tax bill at redemption.

Again, the government allows bond investors to do this if they so choose. In these cases the discount (or gain at redemption), $P - C$, is accumulated over the term of the bond. That is, small "pieces" of the discount are allocated to each bond coupon.

The process of gradually increasing the value of the bond from the purchase price up to the redemption value is called **accumulation of a discount** or **writing up a bond**. A **bond accumulation schedule** is a table that shows the division of the investor's interest (at a yield rate) into the bond interest payment and the increase in the book value of the bond (or the book value adjustment) along with the book value after each bond interest payment is paid.

EXAMPLE 2   A $1000 bond, redeemable at par on December 1, 2012, pays interest at $i^{(2)} = 9\%$. The bond is bought on June 1, 2010, to yield $i^{(2)} = 10\%$. Determine the price and construct a bond schedule.

Solution   The purchase price P on June 1, 2010, can be determined by the alternative purchase-price formula **(16)**:

$$P = 1000 + (45 - 50)a_{\overline{5}|0.05} \doteq \$1000 - \$21.65 = \$978.35$$

The discount is $21.65 and this is the amount of the gain that occurs on December 1, 2012. This amount would be added to the investor's income for 2012, which would result in more tax being owed. Instead, we will accumulate this discount and allocate small "pieces" of it to each of the 5 coupons, much like we did in Example 1.

To construct the accumulation schedule for this bond, we shall calculate the investor's interest at the end of each half-year and gradually increase the book value of the bond by the difference between investor's interest and the bond interest payment.

At the end of the first half-year, on December 1, 2010, the investor's interest should be $978.35 × 0.05 = $48.92. Since the bond interest payment is only $45, we increase the book value of the bond by $48.92 − $45.00 = $3.92. We say $3.92 is used for accumulation of a discount or −$3.92 is the principal adjustment (book value adjustment). You should be able to see that a bond accumulation schedule works exactly the same as a bond amortization schedule, except that the book value adjustment column consists of negative values.

The adjusted value, or book value, after the bond interest payment on December 1, 2010, is $978.35 − (−$3.92) = $978.35 + $3.92 = $982.27. This book value can be computed independently by the alternative purchase-price formula using $F = C = 1000$, $r = 4\frac{1}{2}\%$, $i = 5\%$ and $n = 4$. The above procedure is continued until the bond matures.

The following is a complete bond schedule with $F = C = 1000$, $r = 0.045$, $i = 0.05$, and $n = 5$.

Schedule for a Bond Purchased at a Discount

Date (1)	Time t (2)	Coupon $F \cdot r$ (3)	Interest on Book Value $I_t = B_{t-1} \cdot i$ $(4) = (6)_{t-1} \cdot i$	Book Value Adjustment (5) $= (3) - (4)$	Book Value B_t (6) $= B_{t-1} - (5)$
June 1, 2010	0	—	—	—	978.35
Dec. 1, 2010	1	45.00	48.92	−3.92	982.27
June 1, 2011	2	45.00	49.11	−4.11	986.38
Dec. 1, 2011	3	45.00	49.32	−4.32	990.70
June 1, 2012	4	45.00	49.54	−4.54	995.24
Dec. 1, 2012	5	45.00	49.76	−4.76	1000.00
Totals		225.00	246.65	−21.65	

The five observations that followed Example 1 hold here as well, keeping in mind that the investor would end up paying tax on $246.65 over the term of the bond, as opposed to paying tax on the actual total amount of coupons received, $225.00. However, the investor would not have to claim the discount of $21.65 as interest income at the time of redemption.

The payments made during the term of a bond can be regarded as loan payments made by the borrower (bond issuer) to the lender (the bondholder) to repay a loan amount equal to the purchase price of the bond. The bond purchase price is calculated as the discounted value of those payments (coupons plus redemption value) at a certain yield rate (the interest rate on the loan). Thus the bond transaction can be regarded as the amortization of a loan and an amortization schedule for the bond can be constructed like the general loan amortization schedule in section 5.1.

Also, the first four observations with respect to bond schedules shown in Examples 1 and 2 follow from the general loan amortization schedule and may be summarized as follows:

OBSERVATION:

1. The outstanding principal (the book value of the bond) can be computed as the discounted value of the remaining payments (the purchase price of the bond) at any payment date (coupon date).

2. The sum of the principal repaid (the book value adjustments) is equal to the amount of the loan (the redemption value plus the amount of the premium or the discount).

3. The outstanding principal of the loan is gradually adjusted from the original amount to zero balance after the last payment (last coupon plus redemption value) is paid.

4. Successive principal repayments (book value adjustments) are in the ratio $1 + i$. (Last principal repaid must be reduced by redemption value to satisfy the condition that the last ratio is equal to $1 + i$.)

EXAMPLE 3 Construct the amortization schedule for the loan of a) Example 1; b) Example 2.

Solution a

Date	Payment	Interest Due (at $i = 0.0275$)	Principal Repaid	Outstanding Principal
June 1, 2010	—	—	—	1023.06
Dec. 1, 2010	32.50	28.13	4.37	1018.69
June 1, 2011	32.50	28.01	4.49	1014.20
Dec. 1, 2011	32.50	27.89	4.61	1009.59
June 1, 2012	32.50	27.76	4.74	1004.85
Dec. 1, 2012	1032.50	27.63	1004.87	−0.02*
Totals	1162.50	139.42	1023.08*	

*Each calculation is rounded to the nearest 1¢ and then carried forward at its rounded-off value. This results in an accumulated 2¢ error in the final balance.

Solution b

Date	Payment	Interest Due (at $i = 0.05$)	Principal Repaid	Outstanding Principal
June 1, 2010	—	—	—	978.35
Dec. 1, 2010	45.00	48.92	−3.92	982.27
June 1, 2011	45.00	49.11	−4.11	986.38
Dec. 1, 2011	45.00	49.32	−4.32	990.70
June 1, 2012	45.00	49.54	−4.54	995.24
Dec. 1, 2012	1045.00	49.76	995.24	0
Totals	1225.00	246.65	978.35	

EXAMPLE 4 A $2000 bond is redeemable at 102 in 6 years. The absolute value of the sum of the write-downs (book value adjustment column) is $53.42. What is the price of the bond?

Solution We have $F = 2000$, $C = 1.02(2000) = 2040$. We are also given the absolute value of the sum of the write-downs is 53.42.

When a bond is being "written down," the book value starts at P and gets adjusted down to C. This means $P > C$, or in other words the bond is purchased at a premium. Thus,

$$P = C + \text{Premium}$$
$$= \$2040 + \$53.42$$
$$= \$2093.42$$

EXAMPLE 5   A 5-year bond pays semi-annual coupons and is bought to yield $i^{(2)} = 7\%$. The interest portion of the first coupon is $100.63. The absolute value of the write-up in the book value in the last period (10th coupon) is $14.49. What is the coupon, Fr, paid each period?

Solution   We are given $n = 10$ and $i = 0.035$. Also, since the bond is being "written up," bond values start at P and get adjusted up to C. This means $P < C$, the bond is purchased at a discount.

Using the notation of section 5.1, this means $P_{10} = -14.49$ is the book value adjustment at the time of the 10th coupon. To calculate the book value adjustment in the 1st coupon, P_1, we recognize that the values in the book value adjustment column are in the ratio of $(1 + i)$. Thus,

$$P_1 = P_{10}(1.035)^{-9} = -14.49(1.035)^{-9} = -\$10.63$$

The coupon is equal to the interest paid plus the book value adjustment. Thus,

$$\text{Coupon} = Fr = 100.63 + (-10.63) = \$90.00$$

EXAMPLE 6   Prepare an Excel spreadsheet for the bond from Example 1.

Solution   You should first type in some of the given values. In cell G2, type in the face value, 1000. In cell G3, type in the bond rate, $=0.065/2$. In cell G4, type in the redemption value, 1000. In cell G5, type in the yield rate, $=0.055/2$. In cell G6, we will get the computer to calculate the purchase price by typing in the alternative purchase formula as $=G4+(G2*G3-G4*G5)*(1-(1+G5)^-5)/G5$.

The rest of the entries in an Excel spreadsheet are summarized below.

	CELL	**ENTER**	**INTERPRETATION**
Headings	A1	Time	'Time value for a coupon date'
	B1	Coupon	'Bond interest payment'
	C1	Interest on BV	'Interest on book value'
	D1	Adjustment	'Book value adjustment'
	E1	Book value	'Book value of the bond'
Line 0	A2	0	Time starts
	E2	=G6	Purchase price at time 0
Line 1	A3	=A2+1	Time for coupon 1
	B3	=G2*G3	Semi-annual bond interest payment
	C3	=E2*G5	Interest on book value at time 1
	D3	=B3−C3	Book value adjustment at time 1
	E3	=E2−D3	Book value at time 1

To generate the complete schedule copy A3.E3 to A4.E7

To get totals apply Σ to B3.D7

Below is the bond schedule by an Excel spreadsheet.

	A	B	C	D	E
1	Time	Coupon	Interest on BV	Adjustment	Book Value
2	0				1,023.06
3	1	32.50	28.13	4.37	1,018.69
4	2	32.50	28.01	4.49	1,014.21
5	3	32.50	27.89	4.61	1,009.60
6	4	32.50	27.76	4.74	1,004.86
7	5	32.50	27.63	4.87	1,000.00
8		162.50	139.44	23.06	

Note: All output is rounded to the nearest 1¢ but carried internally to several decimals. Thus the correct final balance is produced, but some columns appear not to add up.

Exercise 6.3

Part A

For problems 1 to 6 in the table that follows, determine logically, before calculation, if the bond is purchased at a premium or a discount. Then determine the purchase price of the bond and make out a complete bond schedule showing the amortization of the premium or the accumulation of the discount.

No.	Face Value	Redemption	Bond Interest Rate	Years to Redemption	Yield Rate
1.	$ 1 000	at par	$i^{(2)} = 10\%$	3	$i^{(2)} = 9\%$
2.	$ 5 000	at par	$i^{(2)} = 6\%$	3	$i^{(2)} = 7\%$
3.	$ 2 000	at par	$i^{(2)} = 6\frac{1}{2}\%$	2.5	$i^{(2)} = 5\frac{1}{2}\%$
4.	$ 1 000	at 105	$i^{(2)} = 10\%$	2.5	$i^{(2)} = 12\%$
5.	$ 2 000	at 103	$i^{(2)} = 7\%$	3	$i^{(2)} = 6\%$
6.	$10 000	at 110	$i^{(2)} = 7\%$	2.5	$i^{(2)} = 8\%$

7. A $1000 par value bond paying interest at $i^{(2)} = 6\%$ has book value $1100 on March 1, 2010, at a yield rate of $i^{(2)} = 4\frac{1}{2}\%$. Determine the amount of amortization of the premium on September 1, 2010, and the new book value on that date.

8. A 20-year bond with annual coupons is bought at a premium to yield $i^{(1)} = 8\%$. If the amount of write-down of the premium in the 3rd payment is $6, determine the amount of write-down of the premium in the 16th payment.

9. A $1000 bond, redeemable at par, with annual coupons at 10% is purchased for $1060. If the write-down in the book value is $7 at the end of

the first year, what is the write-down at the end of the 4th year?

10. A bond with $80 annual coupons is purchased at a discount to yield $i^{(2)} = 7\frac{1}{2}\%$. The write-up for the first year is $22. What was the purchase price?

11. A $1000 bond redeemable at $1050 on December 1, 2012, pays interest at $i^{(2)} = 6\frac{1}{2}\%$. The bond is bought on June 1, 2010. Determine the price and construct a bond schedule if the desired yield is
a) $i^{(12)} = 6\%$; b) $i^{(2)} = 5\frac{1}{2}\%$.

12. A $1000 20-year par value bond with semi-annual coupons is bought at a discount to yield

$i^{(2)} = 10\%$. If the amount of the write-up of the discount in the last entry in the schedule is $5, determine the purchase price of the bond.

13. A bond with $40 semi-annual coupons is purchased at a premium to yield $i^{(2)} = 7\%$. If the first write-down is $4.33, determine the purchase price of the bond.

Part B

1. When $C \neq F$, we define a **modified coupon rate** $g = \dfrac{Fr}{C}$ so $Fr = Cg$. Then

$$P = C + (Cg - Ci)a_{\overline{n}|i} = C + C(g - i)a_{\overline{n}|i}.$$

When a bond is purchased at a premium,
$P - C = C(g - i)a_{\overline{n}|i} > 0$ if $g > i$.
When a bond is purchased at a discount,
$C - P = C(i - g)a_{\overline{n}|i} > 0$ if $i > g$.
Using the above, calculate the price of a $100 2-year bond with bond interest at $i^{(2)} = 9\%$, redeemable at 105 to yield $i^{(4)} = 10\%$. Produce a bond schedule.

2. A $1000 bond pays coupons at $i^{(2)} = 7\%$ on January 1 and July 1 and will be redeemed at par on July 1, 2014. If the bond was bought on January 1, 2006, to yield 6% per annum compounded semi-annually, determine the interest due on the book value on January 1, 2010.

3. A $1000 bond providing annual coupons at $i^{(1)} = 9\%$ is redeemable at par on November 1, 2014. The write-up in the first year was $5.63. The write-up in the 11th year was $19.08. Determine the book value of the bond on November 1, 2010.

4. A $2000 bond with annual coupons matures at par in 5 years. The first interest coupon is $400, with subsequent coupons reduced by 25% of the previous year's coupon, each year.
a) Calculate the price to yield $i^{(1)} = 10\%$.
b) Draw up the bond schedule.

5. A 10-year bond matures for $2000 and has annual coupons. The first coupon is $100, and each increases by 10%. The bond is priced to yield $i^{(1)} = 9\%$. Determine the price and draw up the bond schedule.

6. A $1000 bond with semi-annual coupons at $i^{(2)} = 5\%$ is redeemable for $1100. If the amount for the 16th write-up is $2.50, calculate the purchase price to yield $i^{(2)} = 6\%$.

7. You are told that a $1000 bond with semi-annual coupons at $i^{(2)} = 8\%$ redeemable at par will be sold at $700 to an investor requiring 12% per annum compounded semi-annually.
a) Determine the price of this bond to the same investor if the above coupon rate were changed to $i^{(2)} = 11\%$.
b) Is the 11% bond purchased at a premium or a discount? Explain.
c) For the 11% bond show the write-up (or write-down) entries at the first two coupon dates.

8. A $10 000 15-year bond is priced to yield $i^{(4)} = 12\%$. It has quarterly coupons of $200 each the 1st year, $215 each the 2nd year, $230 each the 3rd year, ..., $410 each the 15th year.
a) Show that the price is $9267.05.
b) Determine the book value after 14 years.
c) Draw up a partial bond schedule showing the first and last year's entries only.

Section 6.4 **Callable Bonds**

Some bonds contain a clause that allows the issuer to redeem the bond prior to the maturity date. These bonds are referred to as **callable bonds**. A bond issuer would "call" a bond early if interest rates fall. This way, they could pay off the old issue and replace it with a new series of bonds with a lower coupon rate.

Callable bonds present a problem with respect to the calculation of the price since the term of the bond is not certain. Since the corporation issuing the bond controls when the bond is redeemed (or called), the investor must determine a price that will guarantee the desired yield regardless of the call date.

EXAMPLE 1 The XYZ Corporation issues a 10-year $1000 bond with coupons at $i^{(2)} = 6\%$. The bond can be called, at par, at the end of 5 years. Determine the purchase price that will guarantee an investor a return of a) $i^{(2)} = 7\%$; b) $i^{(2)} = 5\%$.

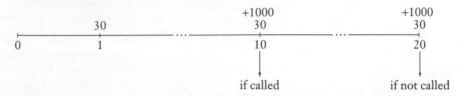

Solution a The bond matures at the end of 10 years but may be called at the end of 5 years. Given a desired yield rate of $i^{(2)} = 7\%$, we calculate the price of the bond for these two different dates using formula **(16)**.

i) If it is called after 5 years,

$$P = 1000 + (30 - 35)a_{\overline{10}|0.035} \doteq \$1000 - \$41.58 = \$958.42$$

ii) If it matures after 10 years,

$$P = 1000 + (30 - 35)a_{\overline{20}|0.035} \doteq \$1000 - \$71.06 = \$928.94$$

The purchase price to guarantee a return of $i^{(2)} = 7\%$ is the lower of these two answers, or $928.94. If the investor pays $928.94 and the bond runs the full 10 years to maturity, the investor's yield will be exactly $i^{(2)} = 7\%$. If the investor pays $928.94 and the bond is called at the end of 5 years, the investor's return will exceed $i^{(2)} = 7\%$.

If the investor pays $958.42 for the bond, however, it will yield $i^{(2)} = 7\%$ only if the bond is called at the end of 5 years. If the bond runs to its full maturity, the rate of return will be less than $i^{(2)} = 7\%$.

Solution b Again we calculate the price of the bonds at the two different dates using a yield of $i^{(2)} = 5\%$ and formula **(16)**.

i) If it is called after 5 years,

$$P = 1000 + (30 - 25)a_{\overline{10}|0.025} \doteq \$1000 - \$43.76 = \$1043.76.$$

ii) If it matures after 10 years,

$$P = 1000 + (30 - 25)a_{\overline{20}|0.025} \doteq \$1000 - \$77.95 = \$1077.95.$$

The purchase price to guarantee a return of $i^{(2)} = 5\%$ is $1043.76. If the bond is called at the end of 5 years, the investor's yield will be exactly $i^{(2)} = 5\%$. If the bond is called any time after 5 years, or if the bond is held to maturity, the investor's yield will exceed $i^{(2)} = 5\%$.

In the above example, we have shown, in effect, that the investor must assume that the issuer of the bond will exercise his call option to the disadvantage of the investor and must calculate the price accordingly. The example above also illustrates a useful principle *for bonds that are callable at par*. That is,

> If the yield rate is less than the coupon rate (if the bond sells at a premium), then you use the earliest possible call date in your calculation.
>
> If the yield rate is greater than the coupon rate (if the bond sells at a discount), then you use the latest possible redemption date in your calculation.

Unfortunately, these guidelines cannot be applied often, since when a bond is called early it is usually done so at a premium. In that case, we are forced to calculate all possible purchase prices and pay the lowest price calculated.

EXAMPLE 2   The ABC Corporation issues a 20-year $1000 par value bond with bond interest at $i^{(2)} = 6\%$. The bond is callable at the end of 10 years at $1100 or at the end of 15 years at $1050. Determine the price to guarantee an investor a yield rate of $i^{(2)} = 5\%$.

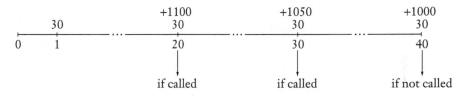

Solution   Calculate the purchase price using formula **(16)**

i) If the bond is called after 10 years,

$$P = 1100 + (30 - 27.50)a_{\overline{20}|0.025} \doteq \$1100 - \$38.97 = \$1138.97$$

ii) If the bond is called after 15 years,

$$P = 1050 + (30 - 26.25)a_{\overline{30}|0.025} \doteq \$1050 - \$78.49 = \$1128.49$$

iii) If the bond is redeemed at par after 20 years,

$$P = 1000 + (30 - 25)a_{\overline{40}|0.025} \doteq \$1000 - \$125.51 = \$1125.51$$

In this case, despite the fact that the desired yield rate is less than the bond coupon rate, the correct answer is found by using the latest possible redemption date. That is because of the premium value in the early call dates.

There also exist debt securities called **extendible** or **retractable bonds**. These bonds are somewhat like a callable bond in that they allow the option of redeeming the bond at a time other than the stated redemption date. The difference between callable bonds and extendible/retractable bonds is that the bond owner, not the issuer, has the option.

An extendible bond allows the owner to extend the redemption date of the bond for a specified additional period. A retractable bond allows the owner to sell back the long-term bond to the issuer at a date earlier than the normal redemption date at par. Savings Bonds are an example of retractable bonds.

Because the option to extend or retract lies with the bond owner, no new mathematical analysis needs to be introduced.

Exercise 6.4

Part A

1. A $2000 bond paying interest at $i^{(2)} = 10\%$ is redeemable at par in 20 years. It is callable at par in 15 years. Determine the price to guarantee a yield rate of a) $i^{(2)} = 8\%$; b) $i^{(2)} = 12\%$.

2. A $5000 bond paying interest at $i^{(2)} = 6\%$ is redeemable at par in 20 years. It is callable at 105 in 15 years. Determine the price to guarantee a yield rate of a) $i^{(2)} = 5\%$; b) $i^{(2)} = 7\%$.

3. A $1000 bond with coupons at $i^{(2)} = 9\%$ is redeemable at par in 20 years. It is callable at the end of 10 years at 110 and at the end of 15 years at 105. Determine the price to guarantee a yield rate of a) $i^{(2)} = 8\%$; b) $i^{(2)} = 10\%$.

4. A bond, paying interest at $i^{(2)} = 5.5\%$, is redeemable at par in 10 years. It is callable at par in 5 years. What date should you use to calculate the purchase price of the bond if you desire a yield of a) $i^{(2)} = 5.5\%$; b) $i^{(2)} = 6.5\%$; c) $i^{(2)} = 5\%$?

5. A $2000 bond is redeemable at par in 12 years and is callable at par in 8 years. The price of the bond to yield $i^{(2)} = 8\%$ is
   • $2076.23 assuming the bond is held to maturity
   • $2058.26 assuming the bond is called at the end of 8 years.
   How will the actual yield rate compare with the desired yield rate (do not calculate the actual yield rate) if an investor pays
   a) $2058.26 and the bond is called early?
   b) $2058.26 and the bond is held to maturity?
   c) $2076.23 and the bond is called early?
   d) $2076.23 and the bond is held to maturity?

Part B

1. A $2000 bond with semi-annual coupons at $i^{(2)} = 6\frac{1}{2}\%$ is redeemable at par in 20 years.
   It is callable at a 5% premium in 15 years. Determine the price to guarantee a yield rate of a) $i^{(4)} = 8\%$; b) $i^{(1)} = 5\frac{1}{2}\%$.

2. A $1000 bond with coupons at $i^{(2)} = 6\%$ is redeemable at par in 20 years. It also has the following call options:

Call Date	Redemption
15 years	105
16 years	104
17 years	103
18 years	102
19 years	101

   Determine the price to guarantee a yield rate of a) $i^{(1)} = 5\%$; b) $i^{(12)} = 7\%$.

3. A $5000 callable bond pays $i^{(2)} = 9\frac{1}{2}\%$ and matures at par in 20 years. It may be called at the end of years 10 to 15 (inclusive) for $5200. Determine the price to yield at least $i^{(2)} = 8\frac{1}{2}\%$.

4. A special callable bond with semi-annual coupons at $i^{(2)} = 10\%$ and a face value of $1000 is sold by the issuer for a purchase price P. The redemption amount is a little unusual in that it is described as $(1200 - 20t)$ during the first 10 years and $[1000 + 20(t - 10)]$ after 10 years, where t is the number of years after issue.
   a) What is the purchase price P to yield 9% per annum compounded semi-annually assuming the bond is called at the end of 6 years?
   b) Is the bond
      i) redeemed at a premium or at a discount? Specify the amount.
      ii) purchased at a premium or at a discount? Specify the amount.
   c) Using the purchase price in a), at what other time point could the bond be called to produce the same yield rate? (Answer to the closest integral number of years n from issue.)

| **Section 6.5** | **Price of a Bond Between Bond Interest Dates** |

The bond purchase-price formulas **(15)** and **(16)** were derived for bonds purchased on bond interest dates. In that case, the seller keeps the bond interest payment due on that date, and the buyer receives all the future bond interest payments. In actuality, bonds are purchased at any time and, consequently, we need a method of valuation of bonds between bond interest dates.

In most cases, bonds are purchased on the bond market (bond exchange), where they are sold to the highest bidder. Trading of bonds is done through agents acting on behalf of the buyer and seller. The seller indicates the minimum price he or she is willing to accept (ask) and the buyer the maximum price he or she is willing to pay (bid). The agents, who work for a commission, try to get the best possible price for their client. Many newspapers publish tables of bond information. The columns describe the bonds as to issuer, bond coupon rate, and date of redemption or maturity. The yields listed are calculated assuming the bond is purchased for the price bid and held to maturity.

When a bond is sold between bond interest dates, the buyer receives all future bond interest payments. However, part of the next bond interest payment really "belongs" to the seller, for the seller owned the bond for part of the bond interest period. We need to calculate the fractional part of the interest period for which the seller owned the bond, and take this into account when determining the price of the bond on the actual purchase date.

We will use the following notation in determining the value of a bond purchased between bond interest dates to yield the buyer interest at rate i.

P_0 = the purchase price of a bond on the preceding bond interest date to yield i

k = the fractional part of the interest period that has elapsed since the preceding bond interest date. $(0 < k < 1)$

$$= \frac{\text{no. of days between preceding bond coupon date and date of sale}}{\text{no. of days between preceding bond coupon date and next bond coupon date.}}$$

P = the **full or dirty** price, which is the total value of the bond on the actual purchase date.

There are two ways to calculate the full price.

1. $P = P_0(1 + ki)$

This formula assumes simple interest for the fractional period of time k. However, this formula is seldom used in practice any more.

2. $P = P_0(1 + i)^k$

This formula assumes compound interest for the fractional period of time, k, and is the formula used in practice, and in this text.

EXAMPLE 1   A $1000 bond, redeemable at par on October 1, 2012, pays bond interest at $i^{(2)} = 10\%$. Determine the purchase (full or dirty) price on June 16, 2010, to yield $i^{(2)} = 9\%$.

Solution   Bond coupons are paid on April 1 and October 1. The preceding bond interest date is April 1, 2010. The exact time elapsed from April 1, 2010, to June 16, 2010, is 76 days. The exact time from April 1, 2010, to the next bond interest date on October 1, 2010, is 183 days. Thus, $k = \frac{76}{183}$.

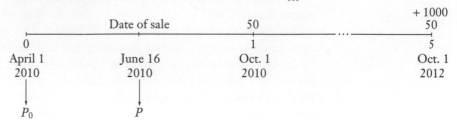

Using formula **(16)**,

$$P_0 = 1000 + (50 - 45)a_{\overline{5}|0.045} \doteq \$1021.95$$

Using the compound interest formula

$$P = P_0(1 + i)^k = 1021.95(1.045)^{\frac{76}{183}} \doteq \$1040.80$$

If we were to graph the full price of a bond, we would see a "sawtoothed" effect, as presented on the following page. As we approach each bond interest date, the full price or actual selling price of the bond increases to give the seller the accrued value of the next bond interest payment or the **accrued bond interest**, which is equal to

$$\boxed{I = k \cdot Fr}$$

In our example,

$$I = \frac{76}{183}(50) = \$20.77$$

At each bond interest payment date, the accrued bond interest is zero and the price of the bond returns to the lower line marked Q. Q is called the **clean price** or **market price** of the bond and is the price that is quoted in the daily paper. Q does not rise and fall as P does.

From the graph, we can see that $P = Q + I$ or

$$\boxed{Q = P - I}$$

In our example,

$$Q = \$1040.80 - \$20.77 = \$1020.03$$

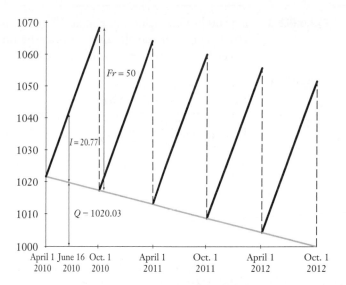

Note that under the compound interest for fractional durations assumption it looks like the value of Q moves along a straight line from one coupon date to the next. This is not quite true as Q actually moves along in a slightly curved fashion, especially as it gets closer to a coupon date.

Since bonds are issued in different denominations, it is customary to give the **quoted price** q on the basis of a $100 bond.

EXAMPLE 2   A $1000 bond paying interest at $i^{(2)} = 9\frac{1}{2}\%$ is redeemable at par on August 15, 2031. This bond was sold on September 1, 2010, at a quoted price of 103.13. What did the buyer pay?

Solution   We have $q = 103.13$. The clean (or market) price is $Q = 10 \times \$103.13 = \$1031.30$.

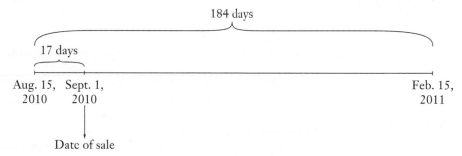

The accrued bond interest from August 15, 2010, to September 1, 2010, is

$$I = \tfrac{17}{184} \times \$47.50 = \$4.39$$

and the full purchase (dirty) price is

$$P = Q + I = \$1031.30 + \$4.39 = \$1035.69$$

EXAMPLE 3 A $500 bond, paying interest at $i^{(2)} = 8\%$, is redeemable at par on February 1, 2019. What should the quoted price be on November 15, 2010, to yield the buyer 9% compounded semi-annually?

Solution

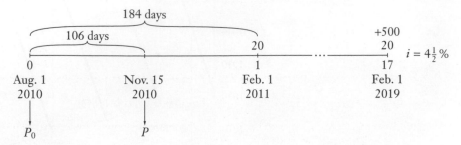

The purchase price on August 1, 2010, to yield $i^{(2)} = 9\%$, would be

$$P_0 = 500 + (20 - 22.50)a_{\overline{17}|0.045} \doteq \$500 - \$29.27 = \$470.73$$

The full (dirty) price on November 15, 2010, to yield $i^{(2)} = 9\%$, would be

$$P = P_0(1 + i)^k = 470.73(1.045)^{\frac{106}{184}} \doteq \$482.82$$

The accrued bond interest from August 1, 2010, to November 15, 2010, is

$$I = \tfrac{106}{184} \times \$20 = \$11.52$$

The clean (market) price on November 15, 2010, would be

$$Q = P - I = \$482.82 - \$11.52 = \$471.30$$

Reducing Q to a $100 bond we get the so-called quoted price

$$q = \tfrac{471.30}{500} \times 100 = 94.26$$

Exercise 6.5

Part A

Determine the full price and the market price of the bonds in problems 1 to 6 in the table below.

No.	Face Value	Redemption	Bond Interest Rate	Yield Rate	Redemption Date	Date of Purchase
1.	$ 1 000	at par	$i^{(2)} = 8\%$	$i^{(2)} = 10\%$	Jan. 1, 2030	May 8, 2010
2.	$ 500	at par	$i^{(2)} = 12\%$	$i^{(2)} = 11\%$	Jan. 1, 2025	Oct. 3, 2010
3.	$ 2 000	at par	$i^{(2)} = 9\%$	$i^{(2)} = 10\%$	Nov. 1, 2021	July 20, 2010
4.	$10 000	at par	$i^{(2)} = 6\frac{1}{2}\%$	$i^{(2)} = 7\%$	Feb. 1, 2028	Oct. 27, 2010
5.	$ 1 000	at 105	$i^{(2)} = 10\%$	$i^{(2)} = 8\%$	July 1, 2021	July 30, 2010
6.	$ 2 000	at 110	$i^{(2)} = 5\frac{1}{2}\%$	$i^{(2)} = 6\frac{1}{2}\%$	Oct. 1, 2025	Apr. 17, 2010

Determine the full price of the following $1500 bonds if bought at the given quoted price.

No.	Redemption Value	Bond Interest Rate	Market Quotation	Redemption Date	Date of Purchase
7.	par	$i^{(2)} = 6\%$	98.50	Sept. 1, 2027	June 8, 2009
8.	par	$i^{(2)} = 11\%$	104.25	Feb. 1, 2023	Oct. 2, 2009
9.	$1575	$i^{(2)} = 9\%$	101.75	Oct. 1, 2023	Nov. 29, 2010
10.	$1600	$i^{(2)} = 13\%$	112.50	Apr. 1, 2023	Jan. 12, 2008

What would be the quoted price on the following $2000 bonds?

No.	Redemption Value	Bond Interest Rate	Yield Rate	Redemption Date	Date of Purchase
11.	par	$i^{(2)} = 11\%$	$i^{(2)} = 8\%$	Nov. 1, 2026	Feb. 8, 2008
12.	par	$i^{(2)} = 12\%$	$i^{(2)} = 10\%$	Mar. 1, 2028	Aug. 19, 2009
13.	$2100	$i^{(2)} = 5\frac{1}{2}\%$	$i^{(2)} = 6\%$	June 1, 2022	Oct. 30, 2007
14.	$2050	$i^{(2)} = 9\%$	$i^{(2)} = 7\%$	Oct. 1, 2018	Nov. 2, 2010

15. A $1000 bond, redeemable at par on October 1, 2012, is paying bond interest at rate $i^{(2)} = 9\%$. Determine the purchase price on August 7, 2010, to yield $i^{(2)} = 10\%$.

Part B

1. Let: P_t be the value of a bond on a coupon date at time t to yield i.
P_{t+1} be the value of a bond on the following coupon date to yield i.

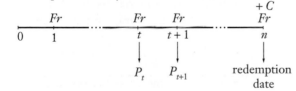

Show that $P_{t+1} = P_t (1 + i) - Fr$.

2. A $1000 bond, redeemable at $1100 on November 7, 2019, has coupons at $i^{(2)} = 7\%$. Determine the purchase price on April 18, 2010, if the desired yield is a) $i^{(12)} = 8\%$; b) $i^{(1)} = 6\%$.

3. An investment company is being audited and must locate the complete records of a specific bond transaction. The bond was a $500 bond with bond interest at rate $i^{(2)} = 12\%$ redeemable at par on January 1, 2025. It was purchased for $550.89 sometime between July 1, 2010, and January 1, 2011. Determine the exact date if the bond was purchased to yield $i^{(2)} = 11\%$.

4. A National Auto Company Limited $1000 bond is due at par on December 1, 2021. Interest is payable at $i^{(2)} = 7\%$ on June 1 and December 1. The bond may be called at 104 on December 1, 2015. Determine the dirty (purchase) price and the clean price for this bond on August 8, 2010 if the yield is to be $i^{(2)} = 6\%$,
a) assuming the bond is called at December 1, 2015;
b) assuming the bond matures at par on December 1, 2021.

5. A $5000 bond with semi-annual coupons at $i^{(2)} = 9\%$ is redeemable at par on November 1, 2030.
a) Determine the price on November 1, 2010, to yield $i^{(4)} = 10\%$.
b) Determine the book value of the bond on May 1, 2013 (just after the coupon is cashed).
c) What should the quoted price of this bond be on August 17, 2013, if the buyer wants a yield of $i^{(1)} = 7\%$?

6. a) A $1000 bond paying interest at $i^{(2)} = 7\%$ is redeemable at par on September 1, 2030. Determine the price on its issue date of September 1, 2010, to yield $i^{(2)} = 9\%$.

b) Determine the book value of the bond on September 1, 2012 (just after the coupon is cashed).

c) Determine the sale price of this bond on September 1, 2012, if the buyer wants a yield of
  i) 6% compounded semi-annually;
  ii) 12% compounded semi-annually.

d) What should the quoted price of this bond be on October 8, 2012, to yield a buyer $i^{(2)} = 8\%$?

7. The ABC Corporation $5000 bond that pays interest at $i^{(2)} = 7\%$ matures at par on October 1, 2022.

a) What did the buyer pay for the bond if it was sold on July 28, 2010, at a quoted price of 89.38?

b) What should the quoted price of this bond be on July 28, 2010, to yield a buyer $i^{(12)} = 6\%$?

c) What should the quoted price of this bond be on December 13, 2012, to yield a buyer $i^{(1)} = 8\%$?

Section 6.6 Determining the Yield Rate

One of the fundamental problems relating to bonds is to determine the investment rate i a bond will give to the buyer when bought for a given price P. In practice, the price is often given without stating the yield rate. The investor is interested in determining the true rate of return on his or her investment, i.e., the yield rate. Based on the yield rate, the investor can decide whether the purchase of a particular bond is an attractive investment or not, and also determine which of several bonds available is the best investment.

There are different methods available for calculating the yield rate. In this section we will calculate the yield rate in two ways. We will also show how to calculate the yield rate using a financial calculator and a spreadsheet.

Note that in the examples that follow, we calculate the yield rate assuming that the bond will be held to maturity unless specifically stated otherwise.

The Method of Averages

This method is simple and usually leads to fairly accurate results. It calculates an approximate value of the yield rate i as the ratio of the average interest payment over the average amount invested.

EXAMPLE 1 A $500 bond, paying interest at $i^{(2)} = 9\frac{1}{2}\%$, redeemable at par on August 15, 2022, is quoted at 109.50 on August 15, 2010. Determine the approximate value of the yield rate $i^{(2)}$ to maturity.

Solution The purchase price is $P = 5 \times \$109.50 = \$547.50$, since the bond is sold on a bond interest date. If the buyer holds the bond until maturity, she will receive 24 bond interest payments of $23.75 each plus the redemption value of $500, in total $24 \times \$23.75 + \$500 = \$1070$. She pays $547.50 and receives $1070. The net gain $\$1070 - \$547.50 = \$522.50$ is realized over 24 interest periods, so that the average interest per period is

$$\frac{\$522.50}{24} = \$21.77$$

The average amount invested is the average of the purchase price (the original value) and the redemption value (the final value), i.e. $\frac{1}{2}(\$547.50 + \$500) = \$523.75$. The approximate value of the yield rate is

$$i = \frac{21.77}{523.75} = 0.0416 = 4.16\% \text{ or } i^{(2)} = 8.32\%$$

If n is the number of interest periods from the date of sale until the redemption date we can conclude that

$$\text{The average interest payment} = \frac{n \times Fr + C - P}{n}$$

$$\text{The average amount invested} = \frac{P + C}{2}$$

$$\boxed{\textbf{The approximate value of } i = \frac{\textbf{the average interest payment}}{\textbf{the average amount invested}}}$$

In most cases the answer is correct to the nearest 10th of a percent. If a more accurate answer is desired, the method of averages should be followed by the interpolation technique described below.

The Method of Interpolation

This method of determining the yield rate consists of calculating two adjacent nominal rates such that the price of the bond lies between the prices determined. The standard method of interpolation between the two adjacent rates is then used to determine $i^{(m)}$. Usually the method of averages is used to get a starting value to be used in the method of interpolation.

EXAMPLE 2 Compute the yield rate $i^{(2)}$ in Example 1 by the method of interpolation.

Solution By the method of averages we determined that $i^{(2)} = 8.32\%$. Now we compute the prices to yield $i^{(2)} = 8\%$ and $i^{(2)} = 9\%$.

$$P(\text{to yield } i^{(2)} = 8\%) = 500 + (23.75 - 20)a_{\overline{24}|0.04} \doteq \$557.18$$
$$P(\text{to yield } i^{(2)} = 9\%) = 500 + (23.75 - 22.50)a_{\overline{24}|0.045} \doteq \$518.12$$

Arranging the data in the interpolation table, we have

	P	$i^{(2)}$
	557.18	8%
	547.50	$i^{(2)}$
	518.12	9%

$39.06 \Big\{ 9.68 \big\{ \quad \big\} d \quad \Big\} 1\%$

$$\frac{d}{1\%} = \frac{9.68}{39.06}$$
$$d = 0.2478238\%$$
$$\text{and } i^{(2)} = 8.2478238\%$$
$$\doteq 8.25\%$$

Check: $P(\text{to yield } i^{(2)} = 8.25\%) = 500 + (23.75 - 20.63)a_{\overline{24}|0.04125} \doteq \$546.97$.

EXAMPLE 3 A $1000 bond paying interest at $i^{(2)} = 11\%$ matures at par on November 15, 2021. On November 15, 2006, it was purchased at 104. On November 15, 2010, it was sold at 97.50. What was the yield rate, $i^{(2)}$?

Solution We have $F = 1000$, $r = 0.11/2 = 0.055$, $Fr = 55$. The bond was purchased on November 15, 2006 for $P = 10 \times 104 = 1040$ and is sold on November 15, 2010 for $C = 10 \times 97.50 = 975.00$. The number of interest periods between the date of purchase and the date of sale is $n = 4 \times 2 = 8$. Using the method of averages, we find

$$\text{The average interest payment} = \frac{8 \times 55 + 975 - 1040}{8} = \$46.875.$$

$$\text{The average amount invested} = \frac{975 + 1040}{2} = \$1007.50.$$

$$\text{The approximate value of } i = \frac{46.875}{1007.50} = 0.0465 \text{ or } 4.65\%.$$

$$\text{The approximate value of } i^{(2)} = 9.30\%.$$

If we want a more accurate answer, we select two rates, $i^{(2)} = 9\%$ and $i^{(2)} = 10\%$, and use them in the following formula:

$$1040 = 55a_{\overline{8}|i} + 975 (1 + i)^{-8}$$

At $i^{(2)} = 9\%$, the right-hand side equals: $362.77 + 685.61 = \$1048.38$

At $i^{(2)} = 10\%$, the right-hand side equals: $355.48 + 659.22 = \$1015.40$

Arranging the data in an interpolation table, we have

		P	$i^{(2)}$	
		1048.38	9%	
32.98	8.38	1040.00	$i^{(2)}$	1%
		1015.40	10%	

$$\frac{d}{1\%} = \frac{8.38}{32.98}$$
$$d = 0.254093389\%$$
$$\text{and } i^{(2)} = 9.25409\%$$
$$\doteq 9.25\%$$

Using a Financial Calculator to Determine the Yield Rate

We will use the notation that was introduced when using the Texas Instruments BA-II Plus calculator to determine the price of a bond in section 6.2.

For Example 2, the steps are as follows:

23.75 $\boxed{PMT}$ 500 $\boxed{FV}$ -547.50 $\boxed{PV}$ 24 $\boxed{N}$ $\boxed{CPT}$ $\boxed{I/Y}$

4.11929

This rate is the yield per half-year. To obtain the nominal yield rate, double this value. Thus, $i^{(2)} = 2(4.11929) = 8.23858 \doteq 8.24\%$. You can see the yield rate obtained using linear interpolation, 8.25%, turned out to be very accurate.

For Example 3, the steps are as follows:

$$55 \;\boxed{PMT}\; 975 \;\boxed{FV}\; -1040 \;\boxed{PV}\; 8 \;\boxed{N}\; \boxed{CPT}\; \boxed{I/Y}$$

$$4.62512$$

Thus, $i^{(2)} = 2(4.62512) = 9.250243 \doteq 9.25\%$.

Using a Spreadsheet to Determine the Yield Rate

Excel has a function called YIELD which will calculate the nominal yield rate of a bond:

YIELD (settlement date, maturity date, rate, price, redemption,
frequency, basis)

where

settlement date = date of purchase
maturity date = date of sale or redemption
rate = nominal bond rate, typed as a decimal
price = price bond was purchased at, in units of $100
redemption = price the bond was sold at, in units of $100

frequency = type '1' if bond has annual coupons, '2' if semi-annual
coupons basis
= type '1' if any fractional period uses actual number of days

For the settlement and maturity dates, they should be typed using the DATE function. This function works even for situations where the bond is purchased in between coupon dates (see Examples 4 and 5).

In Example 2, to calculate the yield rate, $i^{(2)}$, you would type:

=YIELD(date(2010,8,15),date(2022,8,15),0.095,109.5,100,2,1)

This will produce the answer 0.0823858, or $i^{(2)} \doteq 8.24\%$.

In Example 3,

=YIELD(date(2006,11,15),date(2010,11,15),0.11,104,97.50,2,1)

This will produce the answer 0.0925024, or $i^{(2)} \doteq 9.25\%$.

The two methods described in this section apply equally well to bonds purchased between interest dates. The computations are more tedious, as is illustrated in the following example.

EXAMPLE 4   A $5000 bond paying interest at $i^{(2)} = 11\%$ matures at par on June 1, 2020. On February 3, 2010, this bond is quoted at 95.38. What is the yield rate $i^{(2)}$?

Solution   First we use the method of averages to get an estimate of the yield rate assuming that the bond was quoted on the **nearest** coupon date, in this case December 1, 2009, or 21 interest periods before maturity. The clean price on February 3, 2010, is $Q = 50 \times 95.38 = \$4769.00$.

The average interest payment $= \frac{21 \times 275 + 5000 - 4769}{21} = \$286.00$.

The average amount invested $= \frac{5000 + 4769}{2} = \$4884.50$.

The approximate value of $i = \frac{286.00}{4884.50} = 0.058552564$.

The approximate value of $i^{(2)} = 11.71\%$.

If we want a more accurate answer, we select 2 rates, $i^{(2)} = 11\%$ and $i^{(2)} = 12\%$, and compute the corresponding clean prices on February 3, 2010, using the method outlined in section 6.5.

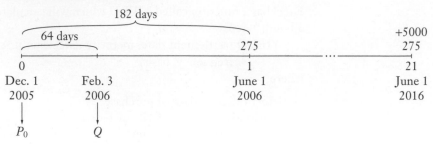

At $i^{(2)} = 11\%$: $P_0 = \$5000$ without calculation.

$$P = 5000(1.055)^{\frac{64}{182}} = \$5095.03$$
$$Q = 5095.03 - \frac{64}{182}(275) = \$4998.33$$

At $i^{(2)} = 12\%$: $P_0 = \$5000 + (275 - 300)a_{\overline{21}|0.06} = 5000 - 294.10 = \$4705.90$

$$P = 4705.90(1.06)^{\frac{64}{182}} = \$4803.32$$
$$Q = P - 1 = 4803.32 - \frac{64}{182}(275) = \$4706.62$$

Arranging the data in an interpolation table, we have

Q on Feb. 3, 2000		$i^{(2)}$
	4998.33	11%
229.33	4769.00	$i^{(2)}$
	4706.62	12%

291.71

$$\frac{d}{1\%} = \frac{229.33}{291.71}$$
$$d = 0.7861575\%$$
$$\text{and } i^{(2)} = 11.7861579\%$$
$$\doteq 11.79\%$$

Note: Using Excel's yield function,

=YIELD(date(2006,2,3),date(2016,6,1),0.11,95.38,100,2,1)

will produce the answer 0.1177894, or $i^{(2)} = 11.78\%$.

Note: Suppose the bond was quoted at 95.38 on April 12, 2010. The nearest coupon date would be June 1, 2010 or 20 interest periods before maturity. You should confirm that the yield rate using the method of averages becomes $i = 0.058665$, or $i^{(2)} = 11.73\%$. Using the method of interpolation, use the same method as shown above but with $n = 20$. Also, when calculating the full price, P, and the clean price, Q, the numerator of k is the number of days between December 1 and April 12 (132 days) and the denominator is the number of days between December 1 and June 1 (182 days). Thus $k = \frac{132}{182}$. You should confirm this leads to $i^{(2)} = 11.82\%$.

EXAMPLE 5   A \$1000 bond paying interest at $i^{(2)} = 12\%$ matures on June 1, 2025. On October 10, 2008, it was purchased for \$1042.50 plus accrued bond interest (i.e., $q = 104.25$). On February 8, 2011, it was sold for \$968.70 plus accrued bond interest (i.e., $q = 96.87$). Estimate the yield rate $i^{(2)}$ by the method of averages.

Solution

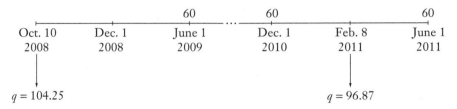

Using the method of averages, we assume that both transactions took place at the *nearest* respective coupon date. That is, we assume a purchase price of \$1042.50 on December 1, 2008, and a sale price of \$968.70 on December 1, 2010. In this period, there would be four coupons of \$60 each.

$$\text{The average interest payment} = \frac{4 \times 60 + 968.70 - 1042.50}{4} = \$41.55.$$

$$\text{The average amount invested} = \frac{968.70 + 1042.50}{2} = \$1005.60.$$

$$\text{The approximate value of } i = \frac{41.55}{1005.60} = 0.0413 \text{ or } 4.13\%.$$

$$\text{The approximate value of } i^{(2)} = 8.26\%.$$

The calculation of the answer using the method of interpolation is left for Part B, problem 9 in Exercise 6.6.

Note: Using Excel's yield function,
=YIELD(date(2008,10,10),date(2011,2,8),0.12,104.25,96.87,2,1)
will produce the answer 0.0868954, or $i^{(2)} \doteq 8.69\%$.

The Yield Curve

One interesting aspect of the bond market is the yield curve. This is a graph showing the current yield-to-maturity of government bonds of different maturities. The yield-to-maturity assumes the investor holds the bonds until redemption and is the yield used in previous sections. Of course, many investors may choose to sell their bond before maturity and in this case their rate of return will depend on both the purchase and the selling prices and not the yield-to-maturity at purchase.

The yield curve shows how interest rates vary for different maturities. That is, it is a visual representation of interest rates for different terms. Before looking at an example, it is important to note that each yield curve should consider bonds of similar risk.

At the time of writing, the longer-term bonds have a higher yield so that the yield curve is upward sloping (as you can see in the graph below). This is a normal or positive yield curve and represents the usual market position. However, sometimes the shorter maturities have higher yields so that the yield curve is known as downward sloping or concave. In these situations, the yield curve is said to be inverted.

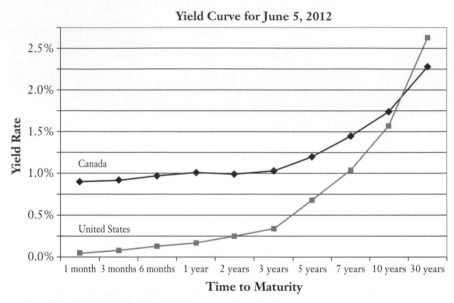

Yield Curve for June 5, 2012

A normal yield curve highlights the fact that if you purchase a bond, hold on to the investment for a period of time, and then sell it, it is likely that your selling yield will be lower than your purchase yield, assuming that other market forces have not changed. This provides investors with the opportunity to obtain a yield in excess of the yield-to-maturity and is known as "riding the yield curve." The next example illustrates this approach.

In Example 6 we will use the yield rates given in the above graph, even though they reflect the yield rates of government bonds*. Corporate bonds would have slightly higher yield rates.

EXAMPLE 6   Mrs. Noori purchases a $1000 bond, paying bond interest at $i^{(2)} = 2\%$ and redeemable at par in 10 years. The price she pays will yield $i^{(2)} = 1.74\%$ if held to maturity. After holding the bond for 3 years, she sells the bond to yield the new purchaser $i^{(2)} = 1.45\%$ (which is the current 7-year yield rate). Calculate Mrs. Noori's yield rate, $i^{(2)}$, over the 3-year investment period.

Solution   Using the bond pricing formula **(15)**, $Fr = 10$, $C = 1000$, $n = 20$, and $i = 0.0087$.

$$\text{Purchase price} = 10a_{\overline{20}|.0087} + 1000(1.0087)^{-20} \doteq \$1023.77$$

*Current and historical Canadian Government yield rates can be found at **www.bankofcanada.ca/en/rates/bonds.html**
Current and historical US Government yield rates can be found at **www.treasury.gov/resource-center/data-chart-center/interest-rates/Pages/TextView.aspx?data=billrates**

After 3 years, the selling price can be calculated using $Fr = 10$, $C = 1000$, $n = 14$, and $i = 0.00725$.

$$\text{Selling price} = 10a_{\overline{14}|0.00725} + 1000(1.00725)^{-14} \doteq \$1036.49$$

Now consider her 3-year investment. She paid $1023.79 for the bond, received a $10 coupon payment every 6 months for 3 years and then $1036.49 when she sold the bond. Therefore, her equation of value at rate i per half-year is:

$$1023.77 = 10a_{\overline{6}|i} + 1036.49(1 + i)^{-6}$$

Using the TI BA-II Plus calculator,

10 $\boxed{PMT}$ 1036.49 $\boxed{FV}$ -1023.77 $\boxed{PV}$ 6 $\boxed{N}$ $\boxed{CPT}$ $\boxed{I/Y}$

1.11778453

Thus, $i^{(2)} = 2(1.11778453)$
$= 2.3556906$
$\doteq 2.36\%$.

Hence, in this example, the investor obtains a yield in excess of 1.74% because she was able to sell at a lower yield.

Exercise 6.6

In the questions that follow, assume that the bond will be held to maturity unless specifically stated otherwise.

Part A

In problems 1 to 4, determine the yield rate, $i^{(2)}$, by the method of averages.

No.	Face Value	Redemption Value	Bond Interest	Years to Redemption	Purchase Price
1.	$2000	at par	$i^{(2)} = 11\%$	12	$1940
2.	$5000	at par	$i^{(2)} = 7\%$	10	$5340
3.	$1000	at 105	$i^{(2)} = 12\%$	15	$1120
4.	$ 500	at 110	$i^{(2)} = 6\%$	11	$ 450

5–8. Determine the yield rate, $i^{(2)}$, in problems 1 to 4 by the method of interpolation. Confirm your answers using a financial calculator or using the yield function in Excel.

9. A $1000 bond paying bond interest at $i^{(2)} = 6\%$ matures at par on August 1, 2017. If this bond was quoted at 92 on August 1, 2010, what was the yield rate $i^{(2)}$
a) using the method of averages;

b) using the method of interpolation;
c) using a calculator or spreadsheet?

10. A $1000 bond redeemable at par at the end of 20 years and paying bond interest at $i^{(2)} = 11\%$ is callable in 15 years at $1050. Determine the yield rate $i^{(2)}$ if the bond is quoted now at 110 assuming
a) it is called;
b) it is not called.

11. A $1000 bond redeemable at par in 20 years pays bond interest at $i^{(2)} = 10\%$. It is callable at the end of 10 years at 105. If it is quoted at 96, determine the yield rate $i^{(2)}$ assuming
    a) it is called;
    b) it is not called.

12. A $1000 bond paying interest at $i^{(2)} = 10\%$ matures at par on June 1, 2026. On August 17, 2010, this bond is quoted at 98.50. What is the yield rate?

13. A $1000 bond paying interest at $i^{(2)} = 7\%$ matures at par on October 1, 2021. On April 28, 2010, this bond is quoted at 102. What is the yield rate?

14. The XYZ Corporation has a $1000 bond that pays bond interest at $i^{(2)} = 8\%$. The bond is redeemable at par on June 1, 2020. On June 1, 2004, an investor buys this bond on the open market at 97. On June 1, 2012, he sells this bond on the open market at 101. Determine the investor's yield rate $i^{(2)}$.

15. Ms. Holman buys a $1000 bond that pays bond interest at $i^{(2)} = 7\%$ and is redeemable at par in 15 years. The price she pays will give her a yield of $i^{(2)} = 8\%$ if held to maturity. After 5 years, Ms. Holman sells this bond to Mr. Dawson, who desires a yield of $i^{(2)} = 6\%$ on his investment.
    a) What price did Ms. Holman pay?
    b) What price did Mr. Dawson pay?
    c) What yield $i^{(2)}$ did Ms. Holman realize? (Use interpolation)

16. A $1000 bond paying interest at $i^{(2)} = 11\%$ matures at par on July 15, 2026. On January 29, 2007, it was purchased for $972.50 plus accrued bond interest (i.e. 97.25). On May 7, 2010, it was sold for $1003.80 plus accrued bond interest (i.e. 100.38). Estimate the yield rate $i^{(2)}$ by the method of averages.

Part B

1. The XYZ Corporation issues a $1000 bond with semi-annual coupons at $i^{(2)} = 7\%$ redeemable at par in 20 years or callable at par in 15 years. Mr. LaBelle buys the bond to guarantee a yield rate $i^{(12)} = 9\%$.
    a) Determine the purchase price.
    b) After 15 years, the XYZ Corporation calls the bond in and pays Mr. LaBelle his $1000. Calculate his overall yield stated as a rate $i^{(12)}$.

2. In our "method of averages" formula we said
$$\text{Average amount invested} = \frac{P + C}{2}$$
A slightly more accurate formula uses
$$\text{Average amount invested} = C + \frac{n + 1}{2n}(P - C)$$
Using this latter modification, repeat problems 1 to 4 in Part A above and see if your approximations improve.

3. The XYZ Corporation has a bond due December 4, 2023, paying bond interest at $i^{(2)} = 10\frac{3}{8}\%$. The price bid on December 14, 2010, is 104. What yield $i^{(12)}$ does the investor desire?

4. Mr. Hunter buys a $1000 bond with semi-annual coupons at $i^{(2)} = 6\%$. The bond is redeemable at par in 20 years. The price he pays will guarantee him a yield of $i^{(4)} = 8\%$ if held to maturity. After 5 years, Mr. Hunter sells this bond to Miss Schnarr, who desires a yield of $i^{(1)} = 5\frac{1}{2}\%$ on her investment.
    a) What price did Mr. Hunter pay?
    b) What price did Miss Schnarr pay?
    c) What yield, $i^{(4)}$, did Mr. Hunter realize?

5. The ABC Corporation issues a $1000 bond, with coupons payable at $i^{(2)} = 7\%$ on January 1 and July 1, redeemable at par on July 1, 2020.
    a) How much would an investor pay for this bond on September 1, 2010, to yield $i^{(2)} = 8\%$?
    b) Given the purchase price from part a), if each coupon is deposited in a bank account paying interest at $i^{(4)} = 6\%$ and the bond is held to maturity, what is the effective annual yield rate $i^{(1)}$ on this investment?

6. A bond paying semi-annual coupons at $i^{(2)} = 8\%$ matures at par in n years and is quoted at 110 to yield rate $i^{(2)}$. A bond paying semi-annual coupons at $i^{(2)} = 8\frac{1}{2}\%$ matures at par in n years and is quoted at 112 on the same yield basis.
   a) Determine the unknown yield rate, $i^{(2)}$.
   b) Determine n to the nearest half-year.

7. An issue of bonds, redeemable at par in n years, is to bear coupons at $i^{(2)} = 9\%$. An investor offers to buy the entire issue at a premium of 15%. At the same time, she advises the issuer that if the coupon rate were raised from $i^{(2)} = 9\%$ to $i^{(2)} = 10\%$, she would offer to buy the entire issue at a premium of 25%. At what yield rate $i^{(2)}$ are these two offers equivalent?

8. In August 1991, interest rates in the bond markets were such that an investor could expect a yield of $i^{(2)} = 10\%$. On August 1, 1991, an investor bought a bond with semi-annual coupons at $i^{(2)} = 9\%$ which was to mature in 20 years at par. By August 1, 1992, interest rates had fallen to $i^{(2)} = 8\%$. This same investor sold his bond on August 1, 1992, on the bond market. Determine the yield $i^{(2)}$ on this investment.

9. For the bond question solved in Example 5 in section 6.6, use the method of interpolation to calculate the yield rate, $i^{(2)}$.

Section 6.7 **Other Types of Bonds**

Zero-Coupon Bonds

A zero-coupon bond is a bond that does not make any periodic interest payments or have any coupons. It is also called a **discount bond** or **deep discount bond**. All that is paid out is the face value of the bond, which is paid out when the bond reaches maturity. As a result, the price paid for a zero-coupon bond is the present value of the face value, discounted at the current yield rate. The price of the bond will thus be lower than the face value. Most governmental bonds, both short term (or Treasury bills, consisting of bonds with a maturity of one year or less) and long term (maturities of more than one year) are zero-coupon bonds. As a matter of fact, the yield curve introduced in section 6.6 is a graph of the current yield rates on government zero-coupon bonds of different maturities.

EXAMPLE 1 An investor buys a $100\ 000 five-year government bond. If the current yield rate is $i^{(2)} = 4.25\%$, what price does the investor pay for the bond?

Solution This would be a zero-coupon bond that pays $100\ 000 at the end of five years. Thus,

$$P = 100\ 000\left(1 + \frac{0.0425}{2}\right)^{-10} = 100\ 000(1.02125)^{-10} = \$81\ 036.24$$

EXAMPLE 2 A $500 000 zero-coupon bond is purchased for $485 325. What yield rate, $i^{(2)}$, does the bond earn if it is a) a six-month Treasury bill; b) a two-year bond?

Solution a
$$485\ 325 = 500\ 000(1 + i)^{-1}$$
This solves for $i = 0.03023747$, or $i^{(2)} = 2i = 6.05\%$.

Solution b
$$485\ 325 = 500\ 000(1 + i)^{-4}$$
This solves for $i = 0.007475133$, or $i^{(2)} = 1.50\%$.

Strip Bonds

Another type of zero-coupon bond is a regular bond in which the coupons have been stripped from the bond, leaving behind only the redemption value. This "redemption only" bond is called a strip bond. This strip bond would sell for a price equal to the present value of the redemption value, discounted at the current yield rate. That is:

$$P = C(1 + i)^{-n}$$

The original buyer of the bond may also sell each coupon as a separate asset or may sell all the coupons as a package. If each coupon is sold separately, the price would be $Fr(1 + i)^{-n}$, where n is the number of interest periods from the time of sale to the time the coupon is payable. If all the coupons are sold as one package, the price would be:

$$Fra_{\overline{n}|i}$$

EXAMPLE 3 A $10 000 corporate bond with bond interest at $i^{(2)} = 9\%$ is redeemable at par in 20 years. Investor A buys the bond to yield $i^{(2)} = 8\frac{1}{2}\%$. Investor A strips the coupons from the bond and sells the remaining "strip" bond to Investor B, who wishes a yield rate of $i^{(12)} = 9\%$.

Determine a) the price Investor B paid for the strip bond; b) the yield rate $i^{(2)}$ realized by Investor A; c) the profit Investor A makes if, in addition to selling the strip bond, the first 10 coupons are sold to Investor C who wishes to yield $i^{(2)} = 8\%$ and the last 30 coupons are sold to Investor D who wishes to yield $i^{(2)} = 7\%$.

Solution a Investor B will pay the discounted value of $10 000 payable in 20 years at $i^{(12)} = 9\%$, or $i = 0.0075$, per month over 240 months.

$$P = 10\ 000(1.0075)^{-240} \doteq \$1664.13$$

Solution b First determine the price Investor A paid for the bond. With $F = C = 10\ 000$, $r = 0.045$, $i = 0.0425$, and $n = 40$,

$$P = 10\ 000 + (450 - 425)a_{\overline{40}|0.0425} \doteq \$10\ 476.93$$

In return for the investment of $10 476.93, Investor A gets 40 coupons worth $450 each over 20 years plus $1664.13 payable immediately from Investor B. That is,

$$10\ 476.96 = 1664.13 + 450a_{\overline{40}|i}$$
$$a_{\overline{40}|i} = 19.5841$$

A starting value to solve $a_{\overline{40}|i} = 19.5841$ (see section 3.6) is

$$i = \frac{1 - (\frac{19.5841}{40})^2}{19.5841} = 0.038821768 \text{ or } i^{(2)} = 2i = 7.76\%.$$

At $i^{(2)} = 7\%$, $a_{\overline{40}|0.035} = 21.3551$.
At $i^{(2)} = 8\%$, $a_{\overline{40}|0.04} = 19.7928$.

We obviously need to proceed to $i^{(2)} = 9\%$.

At $i^{(2)} = 9\%$, $a_{\overline{40}|0.0425} = 18.4016$.

Now we have two rates, $i^{(2)} = 8\%$ and $i^{(2)} = 9\%$, 1% apart, that provide upper and lower bounds for interpolation.

Arranging our data in an interpolation table, we have

	$a_{\overline{40}|i}$	$i^{(2)}$	
1.3912 { 0.2087 {	19.7928	8%	} d
	19.5841	$i^{(2)}$	} 1%
	18.4016	9%	

$$\frac{d}{1\%} = \frac{0.2087}{1.3919}$$
$$d \doteq 0.149938932\%$$
$$\text{and } i^{(2)} = 8.15\%$$

Solution c The price Investor C pays for the first 10 coupons is

$$P = 450a_{\overline{10}|0.04} \doteq \$3649.90$$

The price Investor D pays for the last 30 coupons is

$$P = 450a_{\overline{30}|0.035}(1.035)^{-10} \doteq \$5867.31$$

Total received by Investor A = $(1664.13 + 3649.90 + 5867.31) = $11 181.34
Total paid by Investor A = $10 476.93
Net Profit earned by Investor A = $ 704.41

Exercise 6.7

Part A

1. An investor wishes to buy a government zero-coupon bond. Determine the prices of the following zero-coupon bonds using the given information.
   a) a $10 000 one-year bond, at yield rate $i^{(2)} = 5.45\%$

   b) a $1 000 000 five-year bond, at yield rate $i^{(2)} = 4.50\%$
   c) a $200 000 ten-year bond, at yield rate $i^{(2)} = 6.25\%$

2. Determine the yield rate, $i^{(2)}$, earned on the following zero-coupon bonds.
   a) a $500 000 one-year bond, purchased for $473 595

b) a $10 000 three-year bond, purchased for
   $8750

c) a 1 000 000 ten-year bond, purchased for
   $478 900

3. A corporation issues a $1000 20-year bond with
   bond interest at $i^{(2)} = 10\%$. It is purchased by
   an investor A who wishes a yield of $i^{(2)} = 9\frac{1}{2}\%$.
   This investor A keeps the coupons but sells the
   strip bond to another investor whose desired
   yield is $i^{(2)} = 10\frac{1}{2}\%$. Determine the overall yield
   rate $i^{(2)}$ to investor A.

4. A corporation issues a $1000 15-year zero-
   coupon bond redeemable at par. Determine the
   price paid by an investor whose desired yield is
   $i^{(365)} = 8\%$.

5. Investor A buys a $2500 10-year bond paying
   interest at $i^{(2)} = 6\%$, redeemable at 105, to
   yield $i^{(2)} = 7\%$. She sells the coupons to
   Investor B who wishes to yield $i^{(2)} = 6.25\%$
   and she sells the strip bond to Investor C who
   wishes to yield $i^{(4)} = 6.5\%$. What profit does
   Investor A make?

Part B

1. Another special type of bond is an
   accumulation bond (see exercise B4 in
   section 6.2). For this type of bond, the coupons
   are not paid out every period, but instead are
   reinvested in the bond at the bond interest rate.
   At maturity, the bond holder receives the
   redemption value, C, plus the accumulated value
   of the n-coupons of Fr accumulated at r. The
   price of the bond is equal to the maturity value,
   discounted to the date of sale using the yield

rate, i. That is,

$$\text{Maturity value, } S = C + Frs_{\overline{n}|r}$$
$$\text{Price, } P = S (1 + i)^{-n}$$

Calculate the price of the following accumulation
bonds:

a) A $1000 bond redeemable at par in 12 years,
   paying interest at $i^{(2)} = 6\%$, purchased to
   yield $i^{(2)} = 7\%$.

b) A $5000 bond redeemable at par in 7 years,
   paying interest at $i^{(2)} = 10\%$, purchased to
   yield $i^{(2)} = 8.5\%$.

c) A $2000 bond redeemable at 102.5 in
   15 years, paying interest at $i^{(2)} = 5.75\%$, purchased to yield $i^{(2)} = 6.25\%$.

2. Current yield rates are 3.50% for one-year zero-
   coupon bonds, 3.65% for two-year zero-coupon
   bonds, 3.95% for three-year zero-coupon bonds,
   4.25% for four-year zero-coupon bonds, and
   4.60% for five-year zero coupon bonds. All rates
   are compounded semi-annually.

   a) What type of yield curve do these rates
      suggest?

   b) You create an investment portfolio in which
      you buy $100 000 worth of one-year, two-
      year, three-year, four-year, and five-year
      zero-coupon bonds. How much is the portfo-
      lio worth today?

3. A corporation issues a $10 000 15-year bond
   with bond interest at $i^{(2)} = 4\%$ and redeemable
   at 102. It is purchased by Investor A who wishes
   a yield of $i^{(2)} = 5\%$. Investor A sells the coupons
   to Investor B whose desired yield is $i^{(2)} = 5.5\%$
   and Investor A keeps the strip bond. Determine
   the overall yield rate, $i^{(2)}$, to Investor A.

| *Section 6.8* | **Summary and Review Exercises** |

● Purchase price P of a bond with face value F, redemption value C, and bond
rate r, on a bond interest date n interest periods prior to maturity, to yield rate
i until maturity is given by

$$P = Fra_{\overline{n}|i} + C(1 + i)^{-n} \quad \text{basic formula}$$

or

$$P = C + (Fr - Ci)a_{\overline{n}|i} \quad \text{premium/discount formula}$$

- For par value bonds with $C = F$

$$\text{premium} \quad P - C = (Fr - Ci)a_{\overline{n}|i} = F(r - i)a_{\overline{n}|i}$$
$$\text{premium} \quad C - P = (Ci - Fr)a_{\overline{n}|i} = F(i - r)a_{\overline{n}|i}$$

- For other bonds with $C \neq F$ and modified coupon rate $g = \dfrac{Fr}{C}$

$$\text{premium} \quad P - C = (Fr - Ci)a_{\overline{n}|i} = C(g - i)a_{\overline{n}|i}$$
$$\text{premium} \quad C - P = (Ci - Fr)a_{\overline{n}|i} = C(i - g)a_{\overline{n}|i}$$

- Properties of a bond schedule:
  1. All book values can be reproduced by a purchase price formula.
  2. Book value adjustments add up to the amount of discount (or the amount of premium).
  3. Book values are gradually adjusted from P to C. In the case of a discount, we accumulate the discount or write the bond up from P to C; in the case of a premium, we amortize the premium or write the bond down from P to C.
  4. Successive book value adjustments are in the ratio $(1 + i)$.

- In the bond schedule:

  Book value adjustment at time k
  = Coupon − Interest on book value at time $(k − 1)$.

  - For bonds purchased at a discount, book value adjustments are negative and the bond is written up.

  - For bonds purchased at a premium, book value adjustments are positive and the bond is written down.

- If the bond is purchased between bond interest dates, where k is the fractional part of the interest period that has elapsed since the preceding bond interest date $(0 < k < 1)$ the full or dirty price P is given by

$$P = P_0 (1 + i)^k$$

where P_0 is the price on the preceding bond interest date.

- Clean or market price Q is the full price P less accrued bond interest $I = k(Fr)$

$$Q = P - I$$

- To estimate the yield rate by the method of averages we calculate

$$i \doteq \frac{\text{average income per period}}{\text{average value invested}} = \frac{[n(Fr) + C - P]/n}{(P + C)/2}$$

To obtain a more accurate value of i, we follow the method of interpolation, or use a spreadsheet.

Review Exercises 6.8

1. The Acme Corporation issues $10 000 000 of 20-year bonds on March 15, 2010, with semi-annual coupons at 7%. The contract requires Acme to set up a sinking fund earning interest at $i^{(2)} = 5\%$ to redeem the bonds at maturity; the first sinking-fund deposit is to be made September 15, 2010. Determine
   a) the purchase price of the bond issue to yield $i^{(2)} = 6\%$;
   b) the necessary sinking-fund payment.

2. The XYZ Corporation issues a $1000 bond with coupons at $i^{(2)} = 8\%$ and redeemable at par on August 1, 2025.
   a) How much should be paid for this bond on February 1, 2010, to yield $i^{(2)} = 6\%$?
   b) If the purchase price was $1050, and the bond is held to maturity, determine the overall yield, $i^{(2)}$.

3. A $1000 bond with semi-annual coupons at $i^{(2)} = 10\%$ payable January 1 and July 1 each year matures on July 1, 2015, for $1050.
   a) Determine the price on January 1, 2010, to yield $i^{(2)} = 10\frac{1}{2}\%$.
   b) Is the bond purchased at a premium or a discount?
   c) Calculate the entries in the bond schedule on July 1, 2010, and January 1, 2011.

4. An ABC Corporation $2000 bond, paying bond interest at $i^{(2)} = 8\%$, matures at par on September 1, 2023.
   a) What did a buyer pay for this bond on July 20, 2010, if the market quotation for the bond was 104.75?
   b) Estimate, using linear interpolation, the yield rate for the buyer in part a).
   c) What should the market quotation for this bond be on July 20, 2010, if the desired yield is $i^{(2)} = 7\%$?

5. The ABC Corporation issues a 20-year par value bond on February 1, 2010, with coupons at $i^{(2)} = 8\%$ payable February 1 and August 1. Mr. Kelly buys a $1000 bond from this issue on February 1, 2010 to yield $i^{(2)} = 9\%$. On August 1, 2014, Mr. Kelly sells this bond to Ms.

Quinn, who wants a yield $i^{(2)} = 7\%$.
   a) Determine the original purchase price.
   b) Determine the sale price on August 1, 2014.
   c) What yield, $i^{(2)}$, did Mr. Kelly realize?
   d) Determine the sale price if the transaction took place on September 1, 2014.

6. Ms. Machado invested $10 000 in the Ace Manufacturing Company four years ago. She was to be paid interest on the loan at $i^{(2)} = 11\%$. The principal amount of $10 000 was to be returned after 10 years. Now, having just received the 8th interest payment in full, Ms. Machado has been informed that Ace has just been declared bankrupt. Ms. Machado has been offered, as a settlement, 25% of the present value of all monies due to her, determined at $i^{(1)} = 13\%$. How much can she expect to receive?

7. A $1000 bond has semi-annual coupons at $i^{(2)} = 7\%$. The bond matures after 20 years at par but can be called after 15 years at $1050.
   a) Determine the price to guarantee a yield of $i^{(2)} = 8\%$.
   b) What maturity date was assumed in answering part a)?
   c) Determine the yield, $i^{(2)}$, realized if the bond is redeemed other than anticipated in part a). (Your answer must be larger than $i^{(2)} = 8\%$.)

8. A bond with face value $10 000 pays $i^{(2)} = 9\%$. An investor buys it for $10 500 and sells it 4 years later for $10 200. Calculate the yield rate, $i^{(2)}$, earned by the investor over this period using a) the method of averages; b) interpolation.

9. A $1000 bond with coupons at $i^{(2)} = 10\%$ is redeemable at par in n years. It is purchased at a premium of $300. Another $1000 bond with coupons at $i^{(2)} = 8\%$ is also redeemable at par in n years. It is purchased at a premium of $100 on the same yield basis.
   a) Calculate the unknown yield rate, $i^{(2)}$.
   b) Determine n.

10. A $1000 callable bond pays $i^{(2)} = 10\%$ and matures at par in 20 years. It may be called at $1100 at the end of years 5–9 inclusive. Determine the price to yield at least $i^{(2)} = 9\%$.

11. A $10 000 bond has semi-annual coupons, and matures at par in 15 years. It is bought at a discount to yield $i^{(2)} = 11\%$. The adjustment in book value at the end of 5 years is $25. Determine the purchase price.

12. Calculate the price on Dec. 8, 2010, of a $5000 bond maturing at par on July 2, 2020, paying $i^{(2)} = 6\%$. It is priced to yield $i^{(2)} = 7\%$.

13. A 20-year bond with a par value of $1000, paying $i^{(2)} = 7\%$, and a maturity value of $1100 is bought on December 20, 2007, to yield $i^{(2)} = 6\%$ to the investor.
    a) What is the price of the bond?
    b) How much of the coupon received on June 20, 2011, can be considered as interest income by the purchaser?
    c) If the bond were sold on July 20, 2011, to yield $i^{(2)} = 5\%$ to the purchaser, how much would the seller receive?
    d) Assume the bond is bought for the price calculated in a) and sold for the price calculated in c) on July 20, 2011. What rate, $i^{(2)}$, has the original investor earned? Use the method of averages.

14. A $2000 bond matures at par in 10 years and pays $i^{(2)} = 10\%$. Determine the purchase price to yield to maturity a) $i^{(2)} = 11\%$; b) $i^{(12)} = 9\%$.

15. A $1000 bond matures for $1050 in 2 years and pays $i^{(2)} = 9\%$. Determine the price P to yield $i^{(2)} = 10\%$ to maturity and construct the bond schedule.

16. A $2000 bond with semi-annual coupons at $i^{(2)} = 7\%$ is redeemable for $2100. If the amount for the 10th write-down is $6.50, calculate the purchase price to yield $i^{(2)} = 5.8\%$.

17. For a $2000 bond redeemable at par on February 1, 2025, with bond interest at $i^{(2)} = 8\%$, determine the purchase price on May 8, 2010 to yield $i^{(2)} = 7\%$ until maturity.

18. For a $5000 bond redeemable at 101.75 on May 15, 2017, paying bond interest at $i^{(2)} = 8.5\%$, determine the purchase price on March 7, 2010 at a market quotation of 91.25.

19. For a $2000 bond redeemable at par on April 18, 2019, paying bond interest at $i^{(2)} = 7\%$, calculate the market quotation on June 6, 2010, that would give a yield rate to maturity $i^{(2)} = 8.2\%$.

20. A $2000 bond maturing at par in 16 years, with bond interest at $i^{(2)} = 9\%$, is purchased to yield $i^{(2)} = 10\%$ to maturity. After 4 years the bond is sold to yield $i^{(2)} = 8\%$ to maturity. Determine the yield rate over the 4-year period using interpolation.

Case Study 1   *Callable Bond*

A $5000 callable bond matures on September 1, 2019, at par. It is callable on September 1, 2014, 2016, or 2018 at $5250. Interest on the bond is $i^{(2)} = 8\%$.
   a) Calculate the price on September 1, 2010, to yield an investor $i^{(2)} = 6\%$.
   b) Draw up the bond schedule for the year September 1, 2010, to September 1, 2011.
   c) If the bond was called on September 1, 2016, what yield, $i^{(2)}$, would the investor have earned? Use the method of averages, followed by interpolation.
   d) On November 1, 2012, the bond is sold to yield $i^{(2)} = 7\%$ until maturity.
      i) Determine the purchase price.
      ii) What is the market quotation?

Case Study 2   *Varying Coupons*

The ABC Corporation issues a very unusual type of bond on July 1, 2010. It is issued in units where the face amount is $1000 and the redemption amount is $1500 at July 1, 2020. Semi-annual coupons are payable January 1 and July 1 and are as follows:

	2011	2012	2013	2014	2015
Jan. 1	$60	64	68	72	76
July 1	60	64	68	72	76

	2016	2017	2018	2019	2020
Jan. 1	$80	84	88	92	96
July 1	80	84	88	92	96

a) What should the initial offering price per unit be if the yield to maturity is to be 10% per annum compounded semi-annually?
b) Is this a premium or a discount? Specify the amount.
c) If a purchaser on July 1, 2010, buys a bond at a price as calculated in a), then sells one unit of the bond at July 1, 2012, for $1300, what interest rate $i^{(2)}$ would be realized?

Rates of Return

Learning Objectives

In this chapter we discuss some common methods and financial tools that companies and individuals use to help them make business decisions. These methods basically consist of estimating future income streams, or future cash flows, and then calculating their present value at some desired rate of return. In other situations, the present value is known, leaving the rate of return to be determined. This rate is often referred to as the internal rate of return.

We also include a short section on other securities (e.g., preferred stocks and common stocks). Upon completing this chapter, you will be able to do the following:

- Calculate the net present value of a series of cash flows and use it to make a business decision.
- Calculate the internal rate of return of a series of cash flows and use it to make a business decision.
- Calculate "dollar-weighted" rates of return.
- Calculate "time-weighted" rates of return.
- Calculate prices for common and preferred shares.

Section 7.1   Net Present Value

Most business enterprises and investors are required to decide, on a fairly regular basis, whether a particular business venture or investment is worthwhile and should proceed. In many cases, a comparison among alternative projects is also required. That is, a financial assessment of each proposal is necessary before it commences so that the appropriate decision may be made.

One method of assessing a project that involves future cash flows is to use compound interest and calculate the present value of these cash flows at a particular interest rate. The interest rate used is known as the **cost of capital** and can be considered to be the cost of borrowing money by the business or the rate of return that an investor may obtain if the money is invested with security. The cost of capital can also be thought of as the minimum rate of return required by the investor if they are to undertake the investment or business venture. This process is known as calculating the **net present value** for the project and may be represented by the following equation:

$$\text{Net Present Value (or NPV)} = F_0 + F_1(1 + i)^{-1} + F_2(1 + i)^{-2} + F_3(1 + i)^{-3} + \cdots + F_n(1 + i)^{-n}$$

where F_t = estimated cash inflows − estimated cash outflows (for period t) and i is the cost of capital per period. F_t is commonly referred to as the estimated net cash flow for the project at the end of period t. When $F_t > 0$, the cash inflows for period t exceed the cash outflows and the opposite is true when $F_t < 0$.

The net present value can be used to make a business decision. If NPV ≥ 0, we can conclude that the rate of return from the cash inflows is greater than or equal to the cost of the cash outflows and the project has economic merit and should proceed. If NPV < 0, we conclude that the return for the cash inflows is lower than the cost of the cash outflows and the project should not proceed (as the cost cannot be recovered by the income).

In many examples the first cash flow (namely F_0) is negative, while all future cash flows during the term of the project are positive. However, in other cases, additional funds may be required such that some later F_ts are negative.

EXAMPLE 1 Determine the net present value of a $100 000 investment that is estimated to have the following yearly cash flows (all assumed to occur at the end of each year) if the cost of capital is a) $i^{(1)} = 7\%$; b) $i^{(1)} = 14\%$.

Year End	1	2	3	4
Cash Inflow	$80 000	$70 000	$65 000	$70 000
Cash Outflow	$40 000	$40 000	$35 000	$35 000

Solution a We have $F_0 = -100\,000, F_1 = 40\,000, F_2 = 30\,000, F_3 = 30\,000, F_4 = 35\,000$, and $i = 0.07$,

$$\begin{aligned}\text{NPV at 7\%} &= -100\,000 + 40\,000(1.07)^{-1} + 30\,000(1.07)^{-2} + \\ &\quad 30\,000(1.07)^{-3} + 35\,000(1.07)^{-4} \\ &= +14\,776.61 \doteq +\$14\,777\end{aligned}$$

This result indicates that if the cost of capital is 7%, then the project should proceed, because its profit in present value terms is $14 777.

Solution b With the same values for F_t but with $i = 0.14$,

$$\begin{aligned}\text{NPV at 14\%} &= -100\,000 + 40\,000(1.14)^{-1} + 30\,000(1.14)^{-2} + \\ &\quad 30\,000(1.14)^{-3} + 35\,000(1.14)^{-4} \\ &= -856.30 \doteq -\$856\end{aligned}$$

This negative net present value indicates that if the cost of capital is 14%, then this project will not return as high a rate as the cost of capital and therefore should not proceed.

OBSERVATION:

The following points should be noted.

1. Due to the uncertainty of the future, the cash-flow figures used are normally estimates and therefore the net present value can be rounded to the nearest dollar, or in some cases the nearest hundred or thousand dollars.

2. As the future cash flows are only estimates and may vary with changing circumstances, it is common for at least three different sets of cash flows to be used representing the expected situation as well as an optimistic and pessimistic view, which in turn provides three net present values.

As shown in previous chapters, problems involving cash flows over several periods can be presented in a spreadsheet. The following spreadsheet shows how Example 1 could be calculated at both interest rates.

	A	B	C	D	E	F
1	Year End	Cash Flow	Factor at 7% p.a.	PV at 7% p.a.	Factor at 14% p.a.	PV at 14% p.a.
2	0	−100,000	1.00000	−100,000	1.00000	−100,000
3	1	+40,000	0.93458	+37,383	0.87719	+35,088
4	2	+30,000	0.87344	+26,203	0.76947	+23,084
5	3	+30,000	0.81630	+24,489	0.67497	+20,249
6	4	+35,000	0.76290	+26,702	0.59208	+20,723
7			NPV	+$14,477		−$856

In a spreadsheet, it is also possible to place a variable (say the interest rate) in a particular cell and to set up the table in terms of this cell. This means that when the variable is changed, all the relevant cells change automatically. This process enables the user to see the results at different interest rates quickly.

Most spreadsheets also have an inbuilt function to calculate the net present value. For instance, in Excel it is *NPV* (rate, value 1, value 2, …). This assumes that each value is spaced equally and that the first payment (i.e., value 1) is in one period's time. Using Example 1, we could type the interest rate in cell G1 (0.07) and then the function in the spreadsheet would be:

$$= NPV(\text{G1}, \text{B3} : \text{B6}) - 100\ 000$$

Note that the $100 000 that is paid immediately is subtracted from the function to obtain the correct answer. To see what the net present value becomes when the cost of capital is 14%, you need only change the value of cell G1 to 0.14.

One of the major advantages in calculating net present values is that they enable comparisons to be made between two alternative projects that require the same investment. However, as shown in the following example, the preferred choice may depend on the cost of capital.

EXAMPLE 2 The following data provide the estimated end-of-year net cash flows that will be received from alternative projects A and B for an investment of $200 000. Which project should be adopted if the cost of capital is $i^{(1)} = 6\%$?

Year	1	2	3	4
Project A	$80 000	$70 000	$60 000	$ 35 000
Project B	$30 000	$40 000	$40 000	$150 000

Solution NPV of project A at 6% $= -200\,000 + 80\,000(1.06)^{-1} + 70\,000(1.06)^{-2} +$
$$60\,000(1.06)^{-3} + 35\,000(1.06)^{-4}$$
$$\doteq +\$15\,872$$

NPV of project B at 6% $= -200\,000 + 30\,000(1.06)^{-1} + 40\,000(1.06)^{-2} +$
$$40\,000(1.06)^{-3} + 150\,000(1.06)^{-4}$$
$$\doteq +\$16\,301$$

Both net present values are positive so that both projects would be profitable and could proceed. However, with the higher NPV at 6%, project B is to be slightly preferred.

Using a Financial Calculator to Calculate the NPV

We will illustrate the use of the BA-II Plus calculator to calculate the net present value for Example 2a):

Press $\boxed{CF}$ key, $CF_0 = -200\,000$ hit $\boxed{\text{enter}}$, press $\boxed{\downarrow}$ key
$CO_1 = 80\,000$ hit $\boxed{\text{enter}}$, press $\boxed{\downarrow}$ key
$FO_1 = 1$ hit $\boxed{\text{enter}}$, press $\boxed{\downarrow}$ key
$CO_2 = 70\,000$ hit $\boxed{\text{enter}}$, press $\boxed{\downarrow}$ key
$FO_2 = 1$ hit $\boxed{\text{enter}}$, press $\boxed{\downarrow}$ key
$CO_3 = 60\,000$ hit $\boxed{\text{enter}}$, press $\boxed{\downarrow}$ key
$FO_3 = 1$ hit $\boxed{\text{enter}}$, press $\boxed{\downarrow}$ key
$CO_4 = 35\,000$ hit $\boxed{\text{enter}}$, press $\boxed{\downarrow}$ key
$FO_4 = 1$ then press $\boxed{NPV}$ key
$I = 6$ (interest rate is typed as a number), hit $\boxed{\text{enter}}$, press $\boxed{\downarrow}$ key then press $\boxed{CPT}$

The answer is 15 871.88411, or $15 871.88. You can repeat the above process for Example 2b), entering in the new cash flow values.

EXAMPLE 3 An insurance company has \$1 million to invest. Two investment options are available: the first is an investment in a 4-year 12% corporate bond paying half-yearly interest, redeemable at par and priced at \$95; the second is the purchase of a 4-year lease on a coal mine priced at \$1 million, which is likely to return the following year-end cash flows:

Year	1	2	3	4
Cash Flow	\$400 000	\$600 000	\$500 000	−\$200 000

The net cash outflow in the fourth year is shown as a negative payment and is the cost of land restoration. Which option should the company follow?

Solution In this problem we will calculate the yield obtained on the corporate bond investment (which we assume to be secure) and then use this figure as the cost of capital to calculate the net present value of the mining investment. Using formula **(15)** the equation of value for the bond is

$$95 = 6a_{\overline{8}|i} + 100(1 + i)^{-8}$$

Using the Texas Instruments BA-II Plus calculator, with the following steps

$$6 \boxed{PMT} \ 100 \ \boxed{FV} \ {-95} \ \boxed{PV} \ 8 \ \boxed{N} \ \boxed{CPT} \ \boxed{I/Y}$$

results in $i^{(1)} = 6.831892\%$, or $i^{(2)} = 13.663784\%$.

Then determine $i^{(1)}$ per year equivalent to $i^{(2)} = 13.663784\%$

$$1 + i^{(1)} = \left(1 + \tfrac{0.13663784}{2}\right)^2$$
$$i^{(1)} \doteq 14.13\%$$

We now use $i^{(1)} = 14.13\%$ as the cost of capital for the alternative coal mine lease. (Note that at this cost of capital, the net present value of the corporate bond is equal to 0.)

$$\begin{aligned} \text{NPV at } 14.13\% = &-1\,000\,000 + 400\,000(1.1413)^{-1} + \\ &600\,000(1.1413)^{-2} + 500\,000(1.1413)^{-3} - \\ &205\,000(1.1413)^{-4} \\ \doteq &+\$29\,563 \end{aligned}$$

As the NPV is positive, it indicates that the mining investment will be more profitable than the bond investment; the insurance company should choose the mining investment over the corporate bond based on these estimated cash flows.

EXAMPLE 4   A mining company is considering whether to develop a mining property. It is estimated that an immediate expenditure of $7 000 000 will be needed to bring the property into production. Thereafter, the net cash inflow will be $1 700 000 at the end of each year for the next 10 years. An additional expenditure of $3 200 000 at the end of 11 years will have to be made to restore the property to environmental requirements. On projects of this type the company would expect to earn at least $i^{(1)} = 20\%$. Advise whether the company should proceed.

Solution   The net present value of the project at $i^{(1)} = 20\%$ is

$$\text{NPV at } 20\% = -7\ 000\ 000 + 1\ 700\ 000 a_{\overline{10}|0.20} - 3\ 200\ 000(1.20)^{-11}$$
$$\doteq -7\ 000\ 000 + 7\ 127\ 202.55 - 430\ 681.55$$
$$= -\$303\ 479$$

The negative net present value of the project means that the project will not yield a 20% return per annum and therefore should be rejected. If the above calculations are repeated using a desired rate of 15%, the net present value of the project will be

$$-7\ 000\ 000 + 1\ 700\ 000 a_{\overline{10}|0.15} - 3\ 200\ 000(1.15)^{-11} \doteq \$844\ 088$$

The positive net present value of the project means that the project is earning more than 15% per annum.

Exercise 7.1

Part A

Calculate the net present value for a $100 000 investment in problems 1 to 4 and determine whether the investment should proceed.

End-of-Year Net Cash Flow

No.	Cost of Capital per Year	Year 1	Year 2	Year 3	Year 4
1.	10%	$40 000	$30 000	$40 000	$30 000
2.	7%	$50 000	$60 000	$20 000	—
3.	12%	$15 000	$20 000	$40 000	$60 000
4.	9%	$80 000	$60 000	$20 000	−$20 000

5. A company is considering a $200 000 investment. It is expected that project A will return $50 000 at the end of each year for the next 5 years. On the other hand, it is expected that project B will return nothing for the next 2 years but $100 000 at the end of years 3, 4, and 5. Which project should be chosen if the cost of capital is $i^{(1)} = 4\%$? Do you obtain the same answer if the cost of capital is $i^{(1)} = 7\%$?

Which of the following projects should a company choose if each proposal costs $50 000 and the cost of capital is $i^{(1)} = 10\%$?

End-of-Year Net Cash Flow

	Year 1	Year 2	Year 3	Year 4	Year 5
Project A	$20 000	$10 000	$ 5 000	$10 000	$20 000
Project B	$ 5 000	$20 000	$20 000	$20 000	$ 5 000

6. The Northeast Mining Company is considering the exploitation of a mining property. If the company goes ahead, the estimated cash flows are as follows:

	Cash Inflow	Cash Outflow
Now	0	$3 000 000
End of year 1	$1 000 000	$2 000 000
End of year 2	$1 500 000	$500 000
End of year 3	$1 400 000	$400 000
End of year 4	$1 300 000	$300 000
End of year 5	$1 200 000	$200 000
End of year 6	$1 100 000	$100 000
End of year 7	$1 100 000	$100 000
End of year 8	$1 100 000	$100 000

The project would be financed out of working capital, on which Northeast expects to earn at least 14% per annum. Advise whether Northeast should proceed.

7. A pension fund is able to earn $i^{(2)} = 10\%$ on its investments in corporate bonds. Should it proceed with an investment that costs $100 000 and returns $17 000 at the end of each half-year for the next 4 years?

8. A company is able to borrow money at $i^{(1)} = 8\%$. A new machine costing $60 000 is now available and is estimated to produce the following savings over the next 6 years.

End of Year	1	2	3	4	5	6
Saving	$20 000	$16 000	$14 000	$12 000	$8000	$4000

Should the company borrow money to buy this machine?

Part B

1. A company is able to borrow money at $i^{(1)} = 9\frac{1}{2}\%$. It is considering the purchase of a machine costing $110 000, which will save the company $5000 at the end of every quarter for 7 years and may be sold for $14 000 at the end of the term. Should it borrow the money to buy the machine?

2. An insurance company can invest in corporate bonds to obtain a yield of $i^{(2)} = 12\%$. There are two other investments available. The first is a perpetuity paying $3300 at the end of each quarter, which may be purchased for $100 000. The second is a $100 000 investment, which will return $20 000 at the end of every year for the next 10 years. Which investment provides the company with the highest profit?

3. An investment of $100 000 produces the following year-end net cash flows.

Year	1	2	3	4	5
Cash Flow	$30 000	$30 000	$20 000	$30 000	$20 000

Calculate the net present value for this project if the cost of capital is $i^{(1)} = 2\%, 4\%, 6\%, 8\%, 10\%$, or 12%. Graph your six answers showing the NPV against the cost of capital.

Section 7.2 — Internal Rate of Return

The calculation of the net present value for a proposed investment is one method used to assess whether it ought to proceed. In Example 4 of section 7.1, we determined that the project should not proceed if the cost of capital is $i^{(1)} = 20\%$ (since NPV < 0) but should proceed if the cost of capital is $i^{(1)} = 15\%$. It might be interesting to determine the rate of interest for which the net present value turns from positive to negative. In other words, at what rate of interest is NPV = 0.

The interest rate that produces a zero net present value is called the **internal rate of return** and its calculation is another financial tool that can be used to determine whether or not to proceed with a project. In terms of the estimated cash flows, it may be expressed as the rate of interest that solves the following equation:

$$F_0 + F_1(1 + i)^{-1} + F_2(1 + i)^{-2} + F_3(1 + i)^{-3} + \cdots + F_n(1 + i)^{-n} = 0$$

where i is the internal rate of return (or IRR) or, in terms of compound interest, the yield required to solve this equation of value.

In many instances F_0 is the only cash outflow (or negative net cash flow) so that the equation may be rewritten as

$$F_1(1 + i)^{-1} + F_2(1 + i)^{-2} + F_3(1 + i)^{-3} + \cdots + F_n(1 + i)^{-n} = -F_0$$

or $\qquad F_1(1 + i)^{-1} + F_2(1 + i)^{-2} + F_3(1 + i)^{-3} + \cdots + F_n(1 + i)^{-n} = A$

where A is the initial investment.

EXAMPLE 1 Determine the internal rate of return for an investment costing $10 000 that is expected to produce net cash flows of $5000 at the end of year 1, $3000 at the end of year 2, and $5000 at the end of year 3.

Solution We have $F_0 = -10\ 000$, $F_1 = 5000$, $F_2 = 3000$, $F_3 = 5000$, and

$$-10\ 000 + 5000(1 + i)^{-1} + 3000(1 + i)^{-2} + 5000(1 + i)^{-3} = 0$$

or

$$5000(1 + i)^{-1} + 3000(1 + i)^{-2} + 5000(1 + i)^{-3} = 10\ 000$$

With trial and error, we determine that:

value of left-hand side at 14% = 10 069
value of left-hand side at 14.5% = 9986

As the cash flows are estimated we do not use linear interpolation to obtain a more accurate answer. Instead we choose the interest rate, to the nearest 0.5%, that is closest to $10 000. Since the value of the left-hand side at 14.5% is only $14 off $10 000 (versus $69 off at 14%), we conclude that the internal rate of return is about 14.5%.

Using a Financial Calculator to Calculate the IRR

We will illustrate the use of the BA-II Plus calculator to calculate the internal rate of return for Example 1:

Press $\boxed{CF}$ key, $CF_0 = -10\ 000$ hit $\boxed{\text{enter}}$, press $\boxed{\downarrow}$ key
$\qquad\qquad\qquad CO_1 = 5000$ hit $\boxed{\text{enter}}$, press $\boxed{\downarrow}$ key
$\qquad\qquad\qquad FO_1 = 1,$ hit $\boxed{\text{enter}}$, press $\boxed{\downarrow}$ key
$\qquad\qquad\qquad CO_2 = 3000$ hit $\boxed{\text{enter}}$, press $\boxed{\downarrow}$ key
$\qquad\qquad\qquad FO_2 = 1$ hit $\boxed{\text{enter}}$, press $\boxed{\downarrow}$ key
$\qquad\qquad\qquad CO_3 = 5000$ hit $\boxed{\text{enter}}$, press $\boxed{\downarrow}$ key
$\qquad\qquad\qquad FO_3 = 1$ hit $\boxed{\text{enter}}$,

then press the $\boxed{IRR}$ key, followed by the $\boxed{CPT}$ key.

The answer is 14.41506519, or 14.415%. (**Note:** make sure all other cash flows CO_4, CO_5, etc. are set to 0.)

Using a Spreadsheet to Calculate the IRR

Excel has a function called IRR which will calculate the internal rate of return of a series of current and future net cash flows.

In Example 1, suppose cells B1 to E1 contain the cash flow values: $-10\,000$, 5000, 3000, and 5000 respectively. To calculate the IRR of these cash flows, you would type $=$IRR(B1:E1), which would return a value of 14.41507% which could be rounded to two decimal points, 14.42%.

> **OBSERVATION:**
>
> When calculating IRRs by hand, rounding your answer to the nearest 0.5% is sufficient. When using the BA-II Plus calculator or a spreadsheet to calculate IRRs, you should round your answer to two decimal points.

From our definition of the internal rate of return we know that the net present value for the investment in Example 1 at about 14.5% will be zero. The following table and graph show the NPVs for this investment for various costs of capital.

Cost of Capital	NPV for Example 1
4%	+$2026
8%	+$1171
12%	+$ 415
14%	+$ 69
14.5%	−$ 14
15%	−$ 96
16%	−$ 257
20%	−$ 856

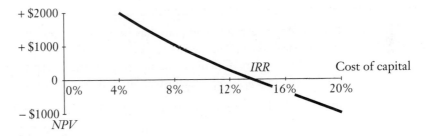

It will be noticed that if the internal rate of return is greater than the cost of capital, then there is a positive NPV and hence the investment should proceed. On the other hand, when the internal rate of return is less than the cost of capital, the NPV is negative and the investment should not proceed. This example leads us to the following relationships, which apply in most cases.

> Let i_c be the cost of capital and i_r be the internal rate of return.
>
> Where $i_r > i_c$, then $NPV > 0$ and the project will return a profit.
> $i_r = i_c$, then $NPV = 0$.
> $i_r < i_c$, then $NPV < 0$ and the project will not return the minimum required rate of return, i_c.

EXAMPLE 2   In Example 2 from section 7.1, calculate the internal rate of return for both project A and project B. Which investment should you choose based on the IRR? Compare your decision to the one made in Example 2 from section 7.1 when the cost of capital is 6%.

Solution

Cost of Capital	NPV for A	NPV for B
6%	+$15 872	+$16 301
8%	+$ 7 444	+$ 4 079
8.5%	+$ 5 424	+$ 1 180
9%	+$ 3 438	−$ 1 659
9.5%	+$ 1 484	−$ 4 440
10%	−$ 437	−$ 7 165

The IRR for project A is about 10% (9.89% to be exact) and the IRR for project B is about 8.5% (8.71% to be exact). If the decision is to be based on the IRR, we would choose project A. However, as can be seen from the above table, if the cost of capital is 6%, we would choose project B since it has the higher NPV.

Which is the correct decision? The answer depends on the cost of capital. If the desired cost of capital is 6%, then project B would be chosen. If the cost of capital is anywhere from 8% to 9.5%, then project A would be preferable.

Remember, we ultimately want to choose a profitable investment, and the project with the higher NPV is the one that is the most profitable, regardless of the IRRs.

EXAMPLE 3   An investment company has been offered an investment that costs $7200 now and $27 000 in 2 years for an estimated return of $24 200 in 1 year and $10 000 in 3 years. Calculate the net present values for this investment at 5% intervals from 0% to 30% inclusive. Show that there exist three internal rates of return.

Solution   We have $F_0 = -7200$, $F_1 = 24\,200$, $F_2 = -27\,000$, and $F_3 = 10\,000$.

$$NPV = -7200 + 24\,200(1 + i)^{-1} - 27\,000(1 + i)^{-2} + 10\,000(1 + i)^{-3}$$

The following table sets out the NPVs for the required rates.

Cost of Capital	Net Present Value
0%	0
5%	− $4
10%	− $1
15%	+ $3
20%	+ $4
25%	0
30%	− $9

As the internal rate of return is the interest rate that provides a zero net present value, we can immediately see that 0% and 25% are both internal rates of return. In addition, there is a third solution between 10% and 15% (actually 11.1%). The reason for these multiple solutions is that the cumulative F_ts change sign more than once. That is, $F_0 < 0$, $F_0 + F_1 > 0$, $F_0 + F_1 + F_2 < 0$, and $F_0 + F_1 + F_2 + F_3 > 0$. In all our previous examples there had been only one change of sign and this is the condition for a single IRR.

Although this particular investment is a little unusual, it highlights the possibility of multiple IRR solutions and the difficulty that may exist in the interpretation of the internal rate of return.

Despite the possible existence of multiple IRRs and the fact that IRRs can lead to different decisions than NPVs do when comparing different investment options, internal rates of return are still frequently calculated and used by companies to assist in making business decisions. The reason is that IRRs are generally easier to understand and easier to communicate than net present values. Stating that "The project will return 13.2%" is much simpler than stating that "At a 12% cost of capital, the net present value of the project is $5000."

Exercise 7.2

Part A

1–4. Having calculated net present values for problems 1–4 in Part A of Exercise 7.1, calculate the internal rate of return in each case using the same data.

5. An investment of $10 000 provides an estimated net cash flow of $3000 for the next 2 years and $3500 for the following 2 years. Calculate this investment's internal rate of return.

6. Determine the internal rate of return for a project that costs $100 000 and is estimated to return the following year-end net cash flows:

Year	1	2	3	4	5
Cash Flow	$10 000	$20 000	$30 000	$40 000	$50 000

Part B

1. An insurance company must choose between two investments, each of which costs $10 000 and produces the following net cash flows at the end of each year.

Year	1	2	3	4	5
Project A	$5000	$4000	$3000	$2000	$1000
Project B	$1000	$3000	$4000	$5000	$6000

Calculate the internal rate of return for each project and their respective net present values at $i^{(1)} = 15\%$ and $i^{(1)} = 25\%$. Which project should be chosen?

2. An investment of $100 000 generates income of $75 000 at the end of the first and second years but requires an outlay of $25 000 at the end of the third year.

a) Calculate this project's internal rate of return.

b) As the final cash flow is negative, a sinking fund is set up at the end of the second year so that this payment will be met. If the sinking fund earns $i^{(1)} = 5\%$ (and not the IRR), what is the project's rate of return under this condition?

Section 7.3   Dollar-Weighted Rates of Interest

Suppose you have an investment portfolio with different amounts earning different interest rates, with new money coming in and withdrawals going out at various points in time. How can you determine the rate of return on the portfolio over a given period of time? To help illustrate this concept, we begin with an example.

EXAMPLE 1   At the beginning of a year, the balance sheet of a small corporation showed assets of $9050. The owner added $2000 at the end of three months, withdrew $1500 at the end of seven months, and withdrew $200 at the end of nine months. The balance sheet at year-end showed assets of $10 000. Calculate the effective rate of interest earned during the year.

Solution

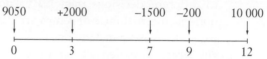

Set up an equation of value with the end of the year (time $= 12$) as the focal date. In the equation below, $i =$ annual rate of interest:

$$9050(1 + i) + 2000(1 + i)^{\frac{9}{12}} - 1500(1 + i)^{\frac{5}{12}} - 200(1 + i)^{\frac{3}{12}} = 10\ 000$$

Using a financial calculator or a spreadsheet, you can solve for $i = 6.581764\%$ $= 6.58\%$.

Alternative Method for Solving for i

We can get a very good approximate answer to this question by first noting that the sum of the beginning balance plus the deposits minus the withdrawals equals:

$$9050 + 2000 - 1500 - 200 = \$9350$$

But, the balance at the end of the year is $10 000. This means that the portfolio earned $650 in interest. Thus, $I = 650$.

Now, if simple interest is assumed over fractional parts of the year, we can set up our equation of value using the end of the year as the focal date:

$$9050(1 + i) + 2000\left(1 + \tfrac{3}{4}i\right) - 1500\left(1 + \tfrac{5}{12}i\right) - 200\left(1 + \tfrac{3}{12}i\right) = 10\ 000$$

We can solve this equation for i. Or, equivalently, we can write things as:

$$I = 9050(i) + 2000\left(\tfrac{3}{4}i\right) - 1500\left(\tfrac{5}{12}i\right) - 200\left(\tfrac{3}{12}i\right)$$

or

$$I = 9875(i)$$

Since $I = 650$, this solves for $i = 0.06582279 = 6.582279\% = 6.58\%$

We see that this alternative method uses an equation that is much easier to solve and yields an answer that is extremely close to the correct answer of $i = 6.581764\%$.

Dollar Weighted Rate of Interest

We can generalize the alternative method of Example 1. To do so, we will use the following the notation:

$$A = \text{amount in fund at } t = 0$$
$$B = \text{amount in fund at } t = 1$$
$$I = \text{interest earned in the year}$$
$$n_t = \text{new principal added at time } t, (0 \le t \le 1)$$
$$n = \sum n_t = \text{total new principal}$$
$$w_t = \text{principal withdrawn at time } t, (0 \le t \le 1)$$
$$w = \sum w_t = \text{total principal withdrawn}$$

We have:

$$B = A + n - w + I$$

If we assume simple interest for any fractional part of the year, we end up with:

$$(1 + i)^{(1-t)} = 1 + (1 - t)i$$

Thus,

$$I = iA + \sum n_t(1 - t)i - \sum w_t(1 - t)i$$

Solving the above equation for i:

$$i \doteq \frac{I}{A + \sum_{t=0}^{1} n_t(1 - t) - \sum_{t=0}^{1} w_t(1 - t)} \qquad (17)$$

This is called the dollar-weighted rate of interest.

Back to Example 1. Recall that $I = 650$, $A = 9050$, a deposit of \$2000 is made at $t = \frac{3}{12}$, a first withdrawal of \$1500 is made at $t = \frac{7}{12}$, and a second withdrawal of \$200 is made at $t = \frac{9}{12}$.

$$i = \frac{650}{9050 + 2000\left(1 - \frac{3}{12}\right) - 1500\left(1 - \frac{7}{12}\right) - 200\left(1 - \frac{9}{12}\right)}$$
$$= \frac{650}{9875}$$
$$= 0.065822785$$
$$= 6.58\%$$

EXAMPLE 2 An initial deposit of $5000 was made into a fund at the beginning of the year. The following transactions also took place throughout the year:

End of Month t	Deposit	Withdrawal
2		700
5	600	
7	600	
10		800

At the end of the year, the fund has a balance of $5125. What rate of return did the fund earn over the year?

Solution $A = 5000, B = 5125, n = 1200, w = 1500$

Thus,

$$I = B - A - n + w = 5125 - 5000 - 1200 + 1500 = 425$$

and

$$i = \frac{425}{5000 - 700\left(1 - \frac{2}{12}\right) + 600\left(1 - \frac{5}{12}\right) + 600\left(1 - \frac{7}{12}\right) - 800\left(1 - \frac{10}{12}\right)}$$

$$= \frac{425}{4883.33}$$

$$= 0.08703$$

$$= 8.70\%$$

Further Simplification

If you have a large number of deposits, n_t, and a large number of withdrawals, w_t, the dollar-weighted formula can be quite cumbersome to use. To cut down on the number of calculations, you may be able to assume (if there are many n_t and w_t) that deposits (n_t) and withdrawals (w_t) occur *uniformly* throughout the year. This is equivalent, mathematically, to a weight of $t = \frac{1}{2}$ for n (total) and w (total). This leads to a much shorter dollar-weighted formula:

$$\boxed{i \doteq \frac{I}{A + \frac{1}{2}n - \frac{1}{2}w}}$$

Since $B = A + (n - w) + I$ or $(n - w) = B - A - I$, this leads to a further simplification:

$$i \doteq \frac{I}{A + \frac{1}{2}(B - A - I)}$$

$$= \frac{I}{\frac{1}{2}(A + B - I)}$$

From this formula, you can see that the effective rate of interest is approximately equal to the total interest earned divided by the average amount of capital "exposed to i".

In summary, if we have a fund in which we assume that all deposits and withdrawals are made uniformly throughout a year, then the yield rate (rate of return) over the year on the fund is approximately equal to:

$$i \doteq \frac{2I}{A+B-I}$$

(18)

EXAMPLE 3   Calculate the effective rate of interest earned in one year on a fund, given the following information:

$$\text{Initial assets} = \$5\ 000\ 000$$
$$\text{Total deposits over the year} = \$500\ 000$$
$$\text{Investment income} = \$265\ 000$$
$$\text{Investment expenses} = \$10\ 000$$
$$\text{Salaries} = \$210\ 000$$
$$\text{Taxes, Fees} = \$90\ 000$$

Solution $A = 5\ 000\ 000$

$\sum n_t = $ total deposits $= 500\ 000$ (assumed to be made uniformly throughout the year)

$I = 265\ 000 - 10\ 000 = 255\ 000$

$\sum w_t = $ total withdrawals $= 210\ 000 + 90\ 000 = 300\ 000$ (made uniformly)

Thus,

$$i = \frac{I}{A + \frac{1}{2}n - \frac{1}{2}w}$$

$$= \frac{255\ 000}{5\ 000\ 000 + \frac{1}{2}(500\ 000) - \frac{1}{2}(300\ 000)} = \frac{255\ 000}{5\ 100\ 000} = 5.0\%$$

or

$$B = A + n - w + I = 5\ 000\ 000 + 500\ 000 - 300\ 000 + 255\ 000 = 5\ 455\ 000$$

$$i = \frac{2I}{A+B-I}$$

$$= \frac{2(255\ 000)}{5\ 000\ 000 + 5\ 455\ 000 - 255\ 000} = \frac{510\ 000}{10\ 200\ 000} = 5.0\%$$

Exercise 7.3

1. A portfolio of investments starts the year with a fund balance of \$1 500 000. By the end of the year the balance is \$6 800 000. Gross interest earned was \$600 000, and there were investment expenses of \$50 000. Determine the effective rate of interest yielded by this portfolio.

2. A fund earning $i = 5\%$ has a balance of \$1 000 000 at the beginning of the year. If \$200 000 is added to the fund at the end of four months and \$300 000 is withdrawn at the end of nine months, calculate the balance in the fund at the end of the year.

3. For a given year, an investment fund starts (January 1) with a balance of $102 000. Deposits of $40 000 are made on March 1 and $10 000 on December 1. A withdrawal of $30 000 is made on June 1. At year-end, the fund balance is $129 800. Calculate the dollar-weighted rate of return of the fund.

4. An investment fund has a balance of $160 000 on January 1. The year-end fund balance is $187 000. The amount of interest earned during the year is $7000 and the annual yield rate on the fund is 4%. If $w = 0$, calculate n and the average date of contributions to the account.

5. The value of a pension fund on January 1 is $1 million. During the year, the pension fund paid out benefits of $50 000 on June 1 and September 1. The fund received contributions of $10 000 on July 1. The year-end balance in the fund was $950 000. Calculate the dollar-weighted rate of return for the given year.

6. A fund earns $1500 of interest during a year and there is $15 000 in the fund at the end of the year. A deposit of $10 000 is made on April 1 and a withdrawal of $11 000 is made on September 1. What yield rate is earned over the year?

Section 7.4   Time-Weighted Rates of Interest

In the previous section, we determined dollar-weighted rates of interest. In fact, all of our previous compound interest rate questions dealt with dollar-weighted rates of interest.

As an alternative to dollar-weighted rates of interest, we can also calculate time-weighted rates of interest.

As will be seen, while the dollar-weighted rate of interest gives the correct rate of return for any actual fund being invested, the time-weighted rate of return gives a more accurate picture of the underlying investment environment.

Consider the following. A fund is worth $2000 on January 1. Halfway through the year, on July 1, the fund drops in value to $1000, but rises back up to $2000 on December 31. If no principal is deposited or withdrawn during the year, then the dollar-weighted yield rate is 0%, since the fund value at the end of the year is the same as it was at the start of the year.

But what if the owner of the fund takes some action on July 1? Consider two cases:

a) The investor adds an additional $1000 on July 1.
b) The investor withdraws $500 on July 1.

To help illustrate what is happening, let's assume that you buy 2000 units at the start of the year at $1 per unit (total = $2000). At the end of the year, the unit value is still $1 per unit. But halfway through the year, the fund value drops to $1000, which means the unit value has dropped to $\frac{\$1000}{2000} = \$0.50$ per unit.

For part a), the investor adds an additional $1000 on July 1 at $0.50 per unit. This means an additional 2000 units are purchased. At the end of the year, the investor has 4000 units at $1 per unit. Using the dollar-weighted method we have $A = 2000$, $n_{0.5} = 1000$, $B = 4000$, and $I = 4000 - 2000 - 1000 = 1000$.

Thus, using equation (**17**),

$$i = \frac{1000}{2000 + 1000\left(1 - \frac{6}{12}\right)} = \frac{1000}{2500} = 40\%$$

For part b), $500 is withdrawn on July 1 at $0.50 per unit. That means that 1000 units are sold, leaving the investor with $2000 - 1000 = 1000$ units, which at the end of the year are worth $1 each. We have $A = 2000$, $w_{0.5} = 500$, $B = 1000$, and $I = 1000 - 2000 + 500 = -500$.

Thus,

$$i = \frac{-500}{2000 - 500\left(1 - \frac{6}{12}\right)} = \frac{-500}{1750} = -28.57\%$$

As you can see, the dollar-weighted approach gives two correct but very different answers that depend on the timing of the cash flow.

Time Weighted Rate of Interest

As mentioned, the rate of return for the actual fund over the year is $i = 0\%$ (since the unit value started the year at $1 per unit and finished the year at $1 per unit). This can be shown in another manner that is neutral, and does not depend on the timing of the cash flow (n_t and w_t). First we calculate a rate of return for the first six months. We use the notation i_1 to represent this (first) rate of return:

$$2000(1 + i_1) = 1000$$
$$i_1 = -50\%$$

Next, we calculate the rate of return for the second six months. We use the notation i_2 to represent this (second) rate of return:

$$1000(1 + i_2) = 2000$$
$$i_2 = 100\%$$

To determine the rate of return i earned over the entire year, (no dollar weights):

$$1 + i = (1 + i_1)(1 + i_2) = (1 - 0.50)(1 + 1) = 1$$
$$i = 0\% \text{ as expected}$$

This is called the *time-weighted* rate of interest. It does not depend on the size of any principal deposited or withdrawn, nor does it depend on when these deposits or withdrawals occur. It does depend on knowing the value or balance of the fund just before a deposit or withdrawal is made.

In General

C_t = Net cash flow at time t
B_t = Fund balance at t just *before* the cash flow is made

If we break up a one-year investment period into m sub-intervals, then the rate of return over the sub-interval $(k - 1, k)$, can be calculated as follows:

$$1 + i_k = \frac{B_k}{B_{k-1} + C_{k-1}}, \quad k = 1, 2, \ldots, m$$

The time-weighted rate of interest, i, earned over the entire year can be calculated as:

$$(1 + i) = (1 + i_1)(1 + i_2)...(1 + i_m)$$

EXAMPLE 1   On January 1, a fund is worth $1000. On May 1, the fund is worth $1120 and investor A adds $300 of new principal. On November 1, the fund value has declined to $1250 and investor A withdraws $420. At year-end the fund is worth $1000.

Compute the annual yield, i, using a) the dollar-weighted method, and b) the time-weighted method.

Solution

Jan. 1	May 1	Nov. 1	Dec. 31
$1000	1120	1250	1000
	+300	−420	

Solution a   We have $A = 1000$, $B = 1000$, $n_{\frac{4}{12}} = 300$, and $w_{\frac{10}{12}} = 420$.

$$B = A + n - w + I$$
$$I = 1000 - 1000 - 300 + 420 = 120$$

Thus, using equation (**17**):

$$i \doteq \frac{120}{1000 + 300\left(\frac{8}{12}\right) - 420\left(\frac{2}{12}\right)}$$
$$= \frac{120}{1130}$$
$$= 10.62\%$$

This is the dollar-weighted rate of return, which depends on the timing of the cash flow. It represents the rate of return the investor earned on the fund based on his/her deposits and withdrawals made throughout the year.

Solution b   For the period (Jan. 1, May 1) = (0, 1), we have $B_0 = A = 1000$, $C_0 = 0$, and $B_1 = 1120$.

Thus,

$$(1 + i_1) = \frac{1120}{1000} = 1.12$$

For the period (May 1, Nov. 1) = (1, 2), we have $B_1 = 1120$, $C_1 = 300$, and $B_2 = 1250$.

Thus,

$$(1 + i_2) = \frac{1250}{1120 + 300} = 0.880282$$

For the period (Nov. 1, Dec. 31) = (2, 3), we have $B_2 = 1250$, $C_1 = -420$, and $B_3 = 1000$.

Thus,

$$(1 + i_3) = \frac{1000}{1250 - 420} = \frac{1000}{830} = 1.204819$$

The overall rate of interest earned by the fund (time-weighted rate of interest) is:

$$(1 + i) = (1.12)(0.880282)(1.204819) = 1.187850136$$
$$i = 0.187850136 = 18.79\%$$

This is the time-weighted rate of return.

OBSERVATION:

In an environment in which *anyone* could have earned 18.79%, *investor A* earned 10.62% because of the *timing* of his/her deposits and withdrawals.

EXAMPLE 2   A pension fund has a value of $1 120 000 on January 1. On May 1, contributions of $100 000 are received, after which the pension fund has a value of $1 150 000. On September 1, benefits of $150 000 are paid out, after which the pension fund has a value of $1 200 000. The value of the pension fund at the end of the year is $1 150 000.

a) What is the time-weighted rate of return on the fund?
b) What is the dollar-weight rate of return on the fund?

Solution a   For the period (Jan. 1, May 1) = (0, 1), we have $B_0 = A = 1\ 120\ 000$, $C_0 = 0$, and $B_1 = 1\ 150\ 000 - 100\ 000 = 1\ 050\ 000$.

Thus,

$$(1 + i_1) = \frac{1\ 050\ 000}{1\ 120\ 000} = 0.9375$$

For the period (May 1, Sep. 1) = (1, 2), we have $B_1 = 1\ 050\ 000$, $C_1 = 100\ 000$, and $B_2 = 1\ 200\ 000 + 150\ 000 = 1\ 350\ 000$.

Thus,

$$(1 + i_2) = \frac{1\ 350\ 000}{1\ 050\ 000 + 100\ 000} = 1.173913043$$

For the period (Sep. 1, Dec. 31) = (2, 3), we have $B_2 = 1\ 350\ 000$, $C_1 = -150\ 000$, and $B_3 = 1\ 150\ 000$.

Thus,

$$(1 + i_3) = \frac{1\ 150\ 000}{1\ 350\ 000 - 150\ 000} = 0.95833333$$

The overall rate of interest earned by the fund (time-weighted rate of interest) is:

$$(1 + i) = (0.9375)(1.173913043)(0.95833333) = 1.0546875$$
$$i = 5.47\%$$

Solution b   We have $A = 1\ 120\ 000$, $B = 1\ 150\ 000$, $n_{4/12} = 100\ 000$, and $w_{9/12} = -150\ 000$.

$$B = A + n - w + I$$
$$I = 1\ 150\ 000 - 1\ 120\ 000 - 100\ 000 + 150\ 000 = 80\ 000$$

Thus, using equation (**17**):

$$i \doteq \frac{80\ 000}{1\ 120\ 000 + 100\ 000\left(\frac{8}{12}\right) - 150\ 000\left(\frac{3}{12}\right)}$$

$$= \frac{80\ 000}{1\ 149\ 166.67}$$

$$= 6.96\%$$

OBSERVATION:

In this example, marketplace rates of return were 5.47% during the year (time-weighted rate of return). However, the person who was actively in charge of the pension fund, depositing and withdrawing money, actually did better, earning a rate of return of 6.96% (dollar weighted rate of return).

Exercise 7.4

1. On January 1, an investment account is worth $200 000. On June 1, the value has increased to $224 000 and $60 000 of new principal is added. On October 1, the value has declined to $250 000 and $84 000 is withdrawn. By December 31, the investment account is again worth $200 000. Compute the yield rate by the time-weighted method.

2. Redo question 1, but assume that an additional $10 000 is withdrawn on July 1.

3. A fund contains $5000 on January 1. On March 15, the fund value is $4000 and a deposit of $2000 is then made. On June 1, the fund value is $8000 and a further $8000 is contributed. On October 1, the fund value is $17 500 and a final deposit of $7500 is made.

   On June 30, the fund value is $15 750 and it is $F(1)$ on December 31. Using the time-weighted method, i_1 over the first six months equals i over the entire one-year period. Calculate $F(1)$.

4. An investment fund has the following values and cash flows. Cash flows occur after the evaluations.

Date	Value of Fund Just Before n_t or w_t, ($)	n_t or w_t
January 1	2000	0
May 1	2050	$w_t = 100$
August 1	2000	$w_t = 100$
October 1	1990	$n_t = 20$
December 31	1900	0

Calculate the time-weighted rate of interest over the year illustrated.

5. Redo question 4 if the fund balance at December 31 is $1800.

6. On January 1, you invest $1000. On April 1, the fund value has increased to $1200, and you deposit an extra $300. On August 1, the fund value has decreased to $1300, and you withdraw $200. The fund value increases to $1200 on October 1, but you withdraw another $200. The fund value on December 31 is $1050. What is the time-weighted rate of return earned over the year? What about the dollar-weighted rate of return?

| Section 7.5 | ## Other Securities |

Bonds are debt securities. That is, if a corporation needs money, it can raise funds by selling bonds. This is analogous to getting a loan, with the coupons representing the loan interest and the redemption of the bond representing the ultimate repayment of the loan.

Bondholders have no ownership rights in the issuing corporation. Bondholders cannot influence the operation of the company.

Should an issuing corporation go bankrupt, creditors are reimbursed in a set order. Secured creditors, normally a bank, are paid first. In loaning the corporation money, secured creditors are given a lien against some defined corporate assets. Thus, these creditors are paid off, in full, before other creditors.

Unsecured creditors are paid next. These include suppliers of goods and services (e.g., office supplies) who have amounts owing to them and all bondholders. Normally, unsecured creditors would expect to receive less than 100% of what they are owed.

Lastly, stockholders (see next section) are paid. Stockholders are owners of the company but have the last claim on assets and may not receive anything until all creditors (secured and unsecured) are paid in full.

Preferred Stocks

As stated above, investors who own stocks in a company are part owners of the company. Issuing stocks (or shares) is just another method a corporation has to raise funds. When a corporation sells shares to an investor, it is agreeing to share future profits of the corporation with the stockholders.

Preferred shares have a risk attribute that lies between bonds and common stocks (which are discussed next).

In the case of bankruptcy, preferred stockholders will be reimbursed after bondholders, but before common stockholders. Preferred stockholders are partial owners of the corporation and their investment return is the payment of dividends out of corporate profits. There is no maturity date for stocks.

The dividends paid on preferred shares are normally fixed and payable quarterly. In most cases, if a dividend payment to a preferred stockholder is missed, those values accrue until they can be paid in total.

EXAMPLE 1   An investor is analyzing the purchase of preferred shares in the IAMBIG Corporation. These shares pay $2 dividend per share at the end of each quarter. Because this is a risky commitment, this investor will evaluate the present value of these dividends at $i = 14\%$ per annum effective.

Calculate the price this investor should be willing to pay per share.

Solution   First calculate i per quarter year such that:

$$(1 + i)^4 = 1.14$$
$$i = 3.3299485\% \text{ per } \tfrac{1}{4} \text{ year}$$

Since shares have no maturity date, the dividends form a quarterly perpetuity of $2 as below:

The price is just the present value of the future cash flows:

$$p = \$2a_{\overline{\infty}|i} \text{ where } i = 3.3299485\%$$
$$= \frac{2}{i}$$
$$= \$60.06$$

Determining the price of a stock by looking at the present value of the dividends is sometimes referred to as the dividend discount model.

Common Stocks

Common stocks are less secure than bonds or preferred stocks. In the case of bankruptcy of the issuing corporation, common stocks are reimbursed last. Common stock dividends are neither pre-defined nor guaranteed. Thus, most purchasers of common stocks are buying these shares in the hope that the corporation will grow and have growing future profits and growing future dividends. Of course, if the value of the corporation rises, the value of the common shares will rise as well, and these shareholders will be able to sell these shares in the future at a profit. This growth potential is usually more important to the investor than the size of current dividends being paid.

EXAMPLE 2   An investor is looking to buy shares in ACME Corporation. Today they are paying a $0.35 dividend per share at the end of each quarter year. The investor expects these dividends to grow at a rate $i^{(4)} = 8\%$ or 2% per quarter. If the investor wants to yield $i^{(4)} = 16\%$, how much per share should she be willing to pay?

Solution   The dividends form a perpetuity, but this time of the form:

$$0.35[(1.02) + (1.02)^2 + (1.02)^3 + \cdots]$$

The present value of this perpetuity at $i^{(4)} = 16\%$ is:

$$P = 0.35\left[\left(\frac{1.02}{1.04}\right) + \left(\frac{1.02}{1.04}\right)^2 + \cdots\right]$$
$$= 0.35\left(\frac{\frac{1.02}{1.04}}{1 - \frac{1.02}{1.04}}\right)$$
$$= 0.35\left(\frac{1.02}{0.04 - 0.02}\right)$$
$$= \$17.85$$

If we assume the first dividend is \$0.35 and the 2% increases begin thereafter, we get:

$$P = 0.35 \left[\frac{1}{1.04} + \left(\frac{1.02}{1.04} \right)^2 + \cdots \right]$$

$$= 0.35 \left(\frac{\dfrac{1}{1.04}}{1 - \dfrac{1.02}{1.04}} \right)$$

$$= 0.35 \left(\frac{1}{0.04 - 0.02} \right)$$

$$= \$17.50$$

Dividend Discount Model

The solution to example 2 can be generalized as:

$$\boxed{P = \frac{D}{i - g}} \tag{19}$$

where: D = Dividend first paid
i = Desired rate of return for investor
g = Growth rate for dividend
P = Price of stock

Note: i and g need to be effective over the same period as the frequency of the dividend payments.

EXAMPLE 3   Redo Example 2 assuming the investor's desired rate of return is $i^{(4)} = 10\%$.

Solution   We can use

$$P = \frac{D}{i - g}$$

$$= \frac{0.35}{0.25 - 0.02}$$

$$= \$70$$

OBSERVATION:

For the dividend discount model to work, we need $i > g$. Also, stock markets are highly sensitive to market interest rates. If these rates drop, we anticipate that stock prices will rise. Much stock market price volatility is based on changing future expectation of interest rates.

Buying Long / Selling Short

For an investor who believes that the stock market will rise in value, it makes sense to borrow money or liquidate existing assets and use that money to buy stocks. This will prove to be wise if the growth in stock values exceeds the rate of interest on the loan or the rate of interest you could have earned on your previous assets. This is referred to as "buying long". Investors who believe stock values will rise are said to be bullish and a market in which stock shares rise is referred to as a bull market.

For an investor who believes that stock values will fall (in general or for some specific stocks) the mirror image transaction is called "selling short". In this transaction, you actually sell shares today, that you do not own, on the promise that you will buy them back eventually (this is called closing your position). Normally, this is done through a broker who holds the shares you are selling and you, in effect, borrow these shares. It may be the broker who decides the date when you have to close your position or cover your short. If the share values rise, you lose money by selling short.

Investors who believe stock values will fall are said to be bearish and a market in which stock values fall is referred to as a bear market.

Exercise 7.5

Part A

1. A stock pays a quarterly dividend (constant) of $2.50 (first dividend due in three months). Calculate the price per share for this stock if $i^{(365)} = 9\%$.

2. A stock paid a quarterly dividend earlier today of $1.75. The company is expected to grow at the rate $i^{(4)} = 6\%$. Calculate the price per share if:
   a) $i^{(4)} = 10\%$
   b) $i^{(2)} = 9\%$

3. RBCIBC paid a $1.50 quarterly dividend earlier today. The company is expected to grow at $i^{(4)} = 1\%$. Calculate the price per share for this stock if:
   a) $i^{(4)} = 8\%$
   b) $i^{(365)} = 9\%$.

4. ACME pays a $2 quarterly dividend with the first dividend payable later today. If its share price is $75, calculate the rate of return $i^{(12)}$ to an investor.

Part B

1. Biglife's stock is currently selling for $28.50. Its next dividend, payable one year from now, is expected to be 0.50 per share. Analysts forecast a long-run dividend growth rate of 7.5% per annum. The next morning, analysts drop the long-run dividend growth rate estimate to 7%. Calculate the new stock price that will result in the same yield rate as today's price of $28.50.

| Section 7.6 | **Summary and Review Exercises** |

● The net present value (or NPV) of a project over n periods with estimated net cash flow F_t at the end of period t, at interest rate i per period, is given by

$$NPV = \sum_{t=1}^{n} F_t(1 + i)^{-t}$$

If NPV > 0, the project will be profitable based on the estimated cash flows.

● The rate of interest that produces a zero net present value is called the internal rate of return (or IRR) and is calculated by solving the equation

$$NPV = \sum_{t=1}^{n} F_t(1 + i)^{-t} = 0$$

● The approximate rate of return on an asset portfolio using the dollar-weighted method is:

$$i \doteq \frac{I}{A + \sum n_t(1 - t) - \sum w_t(1 - t)}$$

● If there are a very large number of deposits (n_t) and withdrawals (w_t) then we assume that n_t and w_t occur uniformly. This gives:

$$i \doteq \frac{I}{A + \frac{1}{2}n - \frac{1}{2}w}$$

$$\doteq \frac{2I}{(A + B - I)}$$

where:

A = amount in fund at $t = 0$

B = amount in fund at $t = 1$

I = interest earned in the year

n_t = new principal added at time t, $(0 \le t \le 1)$

$n = \sum n_t$ = total new principal

w_t = principal withdrawn at time t, $(0 \le t \le 1)$

$w = \sum w_t$ = total principal withdrawn

● The rate of return on an asset portfolio using the time-weighted method is:

$$(1 + i) = (1 + i_1)(1 + i_2)\cdots(1 + i_m)$$

where $1 + i_k = \dfrac{B_k}{B_{k-1} + C_{k-1}}$, B_t is the fund balance at time t, and C_t is the cash flow at time t.

Review Exercises 7.6

1. A pension fund can earn $i^{(1)} = 6\%$ with investments in government securities. Determine which of the following investments the fund should accept if the initial investment required is \$100 000 in each case.

	Estimated Year-End Net Cash Flow				
Project	**Year 1**	**Year 2**	**Year 3**	**Year 4**	**Year 5**
A	25 000	25 000	25 000	25 000	25 000
B	10 000	30 000	40 000	30 000	10 000
C	−80 000	40 000	50 000	60 000	70 000
D	70 000	50 000	30 000	—	−30 000

2. Calculate the internal rate of return for a project that costs $100 000 and returns $30 000 at the end of each of the next 4 years. Compare this rate with the internal rate of return for the following alternative projects.

Estimated Year-End Net Cash Flow

Alternative	Year 1	Year 2	Year 3	Year 4
1	60 000	—	—	60 000
2	—	60 000	60 000	—
3	—	—	—	120 000
4	120 000	—	—	—
5	140 000	−100 000	130 000	−50 000

3. Given the following information about an investment fund:

Date	Value of Fund Just before Deposit	Deposit
January 1	1000	0
July 1	1200	X
December 31	X	

Over the year, the time-weighted return is 0%. Calculate the dollar-weighted return.

4. Given the following information about a portfolio of assets:

Date	Value of Fund Just Before n_t or w_t, ($)	Deposit
January 1	$50 000	0
March 15	40 000	20 000
June 1	80 000	80 000
June 30	157 500	0
October 1	175 000	75 000
December 31	X	0

Using the time-weighted method, the equivalent effective annual rate, i_1, for the first six months is equal to i over the entire one-year period. Calculate X.

5. A fund has value $1000 on January 1. The fund balance is $1200 on June 30 and $2200 on December 31. An additional contribution of $1000 is made on July 1. Compute the annual effective yield rate using:
   a) the dollar-weighted method,
   b) the time-weighted method.

6. Let an asset portfolio have a value of $F(0)$ on January 1, $F\left(\frac{1}{2}\right)$ on June 30, and $F(1)$ on December 31. There are no deposits or withdrawals. Show that the yield rates using the dollar-weighted method and the time-weighted method equal $\frac{F(1) - F(0)}{F(0)}$.

7. Redo question 6 if you allow for one deposit, n,
   a) immediately before calculating the fund balance on June 30
   b) immediately after calculating the fund balance on June 30

8. A mutual fund has a balance of $120 500 on January 1. On May 1, the balance is $123 000. Immediately after this valuation, $80 000 is added to the fund. No further cash flow takes place. If the time-weighted annual yield is 15%, calculate the fund value on December 31.

9. On January 1, 2013, Duane purchases 100 preferred shares of the ACME Corporation. The shares pay dividends of $0.36 per quarter per share at the end of each quarter. Duane wants to earn 4.5% effective per annum on his investment. How much should he pay for the 100 shares?

10. Redo question 9 for common shares where the dividend is expected to grow at rate $i^{(4)} = 4\%$ from time $t = 0$.

11. On January 1, an investment account is worth $10 000. On May 1, the value has increased to $12 000 and $D is deposited. On November 1, the account value is $10 000 and $4000 is withdrawn. On January 1 of the following year, the account value is $6500. The time-weighted rate of interest is 0%. Calculate the dollar-weighted rate.

CHAPTER *8*

YIELD CURVES

Learning Objectives

In this chapter, we discuss yield curves, the term structure of interest rates, spot rates, and forward rates.

Upon completing this chapter, you will be able to do the following:

- Understand the reason for yield curves and the term structure of interest rates.
- Calculate implications of these factors.
- Calculate spot rates and use them in a broader context.
- Calculate forward rates and applications thereof.

Section 8.1 ## Term Structure of Interest Rates

In section 6.6, we introduced the idea of a yield curve, a graph showing the current yield-to-maturities of government issued bonds of different maturities. In other words, the yield curve shows how the rate of return on zero-coupon bonds varies depending on the terms of the bonds.

The yield curve illustrated in section 6.6 is upward sloping, or has a positive slope. As we pointed out, this is the most common type of yield curve. Several theories have been proposed to explain this positive slope:

- The Expectations Theory postulates that more investors expect interest rates to rise in the future than expect them to fall.
- The Liquidity Preference Theory postulates that investors prefer to remain "liquid" and that they will have to be rewarded for larger-term commitments.
- The Inflation Risk Premium theory postulates that no one knows for sure what future rates of inflation will be. Investors worry that inflation will erode their investment values so, again, they seek higher rates of return on longer term investments to counteract the possible impact of rising inflation rates.

It is also possible to have flat yield curves and even inverted yield curves. The latter would occur if there is a strong expectation that future interest rates will fall (perhaps due to falling rates of inflation). This did, in fact, occur in the early 1980s in both Canada and the United States. There was also an inverted yield curve in late 1989 and early 1990.

If we have a yield curve with a positive slope, this will increase the potential investment rates of return. For example, imagine you buy a ten-year bond. Further assume that ten-year bonds are priced to yield 4.25%. If you buy this bond and hold it, the time to maturity will decrease. As that time decreases, the price of this bond will rise since the yield rate for shorter durations is lower. Thus, just by holding the bond, you have the potential for selling it at a future point in time as a profit. This is called "riding the yield curve" as seen in section 6.6.

Exercise 8.1

Part A

1. An investor buys a 10-year $1000 par value bond with coupons at rate $i^{(2)} = 6\%$. The yield rate is $i^{(2)} = 6\%$. He holds this bond for 4 years. He then sells the bond in a market in which interest rates are $i^{(2)} = 4\frac{1}{2}\%$. Calculate:
   a) The price of the 10-year bond.
   b) The sale price of the 6-year bond.
   c) The yield per annum effective over the 4 years the investor held the bond.

2. Given the following yield and coupon rates for $1000 par-value bonds, determine the price for each bond.

Maturity	Annual Coupon	Annual Effective Yield
2	9.0%	6.1%
5	4.5%	4.9%
10	6.0%	6.4%

Section 8.2 **Spot Rates**

Recall that in section 6.7, we introduced strip bonds and zero-coupon bonds. A zero-coupon bond may exist because a normal bond may have been stripped of its coupons (thus you are only purchasing the redemption value) or some entity has issued zero-coupon bonds (i.e., the coupon rate is 0%).

A zero-coupon bond is also referred to as a discount bond or a pure discount bond. Treasury bills are an example of zero-coupon bonds, since a T-bill consists of a single payment made at the time it matures.

For a zero-coupon bond, the yield to maturity is a measure of the yield rate for single payments made at that maturity date. The yield rates of zero-coupon bonds for many maturities, when graphed, will give the yield curve, as mentioned in section 8.1 and in section 6.6.

The yield to maturity of a zero-coupon bond is called the spot rate of interest for that maturity. We will use the notation S_t to denote the spot rate for an t-year zero coupon bond.

Assume we have the following interest rate structure:

Table 8.1: Term Structure of Interest Rates

Length of Investment	Interest Rate
1 year	3.50%
2 years	4.00%
3 years	4.25%
4 years	4.40%
5 years	5.00%

The interest rates listed above are the *spot rates*. For example, the three-year spot rate is $S_3 = 4.25\%$.

Spot rates can be used to determine the price of a fixed income security.

EXAMPLE 1 Calculate the price of a 5-year par value $5000 bond using the spot rates in Table 8.1 if the bond is a) a zero-coupon (strip) bond; b) a bond that pays annual coupons at 7%.

Solution a This bond has one future cash flow and it is the redemption (par) value paid at the end of 5 years. To determine the price, we discount this future cash flow using the 5-year spot rate:

$$P = 5000(1.0500)^{-5}$$
$$= \$3917.63$$

Solution b

$$P = 350(1.0350)^{-1} + 350(1.0400)^{-2} + 350(1.0425)^{-3} + 350(1.0440)^{-4}$$
$$+ 5350(1.0500)^{-5}$$
$$= \$5457.16$$

This answer is more accurate than the one produced by the methods in Chapter 6, which assume constant spot rates.

EXAMPLE 2 Using the spot rates in Table 8.1, calculate the present value of an annuity that pays $100 at the end of each year for three years.

Solution $$P = 100(1.035)^{-1} + 100(1.0400)^{-2} + 100(1.0425)^{-3}$$
$$= \$277.34$$

EXAMPLE 3 Given the following bonds and the effective (level or constant) yield rates, calculate the corresponding one-year, two-year, and three-year spot rates (S_t). Assume a face value of 100.

Maturity	Annual Coupon Rate	Yield to Maturity
1	2.000%	5.000%
2	5.500%	5.487%
3	5.961%	5.961%

Solution For the one-year bond, we would pay a price of

$$P = (2 + 100)(1.05)^{-1}$$
$$= \$97.14$$

This will also be true at spot rate, S_1:

$$97.14 = 102(1 + S_1)^{-1}$$
$$S_1 = 5\%$$

For the two-year bond, we would pay a price of

$$P = 5.50(1.05487)^{-1} + 105.50(1.05487)^{-2}$$
$$= \$100.0240$$

We know $S_1 = 5\%$, so

$$100.0240 = 5.5(1.05)^{-1} + 105.50(1 + S_2)^{-2}$$

Which solves for $S_2 = 5.50\%$.

For the three-year bond, we would pay $100 since it is a par value bond with $r = i$.

Knowing that $S_1 = 5\%$, and $S_2 = 5.50\%$, we get:

$$100 = 5.961(1.05)^{-1} + 5.961(1.055)^{-2} + 105.961(1 + S_3)^{-3}$$

Which solves for $S_3 = 6\%$.

Exercise 8.2

Part A

1. a) Calculate the price of a $1000 two-year par value bond with annual 4% coupons using the spot rates in Table 8.1.
   b) Calculate this price if the annual coupons are at 6%.
   c) Calculate the yield rate to maturity as a constant rate per annum for the bonds in a) and b).
   d) Can you justify the two answers in part c) from general reasoning?

2. Calculate $1000s_{\overline{5}|}$ using the spot rates in Table 8.1.

3. Given the spot rates in Table 8.1:
   a) Calculate the price of a $10 000 four-year zero coupon (strip) bond.
   b) Calculate the price of a $10 000 par value four-year bond with coupons at 5% per annum.
   c) In part b), calculate the effective annual yield (constant) to maturity.

4. Given the following:

Bond	Time to Maturity	Coupon Rate	Yield to Maturity
w	$\frac{1}{2}$ year	3%	5%
x	1 year	4%	8%
y	$1\frac{1}{2}$ years	5%	9%
z	2 years	$5\frac{1}{2}\%$	11%

Assuming that all rates are nominal rates compounded semi-annually, calculate the yield rates of four zero-coupon bonds of the same time to maturity (i.e., determine the four spot rates).

Part B

1. An investor can buy five 5-year bonds with 3% annual coupons to yield 6% effective and can buy three 5-year bonds with 5% annual coupons to yield 4%. Determine the five-year spot rate.

2. You are given the following information about two 10-year bonds. Both bonds have face value $1000 and coupons payable semi-annually, with the next coupon due in 6 months.
   Bond 1: Coupon rate 5% payable semi-annually and price = 992.40
   Bond 2: Coupon rate 9% payable semi-annually and price = 1302.74
   Calculate the yield (spot) rate, $i^{(2)}$, for a 10-year zero-coupon bond.

Forward Rates

As discussed in section 8.1, the expectations theory says that the shape of the yield curve is what the market feels is the direction that interest rates are heading. That means if you have a normal yield curve (upward sloping), the market is expecting that interest rates are likely to rise in the future. An inverted yield curve (downward sloping) indicates that the market is predicting interest rates to fall. A flat yield curve (a horizontal curve) indicates that the market is not sure what direction future interest are heading.

But, can you use the yield curve to predict the actual value of future interest rates? The answer is yes. These future interest rates are referred to as *forward rates*.

We will use the following notation:

S_t = current nominal interest (spot) rate on a t-year zero coupon bond
$_ki_t$ = forward nominal interest rate on a t-year zero coupon bond, k years from now

For example, $_2i_3$ represents the interest rate on a three-year zero-coupon bond that is expected to be in effect two years from now. Similarly, $_5i_2$ represents the interest rate on a two-year zero-coupon bond that is expected to be in effect five years from now.

In order to determine a forward interest rate, $_ki_t$, the relationship is:

$$(1 + S_{t+k})^{t+k} = (1 + S_k)^k(1 + {_ki_t})^t \qquad (20)$$

Formula **(20)** holds if the spot rates and forward rates are annual rates, compounded once a year.

If you have interest rates compounded m times a year (so both the spot rates and the forward rates are $i^{(m)}$), then formula **(20)** becomes

$$\left(1 + \frac{S_{t+k}}{m}\right)^{m(t+k)} = \left(1 + \frac{S_k}{m}\right)^{mk}\left(1 + \frac{_ki_t}{m}\right)^{mt} \qquad (20a)$$

These relationships say:

You can invest \$1 in a $(t + k)$-year zero-coupon bond at the current $(t + k)$ year spot rate, S_{t+k}.

OR

You can invest the same \$1 in a k-year zero-coupon bond at the current k-year spot rate, S_k, followed by reinvesting in a t-year zero-coupon bond at the t-year spot rate in effect k years from now. This latter rate, $_ki_t$, is the forward interest rate that we wish to calculate.

The following examples illustrate how to calculate forward interest rates from a yield curve of current spot rates.

EXAMPLE 1 You are given the following annual spot rates (indicative of a normal yield curve):

Length of Investment	Interest Rate
1 year	3.50%
2 years	4.00%
3 years	4.25%
4 years	4.40%
5 years	5.00%
10 years	5.35%

Calculate the following forward rates.

a) the one-year rate, two years from now
b) the two-year rate, one year from now
c) the two-year rate, three years from now
d) the five-year rate, five years from now

Solution a Let's invest $1 for a total of three years. We can either:
- Invest in a three-year zero coupon bond at 4.25%.

OR
- Invest in a two-year zero-coupon bond at 4.00%, followed by a one-year zero-coupon bond at the one-year rate in effect at that time, $_2i_1$.

In either option, you want to have the same accumulated value at the end of three years. Using equation **(20)**:

$$(1.0425)^3 = (1.0400)^2(1 + {_2i_1})$$

This solves for $_2i_1 = \dfrac{(1.0425)^3}{(1.0400)^2} - 1 = 0.047518043$.

In other words, this yield curve leads us to predict that one-year spot rates will rise from their current level of 3.50% today to 4.75% two years from now.

Solution b The process here is similar to that in part a).
- Invest in a three-year zero-coupon bond at 4.25%.

OR
- Invest in a one-year zero-coupon bond at 3.50%, followed by a two-year zero coupon bond at the two-year rate in effect at that time, $_1i_2$.

$$(1.0425)^3 = (1.035)^1(1 + {_1i_2})^2$$

This solves for $_1i_2 = \left[\dfrac{(1.0425)^3}{1.035}\right]^{\frac{1}{2}} - 1 = 0.04627$.

In other words, this yield curve leads us to predict that two-year spot rates will rise from their current level of 4.00% today to 4.63% one year from now.

Solution c We can solve for $_3i_2$ using a similar method as shown in a) and b). Using equation **(20)**,

$$(1.050)^5 = (1.0425)^3(1 + {_3i_2})^2$$

This solves for $_3i_2 = 6.14\%$, compared to the two-year spot rate today of 4.00%.

Solution d We are being asked to solve for $_5i_5$. Using equation (**20**),

$$(1.0535)^{10} = (1.050)^5(1 + {}_5i_5)^5$$

This solves for $_5i_5 = 5.70\%$, compared to the 5-year spot rate today of 5.00%.

The next example looks at the case of an inverted yield curve, along with the spot rates being nominal rates, compounded semi-annually.

EXAMPLE 2 You are given the following zero-coupon bond nominal yield rates compounded semi-annually (that is, all rates are $i^{(2)}$):

Length of Investment	Interest Rate
1 year	6.25%
2 years	6.00%
3 years	5.50%
5 years	5.25%

What is the three-year rate, two years from now?

Solution We can invest \$1 in a five-year bond at the current spot rate of $i^{(2)} = 5.25\%$, or we can invest the \$1 in a two-year bond at the current spot rate of $i^{(2)} = 6.00\%$, followed by a three-year bond at the future rate of $_2i_3$. Thus using equation (**20a**), we get

$$\left(1 + \frac{0.0525}{2}\right)^{10} = \left(1 + \frac{0.06}{2}\right)^4\left(1 + \frac{{}_2i_3}{2}\right)^6$$

This solves for $\frac{{}_2i_3}{2} = 0.023757588$, or $_2i_3 = 4.75\%$.

What this says is that this yield curve predicts that the yield rate on three-year zero-coupon bonds will drop from its current level of 5.50% to 4.75% in two years.

The next example shows how sometimes you have to use one forward interest rate in order to calculate another.

EXAMPLE 3 Using the data in Example 3, Section 8.2, calculate the corresponding one-year forward rates $_1i_1$ and $_2i_1$.

Solution For a bond with face value $F = 100$, as calculated in Example 3, Section 8.2:

Maturity	Annual Coupon Rate	P	Annual Spot Rate
1	2.000%	97.14	5%
2	5.500%	100.02	5.5%
3	5.961%	100.00	6%

For $_1i_1$ (the one-year rate, one year from now), we use the 2-year bond:

$$100.02 = 5.50(1.05)^{-1} + 105.50(1.05)^{-1}(1 + _1i_1)^{-1}$$
$$_1i_1 = 6.00\%$$

For $_2i_1$ (the one-year rate, two years from now), we need to use the current one-year spot rate *and* the forward one-year rate, one year from now as calculated above and use the 3-year bond:

$$100.00 = 5.961(1.05)^{-1} + 5.961(1.05)^{-1}(1.060)^{-1} +$$
$$105.961(1.05)^{-1}(1.060)^{-1}(1 + _2i_1)^{-1}$$
$$_2i_1 = 0.0700932 = 7.01\%$$

EXAMPLE 4 You are given the following nominal lending rates, compounded quarterly:

Length of Investment	$i^{(4)}$
1 year	3.50%
2 years	4.00%

The XYZ Corporation wants to borrow a sum of money for two years. It can borrow the total amount for two years at $i^{(4)} = 4\%$ or it can borrow the money for one year at $i^{(4)} = 3.50\%$ and then borrow for the second year at the one-year forward rate in effect then (i.e., one year from now).

At what forward rate, compounded quarterly, $_1i_1$, is the XYZ Corporation better off than taking a two-year loan at $i^{(4)} = 4\%$?

Solution Use formula (**20a**) to determine $_1i_1$ such that:

$$\left(1 + \frac{0.04}{4}\right)^8 < \left(1 + \frac{0.035}{4}\right)^4\left(1 + \frac{_1i_1}{4}\right)^4$$

This solves for $_1i_1 = 4.5006\%$. This is a nominal rate, compounded quarterly.

Thus, if XYZ feels that the one-year loan rate one-year from now, $_1i_1$, is likely to be greater than 4.5006%, then XYZ should borrow today at $i^{(4)} = 4\%$, which is guaranteed for two years.

On the other hand, if they feel that the one-year loan rate one-year from today will be less than 4.5006%, then they should borrow today at the one-year rate of 3.5% and then take their chances by refinancing the loan for one more year at the end of the first year at whatever interest rate is in effect at that time (which they hope is less than 4.5006%).

Exercise 8.3

Part A

1. Suppose that current market yield rates, compounded semi-annually, are:
   1-year: 3.25%
   2-year: 3.50%
   3-year: 3.85%
   4-year: 4.25%
   5-year: 4.75%
   Calculate the following forward rates: $_2i_3$, $_3i_2$, $_4i_1$, $_1i_4$

2. A six-month $10 000 Treasury bond can be bought today for $9880 and a one-year Treasury bond can be bought for $9640. Determine the six-month forward rate, six months from now.

3. Given $S_1 = 7\%$, $S_2 = 9\%$, and $S_3 = 10\%$, calculate the following forward rates:
   a) the one-year rate, one year from now
   b) the one-year rate, two years from now
   c) the two-year rate, one year from now

4. Suppose in today's market the annual yield rates on zero-coupon bonds are:
   1-year: 6.00%
   2-year: 7.00%
   3-year: 7.50%
   a) Calculate the corresponding forward rates $_1i_1$ and $_2i_1$.
   b) You are told that the price of a four-year par value bond with face value of $1000 and annual coupons at rate 5% is $900.64. Calculate the one-year forward rate three years from now (i.e., $_3i_1$).

5. You are given the following nominal forward rates, compounded semi-annually:
   $S_1 = 3.9\%$, $_1i_1 = 4.6\%$, and $_2i_1 = 4.4\%$.
   Calculate the corresponding nominal spot rates S_2 and S_3.

6. The following table gives you the actual yield rates of government zero-coupon bonds as of May 30, 1990. The yield rates are the nominal rates, compounded semi-annually. Calculate as many forward rates as you can in the table below (all are nominal rates compounded semi-annually)

Term to Maturity	Yield Rate	Forward Interest Rates			
		1 year from now	2 years from now	3 years from now	5 years from now
1-year rate	13.31%				
2-year rate	12.03%				
3-year rate	11.65%				
5-year rate	11.39%				
7-year rate	11.19%				
10-year rate	10.86%				

7. The ABC company wishes to borrow money for five years. They can borrow money from one financial institution at $i^{(12)} = 6\%$, guaranteed for five years. Or, they can borrow money from a second financial institution at $i^{(12)} = 5.28\%$ guaranteed for only three years, after which time they would have to refinance for the last two years. What maximum forward interest rate would they need to obtain to consider borrowing from the second financial institution?

Section 8.4 **Summary and Review Exercises**

● The present value of a series of cash flows, R_t, using spot rates, S_t, is:

$$A = R_1(1 + S_1)^{-1} + R_2(1 + S_2)^{-2} + \cdots + R_n(1 + S_n)^{-n}$$

● The relationship between a spot rate, S_t, and the corresponding forward rates, $_ki_t$ is:

$$(1 + S_{t+k})^{t+k} = (1 + S_k)^k (1 + {}_ki_t)^t \quad (20)$$

- If the spot rates and forward rates are nominal rates compounded m times a year, then:

$$\left(1 + \frac{S_{t+k}}{m}\right)^{m(t+k)} = \left(1 + \frac{S_k}{m}\right)^{mk}\left(1 + \frac{{}_k i_t}{m}\right)^{mt} \quad (20a)$$

Review Exercise 8.4

1. You are given the following table of spot rates:

t	S_t
0	7.0%
1	6.0%
2	7.5%

   a) Calculate the corresponding forward rates.
   b) Calculate the price of a three-year $1000 par value bond with annual coupons at 8%.

2. Given the following nominal forward rates, compounded semi-annually, calculate the corresponding spot rates, S_2 and S_3.

   $S_1 = 7.00\%$
   ${}_1 i_1 = 5.10\%$
   ${}_2 i_1 = 7.30\%$

3. You are given the following prices for par value bonds paying annual coupons:

Maturity	Annual Coupon	Price per $100
1	10%	104.76
2	7%	103.26
3	8%	108.14

   Determine the price of a $100 three-year par value bond with annual coupons at 9%.

4. The following table provides the prices of four zero-coupon bonds:

Maturity	Price per $1000
1	$956.94
2	907.05
3	863.86
4	814.96

   Determine ${}_3 i_1$.

5. You are given $S_1 = 6\%$ and ${}_1 i_1 = 5\%$. You are also given that the effective yield on a three-year $1000 par value bond with annual 6% coupons is 7%. Calculate ${}_2 i_1$ and S_3.

6. A one-year $1000 par value bond with annual coupons at 9% has an effective yield of 10%. A one-year $1000 par value bond with annual coupons at 8% yields 9.5% per annum. Calculate ${}_1 i_1$.

7. Given the following nominal forward rates of interest, compounded quarterly:
   $S_1 = 4.10\%$, ${}_1 i_1 = 4.8\%$, ${}_2 i_1 = 4.4\%$, calculate the spot rates S_2 and S_3.

8. A two-year $1000 par value bond paying annual coupons at 5% yields 7.4% effective per annum. If $S_1 = 6\%$, calculate S_2.

9. You are given the following nominal spot rates, all of which are compounded semi-annually:

Length of Investment	Interest Rate
1-year	7.00%
2-year	6.75%
3-year	6.35%
4-year	6.00%
5-year	5.65%
7-year	5.35%
10-year	5.00%

   Calculate the following future rates,
   a) the five-year rate, two years from now
   b) the three-year rate, four years from now
   c) the two-year rate, three years from now
   d) the five-year rate, five years from now
   e) the four-year rate, one year from now

CHAPTER *9*

ASSET–LIABILITY MANAGEMENT

Learning Objectives

Often financial institutions have liabilities or promises (e.g. pay-out annuities) that they would like to back with assets (e.g. mortgages). In particular, they would like to have assets whose cash flow (both as to size and timing) is very similar or identical to the required cash flow of the liability.

If you can find an asset whose cash flow explicitly matches the cash flow requirements of the liability, then you can achieve perfect cash flow matching. This may often not be possible. Thus, we seek assets that have attributes that align well with the attributes of the liability. This matching of cash flows is an important part of what is referred to as *asset-liability management*.

Asset-liability management is extremely important, as one real-world example shows. In the late 1970s, interest rates were rising rapidly. In order to attract and retain deposits, banks moved to daily interest savings accounts. These accounts represent the banks' liabilities. The banks' assets were (mainly) loans and mortgages. But most loans and virtually all mortgages at that time had interest rates that were fixed for some defined period (e.g., for mortgages, often up to five years).

As interest rates rose, banks were forced to pay higher rates of return on their daily interest savings accounts (their liabilities) but the interest rates on their assets only rose when a loan or mortgage was refinanced, (which might be as long as five years later). This was obviously an extremely serious problem and some banks came close to bankruptcy because of the lack of asset/liability management.

To understand asset/liability management, we will first introduce the concepts of duration, modified duration (volatility) and convexity. Then we will introduce the concept of immunization, in particular Redington's immunization.

Upon completing this chapter you will be able to do the following:

- Calculate the duration / modified duration (volatility) / convexity of a given portfolio of assets or liabilities and apply these values to real business situations.
- Determine whether an asset portfolio and a liability portfolio are immunized one to the other and the implications of immunization or the lack thereof.

| Section 9.1 | **Duration** |

As we have discussed in our learning objectives, it is desirable to find assets that have highly similar cash flow attributes as promised liabilities. As stated, finding perfect cash flow matching may not always be possible or may be administratively inefficient.

If you only have a few promises (liabilities) to be met, then zero-coupon bonds (introduced in section 6.7) are a natural solution.

EXAMPLE 1 Suppose you have obligations to pay someone $1000 at the end of Year 2 and $2000 at the end of Year 3. To match these obligations, you decide to buy today two zero-coupon bonds (assets), one maturing for $1000 at $t = 2$ and the other for $2000 at $t = 3$. If $i^{(2)} = 6\%$, determine the total cost of these two zero-coupon bonds.

Solution The price is the present value of these two distinct payments at $i^{(2)} = 6\%$.

$$P = 1000\,(1.03)^{-4} + 2000\,(1.03)^{-6}$$
$$= 888.49 + 1674.97$$
$$= \$2563.46$$

Thus, the total cost of these two zero-coupon bonds is $2563.46.

EXAMPLE 2 Juan must pay obligations of $1000 due in six months and another $1000 due one year from now. He can match these obligations by creating a portfolio of bonds from the investments available, which are:
- six-month bonds with face amount $1000 with semi-annual coupons at 8% that can be bought to yield 6% compounded semi-annually, and
- one-year bonds with face amount $1000 with semi-annual coupons at 5% that can be bought to yield 7% compounded semi-annually.

a) What proportion of the asset portfolio should be in six-month bonds and what proportion in one-year bonds?
b) What is the total cost of purchasing the bonds required to exactly match the obligations?

Solution a In 12 months, the six-month bonds will be gone and only the one-year bonds will be available to pay the $1000 obligation. The total payments for the one-year bonds at time 12 months will be a coupon of $25 and the redemption value of $1000 for a total of $1025. To cover the obligation of $1000, the required proportion of one-year bonds would be: $\dfrac{\$1000}{\$1025} = 0.97561$.

Once you have purchased 0.97561 of the one-year bonds, it will provide a coupon payment of $(0.97561)\$25 = \$24.39$ at month 6. To fund a total obligation of $1000 at month 6, the additional amount needed from the six-month bonds is:

$$\$1000 - \$24.39 = \$975.61$$

But at the end of six months, the six-month bonds will pay a coupon of $40 and its redemption value of $1000 for a total of $1040. To cover the net obligation of $975.61, the required proportion of six-month bonds is:

$$\frac{\$975.61}{\$1040} = 0.93809$$

Solution b $1000 six-month bonds can be purchased for:

$$\$1040(1.03)^{-1} = \$1009.71$$

$1000 one-year bonds can be purchased for:

$$\$25(1.035)^{-1} + 1025(1.035)^{-2} = \$981.00$$

So the total purchase price of the desired portfolio of bonds is:

$$(0.97561)\,981.00 + (0.93809)\,1009.71 = \$1904.27$$

Time of an Equivalent Payment

Let cash flow amounts C_1, C_2, ..., C_n be paid at times t_1, t_2, ..., t_n respectively. Suppose we wish to calculate a single point in time, t, such that the total of the payments C_1, C_2, ..., C_n at this point in time is equivalent, at interest rate i, to the separate payments of C_1 at t_1, C_2 at t_2, and so on.

In other words, we need to solve for t, such that:

$$(C_1 + C_2 + \cdots + C_n)(1 + i)^{-t} = C_1(1 + i)^{-t} + C_2(1 + i)^{-t} + \cdots + C_n(1 + i)^{-t}$$

We did a similar question back in Section 2.2, Example 4. We will now repeat that example.

EXAMPLE 3 Payments of $100, $200, and $500 are due at the end of years 2, 3, and 8 respectively. If $i^{(1)} = 5\%$ per annum effective, determine the time, t, at which a single payment of $800 would be equivalent.

Solution

Using time $t = 0$ as our focal date:

$$800(1.05)^{-t} = 100(1.05)^{-2} + 200(1.05)^{-3} + 500(1.05)^{-8}$$
$$800(1.05)^{-t} = 601.89$$
$$(1.05)^{t} = 1.32915$$
$$t = \frac{\log 1.32915}{\log 1.05} = 5.832 \text{ years}$$

Example 3 is nothing new. It just requires us to set up an equation of value, choose a focal date, and solve for the unknown value of t. This is fairly easy to do if you only have a few cash flows to deal with.

But, what if your investment portfolio had hundreds of different assets (e.g., stocks, bonds, mortgages, and real estate)? Is there an easier way to calculate t, even if only approximately?

As a first approximation, t can be calculated as a weighted average of the various times where a payment is made, where the weights are the size of the payments:

$$\bar{t} = \frac{C_1 t_1 + C_2 t_2 + \cdots + C_n t_n}{C_1 + C_2 + \cdots + C_n}$$

This is called the *method of equated time*. In Example 3, this would give:

$$\bar{t} \doteq \frac{100(2) + 200(3) + 500(8)}{100 + 200 + 500}$$

$$= \frac{4800}{800} = 6$$

This is not a bad approximation, since the correct value of t, as we saw in Example 3, is 5.832. However, the method of equated time will always give a value that is too big.

Duration: A Financial Tool

A better estimate for calculating t, when facing far more complex and complicated cash flows (C_t), is called duration. Duration is a tool that can be used to help us find assets with similar cash-flow timing as some known liabilities. We use the symbol $\bar{d}$ to denote the duration of an asset or liability.

The formula for duration is:

$$\bar{d} = \frac{\displaystyle\sum_{t=1}^{n} t C_t (1 + i)^{-t}}{\displaystyle\sum_{t=1}^{n} C_t (1 + i)^{-t}} \tag{21}$$

Duration is a ratio of the present value of the *weighted* future cash flows, weighted by the point in time where the cash flow is to be made (numerator) to the present value of future cash flows (denominator). The interest rate used in this calculation, $i = \frac{i^{(m)}}{m}$, is the current market (spot) rate.

Duration as calculated by formula **(21)** will be given in terms of interest periods. However, it is common to state the duration of an investment in terms of years. To do that, you divide $\bar{d}$ by m.

This type of duration is also commonly referred to as Macaulay duration, so named after the author (Frederick Macaulay) of the 1938 paper that introduced the concept.

Back to Example 3:

$$\bar{d} = \frac{2(100)(1.05)^{-2} + 3(200)(1.05)^{-3} + 8(500)(1.05)^{-8}}{100(1.05)^{-2} + 200(1.05)^{-3} + 500(1.05)^{-8}}$$

$$= \frac{3407.07}{601.89} = 5.661$$

Duration is an important analytic tool in financial analysis. It is the measure of the cash flow interest-weighted "life expectancy" of an asset or liability.

EXAMPLE 4 You invest \$101 461.51 today and expect to receive \$30 000 in 15 months, \$50 000 in 30 months, and \$40 000 in 36 months. If current rates are $i^{(12)} = 7.2\%$, what is the duration of this investment?

Solution Numerator $= 15(30\ 000)(1.006)^{-15} + 30(50\ 000)(1.006)^{-30} + 36(40\ 000)(1.006)^{-36}$
$$= 2\ 825\ 966.95$$

Denominator $= [(30\ 000)(1.006)^{-15} + (50\ 000)(1.006)^{-30} + (40\ 000)(1.006)^{-36}]$
$$= 101\ 461.51$$

Thus,

$$\bar{d} = \frac{2\ 825\ 966.95}{101\ 461.51} = 27.8526 \text{ months}$$

Dividing this value by the number of interest periods per year, $m = 12$, would give the duration in years: $\frac{27.8526}{12} = 2.321$ years.

OBSERVATION:

1. If $i = 0$, then $\bar{d} = \bar{t}$. That is, if the interest rate is zero, then duration and the method of equated time would give the same value for t.

2. $\bar{d}$ is a function of i. As i increases, d decreases and vice versa.

3. One can see from formula **(21)** that if an asset has a single cash flow due in n years (for example, a zero-coupon bond), then $\bar{d} = n$. Otherwise, for assets that have more than one future cash flow and have a term of n years (such as an n-year coupon bond), $\bar{d} < n$.

4. The value of $\bar{d}$, for a bond, will be higher as the term to maturity is longer, as the coupon rate is lower or as the yield to maturity is lower.

5. The value of $\bar{d}$, for a bond, will be lower as the term to maturity is shorter, as the coupons rate is higher or as the yield to maturity is higher.

Duration of an n-period Coupon Bond

For a bond with face value F, redeemable for C, coupons paid m times a year at r per period, bought to yield $i = i^{(m)}/m$ per period for a total of n periods:

Denominator = Price of bond $= Fr a_{\overline{n}|i} + C(1 + i)^{-n}$

Numerator $= \left[Fr(1 + i)^{-1} + 2Fr(1 + i)^{-2} + \cdots + nFr(1 + i)^{-n} \right] + nC(1 + i)^{-n}$
$$= Fr(Ia)_{\overline{n}|i} + nC(1 + i)^{-n}$$
$$= Fr\left[\frac{\ddot{a}_{\overline{n}|i} - n(1 + i)^{-n}}{i} \right] + nC(1 + i)^{-n}$$
$$= Fr\left[\frac{a_{\overline{n}|i}(1 + i) - n(1 + i)^{-n}}{i} \right] + nC(1 + i)^{-n}$$

Duration of an n-period Mortgage with a k-period Interest Rate Guarantee Period

Suppose you have a mortgage loan for A, to be repaid over n months with monthly payments of R, at a monthly interest rate of $i^{(m)} = \dfrac{i^{(m)}}{m} = \dfrac{i^{(12)}}{12}$, with this rate guaranteed for k months $(k < n)$.

$$\left(\begin{array}{l} \textbf{Note:} \text{ If the mortgage is repaid with, say, weekly payments of} \\ R, \text{ then } n, k, \text{ and } i \text{ would be in terms of weeks and } m = 52. \end{array} \right)$$

The investment period will be k months long and the future cash flows will be:

R at the end of every month for k months

PLUS

the outstanding balance of the mortgage at the end of k months, B_k.

Denominator = mortgage amount = A

$$\begin{aligned} \text{Numerator} &= \left[R(1 + i)^{-1} + 2R(1 + i)^{-2} + \cdots + kR(1 + i)^{-k} \right] + kB_k(1 + i)^{-k} \\ &= R(Ia)_{\overline{k}|i} + kB_k(1 + i)^{-k} \\ &= R\left[\frac{\ddot{a}_{\overline{k}|i} - k(1 + i)^{-k}}{i} \right] + kB_k(1 + i)^{-k} \\ &= R\left[\frac{a_{\overline{k}|i}(1 + i) - k(1 + i)^{-k}}{i} \right] + kB_k(1 + i)^{-k} \end{aligned}$$

EXAMPLE 5   Calculate the duration, $\bar{d}$, of a 15-year, $1000 bond paying semi-annual coupons at $i^{(2)} = 8\%$ and redeemable at par if the current yield rate is $i^{(2)} = 7\%$.

Solution $F = C = 1000$

$r = \dfrac{0.08}{2} = 0.04,\ Fr = 40$

$i = \dfrac{0.07}{2} = 0.035,\ n = 30,\ m = 2$

Denominator $= \left[40a_{\overline{30}|0.035} + 1000(1.035)^{-30} \right] = 1091.9602$

Numerator $= 40\left[\dfrac{a_{\overline{30}|0.035}(1.035) - 30(1.035)^{-30}}{0.035} \right] + 30(1000)(1.035)^{-30}$

$= 9539.9025 + 10\ 688.3523$

$= 20\ 228.2548$

Thus,

$$\bar{d} = \frac{20\ 228.2548}{1091.9602} = 18.5247 \text{ half years, or } 9.2624 \text{ years}$$

EXAMPLE 6 A mortgage of \$325 000 is taken out at $i^{(12)} = 6\%$, to be repaid over 25 years. The interest rate is guaranteed for five years. What is the duration of this mortgage?

Solution The monthly payment is $R = \dfrac{325\ 000}{a_{\overline{300}|0.005}} = \$2093.98$.

The outstanding balance at the end of five years, using the retrospective method, is

$$B_{60} = 325\ 000(1.005)^{60} - 2093.98s_{\overline{60}|0.005} = 292\ 279.25$$

Thus,

Denominator $= 325\ 000$

$$\text{Numerator} = 2093.98\left[\frac{a_{\overline{60}|0.005}(1.005) - 60(1.005)^{-60}}{0.005}\right] + 60(292\ 279.25)(1.005)^{-60}$$

$$= 16\ 143\ 010.18$$

and

$$\overline{d} = \frac{16\ 143\ 010.18}{325\ 000} = 49.6708 \text{ months, or } 4.1392 \text{ years}$$

EXAMPLE 7 Calculate the duration of a ten-year \$1000 par value zero-coupon bond if $i = 6\%$ per annum.

Solution From observation 3 above, we know that the duration of a zero-coupon bond is equal to the term. Thus, $\overline{d} = 10$ years.

Note that it does not matter how frequently the yield rate is compounded nor does it matter what the face value, F, of the zero-coupon bond is.

Duration for Loans and Dividend Paying Stock

1. For a loan of A, repaid with periodic payments of R over n-periods at rate i per period:

$$\overline{d} \doteq \frac{\displaystyle\sum_{t=1}^{n} tC_t(1+i)^{-t}}{\displaystyle\sum_{t=1}^{n} C_t(1+i)^{-t}} = \frac{\displaystyle\sum_{t=1}^{n} tR(1+i)^{-t}}{\displaystyle\sum_{t=1}^{n} R(1+i)^{-t}} = \frac{\displaystyle\sum_{t=1}^{n} t(1+i)^{-t}}{\displaystyle\sum_{t=1}^{n}(1+i)^{-t}} = \frac{(Ia)_{\overline{n}|i}}{a_{\overline{n}|i}}$$

The above would also hold for a mortgage loan in which the interest rate is guaranteed for the entire term of the mortgage.

2. Suppose a share of a preferred, dividend paying stock pays a dividend of R at the end of every year forever. If the interest rate is i per period, then,

$$\bar{d} = \frac{\displaystyle\sum_{t=1}^{\infty} tR(1+i)^{-t}}{\displaystyle\sum_{t=1}^{\infty} R(1+i)^{-t}} = \frac{\displaystyle\sum_{t=1}^{\infty} t(1+i)^{-t}}{\displaystyle\sum_{t=1}^{\infty} (1+i)^{-t}} = \frac{(Ia)_{\overline{\infty}|i}}{a_{\overline{\infty}|i}} = \frac{\frac{1}{i} + \frac{1}{i^2}}{\frac{1}{i}} = \left(1 + \frac{1}{i}\right)$$

EXAMPLE 8 A company offers a five year loan of $25\,000 at $i^{(4)} = 8\%$. What is the duration of this loan?

Solution In this example, $n = 5$ years $\times\, 4 = 20$, $i = \frac{0.08}{4} = 0.02$.

Thus,

$$\bar{d} = \frac{(Ia)_{\overline{20}|0.02}}{a_{\overline{20}|0.02}} = \frac{\dfrac{a_{\overline{20}|0.02}(1.02) - 20(1.02)^{-20}}{0.02}}{a_{\overline{20}|0.02}} = \frac{160.9517675}{16.35143334}$$

$$= 9.8433 \text{ quarter years} \quad \text{or} \quad 2.4608 \text{ years.}$$

EXAMPLE 9 A preferred stock offers an annual dividend of $30 per share. What is the duration of this investment if $i = 8\%$?

Solution $$\bar{d} = \left(1 + \frac{1}{0.08}\right) = 13.5 \text{ years}$$

Note that the actual size of the dividend is irrelevant in calculating the duration.

EXAMPLE 10 What is duration of the original $325\,000 mortgage loan in Example 6?

Solution We assume the mortgage interest rate of $i^{(12)} = 6\%$ is in effect for the entire 25-year period. Thus,

$$\bar{d} = \frac{(Ia)_{\overline{300}|0.005}}{a_{\overline{300}|0.005}} = \frac{\dfrac{a_{\overline{300}|0.005}(1.005) - 300(1.005)^{-300}}{0.005}}{a_{\overline{300}|0.005}} = \frac{17\,758.63887}{155.206864}$$

$$= 114.4192 \text{ months} \quad \text{or} \quad 9.5349 \text{ years.}$$

EXAMPLE 11 An investment portfolio contains two bonds, each with $F = C = \$1000$. The first bond matures in two years, with bond rate $i^{(1)} = 5\%$. The second is a five-year zero-coupon bond. If the market rate of return is $i^{(1)} = 4\%$, calculate the duration, $\bar{d}$, of the portfolio.

Solution   The value (price) of each bond is:

$$P_1 = 50(1.04)^{-1} + 1050(1.04)^{-2} = 1018.86$$
$$P_2 = 1000(1.04)^{-5} = 821.93.$$
$$P_{\text{total}} = 1840.79$$

For the first bond:

$$\bar{d}_1 = \frac{50(1.04)^{-1} + 1050(1.04)^{-2}(2)}{50(1.04)^{-1} + 1050(1.04)^{-2}} = 1.95312$$

For the second bond:

$$\bar{d}_2 = \frac{5(1000)(1.04)^{-5}}{(1000)(1.04)^{-5}} = 5$$

For the overall investment portfolio $\bar{d}$:

$$\bar{d} = \frac{1018.86}{1840.79}(1.95312) + \frac{821.93}{1840.79}(5) = 3.3136 \text{ years}$$

Exercise 9.1

Part A

1. You have obligations to pay $5000 in four years and $10 000 in seven years. If $i^{(2)} = 5\%$, calculate the total cost of two zero-coupon bonds that will exactly match the cash flow requirements of these two obligations.

2. Fred and June are proud grandparents of a newborn granddaughter. They decide to set up a fund for her university education. This fund will pay her $15 000 on each of her birthdays from age 18 to age 21 inclusive. If $i^{(4)} = 8\%$, calculate the total price of four zero-coupon bonds that will match the cash flow requirements of this promise.

3. Calculate the duration of a ten-year $10 000 par value bond that pays coupons at $i^{(2)} = 8\%$, purchased to yield $i^{(2)} = 9\%$.

4. Calculate the duration, $\bar{d}$, of the following assets given $i^{(2)} = 6\%$:
   a) a ten-year $10 000 zero-coupon bond
   b) a ten-year $20 000 bond with semi-annual coupons at $i^{(2)} = 7\%$
   c) a ten-year loan of $50 000 repaid with semi-annual payments
   d) a preferred stock paying semi-annual dividends of $50 in perpetuity

5. Calculate the duration of a 20-year par value $10 000 bond with annual coupons at 6% if $i = 5\%$.

6. An investment portfolio holds the following four bonds:
   i) a $50 000 two-year bond with annual coupons at 5%,
   ii) a $40 000 five-year bond with annual coupons at 8%,
   iii) a $60 000 ten-year bond with annual coupons at 6%,
   iv) a $75 000 20-year bond with annual coupons at 9%.
   If $i = 4.5\%$, calculate the duration of this investment portfolio.

7. A ten-year $1000 par value bond with semi-annual coupons at $i^{(2)} = 6\%$ is purchased to yield $i^{(2)} = 4\%$. Calculate the duration.

8. Calculate the duration of a 15-year $5000 par value bond with semi-annual coupons at $i^{(2)} = 7\%$ bought to yield $i^{(2)} = 7\%$.

9. Calculate the duration of $1000 bond paying semi-annual coupons at $i^{(2)} = 8\%$ if the bond is redeemable at 110 in 15 years and the current yield rate is $i^{(2)} = 7\%$.

10. Calculate the duration of:
    a) A 20-year $150 000 mortgage, amortized with level monthly payments at $i^{(12)} = 6\%$.
    b) Redo this question assuming that the interest rate is only guaranteed for four years.

11. The duration of a stock that pays quarterly dividends of $25 per share is 17.6413 years. What is the value of $i^{(4)}$?

Part B

1. The annual payments necessary to repay a loan form a 20-year immediate annuity. If the duration of this annuity is 8.90, what is i?

2. Determine an expression for the duration of an n-year immediate annuity paying $1 per annum at interest rate i.

3. You are given an n-year par value bond ($C = F$) with annual coupons at rate r. Show that if the bond rate equals the yield rate, $r = i$, then $\bar{d} = \ddot{a}_{\overline{n}|i}$.

Section 9.2   **Modified Duration**

Bonds face two variables that make them a risky investment. They are:

1. Reinvestment risk: the risk that if interest rates fall, coupons must be reinvested at a lower rate than i used to determine the price.

2. Interest rate risk: the risk that if interest rates rise, the market value of the bond falls.

It is the latter risk that we wish to investigate. We will use duration to help us assess the risk of the change in the value of our bond (or any fixed income investment) portfolio due to a change in the market interest rate.

First, we define the following:

$P(i)$ = present value of future cash flows, discounted using an interest rate of $i = \dfrac{i^{(m)}}{m}$

$$= \sum_{t=1}^{n} C_t (1 + i)^{-t}$$

We now wish to measure the rate at which the value of our portfolio changes as interest rates change. The rate of change would be:

$$\frac{\dfrac{d}{di^{(m)}} P(i)}{P(i)}$$

Note that $\dfrac{\dfrac{d}{di^{(m)}} P(i)}{P(i)}$ will always be negative for positive cash flows, since present values increase as interest rates fall. We will denote the above positive rate of change as $\bar{v}$, as this is a measure of the volatility of an investment portfolio.

$$\bar{v} = \frac{-\dfrac{d}{di^{(m)}} P(i)}{P(i)} = \frac{-\dfrac{d}{di^{(m)}} \sum_{t=1}^{n} C_t \left(1 + \dfrac{i^{(m)}}{m}\right)^{-t}}{\sum_{t=1}^{n} C_t \left(1 + \dfrac{i^{(m)}}{m}\right)^{-t}}$$

$$= \frac{-\sum_{t=1}^{n} (-t) C_t \left(1 + \dfrac{i^{(m)}}{m}\right)^{-(t+1)} \left(\dfrac{1}{m}\right)}{\sum_{t=1}^{n} C_t \left(1 + \dfrac{i^{(m)}}{m}\right)^{-t}} = \frac{\left(1 + \dfrac{i^{(m)}}{m}\right)^{-1} \sum t C_t (1 + i)^{-t}}{mP}$$

$$= \left(\frac{1}{1 + \dfrac{i^{(m)}}{m}}\right) \sum \frac{t C_t \left(1 + \dfrac{i^{(m)}}{m}\right)^{-t}}{mP} = \left(\frac{1}{1 + \dfrac{i^{(m)}}{m}}\right) \frac{\bar{d}}{m}$$

Thus,

$$\boxed{\bar{v} = \frac{\left(\dfrac{\bar{d}}{m}\right)}{1+i}} \tag{22}$$

where $i = \frac{i^{(m)}}{m}$. This volatility is often referred to as modified duration and it is always given in years.

EXAMPLE 1   In section 9.1, Example 5, we calculated the duration of a 15-year, $1000 bond paying semi-annual coupons at $i^{(2)} = 8\%$ and redeemable at par if the current yield rate is $i^{(2)} = 7\%$ to be 18.5247 half years or 9.2624 years. What is its modified duration (or volatility)?

Solution $$\bar{v} = \frac{\frac{18.5247}{2}}{\left(1 + \frac{0.07}{2}\right)} = \frac{9.2624}{1.035} = 8.9492 \text{ years}$$

How do you use volatility?

Once we have calculated the modified duration, or volatility, what does it mean? What we really want to do is to estimate how the value of an investment port-folio, $P(i)$, changes when interest rates change in the marketplace.

Let $\Delta i^{(m)}$ = change in the interest rate,

where $\Delta i^{(m)}$ = new nominal interest rate – current nominal interest rate

Note: the change in interest rates is the change in the nominal rate, $i^{(m)}$, not the change in the effective rate $i = \frac{i^{(m)}}{m}$.

From a Taylor's series expansion, we have:

$$P(i + \Delta i^{(m)}) = P(i) + \frac{d}{di^{(m)}}P(i)\Delta i^{(m)}$$

$$= P(i)\left[1 - \left(-\frac{1}{P(i)}\frac{d}{di^{(m)}}P(i)\right)\Delta i^{(m)}\right]$$

$$= P(i)(1 - v\Delta i^{(m)})$$

$$\boxed{P(i + \Delta i^{(m)}) = P(i)(1 - \bar{v}\Delta i^{(m)})} \tag{23}$$

This says that if the market interest rate changes by $\Delta i^{(m)}$, the value of an investment portfolio is estimated to be equal to the current value of the portfolio times 1 minus the percentage change in the value of the portfolio, where the percentage change is estimated using the modified duration times the change in the interest rate.

EXAMPLE 2   In Example 1 (originally Example 5 from section 9.1), use the modified duration to calculate the estimated value of the bond if the interest rate (yield rate) changes to a) $i^{(2)} = 7.25\%$, b) $i^{(2)} = 8.25\%$, and c) $i^{(2)} = 6.50\%$.

In addition, calculate the actual value of the bond at the given interest rates and compare your answers to the estimated values.

Solution   From Example 1, we have $\bar{v} = 8.9492$ years, current yield rate $i^{(2)} = 7\%$, and current bond value $P(i) = 1091.96$.

Solution a
$$\Delta i^{(2)} = 0.0725 - 0.07 = 0.0025$$

$$
\begin{aligned}
\text{Estimated new bond value} &= 1091.96\,[1 - (8.9492)(0.0025)] \\
&= 1091.96[1 - 0.022373] \\
&= 1091.96[0.977627] \\
&= \$1067.53
\end{aligned}
$$

If the yield rate rises by 0.25% overnight, the value of the bond falls to $1067.53, a drop of $24.43 (or 2.2373%).

$$
\begin{aligned}
\text{Actual price of bond at } i^{(2)} = 7.25\% \\
&= \left[40a_{\overline{30}|0.03625} + 1000(1.0365)^{-30}\right] \\
&= \$1067.90
\end{aligned}
$$

We see that modified duration does a reasonable job of estimating the new value of the bond (1067.53 vs. 1067.90). It is off by only $0.37 on a $1000 face value bond.

Note: If we had used Macaulay duration instead of modified duration, our estimated bond value would be $= 1091.96[1 - (9.2624)(0.0025)] = \$1066.68$, an error of $1.22 per 1000 of face value).

Solution b
$$\Delta i^{(2)} = 0.0825 - 0.07 = 0.0125$$

$$
\begin{aligned}
\text{Estimated new bond value} &= 1091.96\,[1 - (8.9492)(0.0125)] \\
&= 1091.96[1 - 0.111865] \\
&= \$969.81
\end{aligned}
$$

If the yield rate rises by 1.25% overnight, the value of the bond falls to $969.81, a drop of $122.15 (or 11.1865%).

$$
\begin{aligned}
\text{Actual price of bond at } i^{(2)} = 8.25\% \\
&= \left[40a_{\overline{30}|0.04125} + 1000(1.04125)^{-30}\right] \\
&= \$978.71
\end{aligned}
$$

We see that for a bigger change in the interest rate (1.25% vs. 0.25%), the estimated value of the bond is not as accurate using modified duration as it is using the actual purchase price formula ($969.81 vs. 978.71, which is an error of $8.90 per 1000 of face value). This is due to the fact that the price vs. yield rate is not a straight line relationship, but is, in fact, curved. However, formula **(23)** is assuming that this relationship is linear. We will need to adjust this formula to take into account the convex nature of the price vs. yield rate relationship. This will be done in section 9.3, by introducing another term into our equation: convexity.

Solution c
$$\Delta i^{(2)} = 0.065 - 0.07 = -0.005$$

$$\text{Estimated new bond value} = 1091.96\,[1 - (8.9492)(-0.005)]$$
$$= 1091.96[1 + 0.044746]$$
$$= \$1140.82$$

If the yield rate *falls* by 0.50% overnight, the value of the bond *rises* to $1140.82, an increase of $48.86 (or 4.4746%).

$$\text{Actual price of bond at } i^{(2)} = 6.50\%$$
$$= \left[40a_{\overline{30}|0.0325} + 1000(1.0325)^{-30}\right]$$
$$= \$1142.36$$

OBSERVATION:

As can be seen when comparing the answers to a), b) and c) in Example 2, we can make the following general observations about using modified duration to estimate the change in the value of an investment portfolio when the market interest rates change.
1. Modified duration gives a reasonably accurate answer for changes in the interest of 0.50% or less.
2. For interest rate changes of more than 0.50%, the accuracy of using modified duration decreases. An adjustment to formula **(23)** will be needed to take into account the convexity of the price vs. yield rate relationship. This will be done in section 9.3.

EXAMPLE 3 Referring to Example 6 in section 9.1, calculate the modified duration (volatility) and use it to estimate the value of the mortgage if the interest rate rises to $i^{(12)} = 6.5\%$.

Solution From Example 6 in section 9.1, we have $\bar{d} = 49.6708$ months, $m = 12$, $P(i) = \$325\,000$, and current interest rate $i^{(12)} = 6\%$.

Thus,

$$\bar{v} = \frac{\dfrac{49.6708}{12}}{\left(1 + \dfrac{0.06}{12}\right)} = \frac{4.1392}{1.005} = 4.1186 \text{ years}$$

$$\Delta i^{(12)} = 0.065 - 0.06 = 0.005$$

$$\text{New mortgage value} = 325\,000[1 - (4.1186)(0.005)]$$
$$= 325\,000[1 - 0.020593]$$
$$= \$318\,307.28$$

Note: actual mortgage value $= 2093.98a_{\overline{300}|0.0054166} = \$310\,124.08$

EXAMPLE 4 Calculate the estimated value of a 10-year $1000 zero-coupon bond if interest rates rise from $i = 6\%$ to $i = 6.75\%$.

Solution We have that initial price of bond $= P(i) = 1000(1.06)^{-10} = 558.39$ and $\bar{d} = 10$ years (Recall: duration of a zero-coupon bond = term of bond).

Thus,

$$\bar{v} = \frac{10}{1.06} = 9.4340 \text{ years}$$
$$\Delta i = 0.0675 - 0.06 = 0.0075$$

$$\text{Estimated new value} = 558.39[1 - (9.4340)(0.0075)]$$
$$= \$518.88$$

Note: actual value $= 1000(1.0675)^{-10} = \$520.38$

EXAMPLE 5 In Example 8 of section 9.1, calculate the modified duration of the loan and calculate the estimated value of the loan if the interest falls to $i^{(4)} = 7.15\%$.

Solution From Example 8 in section 9.1, we have current interest rate, $i^{(4)} = 8\%$; current value of loan, $P(i) = \$25\ 000$; and $\bar{d} = 9.8433$ quarter years.

Thus,

$$\bar{v} = \frac{\dfrac{9.8433}{4}}{1.02} = \frac{2.4608}{1.02} = 2.4126 \text{ years}$$
$$\Delta i^{(4)} = 0.0715 - 0.08 = -0.0085$$

$$\text{Estimated market value of loan} = 25\ 000[1 - (2.4126)(-0.0085)]$$
$$= 25\ 000(1.0205071)$$
$$= \$25\ 512.68$$

EXAMPLE 6 If all cash flows are continuous and the investment rate of return is δ, show that $\bar{d} = \bar{v}$.

Solution Given the continuous case:

$$\bar{d} = \frac{\int_a^b tC_t e^{-\delta t}}{\int_a^b C_t e^{-\delta t}}$$

But

$$\bar{v} = \frac{-\dfrac{d}{d\delta}\int_a^b C_t e^{-\delta t}}{\int_a^b C_t e^{-\delta t}}$$

$$= \frac{\int_a^b tC_t e^{-\delta t}}{\int_a^b C_t e^{-\delta t}}$$

$$= \bar{d}$$

Alternative Method

Another method of estimating the new value of an investment portfolio when interest rates change has been suggested by actuary Robert Alps in a Study Note entitled "Using Duration and Convexity to Estimate Change in Present Values". His method uses Macaulay duration and not modified duration, and should lead to more accurate results.

$$P(i + \Delta i^{(m)}) = P(i)\left(\frac{1+i}{1+i^*}\right)^{\bar{d}}$$

(23a)

Where,

i = current rate of interest per mth of a year = $i^{(m)}/m$

i^* = new rate of interest per mth of a year

$P(i)$ = current value of the investment portfolio at i

$\bar{d}$ = Macaulay duration in number of interest periods

EXAMPLE 7   Redo Example 2 using formula **(23a)**. Check to see if this leads to more accurate answers.

Solution   In all three parts, current effective yield rate = $\frac{0.07}{2}$ = 0.0350, $P(i)$ = 1091.96, and $\bar{d}$ = 18.5247 half years.

Solution a
$$i^* = 0.0725/2 = 0.03625$$
$$P(i + \Delta i^{(m)}) = 1091.96\left(\frac{1.035}{1.03625}\right)^{18.5247}$$
$$= \$1067.82$$

Recall from Example 2, actual price at $i^{(2)}$ = 7.25% is \$1067.90, and estimated price using modified duration = \$1067.53.

We see that using formula **(23a)**, we end up with an answer that was off by only \$0.08, versus being off by \$0.37 using modified duration. Thus formula **(23a)** did give a slightly more accurate estimate.

Solution b
$$i^* = 0.0825/2 = 0.04125$$
$$P(i + \Delta i^{(m)}) = 1091.96\left(\frac{1.035}{1.04125}\right)^{18.5247}$$
$$= \$976.72$$

Recall from Example 2, actual price at $i^{(2)}$ = 8.25% is \$978.71, and estimated price using modified duration = \$969.81.

We see that using formula **(23a)**, we end up with an answer that was off by \$1.99, versus being off by \$8.90 using modified duration. Thus formula **(23a)** did lead to a more accurate estimate, although there is still room for improvement (see section 9.3)

Solution c
$$i^* = \frac{0.065}{2} = 0.0325$$
$$P(i + \Delta i^{(m)}) = 1091.96\left(\frac{1.035}{1.0325}\right)^{18.5247}$$
$$= \$1141.99$$

Recall from Example 2, actual price at $i^{(2)} = 6.50\%$ is $1142.36, and estimated price using modified duration = $1140.82.

We see that using formula (**23a**), we end up with an answer that was off by $0.37, versus being off by $1.54 using modified duration. Again formula (**23a**) did give a more accurate estimate.

Exercise 9.2

Part A

1. In exercise 9.1.3, calculate the modified duration of the bond and use it to estimate the value of the bond if the yield rate changes to:
   a) 9.25%; b) 10.50%; c) 8.65%

2. Redo exercise 1 using the Alps modification (that is, using formula (**23a**)).

3. In exercise 9.1.4, calculate the modified duration of each of the four assets and use it to estimate the value of the asset if interest rates rise to $i^{(2)} = 6.50\%$.

4. In exercise 9.1.5, calculate the modified duration of the bond and use it to estimate the value of the bond if the yield rate falls to $i = 4.45\%$.

5. In exercise 9.1.10, calculate the modified duration of the mortgage in both parts a) and b), and use it to estimate the value of the mortgage if interest rates rise to $i^{(12)} = 6.75\%$.

6. In exercise 9.1.11, calculate the modified duration of the stock and use it to estimate the value of the stock if the interest rate rises to $i^{(4)} = 6.10\%$.

Part B

1. Show that the volatility of an immediate perpetuity with annual payments of $1 is equal to the present value of that perpetuity.

| Section 9.3 | **Convexity** |

As we have seen, modified duration works well at estimating the change in the value of an investment portfolio for small changes in the market interest rate (e.g. 0.50% or less).

This figure shows the price vs. yield relationship, $P(i)$.

Convexity Graph

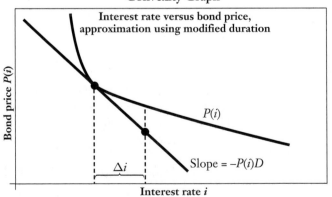

The price vs. yield relationship, $P(i)$, is given by the convex (curve) line. This gives the actual value (or price) of a bond for different interest rates. The straight line, which is tangent to the $P(i)$ curve (at the point of the current interest rate), gives the estimated price of a bond using modified duration as the interest rate goes up or down. As you see, the farther away from the current interest rate you go, the poorer is the estimate of the price using modified duration.

To adjust for this, we need to take into consideration how much curvature there is in the $P(i)$ curve. This curvature is measured by taking the second derivative of the $P(i)$ function and is referred to as convexity.

The convexity of an asset (or liability) is:

$$\bar{c} = \frac{\dfrac{d^2}{d(i^{(m)})^2}P(i)}{P(i)} = \frac{\displaystyle\sum_{t=1}^{n}(-t)(-[t+1])C_t\left(1+\frac{i^{(m)}}{m}\right)^{-(t+2)}\left(\frac{1}{m}\right)^2}{\displaystyle\sum_{t=1}^{n}C_t\left(1+\frac{i^{(m)}}{m}\right)^{-t}}$$

$$\text{OR } \bar{c} = \frac{\displaystyle\sum_{t=1}^{n}t(t+1)C_t\left(1+\frac{i^{(m)}}{m}\right)^{-t}}{m^2\left(1+\frac{i^{(m)}}{m}\right)^2 P(i)} \tag{24}$$

Note, if all cash flows are positive, then $\bar{c}$ will always be positive.

EXAMPLE 1 Consider a four-year $1000 zero-coupon bond. If $i = 6\%$, calculate $\bar{v}$ and $\bar{c}$.

Solution

$$P(i) = 1000(1.06)^{-4} = 792.09$$
$$P'(i) = 1000[-4(1.06)^{-5}] = -2989.03$$

$$\bar{v} = \frac{-P'(i)}{P(i)} = \frac{2989.03}{792.09} = 3.7736$$

$$P''(i) = 1000[20(1.06)^{-6}] = 14\,099.21$$

$$\bar{c} = \frac{P''(i)}{P(i)} = \frac{14\,099.21}{792.09} = 17.8000$$

EXAMPLE 2 Calculate the modified duration, $\bar{v}$, and convexity, $\bar{c}$, for a ten-year $1000 par value bond paying semi-annual coupons at $i^{(2)} = 7\%$ if the current yield rate is $i^{(2)} = 6.5\%$.

Solution

$$P(i) = 35a_{\overline{20}|0.0325} + 1000(1.0325)^{-20} = \$1036.35$$

$$\bar{d} = \frac{35(Ia)_{\overline{20}|0.0325} + 20(1000)(1.0325)^{-20}}{1036.35} = 14.8166 \text{ half years}$$

$$\bar{v} = \frac{\frac{14.8166}{2}}{\left(1 + \frac{0.065}{2}\right)} = \frac{7.4083}{1.0325} = 7.1751 \text{ years}$$

Using formula **(24)**,

$$\bar{c} = \frac{\sum t(t+1)C_t(1+i)^{-t}}{m^2(1+i)^2 P(i)}$$

$$= \frac{[(1)(2)(35)(1.0325)^{-1} + (2)(3)(35)(1.0325)^{-2} + \cdots + (20)(21)(1035)(1.0325)^{-20}]}{2^2(1.035)^2(1036.35)}$$

$$= 65.2392$$

How to Use Convexity

We wish to use convexity, along with modified duration, to get a more accurate estimate of the value of an investment portfolio when the market interest rate changes.

To do this, we expand our Taylor's series to a third term:

$$P(i + \Delta i^{(m)}) = P(i) + P'(i)\Delta i^{(m)} + \frac{P''(i)(\Delta i^m)^2}{2}$$

$$= P(i)\left[1 - \left(-\frac{1}{P(i)}\frac{d}{di^{(m)}}P(i)\right)\Delta i^{(m)} + \frac{1}{2P(i)}\left(\frac{d^2P(i)}{d(i^{(m)})^2}(\Delta i^{(m)})^2\right)\right]$$

Thus

$$\boxed{P(i + \Delta i^{(m)}) = P(i)\left[1 - \bar{v}\Delta i^{(m)} + \frac{1}{2}\bar{c}(\Delta i^{(m)})^2\right]} \tag{25}$$

Where $\Delta i^{(m)} = $ new $i^{(m)}$ – current $i^{(m)}$, $\bar{v} = $ modified duration, and $\bar{c} = $ convexity.

EXAMPLE 3   Suppose in Example 2 that the yield rate rises to $i^{(2)} = 7.5\%$. Calculate the value of the bond using a) the purchase price formula, b) modified duration only, and c) modified duration and convexity.

Solution a $P(i) = 35a_{\overline{20}|0.0375} + 1000(1.0375)^{-20} = \$965.26$

Solution b $\Delta i^{(2)} = 0.075 - 0.065 = 0.01$
$\bar{v} = 7.1751$
Estimated new value $= 1036.35[1 - 7.1751(0.01)] = \$961.99$ (off by \$3.27)

Solution c   Using formula **(25)**
Estimated new value $= 1036.35[1 - 7.1751(0.01) + (0.5)(65.2392)(0.01)^2]$
$= 1036.35 [1 - 0.071751 + 0.00326196]$
$= 1036.35 [1 - 0.06848904]$
$= \$965.37$ (off by only \$0.11)

EXAMPLE 4   An annuity with quarterly payments over 2 years at $i^{(4)} = 4\%$ is purchased today for \$10 000. Calculate the modified duration and convexity of this investment. Then use both of them to estimate the value of the annuity if the interest rate rises to $i^{(4)} = 5\%$.

Solution $P(0.01) = 10\ 000$

Quarterly new payment $= \dfrac{10\ 000}{a_{\overline{8}|0.01}} = \$1306.90$

$$\bar{d} = \frac{(\bar{I}\bar{a})_{\overline{8}|0.01}}{a_{\overline{8}|0.01}} = \frac{\dfrac{a_{\overline{8}|0.01}(1.01) - 8(1.01)^{-8}}{0.01}}{a_{\overline{8}|0.01}} = 4.4478 \text{ quarter years}$$

$$\bar{v} = \frac{\dfrac{4.4478}{4}}{1.01} = 1.1009 \text{ years}$$

$$\bar{c} = \frac{\sum t(t+1)C_t(1+i)^{-t}}{m^2(1+i)^2 P(i)}$$

$$= \frac{1306.90[(1)(2)(1.01)^{-1} + (2)(3)(1.01)^{-2} + \cdots + (8)(9)(1.01)^{-8}]}{4^2(1.01)^2(10\ 000)}$$

$$= \frac{294\ 786.3722}{163\ 216} = 1.8061$$

$\Delta i^{(4)} = 0.05 - 0.04 = 0.01$

Thus, using formula (**25**),

Estimated new value of annuity $= 10\ 000[1 - (1.1009)(0.01) + (0.5)(1.8061)(0.01)^2]$
$= 10\ 000[1 - 0.011009 + 0.000090305]$
$= 10\ 000[1 - 0.010918695]$
$= \$9890.81$

Note: actual annuity value $= 1306.90 a_{\overline{8}|0.0125} = \$9890.78$

EXAMPLE 5   A bond portfolio consists of \$200 000 worth of bonds that are redeemable at par in 20 years. The coupon rate is $i^{(2)} = 7\%$ and they were purchased to yield $i^{(2)} = 9\%$. The portfolio has a duration of 20.202266 half years and a convexity of 128.5. What is the estimated value of the bond portfolio if the yield rate a) rises to $i^{(2)} = 9.75\%$ and b) falls to $i^{(2)} = 8.50\%$?

Solution   The bond portfolio has a current value (price) of

$$P(0.045) = 200\ 000(0.035)a_{\overline{40}|0.045} + 200\ 000(1.045)^{-40} = \$163\ 196.83$$

Solution a $\Delta i^{(2)} = 0.0975 - 0.09 = 0.0075$

$$\bar{d} = \frac{\dfrac{20.202266}{2}}{1.045} = 9.6662 \text{ years}$$

$$\text{Estimated new value} = 163\ 196.83[1 - (9.6662)(0.0075) + (0.5)(128.5)(0.0075)^2]$$
$$= 163\ 196.83[1 - 0.0724965 + 0.003614063]$$
$$= 163\ 196.83[1 - 0.068882438]$$
$$= \$151\ 955.44$$

Solution b
$$\Delta i^{(2)} = 0.085 - 0.09 = -0.005$$

$$\text{Estimated new value} = 163\ 196.83[1 + (9.6662)(0.005) + (0.5)(128.5)(0.005)^2]$$
$$= 163\ 196.83[1 + 0.048331 + 0.00160625]$$
$$= 163\ 196.83[1.04993725]$$
$$= \$171\ 346.43$$

Exercise 9.3

Part A

1. A 25-year mortgage is being amortized with level monthly payments of principal and interest. The interest rate is $i^{(12)} = 6\%$. Determine:
   a) the modified duration (or volatility) of the payments
   b) the convexity of the payments (this may require a spread sheet or computer solution).

2. Calculate the duration, $\bar{d}$, and convexity, $\bar{c}$, for a common stock paying a dividend, D, today. Assume that the size of the dividend grows at 3% per annum and that $i^{(1)} = 5\%$.

3. A loan, L, is to be repaid with three payments: $1000 at the end of one year, $1500 at the end of two years and $2000 at the end of three years. If $i^{(1)} = 7\%$, calculate:
   a) the amount of the loan, L
   b) the duration of the cash flow
   c) the modified duration (or volatility)
   d) the convexity

4. A portfolio of assets contains two bonds:
   - B_1 is a $100 000 ten-year zero-coupon bond, and
   - B_2 is a $40 000 five-year par value bond with semi-annual coupons at $i^{(2)} = 7\%$.
   Calculate the modified duration and convexity of the portfolio at $i^{(2)} = 8\%$. Then use both values to determine the value of the portfolio if the interest rate rises to $i^{(2)} = 8.60\%$.

5. A 10-year $1000 zero-coupon bond is purchased to yield $i^{(1)} = 7\%$
   a) Calculate the duration, the modified duration (or volatility) and the convexity for the bond.
   b) Use these results to estimate the value of the bond at $i^{(1)} = 7.5\%$

6. A preferred stock pays dividends of $50 per annum (first dividend one year from today). If $i^{(1)} = 7.2\%$, calculate the market value, duration and convexity for this stock. Estimate the market value of the stock if $i^{(1)}$ rises to 7.5%.

7. Estimate the value of the following bonds using the given information.
   a) A $10 000 bond, purchased for $10 240 at a yield rate of $i^{(2)} = 5\%$; duration = 18.4524 half years; convexity = 76.8; yield rate rises to $i^{(2)} = 6.25\%$.
   b) A $5000 bond, purchased for $4875 at a yield rate of $i^{(2)} = 7.50\%$; duration = 15.8220 half years; convexity = 65.5; yield rate falls to $i^{(2)} = 7.15\%$.

Part B

1. A $200 000 mortgage at $i^{(2)} = 7\%$ is to be repaid over 25 years with monthly payments of $1400.84. The interest rate is guaranteed for three years. The outstanding balance at the end of the guarantee period (three years) is $189 999.60. The duration is 31.88396 months. Suppose the interest rate rises to $i^{(2)} = 7.5\%$.
   a) Calculate the actual value of the mortgage.

b) Using your answer to a), what should be the value of the convexity?

2. A $1000 bond with semi-annual coupons at $i^{(2)} = 7\%$ is redeemable at par in 2.5 years to yield $i^{(2)} = 8\%$. The price of the bond is $977.74. The duration of the bond is 4.6688 half years. If the yield rate falls to $i^{(2)} = 6.25\%$, what would be the price? Using modified duration and convexity to estimate the price of the bond at this rate, what would you expect the value of the convexity to be?

Section 9.4 **Immunization**

In sections 9.1, 9.2, and 9.3, we introduced the concepts of duration, volatility (modified duration), and convexity, and then used these concepts to estimate the change in the value of an investment portfolio for various changes in market interest rates. In some of our examples, we also showed what the actual value of the investment portfolio would be if you were to ignore duration and convexity and simply calculated the present value of future cash flows using the new market interest rate. This leads to the question, why bother using duration, volatility, and convexity in the first place?

The real importance of duration, volatility, and convexity lies in their role in the process of immunization. Immunization is important, as it is a process that seeks to protect a company from the risk of interest rate changes on both its assets and liabilities. The goal is to allow the company to be somewhat immune to the risk of interest rate changes.

One job an actuary often has is to certify that a corporation (e.g., an insurance company) or a pension fund has assets at least equal to the size of its liabilities. For an insurance company or a pension fund, assets will consist of cash, real estate, stocks, bonds, and mortgages. Liabilities will be future benefits that have accrued to date such as the earned promise to pay a death benefit if a policyholder dies (for a life insurance company) or the promise of a pension fund to pay a retirement pension at age 65 based on years of service already completed.

Having total assets greater than or equal to total liabilities is obviously necessary if the company or pension fund is going to be certified as "solvent".

But just having total assets greater than or equal to total liabilities at time t is not enough. You must also be able to show that your assets can provide continuing cash flow (at any time) that will meet the cash flow demands of the promises represented by the liabilities (remember what happened to the banks in the late 1970s. The cash flow from their assets did not "match" the cash flow required for their liabilities).

A portfolio of assets whose cash flow matches the cash flow of some associated liabilities is known as an immunized portfolio. We will more properly define "immunized" in a moment.

EXAMPLE 1   A small company that is downsizing its operations has decided to provide three employees with early retirement packages that pay $10 000 at the end of each year up to and including age 60, plus a lump sum of $200 000 at age 60. The three employees are now exact ages 51, 53 and 55. The company determines that the payments due under this package can be matched by the income and maturities generated by three 200 000 face amount 5% annual coupon bonds with maturities of 5, 7, and 9 years. Determine the cost to the company to fund this early retirement package if interest rates today are $i = 4.5\%$ per annum effective. (Ignore mortality.)

Solution

$$P_5 = 10\ 000a_{\overline{5}|.045} + 200\ 000(1.045)^{-5} = 204\ 389.98$$
$$P_7 = 10\ 000a_{\overline{7}|.045} + 200\ 000(1.045)^{-7} = 205\ 892.70$$
$$P_9 = 10\ 000a_{\overline{9}|.045} + 200\ 000(1.045)^{-9} = \underline{207\ 268.79}$$
$$= 617\ 551.47$$

In Example 1, we achieve perfect cash flow matching in that the cash requirements of the liabilities were perfectly matched (in both timing and amounts) by the cash flows of the assets. Perfect cash flow immunization (i.e., perfect cash flow dedication) is rarely attainable. However, there are certain principles of immunization we strive for in managing a portfolio of assets and liabilities.

Assume the assets generate a cash flow:

$$A_1, A_2, ..., A_n \text{ at times } 1, 2, ..., n$$

Assume the liabilities require cash flows of:

$$L_1, L_2, ..., L_n \text{ at times } 1, 2, ..., n$$

For perfect cash flow matching,

$$A_1 = L_1, A_2 = L_2, ..., A_n = L_n$$

The technique of immunization is a bit more flexible than perfect cash flow matching in that it does not require the cash flows paid by the assets to exactly match the cash flows demanded by your liabilities. This is also referred to as *Redington immunization*, named after R. M. Redington who first proposed this concept in 1952 in a publication entitled "Review of the Principles of Life-Office Valuations".

Let

$$R_t = A_t - L_t, \text{ for } t = 1, 2, ..., n$$

In this context, R_t represents the net cash flow at time t. Values of $R_t > 0$ mean more money is coming in than going out, while the opposite is true for values of $R_t < 0$.

Define $P(i)$ as the present value of the future net cash flows at i.

$$P(i) = \sum_{t=1}^{n} R_t(1 + i)^{-t}$$

In the process of immunization, the first thing that is required is:

$$P(i) = 0$$

In other words, the present value of the cash inflows from the assets is equal to the present value of the cash outflows for the liabilities.

The second thing that is required is that $P(i)$ have a local minimum at i. This will happen if

$$P'(i) = 0$$

and

$$P''(i) > 0$$

$P'(i) = 0$ can be interpreted as requiring that the modified duration, or volatility, of the net cash flows must equal zero. In other words, the modified duration of the asset cash flows is equal to the modified duration of the liability cash flows.

$P''(i) > 0$ means that the convexity of the net cash flows must be greater than 0.

$$\bar{c} = \frac{P''(i)}{P(i)} > 0$$

Thus, for full immunization, we require that the convexity of the assets be greater than the convexity of the liabilities.

What does all of this mean? Given that $P(i)$ has a local minimum at i, then small changes in the interest rate in *either* direction will *increase* the present value of the net cash flows. Thus, no matter what happens to future interest rates, you are "protected", or "immunized," from any negative effect they might have on your portfolio of assets or liabilities. This is a very desirable result if it can be obtained.

To summarize:

1. The present value of the cash inflow from the assets is equal to the present value of the cash outflow from the liabilities. This condition assures that the correct total amount of assets is utilized to support the liabilities.

2. The modified duration or volatility of the assets is equal to the modified duration or volatility of the liabilities. This condition assures that price sensitivity to changes in interest rates is the same for the assets and the liabilities and average "lifetimes" are equal.

3. The convexity of the assets is greater than the convexity of the liabilities. When this condition is satisfied, a decrease in interest rates will cause asset values to increase by more than the increase in liability values. Conversely, an increase in interest rates will cause asset values to decrease by less than the decrease in liability values.

EXAMPLE 2 To immunize the liabilities in the early retirement package described in Example 1, the company purchases an investment portfolio of two zero-coupon bonds due at times $t_1 = 3$ and $t_2 = 8$, both having a yield to maturity of 5%. Determine the amount of each zero-coupon bond that must be purchased and whether or not the overall asset/liability portfolio is in an immunized position. The current interest rate is $i^{(1)} = 4.5\%$.

Solution The liabilities (in \$000's) are the early retirement payments as follows:

$$
\begin{array}{ccccccccc}
 & & & & 200 & & & 200 & 200 \\
 & & & & + & & & + & + \\
30 & 30 & 30 & 30 & 20 & 20 & 20 & 10 & 10 \\
\hline
0 & 1 & 2 & 3 & 4 & 5 & 6 & 7 & 8 & 9
\end{array}
$$

Let X be the face amount of the three-year bond purchased and Y be the face amount of the eight-year bond purchased.

$P(i) = 0$, therefore

$$\sum R_t (1 + i)^{-t} = \sum (A_t - L_t)(1 + i)^{-t}$$

where, $\quad A_t = X(1.045)^{-3} + Y(1.045)^{-8}$

$$
\begin{aligned}
L_t &= 10\ 000 a_{\overline{9}|.045} + 10\ 000 a_{\overline{7}|.045} + 10\ 000 a_{\overline{5}|.045} + \\
&\quad 200\ 000(1.045)^{-5} + 200\ 000(1.045)^{-7} + \\
&\quad 200\ 000(1.045)^{-9} \\
&= \$617\ 551.47
\end{aligned}
$$

Thus,

$$X(1.045)^{-3} + Y(1.045)^{-8} = 617{,}551.47 \qquad \text{Equation 1}$$

For $P'(i) = 0$, we need

$$\sum t A_t (1 + i)^{-(t+1)} - \sum t L_t (1 + i)^{-(t+1)} = 0$$

As this equation $= 0$, this can be evaluated as:

$$\sum t A_t (1 + i)^{-t} - \sum t L_t (1 + i)^{-t} = 0$$

Thus

$$\sum t A_t (1 + i)^{-t} = 3X(1.045)^{-3} + 8Y(1.045)^{-8}$$

$$
\begin{aligned}
\sum t L_t (1 + i)^{-t} &= 30\ 000(1.045)^{-1} + 2(30\ 000)(1.045)^{-2} + \cdots + 10 \\
&\quad (210\ 000)(1.045)^{-10} \\
&= 3\ 737\ 792
\end{aligned}
$$

Thus,

$$3X(1.045)^{-3} + 8Y(1.045)^{-8} = 3\ 737\ 792 \qquad \text{Equation 2}$$

Solving equation 1 and 2 we get

$$X = 274\ 478 \text{ and } Y = 536\ 171$$

Now check to see if $P''(i) > 0$.

$$\Rightarrow \sum t(t+1)A_t(1+i)^{-(t+2)} - \sum t(t+1)L_t(1+i)^{-(t+2)} > 0$$

$$\Rightarrow \sum (t^2+t)A_t(1+i)^{-(t+2)} - \sum (t^2+t)L_t(1+i)^{-(t+2)} > 0$$

We can multiply through by $(1+i)^2$, without effect, and we can use the fact that $\sum tA_t(1+i)^{-t} = \sum tL_t(1+i)^{-t}$ from above.

Thus, we check to see if

$$\sum t^2 A_t(1+i)^{-t} - \sum t^2 L_t(1+i)^{-t} > 0$$

$$\sum t^2 A_t(1+i)^{-t} = 3^2(274\ 478)(1.045)^{-3} + 8^2(536\ 171)(1.045)^{-8}$$
$$= 26\ 294\ 476$$

$$\sum t^2 L_t(1+i)^{-t} = 30\ 000(1.045)^{-1} + (2^2)(30\ 000)(1.045)^{-2} + \cdots + (10^2)(210\ 000)(1.045)^{-10}$$
$$= 25\ 762\ 277$$

Thus, $P''(i) > 0$ and we can say we are fully immunized.

It can be shown that if we purchase zero-coupon bonds at other than $t_1 = 3$ and $t_2 = 8$ the portfolio might not be fully immunized.

Students are encouraged to do so using an Excel spread sheet.

In practice, there are some issues in the implementation of an immunization strategy. These include:

1. The choice of the interest rate i to calculate $P(i)$, $P'(i)$, and so on, is not always clear. This will have a direct effect on the answer. Further, what may appear to be the correct rate, i, today could change over time.

2. The convexity criterion given only works for very small changes in $i^{(m)}$. This criterion might fail if we have a large change in $i^{(m)}$.

3. The fact that there is a yield curve is not part of the technique outlined. This is the same as assuming that the entire yield curve shifts in parallel when interest rates change. Any other patterns could cause the technique to fail.

4. The calculations may show that a portfolio is immunized at the time at which they are made, but the same portfolio may not necessarily be immunized later on.

5. Exact cash flows may not be guaranteed. For example, a mortgage might be paid off early or a bond called early, not meeting your assumed cash flow.

6. You may not be able to buy exactly the indicated assets either as to amount or time.

Exercise 9.4

Part A

1. You need to pay a debt of $100 000 in five years. You attempt to immunize the financial outcome by buying two zero-coupon bonds, one redeemed in three years and one redeemed in seven years. If $i^{(1)} = 6\%$, calculate the amount of each bond you should buy to theoretically achieve immunization. Also check to see if $P''(i) > 0$ for your portfolio.

2. A company has to pay $5000 in one year, $20 000 in two years, and $10 000 in three years. It wants to immunize its commitment by buying a portfolio of three bonds, which are:
   i) a one-year zero-coupon bond sold to yield $i^{(1)} = 8\%$
   ii) a two-year par value coupon bond with annual coupons at 8%
   iii) a three-year par value bond with annual coupons at 9%.
   How much of each bond offer should be purchased to achieve immunization if $i^{(1)} = 8\%$?

3. Mr. Wang has to pay off an obligation of $60 000 in five years. He decides to achieve immunization by buying two zero-coupon bonds, one due in three years and the other due in six years, each sold to yield an effective rate $i^{(1)} = 5\frac{1}{2}\%$.
   a) How much of each bond should be purchased?
   b) What are the consequences to Mr. Wang if interest rates rise to $i^{(1)} = 6\%$ immediately after the purchase (i.e., is he still immunized?).
   c) Check to see if $P''(i) > 0$.

4. The IMBIG insurance company has an obligation to pay a retiree $20 000 at the end of each year for five years. If $i^{(1)} = 6\%$, then the present value of this obligation is $20\ 000a_{\overline{5}|.06} = \$84\ 247.28$. The company decides to spend $28 082.43 each on three zero-coupon bonds of duration one year, three years, and five years. All bonds yield $i^{(1)} = 6\%$. Is this portfolio immunized?

5. A $1000 obligation is due in ten years. The borrower attempts to immunize this liability by buying two zero-coupon bonds at time t_1 and t_2. She buys $400 worth of Bond A and $900 worth of Bond B. If $i^{(1)} = 9\%$, determine t_1 and t_2.

6. Liability payments of $1000 each are to be made at time $t = 5$, 10, and 15 years. To immunize the liability, the borrower buys two zero-coupon bonds to provide cash flows A_1 at time $t = 7$ and A_2 at time $t = 11$.
   a) If $i^{(1)} = 10\%$, determine A_1 and A_2.
   b) Is the obligation fully immunized?

7. To immunize a liability requiring ten annual payments of $5000, a company acquires a portfolio of assets consisting of $C of cash at time $t = 0$ and $B worth of zero-coupon bonds to be redeemed at time $t = 10$. Determine $C and $B if $i^{(1)} = 7\%$.

Part B

1. Prove that $\frac{d}{di^{(m)}}\bar{v} = \bar{v}^2 - \bar{c}$.

Section 9.5 **Summary and Review Exercises**

● The duration (or Macaulay duration) of an asset or liability is given by:

$$\bar{d} = \frac{\displaystyle\sum_{t=1}^{n} tC_t(1+i)^{-t}}{\displaystyle\sum_{t=1}^{n} C_t(1+i)^{-t}} \quad (21)$$

● The Modified Duration (or volatility) of an asset (or liability) is given by:

$$\bar{v} = \frac{-\frac{d}{di^{(m)}}P(i)}{P(i)} = \frac{\left(\frac{\bar{d}}{m}\right)}{1+i} \quad (22)$$

● The estimated value of an investment portfolio using modified duration when the market interest rate changes by $\Delta i^{(m)} = $ new $i^{(m)}$ – current $i^{(m)}$.

$$P(i + \Delta i^{(m)}) = P(i)(1 - \bar{v}\Delta i^{(m)}) \quad (23)$$

● The convexity of an asset (or liability) is given by:

$$\bar{c} = \frac{P''(i)}{P(i)} = \frac{\sum_{t=1}^{n} t(t+1)C_t\left(1 + \frac{i^{(m)}}{m}\right)^{-t}}{m^2\left(1 + \frac{i^{(m)}}{m}\right)^2 P(i)} \quad (24)$$

● Estimated value of an investment portfolio using modified duration and convexity when the market interest rate changes by $\Delta i^{(m)} = $ new $i^{(m)}$ – current $i^{(m)}$

$$P(i + \Delta i^{(m)}) = P(i)\left[1 - \bar{v}\Delta i^{(m)} + \frac{1}{2}\bar{c}(\Delta i^{(m)})^2\right] \quad (25)$$

● For asset/liability cash flows to be immunized using Redington immunization:

$P(i) = 0$
$P'(i) = 0$
$P''(i) > 0$

where $P(i) = \sum_{t=1}^{n} R_t(1 + i)^{-t}$

and $R_t = A_t - L_t = $ net cash flow at time t
(asset cash flow at time t minus liability cash flow at time t)

Review Exercise 9.5

1. For a ten-year par value bond with annual coupons at $6\frac{1}{2}\%$, calculate the:
   a) duration
   b) modified duration (volatility).

2. An asset portfolio consists of three par value $1000 bonds.
   i) a three-year zero-coupon bond
   ii) a five-year zero-coupon bond
   iii) a five-year par value bond with annual coupons at 8%.
   If $i^{(1)} = 5\frac{1}{2}\%$, calculate the duration of the portfolio and convexity.

3. A preferred stock pays semi-annual dividends of $30 (first one due in six months). If $i^{(1)} = 7\%$, calculate:
   a) the value of the stock
   b) the duration of the stock

c) the exact and approximate market value if interest rates immediately rise to 7.1%

4. A financial institution has an obligation to pay $100 000 in 4 years. This liability can be funded with a combination of three-year zero-coupon bonds and five-year zero-coupon bonds. If $i^{(1)} = 5\%$, determine how much of each bond should be purchased to achieve immunization.

5. The market value of a bond today is $108 at $i^{(1)} = 6.5\%$. The duration, $\bar{d}$, is 6. Estimate the price of the bond if i rises to 6.6%.

6. A ten-year par value bond has annual coupons at 7%. If $i^{(1)} = 5.5\%$, determine:
   a) the price of the bond
   b) the duration of the bond
   c) the modified duration of the bond

7. A five-year bond has semi-annual coupons at $i^{(2)} = 9\%$. If it is purchased to yield $i^{(2)} = 10\%$, determine:
   a) the price of the bond
   b) the duration of the bond
   c) the modified duration or volatility of the bond.

8. A financial institution has a financial obligation of $150 000 due in five years. The institution can fund this liability by buying two types of bonds:
   • B_1 = three-year bonds with annual coupons at 9%
   • B_2 = eight-year zero-coupon bonds
   If $i^{(1)} = 8\%$, determine the amount the institution should invest in each bond to achieve immunization. In this case, is $P''(i) > 0$?

9. A bank must pay $100 000 on a GIC in five years time. The bank can buy two types of bonds: a zero-coupon bond due in three years and a zero-coupon bond due in seven years. If $i^{(1)} = 7\%$, calculate the amount of each bond the bank should purchase.

10. A $1000 zero-coupon bond comes due in ten years. The yield rate on the bond is $i^{(2)} = 6\%$. What is the modified duration of this bond?

11. A loan is paid off with level annual payments over 10 years. If $i^{(1)} = 5\%$, determine:
    a) the duration of the loan
    b) the modified duration of the loan.

12. A preferred stock pays an annual dividend of $15 in perpetuity (first payment in one year). If $i^{(1)} = 6\%$, calculate:
    a) the price of the stock
    b) the duration
    c) the convexity.

13. Interest rates today are $i^{(1)} = 7\%$. A bank must pay an obligation of $150 000 in ten years. The bank determines the present value of this obligation to be $76 252. It buys $38 126 worth of five-year zero-coupon bonds and an equal amount of 12-year zero-coupon bonds. Does this result in immunization?

14. The price of a bond is $95 at $i^{(1)} = 6.5\%$. At this yield rate, the volatility is 5. Estimate the price P if the yield rate falls to 6.4%.

15. a) Calculate the duration of a four-year par value coupon bond with 6% annual coupons, if $i^{(1)} = 5.5\%$.
    b) You have an obligation to pay $5 million in 3.6761 years. If $i^{(1)} = 5.5\%$, how can you use a portfolio of bonds from part a) to immunize the interest rate risk in repaying this obligation?

16. Calculate the duration of a 10-year bond with 7% annual coupons if the yield rate is:
    a) $i^{(1)} = 6\%$
    b) $i^{(1)} = 7\%$
    c) $i^{(1)} = 8\%$

17. a) You have an asset portfolio made up of three zero-coupon bonds:
    i) a $4000 bond due in 2 years
    ii) an $8000 bond due in 3 years
    iii) a $20 000 bond due in 8 years.
    If $i^{(1)} = 5\%$, calculate the duration of your portfolio.
    b) If you had an obligation to pay $25 000 at time $t = 5.661$, how could you use your asset portfolio to protect yourself from changes in interest rates?

18. A financial institution wants to match a portfolio of liabilities with duration $\bar{d} = 2.5$, with a bond portfolio consisting of $p\%$ 4-year annual coupon bonds with 6% coupons and $(100 - p)\%$ two-year annual coupon bonds with 4% coupons. Given $i^{(1)} = 5.5\%$, determine p.

19. A preferred stock pays annual dividends of $10 per year forever (first dividend in one year). If $i^{(1)} = 7\%$, calculate the duration of this stock.

20. Calculate the duration of a 10-year mortgage with monthly payments, P, if $i^{(12)} = 6\%$.

21. The ABC Financial Institution is obligated to pay $60 000 in exactly four years. To provide for this obligation they buy a portfolio of bonds where $p\%$ are two-year zero-coupon bonds and $(100 - p)\%$ are five-year zero-coupon bonds. Determine p if $i^{(1)} = 4.5\%$.

Glossary of Terms

Accumulated Value   The total of the amount of money originally invested plus the interest earned.

Accumulation Function   A mathematical operator that shows the accumulated value of a $1 investment at a given time and at a given rate of interest.

Accumulated Value (of an Annuity)   The equivalent dated value of the periodic payments at the end of the term of the annuity.

Accumulation of Bond Discount   The periodic increase in the book value of a bond bought at a price below redemption so that the book value will equal the redemption value at maturity.

Amortization Schedule   A schedule showing in detail how a debt is repaid by the amortization method.

Amortize   To repay a debt by means of equal periodic payments of interest and principal.

Amortizing a Bond Premium   The periodic reduction of the book value of a bond bought at a price above redemption, so that the book value will equal the redemption value at maturity.

Amount Function   A mathematical operator that shows the accumulated value of a defined investment at a given time and at a given rate of interest.

Annuity   A series of payments made or received at regular intervals of time.

Annuity Certain   A series of payments involving a fixed number of such payments.

Annuity Due   A series of payments in which the payments are made at the beginning of each interval of time.

Asset-Liability Management   The attempt to match as closely as possible the cash flow arising from one's assets to the cash flow requirements or commitments of one's liabilities.

Balloon Payment   An extra payment made at the same time as the final regular payment of an annuity in order to have equivalence.

Bond   A certificate of indebtedness agreeing to reimburse the purchaser and to pay periodic interest payments, called coupons.

Bond Interest Rate   The interest rate specified in a bond, upon which the actual periodic interest payments are based. Also called the coupon rate.

Book Value (of a Bond)   The value of a bond, at any particular time, according to its purchaser's accounting records.

Buying Long   Investing in an asset today in the hope of selling the asset at a future time for a profit.

Callable Bond   A bond that can be redeemed early at the discretion of the borrower.

Call Price   A lump sum of money paid to the purchaser to redeem a bond earlier than its maturity date.

Clean (Market) Price (of a Bond)   The price of a bond without accrued bond interest.

Compound Interest   Interest that is earned upon previously earned interest.

Compound Discount   Analogous to compound interest, except where the cash flows are valued at a rate of discount.

Continuous Compounding   Nominal interest rates in which the conversion frequency becomes infinitely small.

Continuous Annuities   An annuity in which the frequency of payment becomes infinitely small.

Continuous Varying Annuities   A Continuous Annuity in which the definition of the size of payment is a continuous function of time.

Convexity   A measure of the shape of the yield curve that allows one to determine the impact on asset values given a change in the rate of interest.

Coupon   A detachable portion of a bond that represents the bond interest payment.

Coupon Rate   The rate of bond interest per coupon payment period used in determining the amount of the coupon.

Deferred Annuity   A series of payments that has its first payment postponed for one or more periods.

Demand Loan   A loan for which repayment in full or in part may be required at any time.

Dirty Price   *See* Full Price (of a Bond).

Discount (Bond Purchased at)   The amount by which the purchase price of a bond is less than its redemption value.

Discounted Value   The amount of money that must be invested on the evaluation date in order to accumulate a specified amount at a later date.

Discounted Value (of an Annuity)   The equivalent dated value of the periodic payments at the beginning of the term of the annuity.

Discounting   Calculating the discounted value at a specified rate of interest or discount of an amount due in the future.

Dollar-Weighted Rate of Interest   The internal rate of return for a fund based on an equation of value using simple interest for parts of the year.

Drop Payment   A smaller concluding payment made one period after the final regular payment of an annuity in order to have equivalence.

Duration   The interest-weighted average point in time of the payments defined by a given cash flow.

Effective Interest Rate   An annual interest rate that produces the same accumulated values as the nominal rate compounded more frequently than annually.

Equation of Values   The equation obtained when comparing the dated values of the original payments at a focal date to the dated values of the replacement payments at the same focal date.

Equivalent Rates   Two rates of interest that produce the same accumulated value in the same period of time.

Equivalent Single Payment   One payment that can replace several other payments because it equals the dated value of the other payments.

Face Value (of a Promissory Note)   The amount of money specified on the promissory note.

Face Value of a Bond   The par value of a bond, printed on the front of the bond. This is often the amount payable at the maturity date. It is used to define the size of the bond coupons.

Focal Date   A specific point in time selected to compare the dated values of sets of payments. Also called the valuation date.

Force of Interest/Discount   The measure of the intensity of interest/discount at a moment in time.

Forward Rate   The expected spot rate which will come into play in the future. A set of current spot rates will imply a set of forward rates.

Full (Dirty) Price (of a Bond)   The total purchase price of a bond, including any accrued interest.

General Annuity   An annuity in which the payment frequency does not align with the interest conversion frequency.

Immediate Annuity   An annuity in which payments are made at the end of each interest conversion period.

Immunization   A technique to structure assets and liabilities in a manner to avoid adverse effects created by changes in the level of interest rates.

Indexed Bond   A bond in which the coupon and redemption value increase with a specific index such as the Consumer Price Index (CPI).

Interest Conversion Period   The period of time between interest compoundings.

Interest Rate   A measure of the return created by an investment at the beginning of a period in which the interest is paid at the end of the period.

Internal Rate of Return   The rate of interest for which the net present value of a capital investment project is equal to zero.

Market Price   *See* Clean Price (of a Bond).

Maturity Date (of a Note)   The legal due date.

Maturity Value (of a Note)   The face value plus interest that must be paid on the legal due date.

Modified Duration   Sometimes called volatility: a measure of the interest rate sensitivity of a set of cash flows.

Mortgage   A loan backed by the asset value of a piece of real estate, normally a house.

Nominal Interest Rate   An annual interest rate that is quoted with the understanding that interest is compounded more than once a year.

Noninterest-Bearing Promissory Note   A note that does not require the payment of interest (the maturity value of such a note is the same as its face value).

Ordinary Annuity   A series of payments in which the payments are made at the end of each interval of time. Also called an immediate annuity.

Periodic Cost (of a Debt)   The sum of interest paid and the sinking-fund deposit when a debt is retired by the sinking-fund method.

Perpetuity   An annuity for which the payments continue forever.

Premium (Bond Purchased at)   The amount by which the purchase price of a bond exceeds its redemption value.

Proceeds (of a Promissory Note)   The amount of money for which a promissory note is sold.

Promissory Note   A written promise to pay a specified amount of money after a specified period of time with or without interest, as specified.

Quoted Price (of a bond)   The clean price or market price of a bond quoted in the daily newspaper. It is customary to give the quoted price on the basis of a $100 bond.

Real Rate of Interest   The net rate of interest after taking inflation into account.

Redemption Value (of a Bond)   A lump sum of money paid to the bondholder to redeem a bond on or after the day of maturity.

Rule of 70   A quick method to approximate how long an investment will take to double.

Selling Short   Selling an asset today in the hope of purchasing it at a future date at a profit. This is the opposite of buying long.

Simple Discount   The amount of discount earned or paid during any period is constant.

Simple Interest   The amount of interest earned or paid during any period is constant.

Sinking Fund   A fund that is being accumulated by periodic payments for the purpose of attaining a certain amount by a certain date.

Sinking Fund Deposit   A regular periodic payment into a sinking fund.

Spot Rates   The interest rates on a given yield curve.

Stocks   A type of ownership security. Preferred stock provides a fixed rate of return in the form of a dividend. Common stock does not earn a fixed dividend rate.

Strip Bond   A bond that has its coupons removed and sold separately.

Time-Weighted Rate of Interest   The rate of return for a one-year period found by compounding the returns earned over subintervals of the year set each time a deposit or withdrawal is made.

Treasury Bill (T-bill)   A short-term security issued by the federal government.

Volatility   Sometimes called modified duration: a measure of the interest rate sensitivity of a set of cash flows.

Yield Rate   The interest rate that an investor will actually realize on an investment.

Zero-coupon Bond   A bond with no coupons. Its value is the present value of its single redemption payment.

Answers to Problems

Exercise 1.1

1. 20, 125

2. a) $0.2\,t^2 + 0.3\,t + 1$ b) $1 + 4n$

4. a) 30   b) 496

5. 6000

Exercise 1.2

1. a) 2.75%   b) 2.36%

2. a) 40, 3.45%   b) 40, 2.27%

3. a) 6.0775, 5%   b) 12.6348, 5%

4. $678.73

Exercise 1.3

1. a) $2950   b) $1234   c) $10 122.74   d) $5143.84

2. a) 16.8%   b) 14.29%   c) 12%   d) 10.66%

3. a) 1328 days   b) 196 days   c) 82 days

4. $131.25; $129.45   **5.** 60%   **6.** $4880.38

7. $547.59   **8.** $1011.74; $1011.58   **9.** $1042.11

10. $80.14   **11.** 10.37%

12. a) 1.923%   b) 6.14%   **13.** 3.23%

Exercise 1.4

Part A

1. $130.70; $30.70

2. $530.45; $30.45

3. $283.34; $63.34

4. $1677.10; $677.10

5. $63.12; $13.12

6. $1687.57; $887.57

7. $377.91; $77.91

8. $1210; $210

9. a) $520   b) $540   c) $560

10. $2450.09

11. $44.6357 billion; $165 400

Exercise 1.5

Part A

1. $83.96	**2.** $42.47	**3.** $655.56	**4.** $310.46
5. $691.07	**6.** $680.58	**7.** $1486.36	**8.** $999.62
9. $311.80	**10.** $405.30	**11.** $289.25	**12.** $1056.05

Part B

1. A: $41 793.10; B: $29 328.59; Choose A.

Exercise 1.6

Part A

1. a) $921.60   b) $920   **2.** Borrow at 5.1%

3. $8145.06   **4.** $8702.60   **5.** a) $2584.71   b) $2666.67

6. 7.4074%   **7.** $4950   **8.** 8%

9. a) $804.36   b) $790   **10.** 120%

11. a) $4552.88   b) $5491.03   c) 13.18%

12. 5.72%   **13.** 245 days   **14.** 9.24%

15. a) 10.50%   b) 6.83%   c) 4.87%   **16.** a) 4.92%   b) 10.81%   c) 7.23%

Part B

1. a) 3.33%   b) 3.85%   **2.** $d_n = \dfrac{d}{1-d}$

3. a) 3.07%   b) 3.17%   **4.** 10.91%

Exercise 1.7

Part A

1. a) 7.12%   b) 3.03%   c) 8.24%   d) 12.75%   e) 9.38%

2. a) 5.91%   b) 8.71%   c) 9.57%   d) 15.70%   e) 4.40%

3. a) 7.92%   b) 6.05%   c) 18.27%   d) 9.96%   e) 8.08%

   f) 4.04%   g) 5.19%   h) 12.59%

4. 6.02%   **5.** 9.04%   **6.** 23.14%   **7.** $i^{(1)} = 5\%$

8. a) $i^{(2)} = 15\frac{1}{2}\%$ is best; $i^{(365)} = 14.9\%$ is worst

   b) $i^{(2)} = 6.5\%$ is best; $i^{(365)} = 5.9\%$ is worst.

9. $m = 4$; 4.75% will never be equivalent to 5%.

10. a) $146.93   b) $148.02   c) $148.59   d) $148.98   e) $149.18

11. $2936.77   **12.** a) $1061.36   b) $1061.36   c) $1061.36   d) $1061.36

13. $1564.14   **14.** The payment plan is better by $5930.34.

15. $2735.69   **16.** $3258.08   **17.** 7.32%

18. a) $672.97   b) $778.81   c) $598.74   d) $1570.97

19. a) 11 098.20   b) $8193.08   c) $9152.10   d) $10 069.44

20. a) 7.62%   b) 8.25%

Part B

1. a), b), c) $26 764.51; $26 878.33; $26 937.10; $26 977.00; $26 996.51

2. a) 6%   b) 6.70%   c) 6.53%   **3.** 6.14%   **4.** $i^{(2)} = 12.37\%$

6. a) $61.83   b) $60.90   c) $61.69

7. $6920.22; $7037.62; $7098.19; $7139.29; $7155.26; $7159.38

8. $62.19   **9.** $362.84; $367.39; $369.72; $371.29; $371.91; $372.06

Exercise 1.8

Part A

1. a) $1706.99 b) $1715.94 c) $1716.81
2. a) $5383.77 b) $5362.80 c) $5362.56
3. 13.52%; 14.47%   **4.** a), b) November 8, 2015
5. 7.9248125 years   **6.** She should accept offer c).

Part B

1. 8.38%   **2.** 14.624063 years **3.** 4.0612599 years
4. 6.1250454 years   **5.** $328.59   **6.** 6.85%

Exercise 1.9

Part A

1. $6273.74   **2.** $654.06   **3.** $646.28; 5.27%
4. $3810.26; $1810.26; 6.55%
5. $3129.12   **6.** $2351.96   **7.** $81 638.36
8. They should not accept the offer.
9. a) The payments option.   b) The cash option.   **10.** 7.57%
11. 7.21%   **12.** $148 413.16   **13.** 1.005%   **14.** $103.70
15. 1.045   **16.** $1105.17   **17.** 7.12%   **18.** $(1 - 2t)^{-1}$
19. $7.20   **20.** $338.84

Part B

2. $686.76; $2.48   **3.** $2958.57   **4.** $15 903.69   **5.** $3494.79; 5.83%
6. 5.69%   **7.** 7.83%   **8.** a) $-v^2$ b) v c) $v - iv^2$ d) $1 + i$ e) v
9. a) $\dfrac{1}{1 + it}$ b) $\dfrac{d}{1 - dt}$ **10.** 0.0152

Review Exercises 1.10

1. $1892.94   **2.** $3996.16   **3.** $8493.75
4. a) $0.2(n^2 + 4n + 5)$ b) $(2n + 2)/(n^2 + 2n + 2)$ c) $(2n + 4)/(n^2 + 4n + 5)$
5. $827 323.97   **6.** $57.92   **7.** $3388.89   **8.** $i^{(2)}$; $i^{(4)}$; $i^{(12)}$
9. a) 2.941% b) 2.213%
10. a) $1708.14 b) $1814.02   c) $1504.14   d) $2467.96   e) $2013.75
11. a) $1332.61 b) 7.44%
12. a) $2433.31 b) $2838.04   c) $2725.15   d) $2995.77   e) $2568.05
13. a) 4.899% b) 4.762%   c) 4.8494%   d) 4.879%
14. a) 10.460% b) 10.205%; choose 9.6%
15. a) 11.04% b), c) 10.99%
16. $1338.23   **17.** Cash option is better by $1709.88.
18. $2199.72; $146.06   **19.** $715.95; 6.17%
20. $1213.12   **21.** a) $1338.23 b) $1348.85   c) $1349.86
22. $2584 47   **23.** a) $2653.30 b) 10.25%   c) 9.718%
24. a) $850.27 b) $850.46
25. $1036.81   **26.** $1260.50

Exercise 2.1

Part A

1. $1709.14   **2.** $809.40   **3.** a) $1746.54   b) $3271.61
4. $2468.20   **5.** a) $1338.29   b) $1508.69   c) $1700.79
6. $550.21   **7.** $1533.25   **8.** $888.02   **9.** $232.13
10. a) $706.89   b) $459.58   **11.** $226.78   **12.** $193.61
13. $22 593.42   **14.** $840.04   **15.** $932.32
16. a) $1153.68   b) $1193.79   c) $1235.58
17. $428.19   **18.** $529.41; $529.81   **19.** $161.87; $161.96

Part B

2. $3951.33   **3.** $3611.27   **4.** $2504.12   **5.** $106.67

Exercise 2.2

Part A

1. $i^{(4)} = 10.96\%$ **2.** $i^{(12)} = 8.88\%$ **3.** $i^{(1)} = 7.60\%$
4. $i^{(2)} = 13.54\%$ **5.** 8 years 5 months 14 days
6. 2 years 11 months 23 days   **7.** 7 years 10 months 8 days
8. 2 years 6 months 12 days   **9.** $i^{(1)} = 7.18\%$
10. $i^{(4)} = 10.27\%$ **11.** 14.77%   **12.** $i^{(365)} = 13.52\%$
13. a) 15 years 199 days   b) 9 years 330 days   c) 15 years 129 days; 10 years
14. 6 years 208 days   **15.** 8 years 41 days
16. 2.5   **17.** 12.68%

Part B

1. a) $1542.21   b) $2378.41   **2.** 9 years 186 days
4. 34.535 years   **5.** $(1 + i^{(1)})^2 - 1$ **6.** 21 years 31 days
7. 19 years, 233 days   **8.** 7 years, 128 days   **9.** $161.05
10. $1026.94   **11.** 4.53%   **12.** $1.57
13. 2.90%   **14.** a) 3.8145 years   b) 4.7218 years   c) 1.67846 years

Exercise 2.3

Part A

1. 87 645   **2.** 345   **3.** 6.50%
4. 6.6374573 years   **5.** $35 041.15   **6.** $372 556.20
7. a) 3.92%; i real AT = 2.39%   b) 3.85%; i real AT = 1.85%
    c) 3.77%; i real AT = 1.32%
8. $n = 1.61$ days

Part B

1. a) 76 501   b) 0:47 a.m.
2. 36 886   **3.** $0.88425 U.S. = $1 Can.

Exercise 2.4

1. a) USA: $4956.40; Can: $4957.36   b) USA: $4978.34; Can: $4978.44
    c) USA: 4.04%; Can: 3.88%
2. a) 6.45%   b) Other investor = 4.85%; Dealer = 8.90%

Review Exercises 2.5

1. $1892.94   **2.** $228.04   **3.** 15 years 100 days   **4.** 11.14%
5. $8444.68   **6.** September 3, 2012
7. $877.83   **8.** a) 11.04%   b), c) 10.99%
9. $1338.23   **10.** Cash option is better by $17 098.88.
11. a) $850.27   b) $850.46
12. a) 6 years 341 days   b) 6 years 340 days   c) 7 years 7 days   d) 7 years 38 days
    Rule of 70: $n = 7$ years
13. $992.94   **14.** 10.35%   **15.** a) $9797.78   b) $9828.47
16. 3.5023%   **17.** 6   **18.** a) 6.262   b) 4.076
19. 56 years

Exercise 3.2

Part A

1. a) $11 969.42   b) $10 512.66   **2.** $28 760.36   **3.** $3280.87
4. $320.74   **5.** $606.03   **6.** a) $47 551.33   b) $22 300.39
7. $13 031.63   **8.** $62 284.13   **9.** $12 833.69   **10.** $18 038.27
11. a) $8111.34   b) $9281.38   **12.** $204.56   **13.** $5522.36
14. $1039.30   **15.** $49 702.20   **16.** a) $9402.26   b) $8954.24

Part B

2. $25 732.82   **3.** $15 448.11   **5.** 14.2; 30
6. $3515.68   **7.** $24 527.91
10. a) $165.56   b) $195.18   **11.** $529.37
12. a) $6246.21   b) $6686.78   **13.** $103 343.97

Exercise 3.3

Part A

1. a) $3992.71   b) $4579.71   c) $3535.33
2. a) $1992.01   b) $2058.53   c) $1917.10
3. $27 737.28   **4.** $15 569.49   **5.** $6160.42   **6.** $6450.04
7. $670.04   **8.** $7019.27   **9.** $22 096.92   **10.** $12 269.34
11. $13 869.21   **12.** a) $12 795.73   b) $1016.81   c) $8085.63   d) $7218.90
13. $84.39   **14.** $2014.79   **15.** $33.94
16. $118.95, $2137; $111.22, $1673.33; $103.79, $1227.40
17. a) $1012.63   b) $1217.12   **18.** $637.28   **19.** $8331.49

Part B

2. 50; 12   **4.** 17.$\dot{7}$ **5.** 6.57
6. $(1 + i)^{-1} + (1 + 2i)^{-1} + \ldots + (1 + ni)^{-1}$

7. $a_{\overline{2n}|i} - a_{\overline{n}|i} = s_{\overline{n}|i} - a_{\overline{2n}|i} = \dfrac{1}{4i}$ **8.** Ratio = $(1 + i)^n$ **9.** $(1 + i)^n$

10. a) $7758.83   b) $1065.88   c) $8034.50   d) $4717.02; smaller, since 9% > 6%
11. $13 559.93   **12.** $6526.63
13. The company should purchase Machine A.
14. $7384.41   **15.** $12 181.80   **16.** $13 589.73   **17.** $3509.75

Exercise 3.4

Part A

1. $7066.97; $15 484.60   **2.** $895.36   **3.** $10.23
4. $5057.63   **5.** $1080.31   **6.** $576.61   **7.** $73 868.88
8. $910.98   **9.** $4566.77   **10.** $4291.72   **11.** $1842.32
12. $26 093.01   **13.** $23 387.98   **14.** $2532.43   **15.** $4357.35
16. $59.16   **17.** $124 482.59   **18.** a) $3331.74   b) $3678.11

Part B

1. $32 868.66   **2.** a) $4883.88   b) $5006.92   c) $2203.59
5. $17 531.17   **9.** $24 660.89
10. $a_{\overline{7}|i}(1+i)^{-3}$; $a_{\overline{7}|i}(1+i)$; $s_{\overline{4}|i} + a_{\overline{3}|i}$; $s_{\overline{7}|i}(1+i)$; $s_{\overline{7}|i}(1+i)^4$
11. a) $\ddot{s}_{\overline{3}|i}[3(1+i)^6 + 2(1+i)^3 + 1]$ b) $2s_{\overline{3}|i}(1+i)^2 + 3a_{\overline{3}|i}(1+i)$
12. $13 566.11   **13.** $6461.63   **14.** $3096.92

Exercise 3.5

Part A

1. 13; $9.94   **2.** 138; $492.73; $243.95
3. 31; $474.56; $77.93   **4.** 7; $1410.28   **5.** 7; $0
6. 32; $345.58   **7.** 3; $1694.97   **8.** 24; $192.57 on July 1, 2016
9. a) 58; $4732.82   b) $7411.23
10. a) 11; $789.92 on January 1, 2017   b) $525.51
11. 15   **12.** $947.09

Part B

1. January 1, 2018; $92.28   **2.** a) 81   b) $1289.20   c) $1311.76
3. a) 13   b) $5726.60   c) $6012.93   **4.** $151 158.86   **5.** 7; $1494.19

6. $n = \dfrac{\log\left(\frac{S}{R}i + 1\right)}{\log(1+i)}$ **7.** $n = \dfrac{-\log\left(1 - \frac{A}{R}i\right)}{\log(1+i)}$

8. 20; $798.39   **9.** 48

Exercise 3.6

Part A

1. 7.98%   **2.** 18.40%   **3.** 8.70%   **4.** 19.61%; 21.47%
5. 35.07%   **6.** 19.48%   **7.** 5.14%

Part B

1. 21.20%   **2.** 35.07%   **3.** 16.22%   **4.** 17.97%; 19.53%
5. Option 1: $i = 22.73\%$; Option 2: $i = 19.98\%$ is better.
6. $42.65 a month to borrow and buy a TV set.
7. 20.86%   **8.** 7.61%

Review Exercises 3.7

1. a) $96 757.14; $39 470.85   b) $333 943.43; $55 572.48
2. a) $1984.65   b) $2332.09   **3.** $35 719.42
4. a) $2050.63   b) $8649.69   **5.** $57.42

6. $14 631.36; $7214.18   **7.** $71 580.38   **8.** $96 435.44
9. $51 893.87   **10.** $1973.95   **11.** $28 659.99
12. $2569.15   **13.** $28 630.72   **14.** 81; $1441.95; $0
15. 15; $140.88   **16.** February 1, 2012; $41.01   **17.** 65.66%
18. 21.55%   **19.** 17.97%   **20.** 70.04%
21. 14; $111.97 on January 1, 2011   **22.** $376.91
23. May 1, 2011; July 1, 2017   **24.** $14 796.40   **25.** $5394.73
26. a) $7.01   b) $2172   c) 28 months; $473.74
27. 17; May 10, 2012; $61.08   **28.** 19.91%
29. a) $618.26   b) $694.53   c) $4551.60
30. $3263.56   **31.** a) $7520.60; $19 816.34   b) May 1, 2017; $253.07
32. 16.47%   **33.** $4055.39

Exercise 4.1

Part A

1. $1199.86   **2.** $10 239.68   **3.** $2286.27
4. a) $11 469.92   b) $11 386.59   c) $11 629.86   d) $11 300.85
5. a) $2314.08   b) $2312.37   c) $2304.96   d) $2314.94
6. a) $745.60   b) $747.03   **7.** $1133.07
8. a) $221.85   b) $219.36   **9.** $161.71
10. a) $233.51   b) $233.62   c) $233.48
11. $330.67   **12.** $5843.61   **13.** a) $10 863.42   b) $10 863.34
14. a) $6781.37   b) $6782.71   **15.** $1841.59
16. Buying is cheaper.   **17.** $23 691.40   **18.** 14.86%
19. 16.62%   **20.** 59; $0   **21.** $239.89
22. a) $7078.18   b) $21 983.75   c) $7281.59   d) $22 615.51   e) $4498.31
23. a) $17 991.16   b) $1426.50   **24.** $114.33   **25.** 33; $311.62
26. a) $582.07   b) $582.08

Part B

4. a) $1019.62   b) $246.95   **5.** a) $330.85   b) $4106.23
8. $15 495.16   **9.** 11%   **10.** 29.70%   **11.** $4567.34
12. $16 048.08   **13.** a) $47 915.51   b) $49 393.59
14. a) $7804.35   b) $2058.21

Exercise 4.2

Part A

1. $687.48   **2.** $5889.45   **3.** $1534.67   **4.** $1579.05
5. a) $1744.80   b) $2101.26   c) $2483.94
6. $1451.28; $1367.04; $1320.54; $198 307.20; $260 112; $325 394.40
7. a) $1975.81   b) $1995.91   **8.** $1342.71; $1159.74
9. $219.47   **10.** 243; $240.13   **11.** $2332.37; 2255.05; take seller's offer
12. a) $951.93; $1037.94; $1194.69   b) 21.9 years
13. a) $294.73 b) $639.08   **14.** 9.53%
15. 2149.29 + 449.86 = $2599.15

Part B

1. $134 296.84   **2.** 8.00%   **3.** 15 years 9 months   **4.** $3048.63
5. $945.56; $217.73   **6.** $179 095.85   **7.** 11 years; $288.99

Exercise 4.3

Part A

1. a) $10 000   b) $8333.33   c) $6666.67
2. a) $5000   b) $3205.13
3. a) $25 000   b) $26 500   c) $19 802.34
4. a) $2100.12   b) $2363.70
5. a) $1456.31   b) $1639.09   **6.** $13 333.33
7. a) $58 125.94   b) $57 142.86   c) $43 618.37
8. $20 959.18   **9.** 12.5%;12.89%
10. a) $131.16   b) $1508.88   **11.** $2523.65
12. 11%   **13.** $20 548.18   **14.** $460.60

Part B

3. a) 12%   b) $200 000   c) 18
4. $545 145.80   **5.** 20 months; $182.88   **6.** $88 506.21
7. $1652.63   **8.** $161.29   **9.** 68 months; $103.32
10. a) $4912.66   b) $5764.96   **11.** a) $3920.63   b) $4600.83
12. $2222.49   **13.** $623.50   **14.** 14.654 614 years   **15.** $1989.36.

Exercise 4.4

Part A

1. 3.790787; 3.977316   **2.** 32.19 yrs   **3.** 22.2222%
4. 11.64676   **5.** $1157.12   **6.** a) $8374.92   b) $8375.41

Part B

1. $304.45   **2.** $11 434.71   **3.** $\frac{1}{\delta}\ln\left(\frac{\delta}{1-e^{-\delta}}\right)$ **4.** $745.88
5. 6%

Exercise 4.5

Part A

1. $7332.70   **2.** $1 167 898.49   **3.** $20 180.04   **4.** $59 561.47
5. $8323.06   **6.** $137 500   **7.** $8973.78   **8.** $113 990.19
9. $16 082.70   **10.** $2504.44   **11.** $7797.87   **12.** $60 673.97
13. $4780.77   **14.** $15 754.79   **15.** $36.40   **16.** $435.84

Part B

3. b) $100 000   **4.** $22 620.20   **5.** $97 489.02   **9.** $4932.95
10. $16 090.80   **11.** She should choose fund A.
12. $\frac{1}{is_{\overline{2}|i}}\left(p+\frac{q}{is_{\overline{2}|i}}\right)$ **14.** At the end of the 24th year.
15. $442.88; $2708.61   **16.** $147 928.85

Exercise 4.6

Part A

1. $\frac{s_{\overline{n}|i}-n}{\delta}$ **2.** 3   **3.** 400   **4.** 41.336565
5. $10 000   **6.** $3250.42   **7.** $42.61   **8.** $70.25
9. 91.90372

Part B

1. $230.20

2. $\dfrac{1}{\ln\left(\dfrac{1+k}{1+i}\right)}$

3. a) $-(1+i)^{-1}(\bar{I}\bar{a})_{\overline{n}|i}$ b) $-(\bar{I}\bar{a})_{\overline{n}|i}$

4. a) $e^{-\delta n}$ b) $e^{\delta n}$ **5.** $1480.21

Review Exercises 4.7

1. a) $603.73   b) $99.42   **2.** $4892.00; $3281.39
3. $4046.12   b) $4045.61   **4.** a) 27; $88.29   b) 27; $0
5. $1273.45   **6.** 28; $38.03   **7.** 15.74%; 16.36%
8. $22 830.71   **9.** $7006.36; $5202.01
10. a) $9380.77   b) $7606.79   c) $15 705
11. Lease option is cheaper.   **12.** a) $41 884.02   b) $60 795.57
13. a) $1220.61; $1434.20; $2172.62   b) 175 months
14. $123.65   **15.** $2256.98   **16.** $848.07
17. a) $16 435.51   b) $16 517.69   c) $14 654.25
18. $1352.74   **19.** $165.88   **20.** a) $10 716.74   b) $13 048.26
21. a) $750 000   b) $806 189.73   **22.** $14 012.21
24. $10 442.13; $100 727.85   **25.** $380 000   **26.** $6358.35
27. $338 971.64   **28.** $449.21   **29.** $31 787.13
30. $335.92   **31.** $1118.60   **32.** $76 627.98
33. 8.03 years   **34.** 14.294571   b) 14.482182   **35.** 10.512

Exercise 5.1

Part A

1. a) $336.04   b) $335.53   **2.** a) $626.62   b) $623.85
3. $758.05   **4.** $155.30   **5.** Last payment is $3226.91.
6. Last payment is $1842.92.   **7.** $472.82   **8.** $424.91
9. $1190.71; $1297.74   **10.** $2935.54; $111.50
11. a) $43.75   b) $1639.45   **12.** $131.08   **13.** $1516.06
14. 8%
15. a) $274.75   b) 0.0082071   c) 10%   d) $29 738.47   e) 22 years

Part B

1. Debt at the end of 5 months is $2076.13; last payment is $117.38.
2. Last payment is $26.95
3. $1373.79   b) $343.45   c) 19 years 51 weeks
4. 16th   **5.** $8524.76   **6.** $100\left(\dfrac{n}{a_{\overline{n}|i}}-1\right)$
7. U.S. uses $i^{(12)}$; bank statement is correct
8. a) $915.59   b) 24 years 47 weeks   c) $42.65
9. 8.17%   **10.** 8%   **11.** 16.99%   **12.** $1314.67
13. 43rd   **14.** Mortgage A: $111 192.62; Mortgage B: $97 256.92
15. 8.87%

Exercise 5.2

Part A

1. $5607.30; $5607.50   **2.** $5200.37   **3.** $3750.17; $950.33
4. $6383.57   **5.** $1281.01; $245.39   **6.** $1210.01; $82.29
7. $108 166.95   **8.** $184 618.15; $141 381.85
9. $41 738.99; $38 261.01   **10.** $8334.94   **11.** $15 849.33
12. $18 137.44   **13.** $481.02   **14.** $26 528.38

Part B

1. $105 400.67   **2.** Take out $250 000 mortgage at $i^{(2)} = 7.25\%$
3. $153 975.41   **4.** 17 years and 9 months; $205.92   **5.** $2126.40
6. a) 8 years and 5 months; $236.76   b) 7 years and 8 months; $150.40
7. a) $197 015.20   b) $71 082.21   c) $64 572.63
9. November 30, 2012   **10.** $3076.26
11. 11; $93.46   **12.** $123.54
13. a) $915.86   b) $154 754.41   c) i) 17 years and 2 months   ii) $99 091.38
   iii) $108 711.27   iv) $202.91

Exercise 5.3

Part A

1. $154.25; $4.75   **2.** $3.11   **3.** He should not refinance.
4. They should refinance.   **5.** $1009.23   **6.** $248 923.62
7. $422.02   **8.** $3787.21   **9.** $474.79
10. a) 188.68   b) 3580.97   c) Refinance and save 7.42 per month

Part B

1. a) $1114   b) $871.41   c) $15 682.65   d) $97 554.57   **2.** $125.26; $243.76
3. $2062.74   **4.** a) January 1, 2018   b) $442.62   d) $399.84   e) $389.35
5. 1.836017314
6. a) $1291.55; $1281.44   b) $146 666.52; $140 349.12
   c) $1331.73; it would not pay to refinance.
7. a) $1339.65; $1337.86   b) $590 010.50   c) $180 910.94   d) $12 402.25
8. $2974.13   **9.** Choose Mortgage B.
10. a) 6.286496%   b) 7.13388%   **11.** a) $9938.40   b) $5491.33

Exercise 5.4

Part A

1. $3428.87   **2.** $17 045.65   **3.** $184.27; $8711.54
4. $79 589.25; $17 911.00; $136 749.15; $1 256 204.83
5. $41 971.91   **6.** $706.63; $3919.24
7. $64 781.34; $142 906.34   **8.** a) $28 277.87   b) $164 182.71
9. a) $122 036.72   b) $1 070 154.78   **10.** $100.96   **11.** $1370.79
12. a) $325.12   b) $505.12   c) $1618.57   **13.** $5606.85

Part B

1. $5168.85   **3.** a) $24 394.59   b) $1 519 331.88
4. 3 years and 7 months; $95.61   **5.** $13 082.32   **6.** $3460.37
7. 6.5%   **8.** 14.74%
9. a) $1836.42   b) $17 458.03   **10.** a) $6366.56   b) $789.34

Exercise 5.5

Part A

1. a) $7791   b) $7791   c) $8293.40
2. The sinking-fund plan is cheaper by $302.25 per year.
3. Amortization is cheaper by $559.32 semi-annually.
4. 10.04%   5. 9.48%   6. 7.45%
7. a) $15 196.71   b) 8.92%
8. The amortization method is cheaper by $56.52 a month.

Part B

1. Amortization will save $117.61 a month.
2. 13.03%   3. $810.00   4. 7.25%
5. $1278.04 at the end of 12 years.   6. 8.35%

Review Exercises 5.6

1. a) $190.01   b) i) $11 810.25; $88.58; $101.43
2. $966.73; $243.08   3. $4736.06   4. 8.80%
5. $349.41   6. a) $2146.77   b) $229 052.76   c) $276.59   d) $92 097.72
7. a) $1417.46   b) $197 850.59   c) $1654.90   d) $1303.01; $351.89
8. $1198.27   9. Sinking fund will save $10.02 annually.
10. $3900   11. a) $889.19   b) $41 870.31   c) i) $152.88; $736.31   d) $992.59
12. a) $47.60   b) $63.54   13. a) $65.81   b) $3540.41
14. $429 476.31   15. $5387.53
16. a) $662.40   b) $642.66   c) $6754.97   d) i) 22 months sooner   ii) $12 173.89
17. a) $2718.46   b) $14 718.46   c) 13.57%
18. a) $5489.74; $5489.52   b) $445.04   c) $37 277.73
19. a) 7.340352%   b) 7.904388%   20. $30 287.99   21. $174 694.23
22. a) 255 months; $1028.03   b) 229 months; $130.37

Exercise 6.2

Part A

1. $549.48   2. $923.14   3. $1897.17   4. $5857.95
5. $792.96   6. $2539.30   7. $13 191.71   8. $4523.70
9. $1 068 973.16   10. $940.36; $1164.03   11. $107.25
12. a) $4609.49   b) $5204.29

Part B

3. $6000   4. $1214.31   5. $1049   6. $846.28
7. $860.20   8. 10 years   9. $60.08
10. a) $957.88   b) 12 years   11. 7 years   12. $95

Exercise 6.3

Part A

1. Premium; $1025.79   2. Discount; $4866.79   3. Premium; $2046.13
4. Discount; $995.24   5. Premium; $2104.42   6. Discount; $10 599.34
7. $5.25; $1094.75   8. $16.32   9. $9.01   10. $1360
11. a) $1052.76   b) $1068.52   12. $909.91   13. $1019.14

Part B

1. $102.34   **2.** $31.28   **3.** $881.53   **4.** a) $2216.30
5. $1801.07   **6.** $886.82   **7.** a) $925   b) Discount   c) $0.50; $0.53
8. b) $10 408.88

Exercise 6.4

Part A

1. a) $2345.84   b) $1699.07   **2.** a) $5627.57   b) $4466.12
3. a) $1098.96   b) $914.20   **4.** a) $n = 10$ or 20 b) $n = 20$ c) $n = 10$
5. a) equal 8%   b) exceed 8%   c) less than 8%   d) equal 8%

Part B

1. a) $1689.13   b) $2260.08   **2.** a) $1133.76   b) $883.17
3. $5419.36
4. a) $1092.77   b) i) Premium = $80   ii) Premium = $12.77   c) 13 years.

Exercise 6.5

Part A

1. $857.26; $829.19   **2.** $550.69; $535.36
3. $1905.10; $1865.97   **4.** $9655.77; $9502.10
5. $1172.84; $1164.96   **6.** $1885.95; $1881.14
7. $1501.71   **8.** $1591.55   **9.** $1548.01   **10.** $1742.68
11. $128.84   **12.** $116.71   **13.** $97.29   **14.** $113.435
15. $1012.31

Part B

2. a) $1003.60   b) $1167.10   **3.** October 4, 2010
4. a) $1087.03; $1074.02   b) 1094.17; $1081.17
5. a) $4521.50   b) $4543.09   c) 121.15
6. a) $815.98   b) $823.34   c) i) $1109.16   ii) $634.48   d) 90.56
7. a) $4581.84   b) 107.86   c) 94.27

Exercise 6.6

Part A

1. 11.42%   **2.** 6.11%   **3.** 10.64%   **4.** 7.82%
5. 11.48%; 11.466%   **6.** 6.09%; 6.0824%
7. 10.55%; 10.5346%   **8.** 7.97%; 7.9669%
9. a) 7.44%   b) 7.50%   **10.** a) 9.87%   b) 9.86%
11. a) 10.96%   b) 10.50%   **12.** $i^{(2)} = 10.20\%$ **13.** 6.76%
14. 8.62%   **15.** a) $913.54   b) $1074.39   c) 10.44%   **16.** 12.04%

Part B

1. a) $802.71   b) 9.33%   **3.** 9.63%
4. a) $795.37   b) $1058.36   c) 12.32%
5. a) $944.45   b) 7.61%   **6.** a) $5\frac{1}{2}\%$ b) $4\frac{1}{2}$ years
7. $7\frac{1}{2}\%$ **8.** 28.50%   **9.** 8.69%

Exercise 6.7

Part A

1. a) $9476.49   b) $800 510.13   c) $108 081.35
2. a) 5.50%   b) 4.50%   c) 7.50%
3. 8.99%   4. $301.23   5. $95.40

Part B

1. a) $890.27   b) $5527.84   c) $1879.41
2. a) Normal yield curve   b) $442 716.39
3. 4.81%

Review Exercises 6.8

1. a) $11 155 738.60   b) $148 362.33
2. a) $1200.00   b) 7.47%   3. a) $1007.98   b) Discount
4. a) $2156.30   b) 7.44%   c) 108.48
5. a) $907.99   b) $1093.68   c) 12.35%   d) $1100.04
6. $2334.76   7. a) $901.04   b) 20 years   c) 8.36%
8. a) 7.97%   b) 7.95%   9. a) 7%   b) 17.5 years
10. $1092.01   11. $8881.54   12. $4784.84
13. a) $1146.23   b) $34.27   c) $1272.38   d) 8.65%
14. a) Discount ($119.50)   b) Premium ($107.12)
15. $1023.41   16. $2240.50   17. $2224.13   18. $4693.99
19. 92.53   20. 13.12%

Exercise 7.1

Part A

1. +$11 700.02; proceed   2. +$15 461.25; proceed
3. −$4061; not proceed   4. +$25 170.46; proceed
5. At $i^{(1)} = 4\%$: NPV(A) = $22 591.12; NPV(B) = $56 572.77; choose B
   At $i^{(1)} = 7\%$: NPV(A) = $5009.87; NPV(B) = $29 217.93; choose B
6. NPV(A) = −$548.58; NPV(B) = +$2865.55; choose B
7. NPV at 14% = −$115 522; the company should not proceed with the project
8. NPV = +$9874.62; the fund should proceed with the investment
9. NPV at 7% = +$135.29; proceed

Part B

1. NPV = −$130.81; do not borrow
2. NPV of investment 1 = +$11 626; NPV of investment 2 = +$11 358;
   investment 1 provides the company with the highest profit
3.

Rate	2%	4%	6%	8%	10%	12%
NPV	$22 923.25	16 445.44	10 502.14	5037.15	1.24	−4648.79

Exercise 7.2

Part A

1. 15.5%	**2.** 16.5%	**3.** 10.5%
4. 29%	**5.** 11%	**6.** 12%

Part B

1. IRR(A) = 20.5%; IRR(B) = 20%. At 15%: NPV(A) = +$985.63
NPV(B) = +$1609.89. At 25%: NPV(A) = −$757.12; NPV(B) = −$1217.92;
At 15%, project B should be chosen
2. a) 20%   b) 19%

Exercise 7.3

Part A

1. 14.1935%	**2.** $952 930.64	**3.** 6.5739%
4. 20 000; October 1	**5.** 4.1703%	**6.** 8.182%

Exercise 7.4

Part A

1. 18.7850%	**2.** 23.2659%	**3.** $23 625	**4.** 4.0822%
5. −1.3959%	**6.** 13.74%; 19.13%		

Exercise 7.5

Part A

1. $109.88	**2.** a) $175 b) $241.30
3. a) $85.71 b) $74.07	**4.** 10.86%

Part B

1. $22.18

Review Exercises 7.6

1. Accept all (D is best)
2. IRR of the project is 7.5%; for alternative projects: IRR (1) = 8%,
IRR (2) = 7.5%, IRR (3) = 4.66%, IRR (4) = 20%, and IRR (5) = 18%
3. $X = 6000$; −25%   **4.** $236 250
5. a) 13.3333%   b) 20%   **8.** $228 705.06
9. $3253.50   **10.** $34 141.17   **11.** −5%

Exercise 8.1

Part A

1. a) $1000   b) $1078.11   c) 1.8980%
2. a) $1053.09   b) $982.63   c) $971.11

Exercise 8.2

Part A

1. a) $1000.185   b) $1038.001   c) I: 3.990%; II: 3.986%
   d) As expected, the yield rates lie between 3.5% and 4% since these are the spot rates for the first and second years respectively
2. 5.6139   3. a) $8417.79   b) $10 225.36   c) 4.38%
4. 2.50%; 2.00%; 4.56%; 5.60%

Part B

1. 10.13%   2. 5.098%

Exercise 8.3

1. a) 5.59%   b) 6.11%   c) 6.76%   d) 5.13%   2. 4.979253%
3. a) 11.0374%   b) 12.0276%   c) 11.5314%
4. a) 8.009434%, 8.5070203%   b) 9.83%
5. a) 4.25%   b) 4.30%
6. $_1i_1 = 10.76\%$, $_2i_1 = 10.89\%$, $_1i_2 = 10.8249\%$, $_3i_2 = 11.00\%$, $_5i_2 = 10.69\%$, $_2i_3 = 10.9644\%$, $_2i_5 = 10.8549\%$, $_5i_5 = 10.33\%$ 7. 7.08%

Review Exercises 8.4

1. a) 7%; 5.0093458%; 10.563979 6%   b) $1015.32
2. 6.0457%; 6.4622%   3. $115.57   4. 6%
5. a) 10.3257%   b) 7.0838%   6. 8.962%
7. 4.4494%; 4.4329%   8. 7.4363%
9. a) 4.79%   b) 4.49%   c) 4.60%   d) 4.35%   e) 5.32%

Exercise 9.1

Part A

1. $11 181   2. $12 854.03   3. 6.95 years
4. a) 10 years   b) 7.4611 years   c) 4.7614 years   d) 17.1667 years
5. 12.6219 years   6. 7.9596 years   7. 7.8589 years
8. 9.5179 years   9. 6.9144 years
10. a) 8.0928 years   b) 1.1638 years   11. 5.75%

Part B

1. 5%   2. $\dfrac{1}{d} - \dfrac{n}{i s_{\overline{n}|i}}$

Exercise 9.2

Part A

1. a) $9194.05   b) $8416.28   c) $9567.38
2. a) $9195.43   b) $8464.37   c) $9570.12
3. a) 9.7087; $5267.98   b) 7.2438; $20 709.49   c) 4.6227; $48 844.31
   d) 16.6667; $1527.78
4. 12.0208; $11 989.76   5. a) 8.0525; $140 940.94   b) 1.158; $148 697.24
6. 17.3913; $3266.54

Exercise 9.3

Part A

1. a) 9.4875   b) 137.068   2. 51.5; 4904.7619
3. a) $3877.33   b) 2.18   c) 2.0374   d) 6.6051
4. 7.1059; 37.0551; $80 490.47
5. a) mod. duration = 9.3458; 96.0783   b) $485.2052
6. $694.4444; 14.8889; 13.8889; 385.8025; $665.8095
7. a) $9176.72   b) $6326.22

Part B

1. a) $197 453.90   b) 7.8366   2. $1017.11; 6.4549

Exercise 9.4

Part A

1. X = $44 500 and Y = $56 180
2. X = $2754, Y = $17 754 and Z = $9174
3. a) X = $17 969 and Y = $42 200   b) X = $17 800 and Y = $42 400
4. Since 71 056.23 < 84 247.28, this is not an immunized portfolio
5. 4.18; 21.31   6. a) $1536.32; $1305.25   b) not fully immunized
7. C =$17 748.34 and B = 34 168.57

Review Exercises 9.5

1. a) 7.841   b) 7.503   2. 4.11; 20.010
3. a) $871.89   b) 30.062972   c) $859.81; $859.64
4. X = $47 619.05 and Y = $52 500.00
5. $107.3915   6. a) $111.31   b) 7.658   c) 7.259
7. a) $96.14   b) 4.115   c) 3.919
8. X = $57 003.63 and Y = $80 727.96; Yes
9. X = $43 671.94 and Y = $57 245; Yes
10. 9.569   11. a) 5.099   b) 4.856
12. a) $250   b) 17.667   c) 555.556
13. Since 44 111.71 < 76 252.39, this is not an immunized portfolio
14. $95.475   15. a) 3.6761   b) Buy $4.035955 million of these bonds
16. a) 7.6111   b) 7.5152   c) 7.4178
17. a) 5.661   b) Purchase 1.2694 of each of the 3 bonds
18. 31.43% of the 4-year bonds and 68.57% of the 2-year bonds
19. 15.2857   20. 4.5459
21. $\frac{1}{3}$ of 2-year bonds and $\frac{2}{3}$ of 5-year bonds

Index

Jan   31
Feb   28
Mar   31
Apr   30
May   31
Jun   30
Jul   31
Aug   31
Sep   30
Oct   31
Nov   30
Dec   31